SUPERDIVERSITY AND TEACHER EDUCATION

This edited volume addresses the pressing imperative to understand and attend to the needs of the fast-growing population of minority students who are increasingly considered "superdiverse" in their cultural, linguistic, and racial backgrounds. Superdiverse learners—including native-born learners (Indigenous and immigrant families), foreign-born immigrant students, and refugees—may fill multiple categories of "diversity" at once. This volume helps pre- and in-service teachers and teacher educators to move beyond the demographic backgrounds of superdiverse learners to consider not only their ways of being, motivations, and social processes but also the ongoing systemic issues of marginalization and inequity that confront these learners.

Challenging existing teaching and learning paradigms in the K–12 North American context, this volume provides new methods and examples for supporting superdiverse learners in a range of settings. Organized around different conceptual underpinnings of superdiversity, contributors identify the knowledge gaps and effective practices in engaging superdiverse learners, families, and communities. With cutting-edge research on this growing topic, this text will appeal to researchers, scholars, educators, and graduate students in multilingual education, literacy education, teacher education, and international education.

Guofang Li is Professor and Canada Research Chair (Tier 1) in Transnational/ Global Perspectives of Language and Literacy Education of Children and Youth at the University of British Columbia, Canada.

Jim Anderson is Professor of Language and Literacy Education at the University of British Columbia, Canada.

Jan Hare is Associate Dean of Indigenous Education and Canada Research Chair (Tier 1) of Indigenous Pedagogy at the University of British Columbia, Canada.

Marianne McTavish is Professor and Associate Dean of Teacher Education at the University of British Columbia, Canada.

SUPERDIVERSITY AND TEACHER EDUCATION

Supporting Teachers in Working with Culturally, Linguistically, and Racially Diverse Students, Families, and Communities

Edited by Guofang Li,
Jim Anderson, Jan Hare,
and Marianne McTavish

Routledge
Taylor & Francis Group

NEW YORK AND LONDON

First published 2021
by Routledge
52 Vanderbilt Avenue, New York, NY 10017

and by Routledge
2 Park Square, Milton Park, Abingdon, Oxon, OX14 4RN

Routledge is an imprint of the Taylor & Francis Group, an informa business

© 2021 Taylor & Francis

Library of Congress Cataloging-in-Publication Data
Names: Li, Guofang, 1972- editor.
Title: Superdiversity and teacher education : supporting teachers in working with culturally, linguistically, and racially diverse students, families, and communities / Edited by Guofang Li, Jim Anderson, Jan Hare, and Marianne McTavish.
Description: New York, NY : Routledge Taylor & Francis, 2021. | Includes bibliographical references and index.
Identifiers: LCCN 2020040482 (print) | LCCN 2020040483 (ebook) | ISBN 9780367482619 (hardback) | ISBN 9780367482602 (paperback) | ISBN 9781003038887 (ebook) | ISBN 9781000344554 (adobe pdf) | ISBN 9781000344561 (mobi) | ISBN 9781000344578 (epub)
Subjects: LCSH: Teachers--Training of--North America. | Teachers--In-service training--North America. | Multicultural education--North America. | Education, Bilingual--North America. | Minorities--Education--North America.
Classification: LCC LB1719.N67 S87 2021 (print) | LCC LB1719.N67 (ebook) | DDC 370.117097--dc23
LC record available at https://lccn.loc.gov/2020040482
LC ebook record available at https://lccn.loc.gov/2020040483

ISBN: 978-0-367-48261-9 (hbk)
ISBN: 978-0-367-48260-2 (pbk)
ISBN: 978-1-003-03888-7 (ebk)

Typeset in Bembo
by SPi Global, India

CONTENTS

SECTION III
Engaging Practices for Educators for Superdiversity   **219**

FIGURES

TABLES

FOREWORD

There are times, albeit rarely, when the development of a new academic concept breaks through and/or upends existing academic frameworks and discourses. This kind of rare paradigmatic shift is evident in the purchase that "superdiversity", first coined by the British sociologist Steven Vertovec (2007), has had over the subsequent decade or so. Superdiversity, for Vertovec, describes the rapid diversification of many national populations as the result of increased migration and transmigration, particularly to major urban centers in the West, along with the related complexification and increased fluidity of ethnic and linguistic identities in such contexts. Vertovec's initial study focused on multiethnic and multilingual London as an exemplar of these trends, but the concept has since come to be applied in a range of diverse contexts internationally. That said, it is true, as the editors rightly note in their introduction, that North America, and the US in particular, has come somewhat late to the superdiversity party. This is most likely because of the key fissures, and related identity bifurcations, that still pervade many North American academic analyses of "race" and ethnicity. That this volume directly addresses the implications of superdiversity within Canada and the USA is a welcome and timely addition to these wider international debates.

A second key contribution that this volume foregrounds is the increasing interdisciplinary reach of academic discussions of superdiversity. In the intervening years, superdiversity has since reached far beyond its origins in sociology and migration studies. It has been enthusiastically taken up in a wide range of other fields, including political studies, cultural studies, sociolinguistics and applied linguistics, to name but a few. Despite some key work in language education (e.g. Conteh & Meier, 2014; May, 2014), the field of education has, again, been somewhat slower to respond to these developments. Thus, another pivotal and timely contribution of this volume is its in-depth exploration of the implications of superdiversity for education—and, particularly, teacher education. In so doing, the uniformly excellent contributions within it traverse the complex nexus of multicultural, language, and Indigenous education in relation to issues of colonization, racialization, and the normative power of whiteness, along with their ongoing effects in neoliberal education systems.

The focus on a wide range of marginalized groups, including Indigenous students, importantly addresses a key identified weakness of many previous academic discussions of superdiversity, which have tended to focus primarily on urban migrants (May, 2017). The pedagogical implications of the recognition of superdiversity, particularly via related asset-based pedagogies, are also actively explored as a means of effectively addressing ongoing issues of marginalization and inequity for all culturally and linguistically diverse students within education.

The specific implications for teacher education consistently underpin and link all the contributions in this volume. Although not always explicitly stated as such, the volume intersects with, and builds upon, earlier important related work here— notably, critical multiculturalism (e.g. May & Sleeter, 2010; Vavrus, 2014), critical race theory (e.g. Han & Laughter, 2019), and raciolinguistics (e.g. Flores & Rosa, 2015).

Finally, as the editors again rightly note, the global pandemic that is COVID-19 is just the latest development that has disproportionately and deleteriously impacted on communities of color and other marginalized groups. It highlights even further the urgency with which we need to address ongoing systemic inequalities within education, along with their replication and sedimentation in teacher education programs. For all these reasons, this is a volume whose time has come. Read it.

Stephen May

University of Auckland, New Zealand

July 2020

References

Conteh, J., & Meier, G. (Eds.). (2014). *The multilingual turn in languages education: Opportunities and challenges.* Bristol, UK. Multilingual Matters.

Flores, N., & Rosa, J. (2015). Undoing appropriateness: Raciolinguistic ideologies and language diversity in education. *Harvard Educational Review*, 85, 149–171.

Han, K. & Laughter, J. (Eds.) (2019). *Critical race theory in teacher education: Informing classroom culture and practice.* New York, NY: Teachers College Press.

May, S. (Ed.). (2014). *The multilingual turn: Implications for SLA, TESOL and bilingual education.* New York, NY: Routledge.

May, S. (2017). National and ethnic minorities: Language rights and recognition. In S. Canagarajah (Ed.), *Routledge handbook of migration and language* (pp. 149–167). New York, NY: Routledge.

May. S., & Sleeter, C. (Eds.). (2010). *Critical multiculturalism: Theory and praxis.* New York, NY: Routledge

Vavrus, M. (2014). *Diversity and education: A critical multicultural approach.* New York, NY: Teachers College Press.

Vertovec, S. (2007). Super-diversity and its implications. *Ethnic and Racial Studies*, 30, 1024–1054.

CONTRIBUTORS

Andrea Sterzuk is a professor in the Faculty of Education at the University of Regina. Andrea teaches and researches in the area of critical applied linguistics. Her research examines issues of power, identity, and language in schools and higher education as they relate to settler colonialism. Her previous research projects have explored language variation in elementary schools, English-only ideology in higher education, language planning and policy in higher education, and the development of language beliefs in preservice teachers.

Ann Anderson is a professor in the Department of Curriculum and Pedagogy at the University of British Columbia (UBC). Her research and teaching are in mathematics education in the early years, parent mediation of young children's multi-literacies at home, and family literacy. Prior to joining UBC, she worked in the public school system as a classroom teacher. Ann's research includes working with families from diverse cultural backgrounds to understand ways in which young children's multi-literacies are supported prior to, and in the early years of, school. Her research has been funded by the Social Sciences and Humanities Research Council of Canada.

Antoinette Gagné is an associate professor and the Associate Chair for Student Experience in the Department of Curriculum, Teaching, and Learning at the Ontario Institute for Studies in Education (OISE) of the University of Toronto. Her research has focused on teacher education for diversity and inclusion in various contexts. She has explored the experiences of young English language learners and their families as well as internationally educated teachers in Canadian schools and universities. Antoinette is also the convenor of the Network of Critical Action Researchers in Education-NCARE, which brings together university educators from a dozen countries.

April Martin-Ko has worked with families and young children in a variety of educational settings for over 25 years- currently she works as a Pedagogist with the Early Childhood Pedagogy Network. She is also a graduate student (MA) at the University of British Columbia, where her research focuses on land-based learning in the field of early childhood education. She is interested in how young children's embodied and multimodal experiences inform pedagogy and practice. April approaches research and pedagogy thinking with Indigenous and Common Worlds frameworks and utilizes research-creation methodologies such as Poetic Inquiry and A/r/tography. April's ancestry is intersected between Indigenous and settler, and it is with gratitude to the xʷməθkʷəy̓əm (Musqueam), sḵwx̱wú7mesh (Squamish) and səl̓ilwətaʔɬ (Tsleil-Waututh) Peoples as she lives and carries out her work on these unceded traditional territories.

Caroline Locher-Lo earned her Bachelor of Arts in Finance and Commerce in Taiwan, where she was born and raised. She received advanced degrees in Business Administration (MBA) from Eastern Washington University and Education (MEd) with a focus on justice, ethics, and law from Simon Fraser University. She has taught ESL, Mandarin, social justice, methodology, science, math, accounting, and management courses throughout her career and was conferred a doctoral degree (PhD) from the University of British Columbia in 2020. Her research focus is predominantly in the area of immigrant heritage maintenance, with the aim of inciting sustainable systemic change and equity.

Danièle Moore is a Distinguished SFU Professor in educational sociolinguistics at the Faculty of Education, Simon Fraser University in Vancouver, Canada, and a research director at the Sorbonne University, France. Her research interests include issues related to language policies, plurilingualism and plurilingual education, and teacher training in multicultural contexts. She is a past co-editor of the bilingual journal *The Canadian Modern Language Review* and has co-authored several Reference Studies for the Council of Europe on plurilingualism and plurilingual and intercutural education. She is currently a TaC (Training and Consultant) for FREPA/CARAP (Framework of Reference for Pluralistic Approaches to Languages and Cultures), Council of Europe/CELV.

Ester de Jong is the Director of the School of Teaching and Learning and Professor in ESOL/Bilingual Education at the University of Florida in Gainesville, Florida. Prior to coming to the University of Florida, she worked with Spanish-English and Brazilian-Portuguese bilingual programs as the Assistant Director for Bilingual Education and ESL programs in Massachusetts. Her research focuses on equity and integration in the context of dual language education and preparing teachers to work with bilingual learners in K-12 schools. Her book, *Foundations of Multilingualism in Education: From Policy to Practice* published by Caslon Publishing, considers a principled approach to school, program, and classroom decision-making for multilingual learners. Dr. de Jong was President of TESOL International Association (2017–2018).

Guofang Li is a Professor and Tier 1 Canada Research Chair in Transnational/ Global Perspectives of Language and Literacy Education of Children and Youth in the Department of Language and Literacy Education, University of British Columbia, Canada. Her program of research aims to improve the life success of immigrant and minority students by addressing the cultural, linguistic, instructional, and structural barriers in their literacy learning and academic achievement both in school and at home.

Hetty Roessingh is a long-time ESL practitioner in the Calgary Board of Education, working at the high school level. She transitioned to the University of Calgary in 2000 to pursue research interests and to use research findings to inform her work in teacher preparation both at the undergrad and graduate levels. Her program of research reflects a pragmatic approach to understanding early language and literacy, and academic literacy learning over time. This is especially reflected in students' vocabulary growth.

Hua Que obtained her MEd in curriculum, teaching, and learning studies and her PhD in education from Memorial University of Newfoundland. Her research focuses on education and disadvantaged children and young people, including refugee children and youth in Canada and children of migrant workers in urban China. She also examines issues pertaining to the internationalization of higher education. She was a recipient of the SSHRC Doctoral Fellowship and the Mitacs Globalink Research Award.

Jacob S. Bennett taught high school social studies, mainly economics and U.S. history, in Atlanta, Georgia, and Nashville, Tennessee, from 2008 to 2014. Central to his teaching philosophy was that learning best occurs when teachers and students share in trusting and meaningful relationships. To do so, he came to believe teachers must seek to understand the complexities of identity and power. Since leaving the classroom, his research centers on the development of an empirical knowledge base to show how teachers' ideological backgrounds affect decisions of practice related to supporting historically marginalized youth. He earned a PhD in curriculum and instruction from the University of Virginia in 2018 and currently works as a postdoctoral research fellow at Peabody College, Vanderbilt University.

Jan Hare is an Anishinaabe scholar and educator from the MChigeeng First Nation, located in northern Ontario. She is the associate dean for Indigenous Education in the Faculty of Education at the University of British Columbia, the director of the Native Indigenous Teacher Education Program (NITEP), and professor in the Department of Language and Literacy, and she holds the Professorship of Indigenous Education in Teacher Education. As an Indigenous scholar and educator, she has sought to transform education in ways that are more inclusive of Indigenous epistemologies and languages. Her research is concerned with improving educational outcomes for Aboriginal/Indigenous learners and centering Indigenous knowledge systems within educational reform from early childhood education to postsecondary, recognizing the holistic and multidisciplinary nature of Indigenous education. She has developed the Massive Online Open Course (MOOC), Reconciliation Through Indigenous Education.

Jim Anderson is a professor in the Department of Language and Literacy Education at the University of British Columbia. He worked in the public school system as a classroom teacher, reading specialist, language arts consultant and assistant superintendent. His work in family literacy has been funded by the Social Sciences and Humanities Research Council and other agencies. With colleagues, he is currently studying young children's and families' access to and use of digital tools in disadvantaged neighborhoods. He is on the editorial boards of several journals and served on the Literacy Research Panel of the International Literacy Association for 3 years.

Kristen L. White is a former classroom teacher with over a decade of experience working with Grades K to 8. Kristen has a PhD in curriculum, instruction, and teacher education with a language and literacy specialization from Michigan State University. She is an assistant professor of education at Northern Michigan University, where she teaches reading methods courses at the undergraduate and graduate levels. Interested in equity in early childhood contexts, she examines the construction of young children's literate identity/ies and improving the professional preparation of teachers through her research.

Kwesi Yaro is a PhD candidate studying curriculum studies in mathematics education at the Department of Curriculum and Pedagogy, University of British Columbia (UBC), Canada. He has an MA in mathematics education from UBC and a BEd (mathematics focus) from the University of Cape Coast, Ghana. Currently, he is working with researchers from multidisciplinary STEM (science, technology, engineering, mathematics) backgrounds to explore the possibilities and challenges confronting 21st-century teachers in teaching math in STEM for social justice. In his doctoral research, Kwesi is employing Afrocentric worldviews to investigate cultural strategies African immigrant families deploy to support their children's mathematics learning in the Canadian context. He hopes his research will contribute knowledge and insights that will guide teachers and other educators towards more culturally responsive mathematics teaching.

Lilach Marom is a teacher educator and a faculty member in the Department of Educational Studies at Kwantlen Polytechnic University. Her research is focused on questions of diversity, equity, and social justice in education and aims to highlight structural and institutional barriers to the diversification of teacher education and the teaching profession. Lilach has worked as an educator in multiple locations and countries (Israel, the United States, and Canada) with culturally and racially diverse populations. Through these experiences she came to realize that there is no one "right pedagogy," but that education must be grounded in concrete social contexts, and answer to the diverse needs of the communities it is serving. In her teaching Lilach applies a clear focus on social justice, critical inquiry, and cultural sensitivity since she believes these are the foundation of the teaching profession. Lilach's current project explores the experiences of international students in Canadian higher education.

Lisa K. Taylor is a professor of education at Bishop's University. Her research, teaching, and film production explore the affective, cognitive, relational, and ethical dynamics of witnessing and historical memory of ongoing colonial violence within decolonizing pedagogies. She is co-editor with Jasmin Zine of *Muslim Women, Transnational Feminism and the Ethics of Pedagogy* (2014) and with Lynne Davis, Jan Hare, Chris Hiller, and Lindsay Morcom of *Indigenization, Decolonization, and Reconciliation: Critical Considerations and Cross-Disciplinary Approaches in Post-Secondary Classrooms* (Canadian Journal of Native Education, 2018).

Manka Varghese is a professor in the University of Washington's College of Education. She teaches and conducts research on the interaction between identity formation and multilingual learning and teaching and draws on critical perspectives, especially around the intersections of race and language. In doing so, she puts forward an understanding of the historical and current terrain of multilingual youth as complex and rooted in racial, linguistic, and other forms of inequity but with an eye to the possibilities of transformation. She has most recently co-edited a volume and a special issue on language teacher agency and authored articles in various journals on teacher identity, race, and language teaching.

Marianne McTavish is associate dean of Teacher Education in the Faculty of Education, University of British Columbia (UBC). She has taught undergraduate and graduate courses in education at UBC since 1990; her contributions have been recognized with the Murray Elliott Award for Outstanding Contribution to the Teacher Education Program and the Critical Perspectives on Early Childhood Education Emerging Scholar Award of the American Educational Research Association. Her research work with early childhood teacher candidates and digital literacies reconceptualizes the way literacy is taught and practiced. She has authored several professional resources in addition to scholarly articles and chapters on young children's emergent literacy learning, teacher education, and family literacy.

Monica Shank Lauwo is a PhD candidate in Language and Literacy Education at the University of British Columbia. She is the Founder and Director of Cheche Community Library, a multilingual learning centre in Northern

Tanzania. She has extensive experience as an educator in diverse contexts in Tanzania, Kenya, and Canada. Her work explores ways in which translanguaging and multimodality can be used to foster creativity and critical literacy and to reconfigure inequitable power relations. Her research interests include translanguaging, multiliteracies, critical pedagogy, identity, and language ideologies, particularly in East Africa.

Nikki L. Yee is a settler scholar of mixed Chinese and Mennonite ancestry from Saskatchewan, with a PhD in special education from the University of British Columbia. Her research focuses on bringing people together across diversity to examine how educators can better support Indigenous (and all) students in inclusive classrooms. She has taught at all grade levels, from PreK through Grade 12, and provided special education support in both elementary and high school. She has also taught university courses in Indigenous education and special education. Through her work, Nikki aspires to use education as a way to open possibilities for (re)imagining healthy and respectful communities in relationship with Indigenous Peoples.

Patriann Smith is an assistant professor of literacy studies in the Department of Teaching and Learning at the University of South Florida. Her research interests include Black immigrant Englishes/literacies, standardized and nonstandardized English ideologies, multicultural teacher education, literacy assessment, and cross-cultural and cross-linguistic literacy practices. Her recent publications include "How Does a Black Person Speak English? Beyond American Language Norms" published in the *American Educational Research Journal*; "Understanding Afro-Caribbean Educators' Experiences with Englishes across Caribbean and U.S. Contexts and Classrooms: Recursivity, (Re)positionality, Bidirectionality" published in *Teaching and Teacher Education*; *(Re)Positioning in the Englishes and (English)* "Literacies of a Black Immigrant Youth: Towards a 'Transraciolinguistic' Approach" published in *Theory Into Practice*; and "You hear my funny accent?!": Problematizing Assumptions about Afro-Caribbean 'Teachers Turned Educators'" published in the *International Multilingual Research Journal*.

Patricia A. Edwards is a member of the Reading Hall Fame and a Professor of Language and Literacy at Michigan State University. A nationally and internationally recognized expert in parent involvement, home, school, community partnerships, multicultural literacy, early literacy, and family/intergenerational literacy, especially among poor and minority children. She served as the first African American president of the Literacy Research Association in 2006 to 2007 and as the 2010–2011 president of the International Reading Association. She was named as the 2017–2018 Jeanne S. Chall Visiting Researcher at Harvard Graduate School of Education.

Rachel Snyder is a doctoral candidate in Language, Literacy and Culture at the University of Washington. She also holds an MA in anthropology from the University of Chicago and is an experienced bilingual teacher. Rachel is currently working on her dissertation research which examines the emotional journeys of novice bilingual teachers and the emergence of critical consciousness. Her work traces connections between embodied experience, emotional knowledge, and resistance in bilingual teaching.

Renee Shank received her PhD in Multicultural Education at the University of Washington. She is currently the BECA (Bilingual Educator CApacity) program coordinator. Her research focuses on racial discourse in bilingual teacher education, teacher education pedagogy that promotes bilingualism, and teacher education reform to promote multilingualism.

Sara Florence Davidson is a Haida/settler assistant professor in Indigenous education in the Faculty of Education at Simon Fraser University. She has experience teaching in the K–12 system in rural British Columbia and Yukon. Her research interests include Indigenous pedagogies and research methodologies, adolescent literacies, narrative writing and research, and Indigenous education. She is the co-author of *Potlatch as Pedagogy: Learning Through Ceremony*, which she wrote with her father, Robert Davidson.

Sara Hajek is a doctoral candidate in literacy studies at Texas Tech University. Her research interests include literacy, diversity, and teacher education. Her recent publications include "Shifting from Diversity in Multicultural Populations to Teacher/Student Interactions within Transcultural Spaces in an online Literacy Teacher Education Course," published in *Literacy Practice and Research*. In addition to her research, Sara teaches German at a diverse high school in San Antonio. She has also presented multiple professional development sessions for in-service teachers regarding cultural and linguistic issues in the classroom.

Stephen May, PhD, FRSNZ, is a professor of education in Te Puna Wānanga (School of Māori and Indigenous Education) at the University of Auckland, New Zealand. Stephen is an international authority on language rights, language policy, bilingualism and bilingual education, and critical multicultural approaches to education. Additional research interests are in the wider politics of multiculturalism, ethnicity and nationalism, social theory (particularly the work of Bourdieu), sociolinguistics, and critical ethnography. Stephen has published over 100 articles and book chapters, along with numerous books, in these areas, including *The Multilingual Turn* (2014) and *Language and Minority Rights* (2nd ed., 2012). He is the editor-in-chief of the 10-volume *Encyclopedia of Language and Education* (3rd ed., 2017) and the founding co-editor of the journal *Ethnicities*. He is a fellow of the American Educational Research Association and of the Royal Society of New Zealand. His homepage is http://www.education.auckland.ac.nz/uoa/stephen-may.

Teddi Beam-Conroy has been a bilingual educator for over 30 years. In that time, she has gone from paraprofessional to PhD and has worked in five states across the United States as a classroom teacher, a district-level administrator, and a university faculty. She is currently the director of the University of Washington's Elementary Teacher Education Program's Master's in Teaching. Using Critical Race and LatCrit Theory, she centers her research on the preparation of preservice and in-service teachers to serve linguistically and racially minoritized students in K–12 schools.

Xuemei Li is Associate professor in Memorial University's Faculty of Education. She has led and participated in multiple Social Sciences and Humanities Research Council projects (Insight Development Grant, Partnership Development Grant, Partnership Grant) and other funded projects (e.g., MITACS, Canadian Education and Research Institute for Counselling, Pratt Foundation), focusing on newcomer (immigrant, refugee, and international student) language, social, settlement, and career issues in Canada, and particularly in Newfoundland. Her research covers identity issues in additional language contexts, second/additional language writing, TESL/TEFL curriculum and methodology, ESL support in schools and communities, and newcomer integration. She also investigates graduate English writing instruction and teacher education at the tertiary level in China.

Zhuo Sun is a PhD candidate in the Department of Language and Literacy Education, University of British Columbia. She received her master's degree in TESOL from University of Pennsylvania in 2014 and has been involved in ESL/EFL teaching and teacher training since then. She has also been collaborating with community-based heritage-language educators in the Greater Vancouver area to explore and develop localized, inclusive literacy pedagogies for young immigrant learners. Zhuo is currently working on her dissertation research that examines Chinese heritage-language teachers' literacy and pedagogical practices from the theoretical perspectives of transnationalism and situated literacy.

INTRODUCTION

Superdiversity, Emergent Priorities, and Teacher Learning

Guofang Li, Lilach Marom, Jim Anderson, Jan Hare, and Marianne McTavish

This book is an attempt to engage with the growing phenomenon of super-diversity (Schmid et al., 2017; Vertovec, 2007, 2019) in the context of North American K–12 schooling and teacher education. While the concept of superdiversity has been applied in many academic and policy fields (Vertovec, 2019), it has remained relatively underdeveloped in the North American context. Coined more than a decade ago by Vertovec (2007), the notion of superdiversity recognizes the tremendous increase in the categories of migrants in countries such as the United States, the United Kingdom, Canada, and other parts of the world, "not only in terms of nationality, ethnicity, language, and religion, but also in terms of motives, patterns and itineraries of migration, processes of insertion into the labor and housing markets of the host societies, and so on" (p. 1025). These new categories add to the "diversification of diversity" (Vertovec, 2007, p. 1025) and lead to "a multiplication of significant variables that affect where, how and with whom people live—or in schools where, how and with whom people teach and learn" (Gogolin, 2011, p. 241).

Indigenous peoples in countries such as Canada and the United States are caught up in, and a component of, global superdiversity (Moore, 2020). While distinct as sovereign people, they are enmeshed in settler societies through processes of colonization, reconciliation, or self-determination. In Canada, Indigenous people are themselves richly diverse, composed of First Nations, Metis, and Inuit peoples and with more people newly identifying as Indigenous, particularly in urban areas (Statistics Canada, 2018). The population growth rate is more than four times the growth rate of non-Aboriginal people (Statistics Canada, 2016).

Their inclusion in discussions of superdiversity must acknowledge their collective rights to lands, languages, cultures, and traditions (United Nations, 2008) and their rejection of discourses of multiculturalism that reduce their rights and relationships to the government to that of other linguistic and cultural minorities. Therefore, the new reality of superdiversity must attend to a sense of place as colonial states come to terms with their commitments to Indigenous peoples (Chan & Ritchie, 2019). New migrants must acquaint themselves not only with the dominant language and culture of the host society but also be prepared to connect with Indigenous knowledges, cultures, and lands.

Superdiversity does not simply mean more diversity but rather represents a new phenomenon that supersedes traditional conceptions of diversity (Meissner & Vertovec, 2015). It seeks to understand the complexity of new social formations and the public perceptions that accompany them. As such, it is a move away from understanding Western societies as locations in which fixed subcommunities or enclaves coexist side by side and toward unpacking multiple ways of being (some chosen, some forced) in a global, transnational world. Furthermore, whereas immigrant and refugee communities in countries of resettlement were once thought of as ethnic/linguistic enclaves, the concept of superdiversity gives recognition to the diversity within these communities.

Currently, as in many other parts of the world, the demographic trends in Canada and the United States are forming new social formations of diversity patterns with one in four students in K–12 schools coming from a minority-language background. This superdiverse population includes native-born learners (e.g., Indigenous and second- or third-generation students from immigrant and refugee families born in Canada or the United States), foreign-born immigrant students, and refugees, and they are now the majority at many elementary and secondary schools. In the United States, while there had been a decrease of White students (from 62% to 51%) in school between 2000 and 2017, the percentages of school-age children and youth from non-White racial and ethnic groups such as Hispanic, Asian, and mixed race increased, with Hispanic children rising from 16% to 25%; Asian children from 3% to 5%; and children of mixed races, from 2% to 4%. In the meantime, the percentage of children of American Indians/Alaska Natives (1%) and Pacific Islanders (less than 1%) remained unchanged (de Brey et al., 2019). Similarly, in Canada, more than 6% of students are Indigenous and more than 20% of the population are foreign-born (Campbell, 2020; Statistics Canada, 2018). The main groups of immigrants to Canada in 2019 originated from India, China, the Philippines, Nigeria, the United States, Pakistan, Syria, Eritrea, South Korea, and Iran (Assal, 2020). Statistics Canada predicts that, if current immigrations levels to Canada continues, by 2036 nearly half of its population will likely be immigrants or children of immigrants (Statistics Canada, 2017).

These superdiverse groups of students are reported to be most at risk as there remains a persistent and significant gap in achievement in many school districts between these learners and their "mainstream" peers in both Canada and the

United States. For example, in the Toronto District School Board, the largest and most diverse urban school board in Canada and the fourth-largest school board in North America, racial minority students and students of lower socioeconomic backgrounds (these categories often overlap) were reported to face significant gaps (as high as 30% on standardized test scores) compared with White, "mainstream" peers (Campbell, 2020; James & Turner, 2017; McKell, 2010; Shah, 2018). Black, Middle Eastern, Indigenous and Latino boys of lower socioeconomic groups in the Toronto School District were among the lowest in terms of standardized test scores, credit accumulation, and attendance and the highest in dropout rates and suspension (McKell, 2010; Shah, 2018). Similar results were reported in the country's second-largest school district in British Columbia (Gunderson & D'Silva 2016). In the United States, the country's most recent report card based on the 2017 National Assessment of Educational Progress (NAEP), results show that the Black–White and Hispanic–White achievement gaps in fourth- and eighth-grade reading and mathematics had remained significant (e.g., as high as 32 points in eighth-grade mathematics and 26 points in fourth-grade reading in 2017) and not measurably different from the gaps in 1992 (de Brey et al., 2019). Similar to the trends in Canada, minoritized students had the highest suspension rates (the highest among Black students and American Indian/Alaskan students), absentee rates (the highest among American Indian/Alaskan and Pacific Islander students), and dropout rates (the highest among Hispanic and Black students; de Brey et al., 2019). While graduation rates for Indigenous students are improving in various parts of Canada, Indigenous students continue to lag behind their non-Indigenous counterparts due to irrelevant curriculum and the "racism of low expectations" (Auditor General of British Columbia, 2015, p. 37). These achievement gaps are expected to be further exacerbated in 2021 due to extensive school closure in response to the COVID-19 pandemic. Although some continue to do well, many students of minoritized backgrounds may experience a "COVID-19 slide," including "patterns of academic setbacks typical of summers throughout an extended closure and COVID-19 slowdown" (Kuhfeld & Tarasawa, 2020, p. 2).

One key factor that contributes to these racially, linguistically, and culturally diverse students' achievement gaps is the persistent issue of under-preparedness among teachers of these students (Durgunoglu & Hughes, 2010; Dyce & Owusu-Ansah, 2016; Li et al., 2018). Deep preparation for preservice and in-service teachers is crucial to address these issues, keeping in mind that the institutions of schools and structures of teacher education programs were designed for White teachers and with "mainstream" White students in mind (Sleeter & Milner, 2011).

Yet, few teacher education programs require preservice teachers to undertake course work in cultural and linguistic diversity; as a result, teachers generally are not prepared for cultural and linguistic differences they will likely encounter in their classrooms. Indeed, many teachers report a lack of confidence and knowledge to teach diverse learners in their practice (Akiba et al., 2010; Campbell, 2020; Li & Jee, 2020; Li & Sah, 2020). Furthermore, once in their teaching positions, teachers receive little professional development in how to teach students from diverse backgrounds. Teachers sometimes do not have the opportunity to develop sufficient conceptual tools and experiences to understand and work with students' families and communities that often possess different sets of "funds of knowledge" from those in the mainstream (Anderson & Anderson, 2018). It is thus *imperative* that teachers (both in- and preservice) are supported in acquiring what Li (2018) calls, "diversity plus competences"— specific knowledge and skills related to working with culturally, linguistically, and racially diverse learners and their families. This is even more true in a new educational landscape radically changed and disrupted by the COVID-19 pandemic and increasing racial divides in the United States, Canada and elsewhere. It already seems that the first groups to be impacted by crises such as the pandemic are international students and students of marginalized groups. In a post-pandemic educational arena, these groups are likely to continue to suffer both as a result of lack of access and support in online learning spaces and the shift away from "diversity plus competences" in a time of crisis.

As part of Indigenous education reform in countries such as Canada, Australia, and New Zealand, there are a growing number of teacher education programs that now require preservice teachers to receive mandatory coursework in Indigenous histories and incorporate Indigenous knowledges and perspectives into teaching and learning. Consolidation of national policy imperatives (e.g., curriculum reform, and changing standards for the profession by teacher regulating bodies) directed at improving educational outcomes for Indigenous learners and Indigenous–settler relations through a framework of reconciliation has created new conditions under which teacher candidates are being prepared to support Indigenous priorities (Hare, 2020). While there is a growing body of literature advocating for preservice teachers' learning through engaging with Indigenous theories and practices, settler preservice teachers are challenged to find the relevance of Indigenous perspectives within the curriculum. Instead, they engage in "settler moves to innocence" (Tuck & Yang, 2012), which allows preservice teachers to protect their privilege, relieved of feelings of guilt or responsibility towards settler-colonial histories and the impacts for Indigenous learners. Preservice teachers may choose to absolve or distance themselves from their responsibility towards Indigenous education, positioning themselves as perfect strangers (Dion, 2007).

A nuanced analysis of the new patterns of immigration and social formations and their relationships to Indigenous education is important in order both to provide better support to diverse immigrant and marginalized communities and to critique and confront the new forms of resistance and pushback toward immigration that are on the rise in many nation-states. Furthermore, we need to recognize the particular histories of local Indigenous people in colonizing countries and pedagogies and practices that address systemic racism and educational disparities faced by Indigenous learners. Education systems, particularly public schools and teachers, play an important role in both aspects: they are a hub of superdiversity and can affect the perceptions and dispositions of future citizens.

Responding to, and embracing, superdiversity and the complexities it brings to pedagogical practices during the COVID-19 pandemic and its aftermath has become a professional, yet challenging, imperative for educators.

This edited volume addresses these pressing imperatives in education by focusing on the challenges and opportunities afforded by superdiversity in the context of North American K–12 schooling and teacher education. The chapters in this book aim to bridge this gap in multiple ways by (1) considering contextual inequalities and the need in teacher education to recognize and confront challenges and issues that superdiversity presents, (2) reviewing the research that teacher educators are conducting to address superdiversity in these different contexts, and (3) addressing the practical ways in which teachers and teacher educators can support both in-service and preservice teachers in designing instruction for superdiverse learners.

Superdiversity, Migration, and Indigeneity in the North American Context

Superdiversity, as a conceptual tool, urges scholars, policy makers, and practitioners to move beyond one-dimensional analysis of diversity (i.e., mainly focused on overarching ethnic categories), to identify more nuanced patterns that underlie societies nowadays. It is also critical of notions of diversity, when used "as a superordinate term to describe the poor, gathered together discursively to include 'migrants' (documented and undocumented), black and minority ethnic working-class people, and white working-class families" (Blackledge et al. 2018, p. xxi). Alternatively, it calls for a multidisciplinary approach that utilizes new methodological and theoretical tools to analyze and understand better the rapid changes in a given society (King & Bigelow, 2018). For example, in the last three decades, the Greater Vancouver Area in Canada saw a sharp increase in immigration from China (Statistics Canada, 2019). These immigrants, however, widely differ in their socioeconomic status, immigration status, family format, and so forth. The Greater Vancouver Area is also home to an established Chinese Canadian community that dates back to the mid-1800s (Government of Canada, 2017). Thus, there are multiple ways of being Chinese Canadian, and these ways could overlap in some cases and be in juxtaposition in others. Vertovec (2007) urges researchers to use superdiversity to both describe and analyze

> a level and kind of complexity surpassing anything the country has previously experienced. Such a condition is distinguished by a dynamic interplay of variables among an increased number of new, small and scattered, multiple-origin, transnationally connected, socio-economically differentiated and legally stratified immigrants who have arrived over the last decade.
> *(p. 1024)*

In the North American context, the concept of superdiversity is also useful to examine critically the intersections between discourses on diversity and multiculturalism and discourses on settler colonialism and Indigeneity. These tensions apply to the Canadian and American (as well as to the Australian and New Zealandian) context since, unlike the European context in which colonialism was executed outside of the colonizing country, in North America settlers inhabited the colonized land (Tuck & Yang, 2012). Hence, while in Europe colonialism has drastically impacted the colonized countries as well as determined historical routes for immigration, discourses on immigration are in most parts disconnected from discourses of colonialism. However, in North America, particularly in Canada, discourses on Indigenous sovereignty and self-determination are in juxtaposition to discourses of immigration and to the Canadian policy of multiculturalism (St. Denis, 2011). Indigenous peoples argue that they are sovereign nations with historical rights to the land that are "pre-contact, in place before the law of the Settler state" (Paine, 1999, p. 329). This claim stands in tension with Canadian multiculturalism. As St. Denis (2011) explains,

> [m]ulticulturalism erases the specific and unique location of Aboriginal peoples as Indigenous to this land by equating them with multicultural and immigrant groups. Aboriginal people adamantly reject this equating of their Aboriginal position with ethnic minorities as a form of colonialism.
>
> *(p. 311)*

Mindful of this critique, the authors in this book call to engage critically and ethically with superdiversity in ways that explore the complex relations and tensions between immigration, transnationalism, and settler colonialism. They highlight ways for educational institutions to be responsive to the multiple, at times contradicting, at times intersecting, lived experiences of students and communities. Following Blackledge et al. (2018), the authors in this volume use the notion of superdiversity to unpack the complexity of

> people coming into contact or proximity as a result of (inter alia) migration, invasion, colonisation, slavery, religious mission, persecution, trade, conflict, famine, drought, war, urbanisation, economic aspiration, family reunion, global commerce, and technological advances. These phenomena involve the mobility of people, and the mobility of resources. Mobility is not confined to the movement of people across national borders, but includes travel within borders.
>
> *(p. xxii)*

Through the lens of superdiversity, the authors tie the concept of superdiversity to the interplay of multiple intersections and tensions between new and old patterns of immigration in established, changing, and new communities. The works in this volume highlight the complexity and fluidity of these relations and modes of communication and demonstrate the importance of local contexts in formulating how teachers and teacher educators can best respond to the educational needs of individual learners, their communities, and neighborhoods in the context of superdiversity.

Context, Research, and Practices of Teacher Education in a Time of Superdiversity: Overview of the Chapters

Following Vertovec's (2007, 2019) conceptual frames, the content of this book is structured in three sections that speak to the contexts, research, and practice of teacher education in relation to superdiversity. In the first section, "Contexts of Teacher Education in a Superdiverse World," we consider two national contexts of Canada and the United States, as well as multiple local contexts of diverse populations (e.g., immigrants, refugees, Indigenous peoples). Our main focus is on intersections of social justice issues within the context of teacher education such as racial hierarchy, linguistic diversity, and transnationalism.

Specifically, Li's work on diversity among transnational students in North America argues for the need to consider transnational contexts of teacher education in order to attend to challenges and opportunities afforded by increasing mobility, border-crossing, and internationalization brought on by superdiversity. The chapter unpacks the sociocultural, socioeconomic, and sociopolitical complexity that characterizes the superdiverse students and illustrates the experiences of three divergent groups of transnational students in schools: those of involuntary immigrants/refugees, transient migrant students/sojourners, and transilient global elites. The chapter then outlines the instructional, ideological, and structural challenges that transnationalism has brought into light in teachers' classrooms and suggests a genuine "critical transnational curriculum" for teacher preparation. The chapter concludes with suggestions to engage preservice teachers with understandings of transnationalism, acquisition of pedagogical skills to value and support students' multiple identities and transnational educational assets, and development of agency and advocacy for change for superdiverse students in their classrooms.

In the subsequent chapter, Hare discusses the contexts of preparing Indigenous teachers to address the broader needs of Indigenous people. Drawing on the significant cultural being of the Trickster figure observed in Indigenous stories, this chapter describes how, methodologically, the trickster can inform teacher education. The author describes three pedagogical strategies informed by Trickster of how Indigenous teacher education programs can empower Indigenous preservice teachers in advancing their own journeys of decolonization and reclamation and to consider how teacher education can enrich and be enriched by Indigenous communities. These strategies for transforming teacher education to better engage with Indigenous priorities include summoning the imagination, disrupting the order of things, and renewal.

Two chapters that follow address overlapping contextual issues across teacher education programs in both United States and Canada. In her conceptual chapter, Taylor draws on important decolonizing work to propose how teacher education and professional development for teachers might support transformation where inclusion, social justice, and equity are central. The notion of decolonization is especially important in countries such as Canada and the United States where centuries of colonization have so negatively impacted Indigenous peoples.

In the next chapter, Bennett examines how a group of White preservice teachers experienced their teacher education program in relation to their interpretations of diversity and culturally relevant pedagogy at a large public university in the Mid-Atlantic United States. The preservice teachers valued diversity and culturally relevant pedagogy while they simultaneously deemed the pedagogy unnecessary to consider when planning for their future teaching practice. This work contributes to scholarship in both Canada and the United States by adding nuance to the work of scholars who show how Whiteness is often re-centered in teacher education programs.

Situated within the context of an American dual-language teacher education program, Varghese and colleagues explicate intersections of racial and linguistic diversity or the competing "raciolinguistic ideologies" related to dual-language education that are centered on White settler colonialism and demonstrate how collaborative, grassroots-initiated program redesign can challenge these ideologies.

After the discussion of contextual inequalities in the context of superdiversity in teacher education in the initial chapters, Section II, "Research on Teacher Education in a Time of Superdiversity," begins with a teacher educator's self-reflection followed by reports of studies that have begun to document how educators are addressing superdiversity in different contexts. Using an analytic autoethnographic lens with a focus on a graduate teacher education program and one mandatory course in particular, Gagne uncovers how various policies and initiatives in Ontario, at the University of Toronto and the Ontario Institute for Studies in Education (OISE), have aligned recursive program review and renewal in support of preparing prospective teachers to work with immigrant children and youth in Toronto, Canada, a city experiencing superdiversity similar to that of London as described by Vertovec (2007). The self-reflection also provides the opportunity to identify contextual variables and showcase possible contingent responsiveness, and practical solutions that Blackledge et al. (2018) called for.

As Conteh (2018) points out, powerful conservative ideologies still circulate about language learning and teaching that counter efforts to respond to the needs of superdiverse communities. In her chapter, Sterzuk reports on a study that investigated preservice teachers' views of language learners and teachers. Sterzuk's work illustrates that some novice teachers emerge from a teacher education program with the skills and predisposition to work with diverse students but others from the same program regress and take on deficit perspectives. Sterzuk demonstrates how different aspects of the program such as course work and practicum experiences have differential effects on students.

In the chapter that follows, Smith and Hajek examine the degree to which elements of "Culturally Responsive Literacy Pedagogy" (CRLP) and "Linguistically Responsive Literacy Pedagogy" (LRLP) were visible in the practices of in-service teachers as they assessed and instructed superdiverse learners in K–12 schools within the context of an online literacy course. Findings revealed that teachers demonstrated responsiveness across a wide range of literacy instruction and assessment practices. Instances of responsiveness appeared to be more prevalent across lower levels of CRLP and, in comparison, a significantly lower number of instances of responsiveness was visible at each level of LRLP. Based on these findings, they created corresponding informal CRLP and LRLP tools, what they call as "the Culturally and Linguistically Responsive Literacy Prism" to support literacy teachers and educators who wish to identify the degree to which responsiveness occurs and how it might be further cultivated in K–12 literacy classrooms.

Moore's chapter describing PASTEL approaches (Plurilingualism, Art, Science, Technology, and Literacies) is another example of a project that provides practical ways demonstrating how educators have addressed superdiversity. The emphasis on plurilingualism promotes the notion that all languages are resources that learners can leverage. It argues that retaining one's first or home language is highly desirable in an increasingly globalized and transnational world. This perspective is also reflected in the attention to multiliteracies and acknowledges the diverse ways that we communicate for different purposes and functions.

In another empirical study, de Jong reports on a project that aimed to support faculty in infusing ELL (English language learner)–related knowledge and skills in elementary preservice teacher education programs. Underpinning this initiative is the recognition that all teachers will be working with students from diverse backgrounds, not just ELL specialists. This work is important in that it signifies the pressing need for teacher education programs to make changes that will address the challenges of superdiversity that Vertovec and others identify.

Building on these research findings and framings, we believe that educators need to acknowledge "the reality of superdiversity, and look for practical ways to adapt institutions and services" (Blackedge et al., 2018, p. xxvi). Therefore, building on the contextual knowledge and research findings presented in the previous sections, in Section III, "Engaging Practices for Educators for Superdiversity," the chapters offer more practical ways to support both in-service and preservice teachers as well as teacher educators in adapting their instruction for superdiverse learners. Specifically, the chapters focus on how teachers and teacher educators can work within classrooms and schools by revisiting curriculum, pedagogy, and assessments and in collaboration with partners outside the classroom such as parents and communities.

Que and Li report on their study of support services available for refugee students in a small Canadian city where relatively few refugee and immigrant families have resettled until recently. They found that a bridging program designed to assist refugee students transition to a new school system provided some support in one of the high schools and at four middle schools. However, there was a lack of such support for children in elementary schools. Furthermore, instruction in English as a Second Language (ESL) was inadequate across the grade levels. Que and Li identified the need to enhance and expand instruction in ESL and to provide ongoing professional development for teachers working with refugee children and families, particularly in areas such as identifying children with learning disabilities and understanding the impact of trauma.

Two chapters in this section provide engaging practices and valuable lessons learned from working with superdiverse parents and communities as partners in their children's education. Building on ongoing research, the chapters show that family engagement in schools improves student achievement, reduces absenteeism, and restores parents' confidence in their children's education. Students with engaged parents or other caregivers earn higher grades and test scores, have better social skills, and show improved behavior. In their chapter, Edwards and White provide a historical overview of African American families' engagement and involvement in schools and outline the positive outcomes of this involvement by integrating the first author's family histroy. The second author then recounts her experiences as a White teacher, working with African American children and families, highlighting the phenomena of "Whiteness"—seeing children, families, and communities through the lens of White privilege—and "Niceness" or an inability or unwillingness to confront issues of racial and social class inequality. The authors present several models of parental engagement including the "Curriculum and Context-Based Model of Parent Engagement" that Edwards developed. They emphasize the need for teacher education programs and professional development programs to support teachers in gaining confidence and developing sensitivity in interacting with African American caregivers and families who speak different languages and may come from different cultural, racial, and social backgrounds. In the chapter that follows, Anderson and Anderson critically reflect on three decades of working in family literacy programs in superdiverse contexts: (1) in socioeconomically disadvantaged communities, (2) with Indigenous communities, and (3) with immigrant and refugee communities. Through reflecting on some of the challenges that they have encountered, as well as some of the positive lessons that were learned from families, they conclude by proposing some principles for those working with superdiverse children, families, and communities.

Focusing on both curriculum and pedagogy, Roessingh addresses the issue of assessment for superdiverse learners, which is arguably the Achilles' heel of the teaching profession. While there has been increased pressure to diminish large-scale assessment programs in the K–12 years (i.e., assessment of learning), there has been evidence that classroom-based assessment practices and processes are not providing the types of information that are useful for educational institutions to plan for ongoing instruction and learning support when warranted, or for parents and students to benefit and direct their own learning outcomes (assessment as learning). Superdiverse learners (including ELLs) may be especially vulnerable for academic failure if assessment data are not meaningfully communicated and do not offer sufficiently specific feedback for all stakeholders to adjust the learning experiences of diverse students.

Yee and Davison write from the premise that diversity is natural. They draw on their experiences in teaching a mandatory course in Indigenous education required of all preservice teachers in a teacher education program. They indicate the importance of reflecting on their own identities and personal histories and in helping create an ethical space where teacher candidates can engage with decolonizing and Indigenous perspectives, and where vulnerable students feel safe. In selecting resources, Yee and Davidson utilize local material but also material that reflects the diversity in Indigenous perspectives. As they conclude, there is still much to learn as we expand the repertoire of promising practices in helping preservice teachers prepare to work successfully with Indigenous (and all) students.

The Conclusion chapter revisits the conceptual underpinnings of superdiversity and teacher education, draws connections across the chapters, and provides some reflection on moving forward with teacher education in superdiverse contexts.

As a whole, this book advocates a "localized, flexible, non-standardized approach" to teacher education. Such an approach warrants close examinations of the intersections of context, research, and practice that responds to "the fluid, highly variable and ever-changing nature of the relationships across language, power and identity" (King & Bigelow, 2018, p. 469).

Moving from Diversity to Superdiversity in a COVID-19 Eduscape: A Conclusion

Collectively, the chapters in this volume advocate for the need to create better connections between conceptualization of language education, Indigenous education, and transnationalism and weave them with the ongoing efforts to decolonize teacher education in this time of superdiversity. To challenge the marginalization of students and lead to a deep institutional transformation, we argue for a nuanced and contextualized pedagogical weaving of all the components that underlie superdiversity in the North American context. Five principles emerged from our collective endeavor to ensure an institutional transformation in teacher education from a diversity stance to a superdiversity lens. These include prepare teachers to move

1. from continuing colonialism to engaging in decolonization,
2. from implementing superficial multiculturalism to advocating equity and social justice,
3. from endorsing ethnocentric monoculturalism to support learners' multiple dimensions of identity and belonging,
4. from endorsing monolingualism to support learners' multilingual linguistic repertoire, and
5. from local integration to transnationalism in curriculum design and instruction.

Our work in this volume clearly demonstrates that engagement with superdiversity is inherently contextual and should be grounded in the history of the land and the place where teaching and learning occur. The contextual chapters illustrate that teacher education programs in North America were created within the colonial frame of higher education and that a critical examination of Canadian and U.S. colonial history, as well as how colonial structures continue to play out in educational institutions is instrumental to navigate the complex intersection of superdiversity, immigration, transnationalism, and Indigeneity in North America. Reimagining teacher education from colonialism to decolonization is a process of "unlearning colonialism" (Donald, 2016) and undoing colonial practices that have shaped how teachers have been trained in the past and are still being prepared today. The chapters in the research and practice sections point out the need for teachers and teacher educators to self-reflect on their own positioning and stance, reengage with superdiverse communities in equitable approaches, revisit curriculum to restore historically excluded knowledge and ways of knowing, and restructure power dynamics to ensure systemic transformation.

One practice that we need to unlearn and undo is the simplistic multiculturalism that merely celebrates diversity. We concur with Hu-DeHart (2004), who argues that as long as multicultural education in general (and ethnic studies) remains within "the confines of 'sensitivity training' and celebrating diversity," it is safe and uncontested" (p. 848). We therefore advocate that teacher education must engage teachers in critical reflection on societal hierarchies that result in the achievement gaps confronting minoritized learners. Such reflection may entail engaging teachers in deep analyses of why certain social groups are disadvantaged in society and in school and have less access to societal resources and positions of power. This critical engagement requires teacher education to move beyond a superficial "add-ons" approach to address diversity to deep institutional, curricular, and pedagogical shifts that tackle difficult issues of inequity and social injustice that confront minoritized learners in order to liberate and empower these learners, as opposed to reproducing the systemic inequality.

Also, our work on superdiversity in this volume points to the need to unlearn and undo the practice of assimilationist monoculturalism to recognize and understand the complexity that underlies social communities in global, transnational context and in specific locations. It urges teachers and teacher educators to complicate and challenge stereotypes and generalizations that might be embedded in educational systems, and to bring nuanced and inclusive practices in their work with superdiverse students, families, and communities. It calls for teachers to be aware of the role of social media in circulating stereotypes and misinformation and to ask how schools could become spaces of belonging that nourish multiple identities and belongings across contexts.

Associated with undoing ethnocentric monoculturalism, there is a need for teacher education to undo the prevailing monolingualism that reinforces the deficit views of minoritized learners, their families, and communities. Several decades of research and theory have demonstrated the importance and value of acquiring or learning additional languages while maintaining one's first or home language. However, our work in this volume clearly indicates that dominant ideologies undervaluing bilingualism and multilingualism still prevail. Immigrant and refugee students and their families receive little encouragement to maintain their home language. Similarly, Indigenous communities have been experiencing rapid language loss. Related, the cognitive and pedagogical benefits of code-switching or translanguaging are often not leveraged, and in some cases, discouraged. Superdiversity necessitates that teachers are prepared to move from an exclusive focus on assimilating and mainstreaming minoritized learners into the dominant language (e.g., English) and culture. Instead, we propose to enable them with the dispositions of promoting bilingualism/plurilingualism as linguistic and educational assets to the greatest extent practicable, notwithstanding the challenges brought on by heightened nationalism.

Teachers' ability to foster learners' multiple belongings and identities and support their multilingual linguistic repertoire is of critical importance to those with transnational ties. Indeed, providing the necessary infrastructure to support immigrant and refugee families to be successful was an important consideration of Vertovec's original formulation. Teacher education programs must ensure teachers develop a global perspective that values minoritized learners' connectedness to their homelands while seeking belonging to, and social inclusion in the host societies. Teacher education programs must lead teachers in recognizing that "there are many historical, structural, and sociocultural factors at work when students and families cross multiple borders" (Ruiz & Baird, 2013, p. 62) and provide ongoing support in helping them dismantle the barriers that confront minoritized students and families. Teacher education, therefore, must support teachers in gaining pedagogical competence to transform the current subtractive approach to the learners' cultural and transnational education assets into an empowering learning experience.

The principles identified earlier are not stand-alone usnits but rather overlapping ideas that highlight a much-needed transformation in schooling and teacher education. To redo teacher education that is rooted in superdiversity, we need to enrich both our conceptualization of K–12 schooling and teacher education, and the practical implications for teachers, teacher educators, administrators, and policy makers as we demonstrate in the three sections of this book.

Finally, COVID-19 exposed the fragility of North American democracies (with different nuances in Canada and the United States and in different states and provinces) and raised above the surface harsh realities that many people choose to overlook. It clearly exposed the untended and neglected pockets of marginalized people in our society, issues such as racism, economic disparities, tensions between groups, elder and child care, drug addiction, prison, policing, and their multiple intersections are now much more out in the open. While this situation could lead to despair, it can also promote optimism as it clearly demonstrates that we are all connected and that if we want to prosper as humans, we need to care for us all. More specifically, the forced closure of schools and the move to online instruction for universities gives teachers and teacher educators a unique opportunity to reflect on what is lost and what can be done differently post-COVID.

References

Anderson, J., & Anderson, A. (2018). "No peeing on the sidewalk!": Family literacy in culturally, linguistically, and socially diverse communities. *Journal of Family Diversity in Education*, 3(1), 77–91.

Akiba, M., Cockrell, K. S., Simmons, J. C., Han, S., & Agarwal, G. (2010). Preparing teachers for diversity: Examination of teacher certification and program accreditation standards in the 50 states and Washington, DC. *Equity & Excellence in Education*, 43(4), 446–462.

Assal, K. (2020, February 20). *A quarter of Canada's immigrants arrived from India in 2019*. Retrieved on May 12, 2020 *Cic News*. from https://www.cicnews.com/2020/02/a-quarter-of-canadas-immigrants-arrived-from-india-in-2019-0213700.html#gs.6eyqpp

Blackledge, A., & Creese, A., with Baynham, M., Cooke, M., Goodson, L., Goodson, L., Hua, Z., Malkani, B., Phillimore, J., Robinson, M., Rock, F., Simpson, J., Tagg, C., Thompson, J., Trehan, K., & Wei, L. (2018). Language and superdiversity: An interdisciplinary perspective. In A. Cresse & A. Blackledge (Eds.), *The Routledge handbook of language and superdiversity* (pp. xxi–xlv). London: Routledge.

Campbell, C. (2020). Educational equity in Canada: The case of Ontario's strategies and actions to advance excellence and equity for students. *School Leadership & Management*, 1–20. doi:10.1080/13632434.2019.1709165

Chan, A., & Ritchie, J. (2019). Critical pedagogies of place: Some considerations for early childhood care and education in a superdiverse 'bicultural' Aotearoa (New Zealand). *The International Journal of Critical Pedagogy*, 10(1), 51–74.

Conteh, J. (2018). Translanguaging as pedagogy—a critical review. In A. Cresse & A. Blackledge (Eds.). *The Routledge handbook of language and superdiversity* (pp. 473–487). London: Routledge.

de Brey, C., Musu, L., McFarland, J., Wilkinson-Flicker, S., Diliberti, M., Zhang, A., Branstetter, C., & Wang, X. (2019). *Status and trends in the education of racial and ethnic groups 2018* (NCES 2019-038). U.S. Department of Education. Washington, DC: National Center for Education Statistics. Retrieved from https://nces.ed.gov/pubsearch/

Dion, S. (2007). Disrupting molded images: Identities, responsibilities and relationships—teachers and indigenous subject material. *Teaching Education*, 18(4), 329–342.

Donald, D. (2016). Chapter three: From what does ethical relationality flow? An "Indian" act in three artifacts. *Counterpoints*, 478(2016), 10–16.

Durgunoglu, A., & Hughes, T. (2010). How prepared are the US preservice teachers to teach English language learners? *International Journal of Teaching and Learning in Higher Education*, 22(1), 32–41.

Dyce, C. M., & Owusu-Ansah, A. (2016). Yes, we are still talking about diversity: Diversity education as a catalyst for transformative, culturally relevant, and reflective preservice teacher practices. *Journal of Transformative Education*, 14(4), 327–354.

Gogolin, I. (2011). The challenge of super diversity for education in Europe, *Education Inquiry*, 2(2), 239–249,

Government of Canada. (2017). *Immigrants from China, 1885–1949*. https://www.bac-lac.gc.ca/eng/discover/immigration/immigration-records/immigrants-china-1885-1949/Pages/introduction.aspx

Gunderson, L., & D'Silva, R. (2016). Disaggregating secondary-level Chinese immigrants' academic, English, and school success. In W. Ma, & G. Li, (Eds.), *Chinese-heritage students in North American schools: Understanding hearts and minds beyond test scores* (pp. 88–102). New York, NY: Routledge.

Hare, J. (2020). Reconciliation: Hope or hype? In A. Phelan, W. F. Pinar, N. Ng-A-Fook, & R. Kane (Eds.), *Reconceptualizing teacher education. A Canadian contribution to a global challenge* (pp. 19–38). Ottawa, ON: University of Ottawa Press.

Hu-DeHart, E. (2004). Ethnic studies in U.S. higher education: History, development, and goals. In J. A. Banks & C. A. M. Banks (Eds.), *Handbook of research on multicultural education* (pp. 869–881). San Francisco: Jossey-Bass.

James, C. E., & Turner, T. (2017). *Towards race equity in education: The schooling of black students in the Greater Toronto area*. Toronto, Ontario, Canada: York University.

King, A., & Bigelow, M. (2018). Multilingual education policy, superdiversity and educational equity. In A. Creese & A. Blackledge (Eds.), *The Routledge handbook of language and superdiversity* (pp. 459–473). London: Routledge. doi:10.4324/9781315696010

Kuhfeld, M., & Tarasawa, B. (2020). *The COVID-19 slide: What summer learning loss can tell us about the potential impact of school closures on student academic achievement*. NWEA. Retrieved May 11, 2020 from https://www.nwea.org/content/uploads/2020/05/Collaborative-Brief_Covid19-Slide-APR20.pdf

Li, G. (2018). Moving toward a diversity plus teacher education: Approaches, challenges, and possibilities in preparing teachers for English language learners. In A. Polly (Ed.), *Handbook of research on analyzing practices for teacher preparation and licensure* (pp. 215–236). Hershey, PA: IGI Global.

Li, G., Hinojosa, D., & Wexler, L. (2018). Beliefs and perceptions about their preparation to teach English language learners: Voices of mainstream pre-service teachers. *International Journal of TESOL and Learning*, 7(1&2), 1–21.

Li, G., & Jee, Y. (2020). *Pan-diversity integration as an equity trap: Lessons from pre-service teachers' experiences of preparation for teaching English language learners in the U.S* [Manuscript under review].

Li, G., & Sah, P. (2020). Critical pedagogy for preservice teacher education: An agenda for a plurilingual reality. In S. Steinberg et al. (Eds.), *Handbook of critical pedagogy* (pp. 884–898). New York: SAGE Publications.

McKell, L. (2010). *Achievement Gap Task Force draft report for discussion and feedback*. Toronto, ON: Toronto District School Board.

Meissner, F., & Vertovec, S. (2015). Comparing super-diversity. *Ethnic and Racial Studies*, 38(4), 521–555.

Moore, T. (2020). Governing superdiversity: Learning from the Aboriginal Australian case. *Social Identities*, 26(2), 233–249.

Morris, L. (2004). *The control of rights: The rights of workers and asylum-seekers undermanaged migration* (Discussion Paper OFSTED (Office for Standards in Education) 2003. The education of asylum-seeker pupils, Report HMI 453). London: Joint Council for the Welfare of Immigrants.

Paine, R. (1999.) Aboriginality, multiculturalism, and liberal rights philosophy. *Etnos*, 64(3–4), 325–349.

Ruiz, N. T., & Baird, P. J. (2013) Transnational teacher education: Towards theory and practice. *NABE Journal of Research and Practice*, 4(1), 60–100.

Schmid, K., Wölfer, R., Swart, H., Christ, O., Al Ramiah, A., Vertovec, S., & Hewstone, M. (2017). The "wallpaper effect" revisited: Divergent findings on the effects of intergroup contact on attitudes in diverse versus nondiverse contexts. *Personality and Social Psychology Bulletin*, 43(9), 1268–1283.

Shah, V. (2018). Different numbers, different stories: Problematizing "gaps" in Ontario and the TDSB. *Canadian Journal of Educational Administration and Policy*, 187, 31–47.

Sleeter, C. E., & Milner, H. R. (2011). Researching successful efforts in teacher education to diversify teachers. In A. F. Ball & C. A. Tyson (Eds.), *Studying diversity in teacher education* (pp. 81–104). Lanham, MD: Rowman & Littlefield.

Statistics Canada (2016). *Growth rate of population is much higher for Aboriginal peoples.* Retrieved from https://www150.statcan.gc.ca/n1/pub/89-645-x/2010001/growth-pop-croissance-eng.htm

Statistics Canada. (2017). *Study: A look at immigration, ethnocultural diversity and languages in Canada up to 2036, 2011 to 2036.* https://www150.statcan.gc.ca/n1/daily-quotidien/170125/dq170125b-eng.htm

Statistics Canada. (2018). *First Nations people, Métis and Inuit in Canada: Diverse and growing populations.* Ottawa, Ontario: Statistics Canada.

Statistics Canada. (2019). *Focus on Geography Series, 2016 Census.* https://www12.statcan.gc.ca/census-recensement/2016/as-sa/fogs-spg/Facts-pr-eng.cfm?Lang=Eng&GK=PR&GC=59&TOPIC=7

St. Denis, V. (2011). Silencing Aboriginal curricular content and perspectives through multiculturalism: "There are other children here." *Review of Education, Pedagogy, & Cultural Studies*, 33(4), 306–317.

Tuck, E., & Yang, K. W. (2012). Decolonization is not a metaphor. *Decolonization: Indigeneity, Education & Society*, 1(1), 1–40.

United Nations. 2008. *United Nations declaration on the rights of indigenous peoples.* http://www.un.org/esa/socdev/unpfii/documents/DRIPS_en.pdf

Vertovec, S. (2007). Super-diversity and its implications. *Ethnic and Racial Studies*, 30(6), 1024–1054.

Vertovec, S. (2019). Talking around super-diversity. *Ethnic and Racial Studies*, 42(1), 125–139.

Vertovec, S., Schmid, K., Wölfer, R., Swart, H., Christ, O., Al Ramiah, A., et al. (2017). The "wallpaper effect" revisited: Divergent findings on the effects of intergroup contact on attitudes in diverse versus nondiverse contexts. *Personality and Social Psychology Bulletin*, 43(9), 1268–1283.

SECTION I

Contexts of Teacher Education in a Superdiverse World

1

TEACHING SUPERDIVERSE STUDENTS IN A TRANSNATIONAL WORLD

Rethinking Teacher Education

Guofang Li

"Where do the [Chinese] parents want their children to live when they grow up? In Canada or elsewhere?" This question was posed to our research team by a principal when we met in early March 2020 when the school was still open prior to COVID-19 lockdown in British Columbia to try to understand Chinese immigrant parents' expectations for their children in Canadian schools. While the parents were trying to prepare their children for a global future in their culturally specific ways, the principal and the teachers questioned whether the parents knew "what this global future" entailed. Our conversation pointed to a practical need for teachers and schools to grapple with teaching children who may be socialized into loyalty and belonging to multiple nations, states, and cultural groups beyond physical national borders. The goal of this chapter is to address this practical need by unpacking the diversity within transnational students' population in North America, their divergent and convergent experiences in schools, and the implications for teachers and their preparation for teaching these students.

Levitt and Schiller (2008) describe the phenomenon of physical and/or symbolic enactment of sustaining social networks or "multiple worlds" beyond boundaries of nation-states as transnationalism. Transnationalism is enacted as "cultural members learn how to belong to hyper-diverse spaces and learn new ways of participating in transcultural communities of practice across ethno-national groups and languages" (Malsbary, 2018, p. 1240). Precisely because of the coexistence of and aspiration for identities and belongings to multiple worlds beyond national borders, transnational students usually have unique educational orientations and needs and can pose challenges for teachers who were trained to achieve the sole goal of teaching students to become mainstreamed into the host society (Sánchez & Kasun, 2012). Mismatches among teachers' and parents' and students' orientations often lead to conflicts between home and school, resulting in many transnational students' sense of disconnection and resistance to schooling, teachers' negative perceptions of their transnational ties (Lightman, 2018), and schools' neglect of their transnational resources and literacies (Taira, 2019). As Sánchez and Kasun (2012) noted, public school educators and researchers have "neither adequately recognized nor situated this [transnational] lifestyle" (p. 72) in K–12 educational contexts, warranting the need for teacher educators to address the teaching and learning implications of working with transnational students.

However, as transnational mobility and extension of social networks have increased diversity to a new level, there has been minimal research done on how to prepare teachers to address transnationalism in K–12 school settings in North America. In light of this urgent need, this chapter discusses how teacher education might prepare new generations of teachers for the growing complexity brought on by the increasing trend of transnationalism in K–12 schools.

Unpacking Diversity Among Transnational Students in North America

The unprecedented rate of global mobility in the past few decades has resulted in the ever-increasing influx of foreign-born immigrants into North America. Both the U.S. and Canada have reported record-breaking rises in their new immigrant population: the U.S. foreign-born population reached a record 44.4 million (13.7% of the total population) in 2017, more than quadrupled since 1965 (Radford, 2019). Similarly, the recent Canadian national census of 2016 showed that 7.5 million individuals were foreign-born in Canada, accounting for 21.9% of the total population. That is, approximately one out of every five people in Canada is foreign-born (Statistics Canada, 2017). Entailed in these recent statistics is the heterogeneity of transnational students across various axes of differentiation, ranging from gender, race, and religion to national origin, immigration status, and social class. The hyper-diverse demographics among the recent immigrants are also well mirrored in the K–12 context. According to the National Center for Education Statistics (NCES), as of 2015, more than half of school-age youth in public schools in the United States were non-Caucasian ethnic minority and about 9.6% of them were English language learners (ELLs; Geinger, 2018). In some states such as California, more than one-fifth of its K–12 students were classified as English learners (NCES, 2019). Similarly, in Canada, in many schools in British Columbia and Ontario, as many as 65% of the student populations are ELLs (Skelton, 2014).

To date, many terms have been adopted in the field of education to capture the superdiversity within these groups of learners. For instance, over two decades ago, Ogbu and Simon (1998) categorized newcomer minority students into *voluntary/involuntary* immigrants to describe students' reasons for immigration. Voluntary immigrants include those who leave their countries of origin willingly and voluntarily for employment or better life chances. Involuntary immigrants, by contrast, are those forced to relocate due to civil war or other crises in their places of origin and do not plan or choose to settle in the host society. These involuntary immigrants include mainly refugees, migrant workers, undocumented workers, and sometimes binational people who maintain economic and social ties with their places of origin but may be unsure about where best to prepare their children for the future, in the host society or in their places of origin.

In more recent studies, *migrant* and *immigrant* are often used to describe students with plural but temporal geographic attachments (Zúñiga & Hamann, 2009). A migrant refers to any person who lives temporarily in a foreign country, moving from one place to another in search of short-term employment, and who has acquired some significant social ties to this country, whereas an immigrant is an individual who willingly leaves their country of origin and legally enters another country to permanently resettle, thus qualifying to work without restriction (Preemptive Love, 2019). Migrant students, due to their temporary residence status, are sometimes called "sojourners" given the differences they embody from both native-born and immigrant students who intend to stay in their host country for an extended period. Key to this differentiation is the fact that sojourners "need not only learn how to negotiate this place (i.e., the community surrounding their present school), but fundamentally any new place, as the prospect looms that they will sooner or later be headed someplace else" (Hamann, 2001, p. 38).

Lightman (2018) conceptualized newcomer immigrant youths on a *transilient-transient* spectrum based on their divergent family socioeconomic statuses and family material conditions prior to and after immigration. The "transilients" are the prototypical transnational groups, with flexible global citizenships and professional networks of socioeconomic elites (e.g., Kobayashi & Preston, 2007; Ley, 2010; Ong, 1999; Waters, 2006). This group includes both offspring of business or economic immigrants who possess considerable economic resources and "visa students" who can afford high tuition fees to attend schools in Canada or the United States. Transient transnationals, on the other end, are "at the interstices of precarious employment and precarious citizenship" (Ried-Musson, 2014, p. 162). In North America, this group of transnationals consists mainly of migrant workers largely originating from Mexico, Central America, the Caribbean, South-East Asia, or involuntary migrants in the refugee stream.

These attempts to differentiate transnational students in research studies suggest the complexity that exists within these groups. K–12 education in North America needs to embrace such superdiversity and consider how to capitalize on students' diverse motivations and experiences within the global sociopolitical climate to maximize their chances of sociocultural and academic success. The next section focuses on the experiences of three divergent groups of transnational students in North American schools: those of involuntary immigrants/refugees, transient migrant students/sojourners, and transilient global elites.

Transnational Students' Di/Convergent Schooling Experiences in North America

A growing body of research has documented transnational students' experiences of schooling in North America. While the experiences of all transnational students differ due to their particular backgrounds and immigrant histories, many, regardless of their immigration or socioeconomic status, also share similar stories of facing challenges of linguistic and cultural discontinuity between school and home, social discrimination, academic exclusion, and system blockage (i.e., school assignment, school language policy, immigrant language provision policy; Li, 2006, 2008, 2018). Furthermore, few schools or teachers were found to be responsive to the students' full transnational experiences and their desire to using their schooling as "preparatory for persistently transnational adulthood" (Hamann & Zúñiga, 2011, p. 148).

Refugee Students' Experiences

Research with refugee students has consistently revealed the impact of their transnational ties (social, material, and/or political), often negative, on their adjustment to schooling and life in North America. Trauma and loss were the top factors that affect refugee youths' physical and psychological well-being and academic success (Dávila, 2012; Kanu, 2008; McBrien, 2011). For example, McWilliams and Bonet (2016) investigated 90 Bhutanese, Burmese, and Iraqi refugee youths' schooling experiences in the United States and found that they were heavily impacted by the effects of trauma and loss from their experiences prior to resettlement in the United States. They were also caught in "the ubiquitous tension between looking to better their lives through education, while also encountering linguistic and foundational challenges in their classrooms" (McWilliams & Bonet, 2016, p. 164). Similarly, in Canada, refugee youths with interrupted schooling have been found to "fall through the cracks" due to confusion within the educational system, financial pressures to support their families, and the need to deal with traumatic pasts (von Stackelberg, 2020).

A plethora of research on refugee children's adaptation to school indicates that they often experienced trauma, social isolation, loneliness, and widespread depression (that sometimes led to suicide) in U.S. and Canadian schools, even among those who achieved academic success (Jowett, 2020; Li, 2009; McBrien, 2011; Mosselson, 2007). Many of the youths were also confronted with racial discrimination and sociolinguistic and academic marginalization (Dávila, 2012; Kanu, 2008; Li, 2018). Due to the lack of support services, refugee students were often left to sink or swim in "schools in crisis" (McWilliams & Bonet, 2016, p. 164). Both official and social spaces in school have been reported to be unwelcoming to refugee students with different linguistic, cultural, ethnic, or religious backgrounds. Refugee students were often marginalized in school programs, and this marginalization was "motivated by employment issues, the concerns of local businesses, fear of potential violence, and the wish to maintain an academic advantage" (Gitlin et al., 2003, p. 91) among teachers, mainstream students, and the local white community surrounding the school. These experiences of othering significantly shaped refugee students' sense of being and belonging in the mainstream schools (Levitt & Schiller, 2008).

Sojourner Students' Experiences

The majority of relevant studies on transnational migrant students have been conducted in the United States and Mexico. These studies typically focus on the experiences of transient, economically disadvantaged students from Mexico or Central American countries. As noted earlier, these "sojourner students" also faced similar challenges of poverty, language, and cultural differences that were often posed by mobility. As Green (2003) explained, moving from place to place makes it difficult to attend school regularly, learn at grade level, accrue credits, and meet all graduation requirements. It is also difficult to participate in socializing activities and create the social networks critical to change their economic and social status in society. Geographic mobility makes it harder to receive the adult support most young people need academically, socially, psychologically, and emotionally. In a study of 18 migrant secondary school students' experiences in California, Terhorst (2017) found that both academic and migration stresses affected students' self-esteem and attitude towards schooling and parents were unable to provide support to their children academically due to educational, language, or working restrictions. Among students who were mobile transnationally across borders, educational experiences were influenced not only by events related to their daily experiences in the United States but also by experiences that linked them with their places of origin. However, like the transnational literacies of refugee youth (Taira, 2019), migrant students' transnational ties and resource often remain invisible to teachers mainly due to students' unwillingness to share these resources in school or because there is no pedagogical space in the classroom to activate such experience (Sánchez & Kasun, 2012). Even when migrant students' transnational identity is brought to teachers' attention, individual educators may view it as an added component and may or may not feel that it is the school's responsibility to accommodate to the needs of transnational students and their families. Similar to refugee youth, migrant students also confront serious societal and institutional barriers in receiving proper educational services (Green, 2003) and many teachers often lack pedagogical toolkits or curricular resources and are unsure how to provide support or capitalize on students' mobile, transnational experiences regardless of their expression of interest or willingness to make changes (Rendall & Torr, 2008).

International Students' Experiences

A third group of transnational students increasingly gaining attention in research is intimately tied to the broader trend of the globalized knowledge economy, where international education takes the form of "market-driven processes, conceptualized through a neoliberal framework of supply and demand" (Robertson, 2013, p. 40). One distinct characteristic of these students is that they often have one parent present in the host country while the other parent remains in their country of origin to provide financial support. Sometimes, both parents may be absent and the students stay with host families in the host society. One consequence is a propensity for frequent or extended absences during the school year as they travel back and forth between the host country and their country of origin (Hamann & Zúñiga, 2011). These international, visa-holding students (and their families) view a Western educational experience as a globally transferrable asset that is highly instrumental to their upward social mobility (Waters, 2006). Mitchell (2001) provided a Canadian example of how the value of education is more globally oriented for some transnational families and communities:

> For many immigrant Chinese Canadians, the preparation of individuals to become high achievers in a global workplace is more practical and more attainable than their constitution as citizens of a particular nation-state. In this vision, inherently national narratives, such as that of multiculturalism, are willingly sacrificed for a more flexible notion of educational excellence.
>
> *(p. 39)*

Studies with Korean early study abroad students and Chinese study abroad or "parachute" students have revealed that although these students were free of financial pressures or traumatic pasts (unlike their refugee and migrant peers) and enjoyed more family educational investment, they were also confronted with many similar sociolinguistic challenges posed by language and cultural differences (Kang & Kim, 2017; Li, 2019; Lightman, 2018; Waters, 2006). More pronounced than the other two groups, studies with this group of students often reveal high family pressure for academic success, intense parent–child conflicts, and mental health issues (i.e., loneliness and depression). Similar to the other two groups, students' transnational experiences are regarded as a major factor that impedes academic progress (Goldstein, 2003; Hamann, 2001; Zúñiga & Hamann, 2009). Lightman (2018) studied 14 international students' experiences in a Canadian secondary school and found that the students' transnational "ways of being" and multiple ways of belonging were in conflict with the teachers' views on how students ought to act and feel within classroom settings. In some cases, there was a degree of hostility by the teachers toward extended home country visits by transnational students, given that their absence disrupted teachers' instructional plans and necessitated adjustments that added to teachers' workload. However, in many of these cases, the teachers expressed feelings of inadequacy and unpreparedness in assisting students to succeed when they were not physically present in the classroom (Lightman, 2018). Apart from teachers' unpreparedness and lack of resources to tailor their classes to meet the needs of transnational students, Taira (2019) posited that the prescribed curriculum adopted in many schools often allowed very limited space for transnational students to access personally relevant and engaging texts.

The findings of studies across these three groups consistently demonstrate that although these transnational students came with crucial ethno-linguistic and cultural capital, such sociocultural and linguistic resources have not been translated into supporting resources compatible with the assimilationist approach in mainstream schools, where transnational migrant youth are often framed narrowly as "English learners" (Dabach & Fones, 2016). This framing often leads to foregrounding deficits among the learners while turning a blind eye to their linguistic skills and cultural knowledge, leading to neglect of, or even negative reaction to, students' multilingualism and transnational experience and identity (Lightman, 2018; Sánchez & Kasun, 2012).

Educating Transnational Students: Challenges and Promising Practices

Researchers have observed that, given a supportive instructional and curricular environment, transnational youth possess rich reservoirs of multiliteracy resources and knowledge (Goldstein, 2003; Rounsaville, 2014; Taira, 2019), cultural adaptability and flexibility (Kim & Slapac, 2015; Skerrett, 2012), as well as navigational and resistance skills (Pacheco, 2012; Shik, 2015) that enable them to make sense of academic content and to survive a school environment often marked by hostility and loneliness. They are also observed to be able to make use of their transnational experiences in the local context of classroom learning (de la Piedra & Araujo, 2012). However, there are also many reports of current school systems "failing to properly educate and ease the transition and integration" of these transnational students, many of whom "quickly become marginalized as racially, ethnically, religiously and linguistically marked minority groups" (Suárez-Orozco & Sattin, 2007, p. 3). Several layers of challenges of educating transnational students have been identified. One is the lack of teacher preparation for teaching students who possess transnational resources, along with other socioemotional challenges (Jowett, 2020; Li, 2009; McBrien, 2011; Mosselson, 2007). In a study on educators' perspectives on the social and academic integration of Syrian refugees in rural, urban, and suburban schools in Canada, Antoinette Gagné et al. (2018) reported that one of the greatest challenges that educators face is the high number of students who have experienced trauma before their arrival in Canada and how it significantly interferes with their learning. However, many teachers reportedly lack preparation for working with refugee populations and do not understand the effects of trauma, and there is an uneven provision of services for refugee families and support for teachers across different schools and districts. This sense of under-preparedness is also prevalent among teachers who teach migrant or elite international students (Lightman, 2018; Sánchez & Kasun, 2012).

In addition to the lack of preparation, resources, and toolkits among teachers, there also exist ideological, structural challenges. Informed by a traditional, assimilationist conception of immigration, school systems in the receiving country often adopt a one-way accommodation approach that is more focused on changing newcomers' language use and cultural identity to help them successfully transition into the new educational and sociocultural environments (Li & Sah, 2020; Sánchez & Kasun, 2012). However, for the continuous influx of transnational students with strong affiliations to both host and home countries (and others) who envision educational and career prospects in more than one country, the assimilationist model of education becomes limiting, given its roots in "a combination of essentialist notions of identity in general and essentialist ways of relating to national identity specifically" (Erdal, 2013, p. 988).

In reality, it is typical that students who sustain transnational connections display a "dual frame of reference" through which they make continual comparisons about the strengths, weaknesses, and relative worth of their educational experiences in the home and host countries (Ogbu & Simon, 1998; Vertovec, 2007). This dual frame of reference, however, remains "invisible" to many teachers who continue to draw a monolithic association between students' academic achievement and behavioral performances against mainstream monocultural norms and see students' transnational connections as deficits rather than assets for learning (e.g., Lightman, 2018; Sánchez & Kasun, 2012). In a study on transnational students' educational experiences in Mexico and Chicago, Hamann and Zúñiga (2011) found that school curriculum and peers often become a source of everyday ruptures for transnational students that negatively impact their chances of social and academic success in schools. In another study that explored the literacy practices of 12 transnational students in a ninth-grade English classroom, Taira (2019) found that although these students clearly possessed transnational understandings and had lives that included participation in rich and varied literacies, these practices were "rarely visible in the school and classroom, and only surfaced when strategically sought out by the school and teacher to further academic goals" (p. 83).

Many teachers with good intentions may have adopted a superficial form of multicultural education that failed to engage students with critical reflection on their own intercultural experiences for transformative learning (Gutierrez, 2019; Ladson-Billing, 1995). Some mainstream teachers were reported to voice "abstract commitments to diversity" without gaining fundamental understandings of diversity to provide effective instruction for minoritized students (Pezzetti, 2017, p. 131). Others were reported to have become "overwhelmed" and lost their idealistic beliefs about diversity, reverting to "old stereotypical notions about [minoritized] students" (Causey et al., 2000, p. 43). In this sense, multiculturalism-oriented teaching and learning has become "invisible, irrelevant and/or tokenistic in the current milieu, and may even inhibit the integration of students with transnational ties" (Lightman, 2018, p. 131). Therefore, to change the status quo, schools must rethink the fundamental assumption of assimilating students as citizens of the host society and instead become culturally and sociopolitically responsive to students' identities and their sense of belonging that may extend beyond or across national boundaries (Bajaj & Bartlett, 2017).

A few studies have documented such successful practices where teachers are reported to be able to recognize students' transnational funds of knowledge and weave them into the tapestry of classroom activities and interactions through innovative pedagogical planning (de la Piedra & Araujo, 2012; Malsbary, 2018). Based on a study of three urban international high schools in New York and California that served newcomer immigrant and refugee students, Bajaj and Bartlett (2017) identified in the schools "a critical transnational curriculum" that uses diversity as a learning opportunity, engages translanguaging (or students' use of their full linguistic repertoire, including first languages), promotes civic engagement as curriculum, and cultivates multidirectional aspirations. In the focal schools, students from heterogeneous backgrounds were intentionally mixed together to collaborate on projects so they could learn from one another. These schools also valued students' first languages by offering bilingual programs and materials and through allowing students to use their first language for content learning. Furthermore, students were engaged in direct learning experiences connected to social and environmental issues affecting their local and transnational communities. Finally, the schools took into consideration students' multiple current national identifications and different plans for the future by cultivating students' native languages, intentionally extending the curriculum beyond a local, U.S. focus, and working with students to plan a broad spectrum of future possibilities.

In another study that examined one transnational teacher's language arts classrooms in an English–Spanish dual-language program close to the US–Mexico border, de la Piedra and Araujo (2012) revealed that the teacher valued code-switching as a common strategy to engage students in meaningful participation and instructional conversations and designed literacy tasks that promoted students' recontextualization of Mexican school knowledge and discourse as tools to assist with academic learning. More important, a salient practice in her instructional repertoire was making connections, where she reflected how she transferred Mexican schooling experience into navigational tools for the U.S. academic context and encouraged her students to make their own connections to better acclimate themselves to English-dominant U.S. schooling and academic learning.

Similarly, in ethnographic studies of three teachers' practices working with diverse newcomer youths in Los Angeles and New York, Malsbary (2018) found that each teacher engaged in a set of practices in relation to the transnational social field in which they worked. These practices included creating contextually relevant activities that allowed students to use their first languages in subject-specific curriculum that fostered interdisciplinary connections, conducting epistemically open assessment (e.g., a multimodal assessment that encouraged learner talk, generated authentic questioning, allowed students to transfer skills learned to a new problem set, and permitted plenty of time for all learners to complete assessments in comparison with the norms set in traditional district and state-based testing), and sustained critical languaging (e.g., encouraging democratic, equitable talk among students and allowing translanguaging).

Two things must be noted from these studies. First, teachers who are migrants themselves with transnational backgrounds or experiences are few in the current teaching force in North America, in which over 85% of in- and preservice teachers are White, middle class, and monolingual. Not all of the teachers with transnational experiences automatically adopt pedagogies that recognize students' transnational assets. Second, the focal teachers were all veteran teachers (5–28 years) who have been teaching in superdiverse contexts for years and all emphasized the critical role of this "time in context" in helping them learn to become responsive to the students' transnational resources and assets (Malsbary, 2018). Their experiences pose important questions and provide directions on how to best support other teachers and preservice teachers who may not have had much "time in context" yet, which is the focus of the next section.

Implications for Teacher Education

An overwhelming body of research has pointed to the under-preparedness of pre-service teachers across all levels in both Canada and the U.S. (Cummins, 2014; Greenberg et al., 2015; Li et al., 2018; Webster & Valeo, 2011). In a nationwide program review of preservice teacher education institutions in the United States, Greenberg, Walsh, and McKee (2015) concluded that over 76% of the country's programs failed to ready their elementary teacher candidates for teaching ELLs, many of whom are transnational students. In a review of Canadian educational policies regarding diverse learners, Cummins (2014) found that

> [w]ith respect to immigrant-background students, a large majority of teachers and administrators have not had opportunities to access the knowledge base regarding effective instruction for these students nor have they had opportunities for pre-service or in-service professional development regarding effective instructional practices.
>
> *(p. 358)*

Ideologically, federal educational policies in the United States have been pushing for "English only" instruction and a sharp decrease in federal funding to help states and local school districts to provide bilingual support for diverse learners, presenting additional challenges for teachers to educate these students (Goldenberg & Wagner, 2015; Li & Sah, 2020). This policy push for "English only" instruction strongly influences the way teacher education policies and practices are framed. For example, the dominant monolingual educational practices have resulted in little attention to incorporating sociolinguistic issues in teacher education programs (Li, 2018; Lucas & Villegas, 2013). In many teacher education programs, the issue of diversity is often rendered a marginal status in the curriculum, if any, and the superficial, peripheral attention to diversity had produced little or no change in either schools or in teacher education praxis (Ladson-Billings, 1995), and in some cases, resulted in "damage-centered teaching" that intentionally or unintentionally perpetuates white, monolingual, supremacist logics (Andrews et al., 2019, p. 7). As Samson and Collins (2012) argued,

> [a] multisubject elementary school teacher candidate, for example, may be required to take courses in child development, English language arts, math, science, social studies, art, behavior management, and assessment, but not in the pedagogy of teaching ELLs. Without specific required coursework relating to the unique learning needs of ELLs, teachers will not be able to teach these students adequately.
>
> *(p. 8)*

It must be noted that current scholarship on educating diverse newcomers, as shown earlier, has concentrated on preparing teachers to focus on linguistic and cultural diversity with the goal of assimilating newcomers into the dominant language, and has not touched on the issue of transnationalism that is integral to superdiverse newcomers' everyday lives and schooling. With this kind of preparation, many well-intentioned, even social justice–oriented teacher candidates may not have learned to recognize the educational needs of the transnational students that set them apart from U.S.-born, monolingual English-speaking students, leading to classroom practices that are ineffective for preparing learners for multiple futures and belongings. As Lightman (2018) documented, although many teachers have reached an awareness of the need for more culturally diverse and globally transferrable curricula, they may still be challenged with competing demands among students who live a normative life of transnationalism and lack the ability to support those students accordingly.

It is evident that there is a need to prepare teachers for the transnational turn that requires a different kind of teacher education curriculum, one that parallels the critical transnational curriculum enacted in some K–12 schools (see Bajaj & Bartlett, 2017; Malsbary, 2018). Levitt and Schiller (2008) argued for a new analytical lens that centers on transnationalism to revisit the basic assumptions about social institutions such as the family, citizenship, and nation-states in education "because migrants are often embedded in multi-layered, multi-sited transnational social fields, encompassing those who move and those who stay behind"

(p. 1003). Nowadays, as the population of learners becomes increasingly super-diverse, key concepts such as society and culture need to be reinterpreted with growing fluidity and flexibility, unshackled from the traditional bonds of nation-state or territory (Warriner, 2017). Given the uncertainties of immigration status or future family plans, students do not necessarily view Canadian or U.S. education as a means to naturalization; rather, many of them possess greater knowl-edge of, and interest in, sociopolitical issues and history of their home country than those of the (temporary) receiving society (e.g., Mitchell, 2001; Rumbaut, 2002). As the conversation with the principal at the beginning of this chapter indicates, transnational students may be less interested in membership in a par-ticular national community than in a global form of citizenship that allows them to move both locally and internationally in the future (Mitchell, 2001). Teacher education and professional development should therefore support preservice and in-service teachers in examining their own assumptions about the value and goal of education and foster their understanding of students' desire for transnational mobility and portability of education-based cultural capital across borders. This means that focusing on supporting students' English-only development and social integration into the local mainstream society is not enough. As Skerrett (2012) argued, a genuine transnational curriculum must engage preservice teachers with the study of transnational students' evolving language and multiliteracy practices across multiple contexts and over time and foster such transnational literacies by investigating the transnational experiences and concerns of students.

Furthermore, new teacher education curricula must move beyond teach-ers' transnational awareness to underscore the notion that students' globally and internationally transferrable knowledge and identity formations are a desirable asset (rather than barrier) for accommodating students' diverse needs and to bet-ter prepare them with global adaptability (Lightman, 2018). To accommodate transnational students' needs to successfully negotiate and communicate in glo-balized spaces, teacher education curricula must equip preservice teachers with an understanding of how transnational networks function, as well as support them in developing the pedagogical skills to support students' multiple identities within these ever-diversifying contexts by utilizing them as assets in designing plans for teaching (Baker, 2015). This means preparing preservice teachers with effective strategies (e.g., design learning opportunities that capitalize on diver-sity, critical languaging, and flexible assessments) to connect students' academic learning with the actualization of a wide range of meaningful educational goals and encourages collaboration, creativity, and multilingual, as well as multimodal, practices (Skerrett, 2012).

Finally, in addition to the need to recognize and affirm students' multiple identities and transnational educational assets, there is also a need to engage pre-service (and in-service) teachers in learning to become agents of change for transnational students, especially those who are economically and sociopolitically disadvantaged (Li, 2013). To do so, preservice teachers must be provided with authentic opportunities for meaningful experiential contact with diverse learners, and engage with their guiding teachers in dialogue about how these students learn (maybe differently from other students) and how best to facilitate their learning by incorporating their transnational experiences and affirming their complex individual identities with myriad goals for the future.

The attention to transnationalism in teacher education is relatively new. In moving towards operationalizing it in teacher education curriculum, Cochran-Smith's (2003) eight questions on how to integrate diversity into teacher education can serve as a theoretical frame. Rethinking teacher education curriculum for transnationalism can begin with the ideology question that reexamines the existing English-only, assimilationist approach to diversity. Accompanying this ideological reexamination is the knowledge question, which addresses teachers' knowledge base and disposition toward superdiverse learners. The teacher learning question addresses the challenges of incorporating content of transnationalism into the teacher education curriculum and where and how to engage learners in meaningful practices. Another question, the recruitment/retention question, provides pathways to diversify the teaching force. The outcome question discusses the assessment of such preparation; and finally, the coherence question addresses how these seven components are connected as a holistic system internally and externally from policy to practice for teacher preparation.

A Concluding Remark

This chapter was completed during Canada's stay-home order to combat COVID-19 pandemic. Like Canada, many countries such as the United States temporarily suspended international travels, as well as immigrant and refugee admissions, and moved all education activities, including K–12 and higher education, to online platforms. Due to these drastic changes globally, teacher education, as well as K–12 education, will need to grapple with the changing transnational patterns post-COVID-19 and address them virtually by using new technologies.

References

Andrews, D. J. C., Brown, T., Castillo, B. M., Jackson, D., & Vellanki, V. (2019). Beyond damage-centered teacher education: Humanizing pedagogy for teacher educators and preservice teachers. *Teachers College Record*, 121(6), 1–28.

Bajaj, M. & Bartlett, L. (2017). Critical transnational curriculum for immigrant and refugee students. *Curriculum Inquiry*, 47(1), 25–35. doi:10.1080/03626784.2016.1254499

Baker, J. (2015). *Imagining the cosmopolitan classroom: Education in transnational spaces.* Center for Education Enterprise. Retrieved from https://cee.mggs.vic.edu.au/wp-content/uploads/2016/06/Education-in-Transnational-Spaces.pdf

Causey, V. E., Thomas, C. D., & Armento, B. J. (2000). Cultural diversity is basically a foreign term to me: The challenges of diversity for preservice teacher education. *Teaching and Teacher Education*, 16(1), 33–45.

Cochran-Smith, M. (2003). Learning and unlearning: The education of teacher educators. *Teaching and Teacher Education*, 19(1), 5–28.

Cummins, J. (2014). To what extent are Canadian second language policies evidence-based? Reflections on the intersection of research and policy. *Frontiers in Psychology*, 5. doi:10.3389/fpsyg.2014.00358

Dabach, D. B., & Fones, A. (2016). Beyond the "English Learner" frame: Transnational funds of knowledge in social studies. *International Journal of Multicultural Education*, 18(1), 7–27.

Dávila, L. T. (2012). 'For them it's sink or swim': Refugee students and the dynamics of migration, and (dis)placement in school. *Power and Education*, 4(2), 139–149.

de la Piedra, M. T., & Araujo, B. (2012). Transfronterizo literacies and content in a dual language classroom. *International Journal of Bilingual Education and Bilingualism*, 15(6), 705–721.

Erdal, M. B. (2013). Migrant transnationalism and multi-layered integration: Norwegian-Pakistani migrants' own reflections. *Journal of Ethnic and Migration Studies*, 39(6), 983–999.

Gagné, A., Al-Hashimi, N., Little, M., Lowen, M., & Sidhu, A. (2018). Educator perspectives on the social and academic integration of Syrian refugees in Canada. *Journal of Family Diversity in Education*, 3(1), 48–76.

Geinger, A. W. (2018, August, 27). *America's public school teachers are far less racially and ethnically diverse than their students*. Pew Research Center. Retrieved from https://www.pewresearch.org/fact-tank/2018/08/27/americas-public-school-teachers-are-far-less-racially-and-ethnically-diverse-than-their-students/

Gitlin, A., Buendía, E., Crosland, K., & Doumbia, F. (2003). The production of margin and center: Welcoming–unwelcoming of immigrant students. *American Educational Research Journal*, 40(1), 91–122.

Goldenberg, C., & Wagner, K. (2015). Bilingual education: Reviving an American tradition. *American Educator*, 39(3), 28–44.

Goldstein, T. (2003). Contemporary bilingual life at a Canadian high school: Choices, risks, tensions, and dilemmas. *Sociology of Education*, 76(3), 247–264. doi:10.2307/3108468

Green, P. E. (2003). The undocumented: Educating the children of migrant workers in America. *Bilingual Research Journal*, 27(1), 51–71.

Greenberg, J., Walsh, K., & McKee, A. (2015). *2014 Teacher prep review: A review of the nation's teacher preparation programs*. Washington, DC: National Council on Teacher Quality.

Gutierrez, K. D. (2019). Rupturing white innocence in teacher education: Designing teacher education as a proleptic activity through social design experiments. *Teachers College Record*, 121(6), 1–7.

Hamann, E. T. (2001). Theorizing the sojourner student (with a sketch of appropriate school responsiveness). *Faculty Publications: Department of Teaching, Learning and Teacher Education*, 73, 32–71.

Hamann, E. T., & Zúñiga, V. (2011). Schooling and the everyday ruptures transnational children encounter in the United States and Mexico. In C. Coe, R. Reynolds, D. Boehm, J. M. Hess, & H. Rae-Espinoza (Eds.), *Everyday ruptures: Children and migration in global perspective* (pp. 141–160). Nashville, TN: Vanderbilt University Press

Kang, H., & Kim, H. (2017). Korean transnational students' school adjustment: An ecological perspective. *Middle Grades Review*, 3(2). Retrieved from https://scholarworks.uvm.edu/mgreview/vol3/iss2/3

Kanu, Y. (2008). Educational needs and barriers for African refugee students in Manitoba. *Canadian Journal of Education*, 31(4), 915–940.

Kim, S., & Slapac, A. (2015). Culturally responsive, transformative pedagogy in the transnational era: Critical perspectives. *Educational Studies*, 51(1), 17–27.

Kobayashi, A., & Preston, V. (2007). Transnationalism through the life course: Hong Kong immigrants in Canada. *Asia Pacific Viewpoint*, 48(2), 151–167.

Ladson-Billings, G. J. (1995). Multicultural teacher education: Research, practice, and policy. In J. A. Banks & C. A. McGee Banks (Eds.), *Handbook of research on multicultural education* (pp. 747–759). New York: Macmillan.

Levitt, P., & Schiller, N. (2008). Conceptualizing simultaneity. In A. Portes & J. DeWind (Eds.), *Rethinking migration: New theoretical and empirical perspectives* (pp. 181–218). Oxford, UK: Bergbabn Books.

Ley, D. (2010). *Millionaire migrants: Trans-pacific life lines*. Malden, MA: Wiley Blackwell.

Li, G. (2006). *Culturally contested pedagogy: Battles of literacy and schooling between mainstream teachers and Asian immigrant parents*. Albany, NY: SUNY Press.

Li, G. (2008). *Culturally contested literacies: America's "rainbow underclass" and urban schools*. New York: Routledge

Li, G. (2013) Promoting teachers of culturally and linguistically diverse (CLD) students as change agents: A cultural approach to professional learning. *Theory Into Practice*, 52(2), 136–143.

Li, G. (2018). Moving toward a diversity plus teacher education: Approaches, challenges, and possibilities in preparing teachers for English language learners. In A. Polly (Ed.), *Handbook of research on analyzing practices for teacher preparation and licensure* (pp. 215–236). Hershey, PA: IGI Global.

Li, G. (2019). Resource diversity in Asian immigrants and refugees: Implications for language arts instruction. *Language Arts*, 96(6), 370–383.

Li, G., Hinojosa, D., & Wexler, L. (2018). Beliefs and perceptions about their preparation to teach English language learners: Voices of mainstream pre-service teachers. *International Journal of TESOL and Learning*, 6(3&4), 41–61.

Li, G., & Sah, P. (2020). Critical pedagogy for preservice teacher education: An agenda for a plurilingual reality. In S. Steinberg et al., (Eds.), *Handbook of critical pedagogy*. New York: SAGE Publications.

Lightman, N. (2018). Situating secondary schooling in the transnational social field: contestation and conflict in Greater Toronto Area classrooms. *Critical Studies in Education*, 59(2), 131–148.

Lucas, T., & Villegas, A. M. (2013). Preparing linguistically responsive teachers: Laying the foundation in preservice teacher education. *Theory Into Practice*, 52(2), 98–109.

Malsbary, C. B. (2018). Teachers as creative designers in transnationalism. *Urban Education*, 53(10), 1238–1264.

McBrien, J. L. (2011). Including immigrant and refugee students. In J. Fauske, J. Carr, & P. Jones (Eds.), *Leading for inclusion: Meeting the needs of all learners in a diverse society* (pp. 136–149). New York: Teachers College Press.

McWilliams, J. A., & Bonet, S. W. (2016). Continuums of precarity: Refugee youth transitions in American high schools. *International Journal of Lifelong Education*, 35(2), 153–170.

Mitchell, K. (2001). Education for democratic citizenship: Transnationalism, multiculturalism, and the limits of liberalism. *Harvard Educational Review*, 71(1), 51–78.

Mosselson, J. (2007). Masks of achievement: An experiential study of Bosnian female refugees in New York City schools. *Comparative Education Review*, 51(1), 95–115.

National Center for Education Statistics. (2019). *English language learners in public schools*. Retrieved from https://nces.ed.gov/programs/coe/indicator_cgf.asp

Ogbu, J. U., & Simons, H. D. (1998). Voluntary and involuntary minorities: A cultural-ecological theory of school performance with some implications for education. *Anthropology & Education Quarterly*, 29(2), 155–188.

Ong, A. (1999). *Flexible citizenship: The cultural logics of transnationality*. Durham, NC: Duke University Press.

Pacheco, M. (2012). Learning in/through everyday resistance: A cultural-historical perspective on community 'resources' and curriculum. *Educational Researcher*, 41(4), 121–132.

Pezzetti, K. (2017). 'I'm not racist; my high school was diverse!' White preservice teachers deploy diversity in the classroom. *Whiteness and Education*, 2(2), 131–147.

Preemptive Love. (2019, Oct. 30). *Migrant vs. immigrant: what's the difference?* Retrieved from https://preemptivelove.org/blog/migrant-vs-immigrant/

Radford, J. (2019, June, 17). *Key findings about U.S. immigrants*. Pew Research Center. Retrieved from https://www.pewresearch.org/fact-tank/2019/06/17/key-findings-about-u-s-immigrants/

Rendall, M. S., & Torr, B. M. (2008). Emigration and schooling among second-generation Mexican-American children. *International Migration Review*, 42(3), 729–738.

Reid-Musson, E. (2014). Historicizing precarity: A labour geography of 'transient' migrant workers in Ontario tobacco. *Geoforum*, 56, 161–171.

Robertson, S. (2013) *Transnational student-migrants and the state: The education-migration nexus*. New York: Palgrave Macmillan.

Rounsaville, A. (2014). Situating transnational genre knowledge: A genre trajectory analysis of one student's personal and academic writing. *Written Communication*, 31(3), 332–364.

Rumbaut, R. G. (2002). Severed or sustained attachments? Language, identity, and imagined communities in the post-immigrant generation. In P. Levitt & M. C. Waters (Eds.), *The changing face of home: The transnational lives of the second generation* (pp. 43–95). New York: Russel Sage Foundation.

Samson, J. F., & Collins, B. A. (2012). *Preparing all teachers to meet the needs of English language learners: Applying research to policy and practice for teacher effectiveness*. Center for American Progress. Retrieved from https://files.eric.ed.gov/fulltext/ED535608.pdf

Sánchez, P., & Kasun, G. S. (2012). Connecting transnationalism to the classroom and to theories of immigrant student adaptation. *Berkeley Review of Education*, 3(1), 71–93.

Shik, A. W. (2015). Transnational families: Chinese-Canadian youth between worlds. *Journal of Ethnic and Cultural Diversity in Social Work*, 24(1), 71–86.

Skelton, C. (2014, August, 07). *ESL students in majority at more than 60 schools in Metro Vancouver*. Vancouver Sun. http://www.vancouversun.com/health/students+majority+more+than+schools+Metro+Vancouver/10005768/story.html

Skerrett, A. (2012). Languages and literacies in translocation: Experiences and perspectives of a transnational youth. *Journal of Literacy Research*, 44(4), 364–395.

Statistics Canada. (2017). *Focus on geography series, 2006 census: Immigration population*. Retrieved from https://www12.statcan.gc.ca/census-recensement/2016/as-sa/fogs-spg/Facts-can-eng.cfm?Lang=Eng&GK=CAN&GC=01&TOPIC=7

Suárez-Orozco, M. M., & Sattin, C. (2007). Wanted: Global citizens. *Educational Leadership*, 64(7), 58–62.

Taira, B. W. (2019). (In)Visible literacies of transnational newcomer youth in a secondary English classroom. *Global Education Review*, 6(2), 74–93.

Terhorst, A. (2017). *Academic barriers for migrant middle school students in Salinas, California* [Unpublished master's thesis]. Master's Theses. San Jose State University.

Vertovec, S. (2007). Super-diversity and its implications. *Ethnic and Racial Studies*, 30(6), 1024–1054.

von Stackelberg, M. (2020, February, 12). *Refugee youth 'falling through the cracks' in Manitoba's education system, report finds*. CBC News. Retrieved from https://www.cbc.ca/news/canada/manitoba/refugee-youth-education-winnipeg-report-1.5460507

Warriner, D. (2017). Theorizing the spatial dimensions and pedagogical implications of transnationalism. *Curriculum Inquiry*, 47(1), 50–61.

Waters, J. L. (2006). Geographies of cultural capital: Education, international migration and family strategies between Hong Kong and Canada. *Transactions of the Institute of British Geographers*, 31(2), 179–192.

Webster, N., & Valeo, A. (2011). Teacher preparedness for a changing demographic of language learners. *TESL Canada Journal*, 28(2), 105–128.

Zúñiga, V., & Hamann, E. T. (2009). Sojourners in Mexico with US school experience: A new taxonomy for transnational students. *Comparative Education Review*, 53(3), 329–353.

2

TRICKSTER COMES TO TEACHER EDUCATION

Jan Hare

Indigenous teacher education (ITE) is a critical area of development in countries such as Canada, the United States, Australia, and New Zealand mobilized by international, national, and local policy directives aimed at increasing success of Indigenous learners, incorporating Indigenous knowledges in teaching and learning, and enhancing educational capacity within Indigenous communities and public schools (e.g., Australian Curriculum and Assessment Reporting Authority, 2014; Truth and Reconciliation Commission Canada, 2015; National Congress of American Indians, 2019; United Nations Declaration of the Rights of Indigenous Peoples, 2007; MATSITI—More Aboriginal and Torres Strait Island Teachers Initiative, 2017). Such educational transformation requires addressing educational barriers for Indigenous students and families and mobilizing Indigenous education policies, curriculum, and professional development. Indigenous teachers play a significant role in creating educational environments that are culturally responsive, tribally specific, and inclusive of Indigenous knowledge approaches. Furthermore, Indigenous teachers can advance comprehensive, Indigenous-focused educational opportunities within Indigenous communities by promoting educational sovereignty and improving the life worlds of Indigenous communities (National Congress of American Indians, 2019).

Preparing Indigenous teachers to address the broader needs of Indigenous peoples as learners, parents, teachers, and communities requires teacher education programs to take up their responsibilities of advancing Indigenous education priorities, including recruiting, retaining, and ensuring the successful completion of Indigenous teachers. Faculties of education must consider ways to be responsive to the educational aspirations of Indigenous learners and accountable to Indigenous communities (McCarty & Lee, 2014). This chapter focuses on the ways that teacher education policies, practices, and curriculum can be reconstructed to address the significant priority of increasing the number of

Indigenous educators in the workforce, as well as reimagined to create support-ive learning environments and innovative career pathways to teacher education for Indigenous students. It draws on the significant cultural being of the trick-ster in Indigenous story traditions to help bring to light how teacher education programs situated within Western institutions can be reconceptualized so they reflect Indigenous visions of what it means to be a teacher serving Indigenous communities and learners (Garcia & Shirley, 2019).

The trickster figure appears in the stories of many different cultures, so it is not inherently Indigenous (Womack, 2008). Rather, Indigenous people con-struct this notion of the trickster from their own languages, lands, and stories. Nongendered, the trickster is a transformer, shape-shifter, spiritual being, or supernatural figure. The deeds and antics of the trickster, for which the trickster is known and how listeners come to understand their world, offer a response to what teacher education programs can learn from Indigenous perspectives. Readers may hear of Ableegumooch if they are to visit Miq'maw territory on the East Coast of Canada, Nanaboosho among the Anishinaabek, Weeesageesic adventuring in Cree worlds, Napi taking journeys on the Plains, sometimes col-liding with Coyote in western Canada, who may bump up against Raven on the West Coast.

In drawing on the trickster, I am not trying to define the trickster as anthropol-ogists, historians, or scholars of literary studies have. Rather, I consider the trick-ster as an embodiment of Indigenous people's worldview, known to us through stories and learning traditions. In doing so, I wish to explore how methodically the trickster can be in coming to teacher education, demonstrating how ITE programs can empower Indigenous preservice teachers in advancing their own journeys of decolonization and reclamation and to consider how mainstream teacher education can enrich and be enriched by Indigenous communities. Three trickster strategies are presented as a means to contemplate much-needed trans-formation in teacher education and mobilize the goals of recruitment, retention, and successful completion of Indigenous pre-service teachers.

Achieving Parity in the Teacher Education Workforce

Indigenous educators are profoundly underrepresented in public, on-reserve/tribal, and other school settings. There is urgent need to increase the low num-ber of Indigenous educators in classrooms and schools. In the United States, while the population of teachers of color overall is growing, the number of Native American teachers is a declining share of the teacher workforce (Carver-Thomas, 2018). In fact, less than 1% of teachers in the United States identify as American Indian, Alaska Native, and Native Hawaiian (National Center for Educational Statistics, 2016). Across Canada, similar trends for the Indigenous teacher workforce suggest Indigenous people's participation as teachers and preservice teachers represent a very small total of the teacher workforce.

For example, the province of Saskatchewan has reported an under-representation of Aboriginal teachers at all levels of a school division, with even greater disparities in the school administrative levels (Saskatchewan School Boards Association, 2015). In British Columbia, where just over 63,000 Indigenous students attend public schools, comprising nearly 12% of the student population, statistics suggest Indigenous educators make up less than 2% of the 42,000 certified public school teachers in the province (Auditor General of British Columbia, 2015). More recently, the British Columbia Supreme Court ruling to restore class size and composition language that was removed from the 2002 teachers' contracts has created a pressing need for more teachers in the classrooms, resulting in teachers in First Nations band-operated schools leaving communities for opportunities in public school classrooms. Chronic shortages of Aboriginal teachers have also been reported in public school systems in Ontario and Manitoba (Cherubini et al., 2010).

The situation with the Indigenous teacher workforce in on-reserve/tribal communities is even more exacerbated. In Canada, northern First Nations schools are forced to rely on nonprofit organizations such as Teach for Canada to address the significant gaps. Within Australia, Aboriginal and Torres Strait Island teachers are significantly underrepresented in teaching positions in schools relative to the proportion of Indigenous students, motivating the national five-year (2012–2016) collaborative project MATSITI—More Aboriginal and Torres Strait Island Teachers Initiative. At the completion of this project, there were only 3,100 teachers who identified as Indigenous in the country. Although an increase of 439 teachers (16%) was observed over the course of the project, the Australian teacher workforce is still composed of less than 1% of Indigenous teachers (Buckskin, 2016).

The Role of Indigenous Teachers

Increasing the number of Indigenous educators in classrooms and communities is important as they can help ameliorate persistent and significant academic disparities that Indigenous learners experience (Mueller et al., 2013). Research suggests that when Indigenous students are taught by Indigenous educators, they are likely to engage more deeply in learning and experience better outcomes (Buckskin, 2017; Egalite et al., 2015; Perso & Hayward, 2015). This is because Indigenous educators may serve as role models and are more likely to understand Indigenous students' languages, cultures, worldviews, and learning needs (Santoro & Reid, 2006). They are more able to enact culturally relevant teaching and assist Indigenous learners to feel more welcome. Indigenous teachers are motivated by their own experiences of schooling, wanting the education of future generations of Indigenous children to be markedly different from their own experiences of schooling (Martineau et al., 2015). As the Council of the Ministers of Education (CMEC, 2016) states, having "dedicated teachers who understand and can support Aboriginal students, and increasing the number of Aboriginal teachers who are members of the same communities and share the same culture and traditions as their students, are powerful vehicles of change" (p. 4). Any commitments to improve educational outcomes for Indigenous learners must focus on increasing the number of Indigenous educators.

Several U.S. and Canadian studies have revealed that many teacher education programs do not sensitize preservice teachers to cultural and linguistic differences they will likely encounter in their future classrooms nor provide them with knowledge, strategies, and pedagogical knowledge to address to these disparities (Faez, 2012; Webster & Valeo, 2011). As teacher education moves beyond preparing only Indigenous preservice teachers to work largely in tribal/ on-reserve schools toward preparing all teacher candidates for teaching all students about Indigenous histories and perspectives in accordance with international curriculum reform and changing standards for the profession by teacher regulating bodies, Indigenous teachers bring valuable knowledge and experience to the professional development of other educators. Caution needs to be paid to the burden that Indigenous educators carry when ascribed the role of expert and given responsibility for all aspects of education. However, Indigenous teachers can provide valuable mentoring to their non-Indigenous colleagues through pedagogical support, advice about Indigenous cultures and ways of knowing, and establishing and maintaining home-school relationships (Santoro et al., 2011).

Experiences of Indigenous Preservice Teachers

While Indigenous preservice teachers may have the option to attend Indigenous-led teacher education programs, these programs are generally part of mainstream teacher education. ITE programs allow Indigenous students to remain in their communities for a portion or all of their programming, but many Indigenous students must transition to a university campus to complete their professional certification. To help readers understand Indigenous pre-service experiences of teacher education, I turn to the trickster story "Coyote Takes Water From The Frog People." Stolo scholar Dr. Jo-ann Archibald (2008) describes the power of Indigenous stories to heal and teach but reminds us to attend to protocols associated with storytelling such as locating the story in its territorial origin. In the case of the trickster stories, in particular, I want to reference the cultural and historical specificity of this trickster figure from where this trickster story emerges (Fagan, 2010).

This is a Kalapuya story from the Indigenous people whose traditional homelands are in the Willamette Valley in western Oregon of the United States. It is an oral story documented by anthropologists Erdoes and Ortiz (1984). It can also be found on educational and cultural websites supported by Indigenous communities and organizations. There may be slight variations in the retellings, but with Indigenous stories, it is the responsibility of reader/listener to make meaning. However, this pedagogical narrative has been selected for the perspectives it brings to bear on ITE:

> Coyote was out hunting and he found a dead deer. One of the deer's rib bones looked just like a big dentalia shell, and Coyote picked it up and took it with him. He went up to see the frog people. The frog people had all the water. When anyone wanted water any water to drink or cook with or wash, they had to go and get it from the frog people.
>
> Coyote came up. "Hey frog people, I have a big dentalia shell. I want a big drink of water—I want to drink for a long time."
>
> "Give us that shell," said the frog people, "and you can drink all you want."
>
> Coyote gave them the shell and began drinking. The water was behind a large dam where Coyote drank. "I'm going to keep my head down for a long time," said Coyote, "because I'm really thirsty. Don't worry about me."
>
> "Okay, we won't worry," said the frog people.
>
> Coyote began drinking. He drank for a long time. Finally one of the frog people said, "Hey Coyote, you sure are drinking a lot of water there. What are you doing that for?"
>
> Coyote brought his head up out of the water. "I'm thirsty."
>
> "Oh."
>
> After a while one of the frog people said, "Coyote, you sure are drinking a lot. Maybe you better give us another shell."
>
> "Just let me finish this drink," Coyote said, putting his head back under water.
>
> The frog people wondered how a person could drink so much water. They didn't like this. They thought Coyote might be doing something.
>
> Coyote was digging out under the dam all the time he had his head under water. When he was finished, he stood up and said, "That was a good drink. That was just what I needed."
>
> Then the dam collapsed, and the water went out into the valley and made the creeks and rivers and waterfalls. The frog people were very angry. "You have taken all the water, Coyote!"
>
> "It's not right that one people have all the water. Now it is where everyone can have it."
>
> Coyote did that. Now anyone can go down to the river and get a drink of water or some water to cook with, or just swim around.
>
> *(Erdoes & Ortiz, 1984, pp. 355–356)*

This story brings to mind the enormous challenges Indigenous preservice teachers face becoming educators. They may need to transition to a university campus for remaining professional certification requirements, leaving behind family, community, and cultural commitments (Martineau et al., 2015). ITE programs can be regarded as not entirely legitimate, therefore, Indigenous students are viewed as less able than their non-Indigenous peers and their qualifications devalued (Santoro et al., 2011). They confront racism directed at them by their non-Indigenous counterparts or by teacher educators complicit by perpetuating or by failing to address discrimination in course work. In mixed classrooms, Indigenous preservice teachers are relied on to educate settler students and teacher educators on the histories of colonialism and ongoing forms of systemic racism, adding to the emotional burden they already carry in their encounters with mainstream teacher education. They are too often called on in classroom discussions to support the teaching of Indigenous content, as well as share their experiences of Indigeneity.

The curriculum of teacher education is shaped by dominant/Eurocentric theories and practices, marginalizing Indigenous preservice teacher's knowledge and experiences in university settings (Brayboy & Maughan, 2009). In fact, ITE programs situated in White, mainstream institutions can be constrained by larger systems of assimilation. Rather than preparing Indigenous students to teach in tribally specific ways, Indigenous preservice teachers become vulnerable to reproducing mainstream approaches to education in Indigenous classrooms and communities driven by government curriculum, testing, and standardization (Castagno, 2012). Furthermore, if the financial resources and trusting relationships needed for Indigenous community and university collaborations are lacking, Indigenous preservice teachers are put at risk for completion of their program (Hobson et al., 2018).

I return to the story of Coyote, who breaks with social and physical boundaries of the dam created by the Frog People. Indigenous preservice teachers cross the social and physical confines that separate postsecondary institutions from Indigenous communities and cultures; institutions that were not created for Indigenous peoples. Sami scholar Kuokkanen (2007) argues that programs intended to bridge mainstream education with Indigenous cultures and communities ignore their ontological and epistemic difference and, while offering support and assistance, place responsibilities solely on Indigenous students to succeed. Coyote, who appears to be engaged in an act of self-interest by drinking up the water, is strategically breaking the dam to ensure water is available for the people, the land, and animals. Like Coyote, Indigenous preservice teachers are also confronting and breaking institutional barriers, using education as a tool for self-determination, nationhood, and transformation of educational systems.

Trickster Strategies

If we were only to focus on the foibles or successes of Coyote in the Kalapuya story shared, we may come to understand Indigenous preservice teachers' motivations and experiences in becoming a teacher. But this would be reductive and limit the possibilities of Indigenous stories to help us theorize ITE. Instead, I wish to focus on the way Coyote functions in the story, emphasizing three pedagogical strategies within Indigenous narratives to create a framework that demonstrates the way dominant/mainstream postsecondary education structures can be dismantled to advance practices of recruitment, retention, and success of Indigenous students. These strategies deployed by the trickster are aimed at re-centering Indigenous priorities within Western mainstream teacher education programs.

Strategy 1: Summoning the Imagination

The pedagogy of the trickster relies on summoning our imagination. This occurs through the trickster's wanderings, the ability to assume different forms, and possessing human and more-than-human qualities. As Coyote demonstrates in the story earlier, the trickster often utilizes humor, self-mocking, or absurdity to help teach us lessons. Anishinaabe writer Gerald Viznor (1986), takes issue with the reductive caricature of the trickster as buffoon created by anthropologies who view the trickster as a source of entertainment. Rather, he suggests that Indigenous interpretations of the trickster are culturally centered, communally grounded, highly complex, and comedic. As Archibald (2008) describes, Trickster is someone who "often gets into trouble ignoring cultural rules and practices ... . At the same time, Trickster has the ability to do good things for others ... and given much respect" (p. 5). As Indigenous writers, scholars, and storytellers surmise, the antics of the trickster are strategic, used to make people think, form new ideas, and educate.

Supporting Indigenous student success in teacher education is about summoning the imagination so that Indigenous preservice teachers engage in cultural sustainability and revitalization (McCarty & Lee, 2014). This means assisting Indigenous preservice teachers to find their gifts, maintain their cultural integrity, and fulfill their responsibilities towards the broader Indigenous community (Pidgeon, 2008). In particular, ensuring Indigenous pre-service teachers find their gifts does not always emphasize academic success. Instead, it is about structuring learning that validates Indigenous student experience as a legitimate source of knowledge and decolonizing the curriculum of teacher education in respectful and productive ways. Brayboy and Maughan (2009) remind us that it is

> not enough for teacher education programs to simply claim commitments to the training of Indigenous educators. They must also be able to see that the construction of knowledge is socially mediated and that Indigenous students bring other conceptions of what knowledge is and how it produced in their teaching.
>
> *(p. 19)*

ITE programs need to innovate, creating distinctive practices that prepare Indigenous preservice teachers for community contexts, while working within the dominant paradigm of teacher education. Castagno et al. (2015) promote an approach to ITE in mainstream institutions as one that engages Indigenous students in practical experiences as modeled by highly qualified teachers of Indigenous youth. While the theory of culturally responsive schooling may form part of the curriculum, transferring this knowledge to classroom practice is important for Indigenous preservice teachers. Hale and Lockard (2018) under-score the role of mentor teachers preparing Indigenous preservice teachers for the field. Mentor teachers possess excellence in classroom experience and Dine language instruction and build the practices of Dine preservice teachers from the Navajo Nation in the southwestern United States. Mentors share lesson plans, materials, and teaching strategies. In turn, Dine preservice teachers are culturally responsive to Dine students and families, increasing student academic achieve-ment. This example of the trickster as imaginative is particularly helpful in reten-tion of Indigenous preservice teachers and assisting them in their transition to classrooms and communities where they will work.

Trickster Strategy 2: Disrupting the Order of Things

Another pedagogical strategy of the trickster with implications for transform-ing teacher education is the ability of the trickster to disrupt the social order of things. Using this technique, the trickster transforms present realities to cre-ate something more habitable. Anishnaabe scholar Niigonwedom James Sinclair, tell us that "[h]is presence usually ensures that something interesting, divergent, and potentially world-altering will occur" (2010, p. 25). Trickster's tendency to disrupt usually means bridging stability with absurdity. In doing so, Trickster expands the limits of what is possible for listeners of these stories. In the Coyote story, the Frog people think Coyote is drinking up the water when, really, he is submerged for so long with the goal of ensuring water can be shared among everyone. What we can all appreciate about Coyote, and other tricksters, is their ability to change reality by flouting social conventions.

As trickster wanders through the landscape of teacher education, trickster can "manipulate and subvert the colonial world" (Cox, 2005, p. 252), helping us see new and innovative pathways to becoming an Indigenous teacher through ITE programs. The demand for Indigenous teachers requires contextual responses to recruitment and retention. Disrupting the current models of ITE to account for these priorities, we can look to a growing number of promising programs being developed through community–university collaborations. One program taking a new approach is the Build From Within—Ozhitoon Onji Peenjiiee Teacher Education Program, located in situ at a local high school. It is result of a collabo-ration between Winnipeg School Division and the University of Winnipeg, both located in central Canada, and Indspire, a national Indigenous education organi-zation. It transitions Indigenous students from high school through to university with the goal of becoming educational leaders within the urban community.

Students begin with education assistant (EA) training starting in Grade 11 and complete EA certification by Grade 12. Once they graduate, they begin paid employment as EAs in the Winnipeg School Division. Tuition is provided, along with mentorships, summer job opportunities, and cultural activities.

Build From Within inspires among Indigenous students to consider teaching as a career in high school. Reports and studies suggest that the recruitment of Indigenous students should occur in earlier grades, as early as middle school (Francis et al., 2018; Hare, 2018). High school students might also be recruited through mentoring initiatives, such as introducing students to high-achieving Indigenous teacher role models (CMEC, 2016) and developing partnerships with schools and professional organizations to promote teacher education and support outreach activities (Association of Canadian Deans of Education, 2010). For example, the More Aboriginal and Torres Strait Islander Teachers Initiative (MATSITI) in Australia developed a Teach Team, which consisted of a group of Indigenous teaching ambassadors, who could go out and talk to groups of students in schools and Indigenous communities (Buckskin, 2016). Teach New Zealand and MATSITI have developed websites to lift the recruitment and retention of Indigenous educators, promoting videos of Indigenous educators.

Another program, NITEP—the Indigenous Teacher Education Program at the University of British Columbia in western Canada—has been innovating over the last 44 years. Established in 1974 by a group of Indigenous educators, NITEP was distinct from the mainstream institution. Archibald and LaRochelle (2018) describe key features that contribute to the long-standing success of this program. They describe the community-based nature of the program that relies on strong partnerships with Indigenous communities and organizations, whereby community has a voice in decision-making. Those relationships are maintained through NITEP staff and faculty. The program uses a cohort model to create a feeling of family and belonging. Course work emphasizes Indigenous knowledges and invites Elders and cultural resource speakers to be part of programming and course work. Education courses are taken each year of the 4-year program, constituting an Indigenous Education concentration within a Bachelor of Education degree. There are seminars and school placements that allow Indigenous students to develop professional teaching expectations. A portion of the courses are offered online and in blended-learning formats, enhancing student's digital practices. Supports and services for students take a holistic approach, whereby advisors, staff, and faculty nurture the academic, social, physical, and spiritual aspects of Indigenous teacher candidates. Even as the program undergoes change through leadership, governance, new pathways to the program, and curriculum initiatives, "the program remains Indigenous in philosophy and practice" (Archibald & LaRochelle, 2018, p. 210).

Some of the changes that NITEP has experienced in the last few years continue to enhance Indigenous preservice teacher experiences. NITEP has changed its approach to recruitment, allowing for a longer time to develop relationships with communities before students come into the program. A 2-year approach to recruitment gives NITEP time to build strong community–university collaborations through regular visits to the community. Students who learn of the program coming to their territory have more time to prepare themselves to meet admission criteria. Furthermore, the program has eliminated the university application fee and created broader admission policies. As a result, NITEP is seeing increased applications to the program. NITEP is developing new pathways that include a postdegree specialization, a dual-credit course for high school students that will count for credit once admitted to NITEP, and partnering with an Indigenous higher educational institution to create a dual-degree program. This ITE program is challenging existing professional certification approaches that rely on face-to-face instruction in course work. Instead, it is piloting blended learning that allows students to remain in community-based settings for course work to reduce the attrition that happens when students must transition to a large urban campus. Increasing support services to include Indigenous mentoring initiatives that draw on faculty, alumni, and Elders, a wellness program, hiring a digital peer mentor, enhancing practicum experiences, increasing funding and bursaries, and land-based curriculum experiences are enhancements to NITEP aimed at Indigenous teacher candidate belonging and retention. Also, it has been important to provide professional development for teacher education staff who interact with Indigenous students concerning systemic racism and oppressive practices that create barriers to student success. NITEP, whose program logo is represented by the Raven trickster figure, upholds its guiding values through the trickster feat of balancing both tradition and change.

Trickster Strategy 3: Renewal

The final trickster approach is the strategy of renewal. Archibald (2008), who has developed a framework for storytelling for both research and practice, explains, "People keep the spirit of a story alive by telling it to others and by interacting with the story" (p. 149). In the retelling of stories, meaning unfolds in relationship to personal lives. And each retelling prompts new meaning as each person interprets the story. Indigenous people need to continue to tell their trickster, shapeshifter, and transformer stories. We tell these stories in the interest of continuing our intellectual, spiritual, and social traditions. However, it is in the telling and retelling of trickster stories, such as "Coyote Takes Water From The Frog People," that change and growth can occur.

Few teacher education programs require course work in cultural and linguistic diversity. There is wide variability in how preservice teachers are prepared to address diversity, and we still know relatively little about how differences in preparation affect teacher quality (Boyd et al., 2009; Cochran-Smith et al., 2015). Renewal in teacher education is being mobilized through mandatory/ foundational course instruction in Indigenous education for all teacher candidates.

In Canada, the Association of Canadian Deans of Education (2010) expressed its commitment to increasing future teacher's knowledge and competencies to take up Indigenous education practices in its Accord on Indigenous Education. Large-scale reform of teacher education in Canada is also being assisted by the Truth and Reconciliation Commission (TRC) of Canada (2015), which put forward 94 Calls-to-Action. Specifically, recommendations of the TRC confer responsibilities for teacher education through recommendations that include, "educat[ing] teachers on how to integrate Indigenous knowledge and teaching methods into classrooms," and "identifying teacher training needs" (TRC of Canada, 2015, p. 5) specific to Indigenous histories and worldviews. As a result, an increasing number of teacher education programs require coursework in Indigenous education or integrate Indigenous perspectives across the teacher education curriculum. Similarly, the New Zealand Ministry of Education has developed a Maori education strategy, which includes cultural competencies for teachers of Maori learners with implications for teacher education programs (Clarke et al., 2018) and Australia has developed standards that require teachers at any level of career to demonstrate knowledge of Indigenous histories, cultures, and languages in their practice (Australian Curriculum and Assessment Reporting Authority, 2014).

Given critiques of teacher education have established how commonly the classroom operates as a colonized space in which Indigenous students experience racism and exclusion in content, learning approaches, and classroom interactions (Cote-Meeks, 2014), teacher education must become a space of renewal, where Indigenous knowledges, worldviews, and histories become part of teaching and learning for all preservice teachers. There is exciting scholarship describing the practices of Indigenous and ally teacher educators taking up Indigenous education with pre-service teachers, including learning from Indigenous knowledge theories (Battiste, 2013; Brayboy & Maughan, 2009; Grande, 2015; Kovach et al., 2015), engaging in pedagogical practices that draw from traditions of land education, storytelling, or experiential and relational learning (Calderon, 2014; Brayboy, 2008; Scully, 2015), and drawing from the wisdom and guidance of Indigenous community members, Elders, and knowledge keepers (Archibald, 2008; Hare, 2015). Preservice teachers learning from Indigenous knowledge systems, perspectives, histories, and pedagogies have experienced deep transformation in their social understandings, as well as knowledge to assist them in enhancing their own classroom practices (Dion, 2007; Garcia & Shirley, 2013; Kitchen & Raynor, 2013).

Decolonizing and Indigenous approaches require teacher educators and the preservice teachers with whom they work to examine their own engagements with colonial histories and ongoing manifestations of how colonialism operates in schools and society. Teaching Indigenous perspectives and knowledges to largely non-Indigenous students involves unsettling prior knowledge and assumptions, which can trigger deep resistance (McLaughlin, 2013). The challenge is for teacher educators "to facilitate the transformation of students' feeling of 'guilt and resistance' into a critique of existing knowledge towards developing competencies for social justice and responsibility" (p. 258). Teacher educators have taken up a number of strategies to move preservice teachers beyond their estrangement with Indigenous people, histories, and contemporary realities. For example, as a critical pedagogy of remembrance, Lenape scholar, Susan Dion (2007) invited teachers learn from biography of their relationship with Aboriginal people by drawing together images from their past and holding these images up against representations of Indigenous storytellers, filmmakers, and visual artists as a means to explore how their investments in colonial and dominant discourses. Scully (2015) used an experiential approach, describing a "Local Assignment," whereby preservice teachers find out which treaty land they live on, researching Indigenous communities and histories, and engaging with Indigenous community members. In my previous work with colleagues (Davis et al., 2018), we see that for instructors,

> elevating the status of Indigenous knowledges among learners requires they make significant changes in the classroom atmosphere; they strive to create classrooms that are spaces of truth-telling and compassion, places of empowerment for Indigenous students, and places where students of settler heritage are able to engage in opportunities to be unsettled in their thinking and behaviour.
>
> *(p. 23)*

Conclusion

Indigenous stories carry with them moral and social responsibilities for the listener. For these stories to take hold in our lives, giving us new insights and new directions for living and learning, listeners must learn to make meaning from them. Meaning-making comes from understanding how Indigenous stories are organized in their structures, themes, features, and the many purposes that they serve. Trickster stories aim to teach us about our world. They are pedagogical narratives, whereby the trickster may be seemingly ridiculous, playful, or mischievous. Yet, these stories employ deliberate strategies that summon the imagination, disrupt the social order of things, and create renewal allowing us to see transformational possibilities for our world. If Indigenous stories are to matter,

> the relationship between the storyteller and the listener implies that, as a result of hearing the story, some action will be taken and transformation will take place. Real transformative action requires more than sympathetic listening; it demands taking responsibilities for the stories we are told.
>
> *(Johnson, 2010, pp. 200–201)*

ITE programs have a critical role to play in the development of Indigenous preservice teachers. In these programs, students can be grounded in teaching and learning that nurtures and validates their identity and prepares them for not only Indigenous communities and schools, but also for public education. The long history of ITE programs to contribute to language revitalization, incorporating Indigenous knowledges and pedagogies in classrooms, enhancing Indigenous student achievement, and building capacity within Indigenous communities demonstrates the limitations of mainstream conventional/initial teacher education programs to address Indigenous priorities. Given the educational agendas of decolonization, reconciliation, sovereignty shaping curriculum and policy reform, teacher education must attend to trickster strategies to better serve Indigenous communities and learners, and enhance the competencies of all preservice teachers to take up their roles and responsibilities toward Indigenous education.

References

Archibald, J. (2008). *Indigenous storywork: Educating the heart, mind, body, and spirit.* Vancouver: University of British Columbia Press.

Archibald, J., & LaRochelle, J. (2018). Raven's response to teacher education: NITEP, an Indigenous story. In P. Whitinui, M. Rodriguez de France, & O. McIvor (Eds.), *Promising practices in Indigenous teacher education* (pp. 207–220). Singapore: Springer Nature Singapore Pte Ltd.

Association of Canadian Deans of Education (ACDE). (2010). *Accord on Indigenous education.* Retrieved from http://mediarelations.concordia.ca/pdf/Accord%20June1%20 2010.pdf

Auditor General of British Columbia. (2015). *An audit of the education of Aboriginal students in the B.C. public school system.* Author: Victoria, BC. Available at http://www. bcauditor.com/sites/default/files/publications/reports/OAGBC%20Aboriginal%20 Education%20Report_FINAL.pdf

Australian Curriculum and Assessment Reporting Authority. (2014). Aboriginal and Torres Strait Islander histories and cultures. Retrieved from https://www. australiancurriculum.edu.au/f--10--curriculum/cross--curriculum--priorities/ aboriginal--and--torres--strait--islander--histories--and--cultures?

Battiste, M. (2013). *Decolonizing Education: Nourishing the Learning Spirit.* Saskatoon, SK: Purich Publishing Ltd.

Boyd, D. J., Grossman, P. L., Lankford, H., Loeb, S., & Wyckoff, J. (2009). Teacher preparation and student achievement. *Educational Evaluation and Policy Analysis,* 31(4), 416–440.

Brayboy, B. M., & Maughan, E. (2009). Indigenous knowledges and the story of the bean. *Harvard Educational Review,* 79(1), 1–21.

Buckskin, P. (2017). *More Aboriginal and Torres Strait Islander Teachers Initiative Final Report. 1.0 Vol.* Adelaide, South Australia: University of South Australia. http://matsiti.edu.au/ wpcontent/uploads/2017/02/MATSITI-Final-Report-1.0.pdf

Calderon, D. (2014). Speaking back to manifest destinies: A land education-based approach to critical curriculum inquiry. *Environmental Education Research,* 20(1), 24–36.

Carver-Thomas, D. (2018). *Diversifying the teaching profession: How to recruit and retain teachers of color.* Palo Alto, CA: Learning Policy Institute. Retrieved from https://learningpolicyinstitute.org/product/diversifying-teaching-profession

Castagno, A. E. (2012). "They prepared me to be a teacher, but not a culturally responsive Navajo teacher for Navajo kids": A tribal critical race theory analysis of an Indigenous teacher preparation program. *Journal of American Indian Education*, 51(1), 3–21.

Castagno, A. E., Brayboy, B. M. J., Chadwick, D., & Cook, L. (2015). "Learning to teach" in and for Indian Country: The promise and paradox of preparing culturally responsive teachers for schools serving Indigenous students. Retrieved from http://jan.ucc.nau.edu/jar/HOE/HOE5.pdf

Clarke T., Macfarlane, S., & Macfarlane, A. (2018). Integrating Indigenous Maori frameworks to ignite understandings within initial teacher education—beyond. In P. Whitinui, M. Rodriguez de France, & O. McIvor (Eds.), *Promising practices in Indigenous teacher education* (pp. 71–85). Singapore: Springer Nature Singapore Pte Ltd.

Cherubini, L., Niemczyk, E., Hodson, J., & McGean, S. (2010). A grounded theory of new Aboriginal teachers' perceptions: The cultural attributions of medicine wheel teachings. *Teachers and Teaching: Theory and Practice*, 16(5), 545–557.

Cochran-Smith, M., Villegas, A. M., Abrams, L., Chavez-Moreno, L., Mills, T., & Stern, R. (2015). Critiquing teacher preparation research: An overview of the field, part II. *Journal of Teacher Education*, 66(2), 109–121.

Cote-Meek, S. (2014). *Colonized Classrooms: Racism, Trauma and Resistance in Post-Secondary Education.* Halifax, NS: Fernwood Publishing.

Council of Ministers of Education Canada. (2016). *Aboriginal educators' symposium. Summary report.* Author: Toronto, ON. Available at https://www.cmec.ca/Publications/Lists/Publications/Attachments/359/CMEC-Aboriginal-Educators-Symposium-2015-EN.pdf

Cox, J. (2005). Living sideways: Tricksters in American Indian oral traditions. *MELUS*, 30(2), 252–255.

Davis, L., Hare, J., Morcom, L., Hill, C., & Taylor, L. (2018). Critical considerations and cross-disciplinary approaches to pedagogy in the post-secondary classroom. *Canadian Journal of Native Education*, 40(1), 13–35.

Dion, S. D. (2007). Disrupting molded images: Identities, responsibilities and relationships—teachers and indigenous subject material. *Teaching Education*, 18(4), 329–342.

Egalite, A. J., Kisida, B., & Winters, M. A. (2015). Representation in the classroom: The effect of own-race teachers on student achievement. *Economics of Education Review*, 45, 44–52.

Erdoes, R., & Ortiz, A. (Eds.). (1984). *American Indian myths and legends.* Pantheon.

Faez, F. (2012). Diverse Teachers for diverse students: Internationally educated and Canadian-born teachers' preparedness to teach English language learners. *Canadian Journal of Education*, 35(3), 64–84.

Fagan, K. (2010). What's the trouble with the trickster? An introduction. In D. Reder & L. M. Morra (Eds.), *Troubling tricksters: Revisioning critical conversations* (pp. 3–20). Waterloo, ON: Wilfrid Laurier Press.

Francis, L., Torez, C. A., & Krebs, M. (2018). 'Hold strongly to one another': The development of an Indigenous teacher preparation and professional development program. In P. Whitinui, M. Rodriguez de France, & O. McIvor (Eds.), *Promising practices in Indigenous teacher education* (pp. 221–235). Singapore: Springer Nature Singapore Pte Ltd.

Garcia, J., & Shirley, V. (2013). Performing decolonization: Lessons learned from Indigenous youth, teachers and leaders' engagement with critical Indigenous pedagogy. *Journal of Curriculum Theorizing, 28*(2).

Garcia, J., & Shirley, V. (2019). *Indigenous education reconstructed and reimagined: Countering "post-truths" through Indigenous teacher education.* Toronto, ON: American Education Research Association.

Grande, S. (2015). *Red pedagogy: Native American social and political thought.* Lanham: Rowman & Littlefield.

Hale, V. M., & Lockard, L. (2018). Diving into the language work: Preparing tachers for the Dine language classroom. In P. Whitinui, M. Rodriguez de France, & O. McIvor (Eds.), *Promising practices in Indigenous teacher education* (pp. 163–174). Singapore: Springer Nature Singapore Pte Ltd.

Hare, J. (2015). *"All of our responsibility"*: Instructor experiences with required Indigenous education courses. *Canadian Journal of Native Education, 38*(1), 101–120.

Hare, J. (February, 2018). *Report on the Aboriginal student retention and recruitment in teacher education [Symposium].* Association of BC Deans of Education, Vancouver, British Columbia, Canada

Hobson, J., Oakley, K., Jarrett, M., Jackson, M., & Wilcock, N. (2018). In P. Whitinui, M. Rodriguez de France, & O. McIvor (Eds.), *Promising practices in Indigenous teacher education* (pp. 207–220). Singapore: Springer Nature Singapore Pte Ltd.

Johnson, D. M. (2010). (Re) Nationalizing Naanabozho: Anishinaabe Sacred Stories, Nationalist Literary Criticism, and Scholarly Responsibility. In D. Reder and L. Morra (Eds.) *Troubling Tricksters: Revisioning Critical Conversations,* pp. 200–204, Waterloo, ON: Wilfrid Laurier University Press.

Kitchen, J., & Raynor, M. (2013). Indigenizing teacher education: An action research project. *Canadian Journal of Action Research, 14*(3), 40–58.

Kovach, M., Carrier, J., Montgomery, H., Barret, M. J., & Giles, C. (2015). *Indigenous presence. Experiencing and envisioning Indigenous knowledges within selected post-secondary sites of education and social work.* http://www.usask.ca/education/profiles/kovach/Indigenous-Presence-2014-Kovach-M-et-al.pdf

Kuokkanen, R. J. (2007). *Reshaping the university: Responsibility, Indigenous epistemes, and the logic of the gift.* Vancouver: University of British Columbia Press.

Martineau, C., Steinhauer, E., Wimmer, R., Vergis, E., & Wolfe. A. (2015). Alberta's Aboriginal Teacher Education Program: A little garden where students blossom. *Canadian Journal of Native Education, 38*(1), 121–148.

McCarty, T. L., & Lee, T. S., (2014). Critical culturally sustain/revitalizing pedagogy and Indigenous education sovereignty. *Harvard Education Review, 84*(1), 101–123.

McLaughlin, J. (2013). "Crack in the pavement": Pedagogy as political and moral practice for educating culturally competent professionals. *International Education Journal: Comparative Perspectives, 12*(1), 249–265.

Mueller, R., Carr-Stewart, S., Steeves, L., & Marshall, J. (2013). Teacher recruitment and retention in select First Nations schools. *In Education, 17*(3). Retrieved from http://ineducation.ca/ineducation/article/view/72/553

National Center for Educational Statistics. (2016). *Number and percentage distribution of teachers in public and private elementary and secondary schools, by selected teacher characteristics: Selected years, 1987–88 through 2015–16.* Retrieved from https://nces.ed.gov/programs/digest/d17/tables/dt17_209.10.asp

National Congress of American Indians. (2019, September). *Becoming visible: A landscape analysis of state efforts to provide Native American education for all.* Washington, DC. September 2019. Retrieved from Retrieved from http://www.ncai.org/policy-research-center/research-data/prc-publications/NCAI-Becoming_Visible_Report-Digital_FINAL_10_2019.pdf

Perso, T., & Hayward, C. (2015). Teaching Indigenous students—cultural awareness and classroom strategies for improving learning outcomes. *Australian Journal of Eduucation,* 59(3), 329–331. doi:10.1177/0004944115602370

Pidgeon, M. (2008). Pushing against the margins: Indigenous theorizing of "success" and retention in higher education. *Journal of College Student Retention: Research, Theory & Practice,* 10(3), 339–360.

Santoro, N., & Reid, J. A. (2006). 'All things to all people': Indigenous teachers in the Australian teaching profession. *European Journal of Teacher Education,* 29(3), 287–303.

Santoro, N., Reid, J. A., Crawford, L., & Simpson, L. (2011). Teaching Indigenous children: Listening to and learning from Indigenous teachers. *Australian Journal of Teacher Education,* 36(10), 65–76.

Saskatchewan School Boards Association. (2015). *Attitudes and perceptions of Saskatchewan educators and non-educators towards the importance of First Nations and Metis achievement.* Author: Saskatoon, SK. Available at https://saskschoolboards.ca/wp-content/uploads/2015/08/13-01.pdf

Scully, A. (2015). Unsettling place-based education: Whiteness and land in Indigenous education in Canadian teacher education. *Canadian Journal of Native Education,* 38(1), 80–100.

Sinclair, N. J. (2010). Trickster Reflections: Part 1. In D. Reder and L. M. Morra (Eds.) *Troubling tricksters: Revisioning critical conversations* (pp. 21–58). Waterloo, ON: Wilfrid Laurier Press.

Truth and Reconciliation Commission of Canada. (2015). *The survivors' speak. A report of the Truth and Reconciliation Commission of Canada.* http://www.trc.ca/websites/trcinstitution/File/2015/Findings/Calls_to_Action_English2.pdf

United Nations Declaration on the Rights of Indigenous Peoples. 2007. *UN Declaration on the Rights of Indigenous Peoples.* United Nations. www.un.org/esa/socdev/unpfii/en/drip.html

Vizenor, G. (1986). Woodland word warrior: An introduction to the works of Gerald Vizenor. *Melus,* 13(1/2), 13–43.

Webster, N. L., & Valeo, A. (2011). Teacher preparedness for a changing demographic of language learners. *TESL Canada Journal,* 105–105. doi:10.18806/tesl. v28i2.1075

Womack, C. S. (2008). A single decade: Book-length Native literary criticism between 1986 and 1997. In C. S. Womack & D. Heath Justice (Eds.), *Reasoning together: The Native critics collective* (pp. 3–104). Norman: University of Oklahoma Press.

3

GETTING PAST THE WHITE PAPER

Inclusion, Antiracism and Decolonial Inheriting in Teacher Education

Lisa K. Taylor

I begin with a question that, when it was given to me, marked a moment of clarity that continues to ripple through my teaching. It happened in the 2015 conference of the Canadian Association for Indigenous Education (CASIE) as I presented on pedagogies of unsettling settler consciousness in the context of a non-mandatory Bachelor of Education course titled "Settler Colonialism, Education, and Decolonization". "Nice title", said Mark Aquash, Potawatomi Anishinaabe scholar and generous programme chair of CASIE that year. "Have your students gotten past the White Paper?"

Tabled in 1969, the "Statement of the Government of Canada on Indian Policy" defined all policies pertaining to First Nations as discriminatory and exclusionary: the distinct legal status of "Indian" itself was defined as a barrier to equality that would best be eliminated altogether. It also proposed to repeal the Indian Act that governs every aspect of life for recognized First Nations and to dissolve the Department of Indian Affairs within 5 years. A commissioner would be appointed to address any outstanding land claims, provide funds for economic development, and gradually terminate all treaties between First Nations and Canada, including ending the legal and financial responsibilities of the Crown as signatory to those treaties. The responsibility for all services would be transferred to provincial governments and reserve lands would be converted to private property owned by the band or its members.

Abolishing the distinct legal definition of First Nations under a discriminatory act would, in Trudeau's vision of a "just society", eradicate the discrimination itself and "enable the Indian people to be free—free to develop Indian cultures in an environment of legal, social and economic *equality* with other Canadians" (cited in First Nations Studies Program, 2009, n.p.).

The rejection and opposition were overwhelming, including The Indian Association of Alberta's *Red Paper* (see Cardinal, 1969), and the Union of BC Indian Chief's *Brown Paper,* and a momentous pan-Indigenous movement for establishing aboriginal land title (see the Cardinal case, 1973) and control of education (National Indian Brotherhood, 1972).

But half a century on, Mark's question is one I find useful to ask myself in all my work as a White settler scholar and a teacher educator. Are we getting past the White Paper? Or are we working within a framework that equates the struggles and aspirations of Indigenous people with those of other communities facing racial discrimination or that presumes the ameliorability of this settler-colonial society, through the curricular and pedagogical removal of barriers to Indigenous student empowerment, educational success, and upward mobility? Are our projects—supporting teachers to engage in curriculum inclusion and culturally responsive pedagogy—framed within settler futurities or Indigenous ones (Tuck et al., 2014; Tuck & Yang, 2012)? What's the difference, and why does it matter?

Teacher education in Canada is at a complex moment, full of contradiction and potential: discourses of reconciliation, decolonization and Indigenization (each of these heterogeneous and differently situated, contested, and institutionally sanctioned) have been gaining institutional traction within a field historically and predominantly framed by progressive discourses of multi-cultural education, culturally responsive pedagogy, integrative or intersectional antiracism, antidiscrimination and equity or social justice education.[1] These more established formations are broadly oriented to education's role in supporting the success of diverse learners and communities as part of building the sociopolitical infrastructure for societal change. It's important at this juncture to distinguish between the ways these different perspectives engage with difference and disparity and the societal visions and futurities framing their agendas for education-led change. What is at issue in this exercise is the tendency for the unexamined premises, referents, and agendas of more established discourses of education for social change to be used as the 'box' into which student teachers insert what they may experience as 'new perspectives'.

In this chapter, I explore some of the premises and frames of what we might broadly refer to as equity, antiracism and social justice education that come into question when educators take up pedagogies oriented towards reconciliation, decolonial, anticolonial, or treaty education. I do this through the unpacking and discussion of one critical moment in teacher education. I turn to settler colonial studies and theories of racial and colonial capitalism to clarify how racism figures within colonial modernity and the implications for antiracism and decolonial education, specifically for the role we each are called to play in this historical moment of reckoning and potential transformation.

Who Do I Think I Am? Who Do I Think I'm Talking To?

The previous paragraph sits uneasily with me. There is the epistemic violence of throwing around these broad umbrella terms as if they had a stable finite coherent referent; for example, Tuck and Yang (2012) contend with decolonial theory that any use of the word *decolonization* is a harmful metaphor unless it pursues an agenda of returning Indigenous Land to Indigenous stewards. There is also a keen sense of my own positionality and limited knowledge claims: any claim—including rigorously grounded scholarly claims—is partial; this is especially the case but particularly by those of us whose subject location is buttressed by the institutional hegemonies of colonial modernity and the experiential solipsism and privileged insularity of living in a racially segregated White supremacist settler colony.

I explore the implications of different educational agendas as a White settler scholar whose work has been nourished by deepening relationships with the traditional Abenaki stewards of the unceded territory where I have the responsibility of teaching as well as Indigenous educators with whom I've been privileged to collaborate (Davis et al., 2018). I am also conscious of the limited, particular roles I'm positioned to take up. While I'd prioritize Indigenization as part of transforming our institution, as a settler scholar and educator, I don't see it as my role to teach Indigenous knowledge within my courses: Coulthard (2014) reminds us that within institutional politics of recognition, making Indigenous subjects the object of concern can work to divert attention to the colonial relationships of power structuring that very concern. I wonder if there are real limits to settler-educators' decolonizing curriculum or pedagogy: I take this caution from Sium et al. (2012: 10) who write that "[d]ecolonization is indeed oppositional to colonial ways of thinking and acting but demands an Indigenous starting point and an articulation of what decolonization means for Indigenous peoples around the globe." My preferred focus, then, is on centring Indigenous–settler relationships and problematizing settler-colonial frames of reference, epistemes, imaginaries, and desires (Snelgrove et al., 2014) so that my students come to appreciate and respectfully seek out (or expect from our university) teachings from Indigenous knowledge holders as part of discerning their responsibility and role within the greater challenge of transforming relationships between this settler colony, Indigenous peoples, Turtle Island, and our Mother Earth.

This focus foregrounds the necessarily limited and particular value of this chapter: it is a critique of colonial modernity from within (Battiste, 2013; Mignolo, 2002), a critique structurally and endemically prone to re-centring White settlerhood (Jafri, 2012) and damage-centred or celebrational narratives of Indigenous people (Tuck, 2009). It is a critique that learns from and points to the work of Indigenous educators writing from Indigenous knowledge and teaching traditions. It's my hope, then, that the chapter may be of particular value to colleagues and audiences working in contexts in which colonial modernity and settler colonial frames are implicit and unchallenged.

'Haven't we already covered this?': Distinguishing Between Education for Inclusion, Equity, and Transformation

The critical moment under examination occurred in the context of an undergraduate teacher education programme in a small liberal arts teaching-focused university serving a heterogeneous but predominantly White-identified, settler student population of varied ethnolinguistic, socioeconomic, gender and sexual identity and ability from across Canada.

The education faculty's response to the Truth and Reconciliation Commission on mandatory residential schools for First Nations and Inuit children has created the institutional momentum for the ongoing development of two current courses, one focused on settler colonialism and decolonizing, and one on Indigenous education. It is in the context of promoting the first course that the student comment has repeatedly arisen over the years, "Haven't we already covered this? Didn't we study racism in the social justice/antidiscrimination course?" (reference has also been made to having "covered Indigenous issues" in other foundational and methods courses).

What are the unexamined premises when questions of (de)colonization and Indigeneity are reduced to an extension or component of antiracism or social justice education? To begin, Whiteness is the unmarked centre when racism and settler colonialism are conflated (if two courses are too many, this implies that Eurocentrism is a norm under attack).

This critical moment raises related questions of intersectionality and incommensurability, including the particular utility and purchase that concepts from social justice, anti-discrimination, and equity education hold and their relevance for decolonial educational approaches aimed at shifting this settler-colonial nation's relationship with traditional land stewards and Land. We can ask if the goals of equity and diversity within social justice education are commensurable with goals of decolonization, and the place of pedagogies for promoting academic success for marginalized learners and affirming intersectional identity (including culturally responsive pedagogy, inclusive curriculum, differentiated and inclusive pedagogy).

In preparing teachers to support racially, culturally, and linguistically diverse K–12 students, the term *diversity* is both valuable and problematic. For example, given the ways racism works to homogenize racialized populations, Vertovec's (2016) concept and method of super-diversity is extremely helpful in pushing educators to understand the wide range of student identifications and experiences, home cultures and capacities in complex ways that exceed flat, two-dimensional demographic categories (including categories of ethnicity or visible forms of sociocultural identity and organization) and to recognize complex social formations and movements of families within and across borders, traditional territories and communities that are experiencing new dynamics of spatial segregation, displacement, and contact (Vertovec, 2016).

In no way am I diminishing the importance of strengthening and promoting complex forms of K–12 learner identity, cultural ways of knowing and learning, and success through curriculum, resource and pedagogical reform. But for the purposes of this collection, I want to distinguish between the implicit agendas of education for *diversity* and equity (including antiracism education), and education for *decolonization*, that is, the implicit agendas of *reform* and *transformation*. Andreotti et al. (2015, 2017) have helpfully mapped these distinctions as approaches aimed at soft reform of current sociopolitical regimes, radical reform (including re-distribution of access to resources and mobility within current systems of power), and those that envisage transformation beyond reform. Stein and de Oliveira Andreotti (2016) have also suggested that there are ways in which different approaches can be strategically complementary or performative (e.g., promoting Indigenous students as future leaders of ongoing movements for sovereignty) even while there is also a way that approaches reforming and propping up one system foreclose the imaginability and thinkability of alternatives beyond reform (cf. Coulthard, 2014).

While schools play a key role in redistributing access to mobility, for example, decades of social justice and anti-discrimination education practice remind us that supporting marginalized and disadvantaged individual students to succeed is not the same as transforming the structures, organization, and ethos of a discriminatory society. We could consider this in terms of educational agendas aimed at challenging different particular systems of discrimination. Supporting the academic success of low-income learners, for example, can indeed happen even as wealth inequality grows and polarizes. Supporting the advancement of female and Muslim students can happen even as toxic masculinity, militarism, and Islamophobia win elections and inform national policies. Similarly, hegemonic approaches to inclusion tend to focus on the success of individual Indigenous students or the insertion of selective isolated elements of Indigenous cultural or knowledge into Eurocentric disciplines and epistemologies that are left untouched (Ahmed, 2012; Battiste & Henderson, 2009; Coulthard, 2014; Gaudry & Lorenz, 2018; Kuokkanen, 2007; Pidgeon, 2016; Stein, 2020). Gaudry and Lorenz (2018), for example, assert that Indigenization is a three-part spectrum. On one end is Indigenous inclusion, in the middle is reconciliation Indigenization and, on the other end, decolonial Indigenization. They conclude that despite using reconciliatory language, post-secondary institutions in Canada focus predominantly on Indigenous inclusion and propose treaty-based and resurgence-based decolonial Indigenization, avoiding questions of sovereignty and Land.

I return to Mark's question: While future teachers are rightly eager to learn pedagogies for promoting academic success for marginalized learners (including culturally responsive pedagogy or inclusive curriculum, differentiated and inclusive pedagogy, of affirming intersectional identity), are we getting past the White Paper? Are we both building inclusive curriculum and culturally responsive pedagogy while recognizing the limits of inclusion as an educational agenda?

If 'Inclusion into what?' means inclusion into settler multiculturalism in which access to greater ethno-racial and class mobility is secured through and financed by extractive economies and increasing expropriation of Indigenous land underwritten by colonial violence, this is incommensurable with decolonizing and Indigenous education (Lawrence, 2010; Tuck & Yang, 2012). As Verna St. Denis (2007, 2011) has argued, curriculum and pedagogical reform framed within agendas of the inclusion/recognition of Aboriginal culture, history, societal and family structures are not enough if they don't help teachers critically analyze how systemic racism and economic exclusion interlock to recreate colonial power. Put differently, we might distinguish between, on one hand, preparing teachers who see their role as supporting Indigenous learners to succeed within an increasingly diverse settler-colonial society and, on the other, preparing all teachers and students in ways that learn from Indigenous struggles to transform a settler-colonial society and shift its nation-to-nation relationship with First Nations.

The call for educators to attend to the particularities and tensions of racial dynamics has long informed conversations amongst Indigenous scholars. Verna St. Denis (2007) underlines the importance of antiracist analysis as part of movements pursuing and supporting Indigenous resurgence. She argues that critical race theory (CRT) can clarify the ways movements focused on Indigenous cultural revitalization and sovereignty need vigilance against cultural racism that essentializes, fundamentalizes, and depoliticizes ethnic and national identity, obscuring processes of racial identity formation and everyday racism faced by Indigenous students--processes that work through psychosocial emotional dynamics of shame, purity, and belonging. She reminds Indigenous and non-Indigenous educators that without an antiracist analysis, Whiteness and settler nationalism can be left unmarked and normalized in ways that shift the focus of attention away from structural exclusion and toward individualized and psychologized victim blaming.

As a methodology developed within CRT and Black feminism (Collins & Chepp, 2013; Crenshaw et al., 1995; Ladson Billings, 1998), *intersectionality* approaches distinctions between racism and colonialism as conditioned by the *particular* histories and imaginaries of interlocking systems of conquest, genocide, and supremacy that "fundamentally gave one another their structure, form, shape, and even momentum" (Lethabo King, 2015). Intersectionality implies, for example, historicizing the particular discursive and legal frameworks that define humanness, bodily fungibility and social death in histories of anti-Black racism in the afterlife of slavery (Hartman, 1997, 2008; Mbembé & Meintjes, 2003; Sharpe, 2016; Walcott, 2014; Wynter & McKittrick, 2015); and understanding the ways that relationships to and control of land are central to settler colonialism (Tuck & Yang, 2012; Veracini, 2010; Wolfe, 2006) even as gender is central to these processes (Maile et al., 2013).

At the same time, Bonita Lawrence and Enaksha Dua (2000, 2005) have called on educators to decolonize antiracism, especially as it has become institutionalized in education. They caution against folding anticolonial, decolonial, and Indigenous education and politics into antiracism, arguing that challenging racism is a *tactical step* necessary but insufficient for larger projects of nationhood, sovereignty, and self-determination and the concrete, non-rhetorical question of land at the heart of Indigenous spiritual as well as political struggles of survival (Lawrence & Dua, 2005; Rutherford, 2010). Hokowhitu (2012) underlines this concern that CRT and antiracism can be pursued in ways that remain state-centred—reforming society to achieve greater racial equality and missing the deeper colonial logics of settler colonialism and imperialism as political, economic, ecological, episte-mological, and ontological projects (see also Styres, 2017). Brayboy (2005, p. 427) address this disjuncture, proposing nine tenets of Tribal Critical Race Theory to distinguish Indigenous peoples' distinct legal/political projects and relationships to the settler-colonial state from their "embodiment as racialized beings".

These conversations point to practical questions as to how decolonization projects intersect with racial and other justice agendas even as they are irreducible and incommensurable with them (Snelgrove et al., 2014; Stein & Andreotti, 2016; Tuck & Yang, 2012).

Intersectionality and Incommensurability: Understanding the productiveness of Racial Logics within Coloniality and Decoloniality in the Preservice Classroom

My teaching history convinces me that preservice teachers need an understand-ing of settler colonialism that both distinguishes it from, and contextualizes it within, other systems of imperialism, Orientalism, anti-Black racism and White supremacy, all of which *share a common organizing grammar of race* (Wolfe, 2006, p. 387) to produce hierarchically variegated identities, labour formations, and modes of dispossession (Quijano, 2007).

Students may be familiar with racism but conflate racism and colonization. They need a framework to understand how racial grammars and racial oppres-sion figure within colonization and coloniality as discursive, psychosocial, and material systems that support *colonial relations of production*, that is, in the ongoing colonial project of expropriation, extraction of resources and extermination of treaty obligations that includes the division of labour within colonial-racial capi-talism (Robinson, 2000; Stein, 2018).

Racial grammars are part of the "colonial division of humanity" (Lowe, 2015) into racial identity categories historically forged in the crucible of European imperial and settler colonial projects, defined in terms of different groups' rela-tionship to ownership of violently expropriated Indigenous Land—delineating who is qualified to own, who is owned, who is disposable or qualified to be exploited labour (Wynter, 2003). Racism sets the unequal terms of access, privi-lege, complicity and ex/inclusion into settlerhood (Jafri, 2012) as first and fore-most a relationship to Land and Indigenous people, an "ongoing structure of people, land, and wellbeing" (Patel et al., 2014, p. 358). The racial identity categories in circulation and currency today emerged alongside philosophies of liberal humanism and citizenship within the colonial relations of production as persistent normative categories of governance for managing settler and slave capitalism (Lowe, 2015).

The imbrication of racial logics and categories of humanity within settler citizenship is the reason why educational approaches to overcoming racial discrimination and expanding access won't necessarily question or transform the structure and project of settler colonialism. An educational focus on greater racial mobility might even justify Canada's claims to immigrant multicultural exceptionalism and the disavowed colonial violence against Indigenous peoples and Land underwriting an extractive economy with its promises of opportunity and property. Chatterjee (2018) has compellingly argued that racialized immigrant labour exploitation and Indigenous dispossession are the inseparable "lifeblood" of settler-colonial nationalism and capitalist accumulation that redefine citizenship, civil rights, and economic opportunity in terms of the ownership of appropriated, commodified Indigenous land (see also Byrd, 2011).

Decolonial approaches include understanding settler colonialism (not as a historic event but) as an *organizing logic and structure of governance* (Wolfe, 2006) that "continues to shape the everyday lives of Indigenous and non-Indigenous peoples" (Arvin et al., 2013, p. 27; Tuck & Gaztambide-Fernández, 2013). Coloniality scholars delineate three main logics or pillars to settler colonial structures of governance (Battell-Lowman & Barker, 2016): the *elimination* of Indigenous peoples "if not physically, then as cultural, political, and legal peoples distinguishable from the rest of Canadian society" (Coulthard, 2014, p. 4); their *replacement* by settler societies and extractivist, ecocidal and expansionist economies based on racialized labour formations; and the discursive and institutional *erasure* or *transcendence* of colonization within historical narratives or consciousness that centre settler perspectives and edit out ongoing colonial violence and Indigenous resistance (Battell-Lowman & Barker, 2016).

Framing settler colonialism first of all as a persisting *structure of elimination* is, in my teaching experience, essential to (1) understanding the structural dimensions of individual experiences of racial prejudice, stereotyping, and discrimination (St. Denis, 2007), specifically (2) discerning what has been a consistent agenda of Canadian state policy towards Indigenous people, that is, to evade or extinguish nation-to-nation treaty obligations and expand land access. This allows a clearer understanding of how anti-Indigenous racism specifically targets First Nations as Land stewards and defenders, through a whole range of policies that work towards Indigenous peoples' disappearance as sovereign nations and contemporary treaty partners. In different ways for Indigenous and non-Indigenous students, this structural focus is the first step in understanding the system of mandatory residential schools for First Nations and Inuit children, not as an aberration or product of individual racist bureaucrats and teachers but rather as part of a *historically consistent* state agenda of political exclusion, assimilation (TRC, 2015) and what Jasbir Puar (2017) has theorized as *colonial debilitation*.[2] This implies that residential schools need to be understood and studied in the context of the Gradual Civilization Act (1857), the Gradual Enfranchisement Act (1869), the Indian Act (1876) and all its amendments, the White Paper, and the contemporary context of ongoing racial violence and injustice (Hubbard, 2019; Starblanket & Hunt, 2018).

Understanding the logic of *replacement* through which settler colonies naturalize and *Indigenize* White settler identities as founding nations, new natives and inevitable inheritors of this land expands antiracism discussions of White supremacy to encompass the entire range of cultural and legal mythologizations that constitute the "curriculum of replacement" (Tuck & Gaztambide-Fernández, 2013) across K–12 subjects (most clearly in the social sciences and language arts canons).

Future teachers need spaces in their preservice programmes to discern this curriculum of replacement for the colonial project that it is. They need opportunities to conduct inventories of their own institutional miseducation, not as a series of omissions and 'silenced voices' but as an organized *erasure and transcendence* of the violence of colonization—as essential to and part of the everyday workings of settler colonialism (Schick & St. Denis, 2005). Non-Indigenous students, in particular, need a framework to help them answer the most urgent question that arises for those who listen deeply and invest in this learning sincerely: "Why have I never been taught this? If I'm implicated, why am I ignorant?" I can echo Pam Palmater's recent video on the three main emotional responses she has observed in her teaching (Palmater, 2019), namely tears, shock, and anger. I'd argue that Non-Indigenous preservice students *need* to start from an understanding of settler colonialism as an ongoing project of *disappearing Indigenous people* from collective imaginaries and political processes of contemporary Canada if they're going to make sense of their own feelings of shock and surprise, even doubt, when forced to face the ongoing violence of colonization. This shock is, in fact, constitutive of settler consciousness and the felt sense of living in a society profoundly racially segregated *by design*. Beyond experiencing shock, non-Indigenous students need the opportunity to articulate and problematize a personal sense of investment in discourses of Canadian innocence, benevolence, exceptionalism, liberal rights, and recognition (Battell-Lowman & Barker, 2016; Coulthard, 2014; Regan, 2010; Suša, 2016; Tuck & Yang, 2012) and discern the ways these discourses do the work of invisibilizing and sanctioning violence.

Settler-colonial studies provide a framework that goes beyond antiracism to reverse the workings of settler-colonial erasure, replacement, and transcendence. To reverse this erasure and peel back the unquestioned stature and universalized authority of Western knowledge systems, future teachers need to not only develop an awareness of colonial violence but to also see how colonial governance functions to protect institutions that disavow and erase that very violence (Kerr, 2014; Stein, 2020). Put differently, there are two erasures to be reversed: the erasure of violence and of the erasure of the erasure. Returning to Palmater's example, student feelings of surprise, shock, and anger offer a springboard to move from "Why haven't I learned this? Why don't I know about this?" to "What agendas are served by this 'not-knowing'? What violence does it make possible and acceptable? What else do I 'not-know'? What does 'not-knowing' protect me from facing? Is more knowledge the solution? Is my learning 'more' going to change the violence financing my quality of life?"

The final questions point away from education's redemptive faith in knowledge- and access-based solutions and point toward what Indigenous educators have always emphasized: relationships. The salience of this distinction can be illustrated by considering two differently inspired learning activities to be found in many teacher education courses in Canada.

Critical anti-oppression, social justice exercises like unpacking one's knapsack of racial, gender, class, and other privilege is a useful step in cultivating critical reflexivity and interrupting the normalization and projection of one's own schooling experiences onto future K–12 students under one's care. Critical reflexivity is essential when teacher demographics do not reflect those of K–12 students and their communities. While essential, it is not sufficient. It does not necessarily unsettle settler consciousness nor unravel investments in settlerhood and extractive relations to Land. Learning to condemn or even critically implicate yourself within systems of discrimination is not the same as comprehending the utility of racism within a larger colonial project of expropriation, extraction, commodification, and differential exploitation of life, labour, and Land.

In decolonizing pedagogies, exercises in centring one's individual, family, and ancestral relationships to Land, territory, and Indigenous land protectors and treaty partners can go a long way in refusing colonial logics of elimination, replacement, and erasure. Haig-Brown (2012) begins with the question, "Whose traditional land are you on?" centring this relationship to the more-than-human web of life honoured in treaty as the frame that encompasses entire family histories, that holds all other relationships of migration, displacement, and settling in Indigenous territory. Freeman (2002, 2018) places her answerability to this relationship to Land at the heart of her personal example of tracing generational layers of implication and the accretion of attachments to settler-colonial formations of desire, belonging, benevolence, and futurity (Dion, 2009; Freeman, 2018; Haig-Brown, 2012; Taylor, 2014).

For students targeted by racism who trace family histories and ancestry to European colonies, it's valuable to have a clear analysis of the settler-colonial project, to discern the exact nature Canadian citizenship as a differentiated structure of belonging that is premised on continuing Indigenous dispossession, on extractive economies of racialized labour and land commodification (Lethabo King, 2015; Amadahy & Lawrence, 2009; Hampton & DeMartini, 2017; Phung, 2011; Sarannillio, 2013; Simpson et al., 2011). This exercise allows students to research and interpret the ways the coloniality of power and of being (Maldonado-Torres, 2007; Quijano, 2007) has shaped and continues to shape the intimate conditions of personal and family history—the forces and narratives of exile, escape, sacrifice, hopes, and opportunity. Understanding the structuring violence and unequal inclusions of settler-colonial citizenship can be helpful, distinguishing between, for example, settler privilege and settler complicity. Jafri (2012) defines the former as "unearned benefits" accrued by all non-Indigenous people in racially unequal ways through the rights and protections of citizenship within the settler state, including the right to make a living and home on Indigenous lands. She distinguishes settler privilege from complicity as different orientations and relations to the settler-colonial project that circulate differently within "settlerhood", a "field of operations into which we become socially positioned and implicated" (2012, n.p.). These are subtle but significant distinctions, and there are many stories to tell of making home on ex-propriated land.

To begin this family research, I ask students to investigate the full range of relationships that have made it possible for them to have grown up where they did (with varying degrees of security, health, wellbeing), and to live in our shared place of study. These relationships can include: ancestral and intergenerational sacrifice and care; family histories of "voluntary and forced arrivals and departures" (Dhamoon, 2015) and the geopolitical forces behind them; histories of complicity, privilege, opportunity, and exploitation within continuing settler-colonial political, juridical, economic, and epistemic structures of expansionism and dispossession; colonial policies of treaty making and breaking, of ongoing material, juridical, economic, cultural, and epistemic violence aimed at Indigenous dispossession and settler; the interdependence and treaty relations amongst all beings visible and microbial, organic and inorganic (including water, air/atmosphere and other 'natural elements') honoured and defended by Indigenous stewards. This research can form the basis of writing a comprehensive implicated history of their family in relation to Land and Indigenous Land protectors, organized by the question, "What stories from my family history are worthy of passing on as the full, complicated truth in order to guide future generations?" (Taylor, 2019).

This exercise takes us to the limits of modern/colonial, Eurocentric Enlightenment, humanist, individualist, and materialist ways of knowing, being, perceiving, and imagining (Sheridan & Longboat, 2006; Styres, 2017). These limits are set in relief by a set of questions:

> What if the dominant worldviews that I've been raised with blind me to the most important relationships I'm part of? What if they blind me to any possibility of living in radically less harmful, more respectful and reciprocal ways? What if I'm not at the centre of the most important relationships that I'm part of? If my life is made possible by relationships, what forms of life do I make possible? What relationships of regeneration does (or could) my living support and nourish.
>
> *(Taylor, 2019)*

This set of questions are designed to connect a sense of personal and familial implication to relationships of responsibility and reciprocity, here to honour the knowledge traditions that Indigenous students bring, and to encourage in non-Indigenous students a conscious stance of epistemic and ontological humility, critical reflexivity, and respect (Kirkness & Barnhardt, 1991). The questions aim to signal that learning from Indigenous knowledge holders demands something other and more than inclusion and equity. They are offered in order to clearly mark the insufficiency of settler multiculturalism, liberal pluralism, and other humanist, materialist and civic frameworks of equity and social justice, in recognition that the project of transforming colonial relations of being and knowing can only ever be Indigenous-led and informed by Indigenous projects of healing, resurgence, and self-determination (Ahenakew, 2019; Battiste, 2013; L. Simpson, 2014; Snelgrove et al., 2014; Styres, 2017).

Conclusion: The Limits of Teacher Education

What happens when we shift our focus from racism and antiracism to settler colonialism and Eurocentric colonial modernity? Certainly, coloniality is co-constitutive and dependent on the ideological justification and organizational logics of racism. But it's only in facing the full extent of the epistemic, politico-economic, and ecological dimensions of modernity/coloniality that (future) educators might develop a healthy skepticism toward the limits of liberal and even critical agendas of educational inclusion. This is the essential ground of listening to the full extent and depths of the calls for societal and existential transformation that I hear from Indigenous educators, knowledge holders, and communities. This is the essential ground of discerning the particular, non-innocent, non-redemptive, and non-guaranteed role that each of us is called to actively take up in the potential implosion of racial and colonial global capitalism we are witnessing, and the call for transformation towards ways of being with the more-than-human web that is Gaia.

I return to the provocation offered 15 years ago by Indo-Canadian scholar Enaksha Dua and Mi'kmaq scholar Bonita Lawrence (2005, p. 126): If the central issue of sovereignty and self-determination and the concrete, non-rhetorical question of land lie at the heart of Indigenous spiritual, as well as political struggles of survival", then they challenge antiracist educators to "begin to think about their personal stake in this struggle, and about where they are going to situate themselves". To do so, future teachers need to be able to situate the racial grammars and racial violence of settler colonialism within the longer projects of the Capitalocene and Plantationocene (Haraway, 2015), world ecologies founded on both the human–nature division and the relegation of colonized and racialized people to economies of unbridled extraction (Moore, 2018). Antiracism can ground a critically implicated appreciation for the absolutely central place of Indigenous people and wisdom traditions in the challenge of transforming an ecocidal world ecology that, as of March 2020, refuses to be ignored any longer. Only then might they teach in ways that begin with the question, "What kinds of relationships are we honouring and (re)generating in our learning?"

Notes

1 I beg the reader's indulgence as I treat these heterogeneous educational movements with these umbrella terms: I will necessarily do them injustice for the purposes of surfacing particular distinctions and hope this strategy yields insights that justify the inevitable violence of reductive broad gestures.
2 Puar (2017) uses the concept of *colonial debilitation* to analyse processes that structure colonized nations in conditions of *debility* and reduce this condition to apolitical rights-based programmes of sustenance-level aid.

References

Ahenakew, C. (2019). *Towards scarring our collective soul wound.* Gesturing Towards Decolonial Futures Collective and Musagetes. https://decolonialfutures.net/towardsscarring/.

Ahmed, S. (2012). *On being included: Racism and diversity in institutional life.* Duke University Press.

Andreotti, V.O., Stein, S., Ahenakew, C., & Hunt, D. (2015). Mapping interpretations of decolonization in the context of higher education. *Decolonization: Indigeneity, Education & Society,* 4(1), 21–40.

Arvin, M., Tuck, E., & Morrill, A. (2013). Decolonizing feminism: Challenging connections between settler colonialism and heteropatriarchy. *Feminist Formations,* 8–34.

Battell-Lowman, E., & Barker, A. J. (2016). *Settler: Identity and colonialism in 21st century Canada.* Nova Scotia, Canada: Fernwood.

Battiste, M. (2013). *You can't be the doctor if you're the disease: Eurocentrism and indigenous renaissance* [CAUT Distinguished Academic Lecture]. https://www.caut.ca/sites/default/files/you-cant-be-the-doctor-if-youre-the-disease-eurocentrism-and-indigenous-renaissance.pdf.

Battiste, M., & Henderson, J. S. Y. (2009). Naturalizing Indigenous knowledge in Eurocentric education. *Canadian Journal of Native Education,* 32(1), 5–18.

Brayboy, B. M. J. (2005). Toward a tribal critical race theory in education. *The Urban Review,* 37(5), 425–446.

Byrd, J.A. (2011). *The transit of empire: Indigenous critiques of colonialism.* U of Minnesota Press.

Cardinal, H. (1969). *Red Paper on Native Development.* Edmonton, Alberta. Indian Chiefs of Alberta.

Chatterjee, S. (2018). Teaching immigration for reconciliation: A pedagogical commitment with a difference. *Intersectionalities: A Global Journal of Social Work Analysis, Research, Polity, and Practice,* 6(1), 1–15.

Collins, P. H. & Chepp, V. (2013). Intersectionality. In G. Waylen, K. Celis, J. Kantola, & S. Laurel Weldon (Eds.), *Oxford handbook of gender and politics* (pp. 57–87). Oxford; New York: Oxford University Press.

Coulthard, G. (2014). *Red skin, White masks: Rejecting the colonial politics of recognition.* Minneapolis: University of Minnesota Press.

Crenshaw, K., Gotanda, N., Peller, G., & Thomas, K. (1995). *Critical race theory. The key writings that formed the movement.* New York: The New Press.

Davis, L., Hare, J., Hiller, C., Morcom, L., & Taylor L. K. (Eds.). (2018). Critical Considerations and Cross-Disciplinary Approaches in Post-Secondary Classrooms [Special issue]. *Canadian Journal of Native Education, Indigenization, Decolonization, and Reconciliation.*

Dhamoon, R. K. (2015). A feminist approach to decolonizing anti-racism: Rethinking transnationalism, intersectionality, and settler colonialism. *Feral Feminisms*, 4, 20–37.

Dion, S. D. (2009). *Braiding histories: Learning from Aboriginal peoples' experiences and perspectives.* Vancouver: University of British Columbia Press.

Dua, E., & Lawrence, B. (2000). Challenging white hegemony in university classrooms: Whose Canada is it? *Atlantis: Critical Studies in Gender, Culture & Social Justice*, 24(2), 105–122.

Essed, P. (1991). *Understanding everyday racism: An interdisciplinary theory* (Vol. 2). Newbury Park, Calif: Sage Publications.

First Nations Studies Program. (2009). Indigenous foundations—The White Paper 1969. University of British Columbia Press. https://indigenousfoundations.arts.ubc.ca/the_white_paper_1969/

Freeman, V. (2002). *Distant relations: How my ancestors colonized North America.* Toronto: McClelland & Stewart.

Freeman, V. (2018). Becoming real on Turtle Island: A pedagogy of relationship. *Canadian Journal of Native Education*, 40(1), 111–124.

Gaudry, A., & Lorenz, D. (2018). Indigenization as inclusion, reconciliation, and decolonization: navigating the different visions for indigenizing the Canadian Academy. *AlterNative: An International Journal of Indigenous Peoples*, 14(3), 218–227.

Haig-Brown, C. (2012). Decolonizing diaspora. In *Decolonizing philosophies of education* (pp. 73–90). SensePublishers.

Hampton, R., & DeMartini, A. (2017). We cannot call back colonial stories: Storytelling and critical land literacy. *Canadian Journal of Education/Revue canadienne de l'éducation*, 40(3), 245–271.

Haraway, D. (2015). Anthropocene, capitalocene, plantationocene, chthulucene: Making kin. *Environmental Humanities*, 6(1), 159–165.

Hartman, S. (2008). *Lose your mother: A journey along the Atlantic slave route.* Macmillan.

Hartman, S. V. (1997). *Scenes of subjection: Terror, slavery, and self-making in nineteenth-century America.* Oxford University Press on Demand.

Hokowhitu, B. (2012). Book Review: Racism, Colonialism, and Indigeneity in Canada: A Reader, Edited by Martin J. Cannon and Lina Sunseri. Toronto: Oxford University Press Canada, 2011. *Junctures: The Journal for Thematic Dialogue*, (15).

Hubbard T. (2019). nîpawistamâsowin: *We Will Stand Up. [Motion Picture].* Canada. National Film Board of Canada.

Jafri, B. (2012). Privilege vs. complicity: People of colour and settler colonialism. *Equity Matters.* http://www.ideasidees.ca/blog/privilege-vs-complicity-people-colour-and-settler-colonialism

Kerr, J. (2014). Western epistemic dominance and colonial structures: Considerations for thought and practice in programs of teacher education. *Decolonization: Indigeneity, Education & Society*, 3(2).

King, T. L. (2015). Interview with Tiffany Lethabo King. *Feral Feminisms*, 4, 64–68.

Kirkness, V. J., & Barnhardt, R. (1991). First Nations and higher education: The four R's: Respect, relevance, reciprocity, responsibility. *Journal of American Indian Education*, 30(3), 1–15.

Kuokkanen, R. (2007). *Reshaping the university: Responsibility, Indigenous epistemes, and the logic of the gift.* Vancouver: University of British Columbia Press.

Ladson-Billings, G. (1998). Just what is critical race theory and what's it doing in a nice field like education? *International Journal of Qualitative Studies in Education*, 11(1), 7–24.

Lawrence, B., & Dua, E. (2005). Decolonizing antiracism. *Social Justice*, 32(4), 120–143.

Lowe, L. (2015). *The intimacies of four continents*. Duke University Press.

Maile, A., Tuck, E., & Morrill, A. (2013). Decolonizing feminism: Challenging connections between settler colonialism and heteropatriarchy. *Feminist Formations*, 25(1), 8–34.

Maldonado-Torres, N. (2007). On the coloniality of being: Contributions to the development of a concept. *Cultural Studies*, 21(2–3), 240–270.

Mbembé, J. A., & Meintjes, L. (2003). Necropolitics. *Public Culture*, 15(1), 11–40.

Mignolo, W. (2002). The geopolitics of knowledge and the colonial difference. *The South Atlantic Quarterly*, 101(1), 57–96.

Moore, J. W. (2018). The capitalocene part II: Accumulation by appropriation and the centrality of unpaid work/energy. *The Journal of Peasant Studies*, 45(2), 237–279.

Palmater, P. (2019). *Why do Indigenous topics cause such emotional discomfort?* TVO Indigenous. https://www.tvo.org/video/why-do-indigenous-topics-cause-such-emotional -discomfort

Patel, S., Moussa, G., & Upadhyay, N. (Eds.) (2014). Complicities, connections, and struggles: Critical transnational feminist analysis of settler colonialism [Special issue]. *Feral Feminisms*, 4.

Phung, M. (2011). Are people of colour settlers too? In A. Mathur, J. Dewar, & M. DeGagne (Eds.), *Cultivating Canada: Reconciliation through the lens of cultural diversity*. Ottawa, ON: Aboriginal Healing Foundation.

Pidgeon, M. (2016). More than a checklist: Meaningful Indigenous inclusion in higher education. *Social Inclusion*, 4(1), 77–91.

Puar, J. K. (2017). *The right to maim: Debility, capacity, disability*. Durham: Duke University Press.

Quijano, A. (2007). Coloniality and modernity/rationality. *Cultural Studies*, 21(2–3), 168–178.

Regan, P. (2010). *Unsettling the settler within: Indian residential schools, truth telling, and reconciliation in Canada*. Vancouver: University of British Columbia Press.

Robinson, C. J. (2000). *Black Marxism: The making of the Black radical tradition*. Chapel Hill, NC: University of North Carolina Press.

Rutherford, S. (2010). Colonialism and the Indigenous present: An interview with Bonita Lawrence. *Race & Class*, 52(1), 9–18.

Saranillio, D. I. (2013). Why Asian settler colonialism matters: A thought piece on critiques, debates, and Indigenous difference. *Settler Colonial Studies*, 3(3–4), 280–294.

Schick, C., & St. Denis, V. (2005). Troubling national discourses in anti-racist curricular planning. *Canadian Journal of Education*, 28(3), 295–317.

Sehdev, R. K. (2011). People of Colour in Treaty. In A. Mathur, J. Dewar, & M. DeGagne (Eds.), *Cultivating Canada: Reconciliation through the lens of cultural diversity*. Ottawa, ON: Aboriginal Healing Foundation.

Sharpe, C. (2016). *In the wake: On Blackness and being*. Durham: Duke University Press.

Sheridan, J., & Longboat, R.D. (2006). The Haudenosaunee imagination and the ecology of the sacred. *Space and Culture*, 9, 365–381. doi:10.1177/1206331206292503

Simon Roger, I. (2013). Towards a hopeful practice of worrying: The problematics of listening and the educational responsibilities of the IRSTRC. In P. Wakeham & J. Henderson (Eds.), *Reconciling Canada* (pp. 129–142). Toronto: University of Toronto Press.

Simpson, J. S., James, C. E., & Mack, J. (2011). Multiculturalism, colonialism, and racialization. *Review of Education, Pedagogy, and Cultural Studies*, 33(4), 285–305.

Simpson, L. B. (2014). Land as pedagogy: Nishnaabeg intelligence and rebellious transformation. *Decolonization: Indigeneity, Education & Society*, 3(3), 1–25.

Sium, A., Desai, C., & Ritskes, E. (2012). Towards the 'tangible unknown': Decolonization and the Indigenous future. *Decolonization: Indigeneity, Education & Society*, 1(1).

Snelgrove, C., Dhamoon, R. K., & Corntassel, J. (2014). Unsettling settler colonialism: The discourse and politics of settlers, and solidarity with Indigenous nations. *Decolonization: Indigeneity, Education & Society*, 3(2).

St. Denis, V. (2007). Aboriginal education and anti-racist education: Building alliances across cultural and racial identity. *Canadian Journal of Education/Revue canadienne de l'éducation*, 1068–1092.

St. Denis, V. (2011). Silencing Aboriginal curricular content and perspectives through multiculturalism: "There are other children here." *Review of Education, Pedagogy, and Cultural Studies*, 33(4), 306–317.

Starblanket, G., & Hunt, D. (2018). How the death of Colten Boushie became recast as the story of a knight protecting his castle. Globe and Mail.

Stein, S. (2018). Confronting the racial-colonial foundations of US higher education. *Journal for the Study of Postsecondary and Tertiary Education*, 3, 77–98. doi:10.28945/4105

Stein, S. (2020). 'Truth before reconciliation': The difficulties of transforming higher education in settler colonial contexts. *Higher Education Research & Development*, 39(1), 156–170.

Stein, S., & de Oliveira Andreotti, V. (2016). Postcolonial insights for engaging difference in educational approaches to social justice and citizenship. In *The Palgrave international handbook of education for citizenship and social justice* (pp. 229–245). London: Palgrave Macmillan.

Styres, S. D. (2017). *Pathways for remembering and recognizing Indigenous thought in education: Philosophies of Iethi'nihsténha Ohwentsia'kékha (land)*. Toronto; Buffalo; London: University of Toronto Press.

Suša, R. (2016). Modern global imaginaries, modern subjects, enduring hierarchical relations and other possibilities. *Postcolonial Directions in Education*, 193.

Taylor, L. K. (2014). Inheritance as intimate, implicated publics: Building practices of remembrance with future teachers in response to residential school survivor testimonial media and literature. *Canadian Social Studies*, 47(2), 110–126. https://canadian-social-studies-journal.educ.ualberta.ca/content/articles

Taylor, L. K. (2019). *Instructions, Colonial Family History Project* [Unpublished course materials]. Bishop's University.

Tuck, E. (2009). Suspending damage: A letter to communities. *Harvard Educational Review*, 79(3), 409–428.

Tuck, E., & Gaztambide-Fernández, R. A. (2013). Curriculum, replacement, and settler futurity. *Journal of Curriculum Theorizing*, 29(1).

Tuck, E., Guess, A., & Sultan, H. (2014). Not nowhere: Collaborating on selfsame land. *Decolonization: Indigeneity, Education & Society*, 26, 1–11.

Tuck, E., & Yang, K. W. (2012). Decolonization is not a metaphor. *Decolonization: Indigeneity, Education & Society*, 1(1), 1–40.

Veracini, L. (2010). *Settler colonialism*. Basingstoke: Palgrave Macmillan.

Vertovec, S. (2016). *Super-diversity as concept and approach: Whence it came, where it's at, and whither it's going. Super-Diversity: A Transatlantic Conversation.*

Walcott, R. (2014). The problem of the human: Black ontologies and 'the coloniality of our being'. *Postcoloniality-decoloniality-black critique: Joints and fissures*, 93–105.

Wolfe, P. (2006). Settler colonialism and the elimination of the Native. *Journal of Genocide Research*, 8(4), 387–409.

Wynter, S. (2003). Unsettling the coloniality of being/power/truth/freedom: Towards the human, after man, its overrepresentation—An argument. *CR: The New Centennial Review*, 3(3), 257–337.

Wynter, S., & McKittrick, K. (2015). *Sylvia Wynter: On being human as praxis*

4

IMPORTANT AND UNNECESSARY

The Paradox of White Preservice Teacher Perceptions of Culturally Relevant Pedagogy

Jacob S. Bennett

In this chapter, I present interview data from a group of White preservice teachers (PSTs) attending a large public Mid-Atlantic university in the United States. Using Engeström and Sannino's (2010) concept of expansive learning as an analytical tool, I aimed to uncover participant understanding and perceptions of diversity, particularly as it related to usefulness of implementing culturally relevant pedagogy (CRP) to inform their future teaching practice. I hoped to answer the following question:

- How do White PSTs who attend the same large public Mid-Atlantic university perceive the need for CRP to inform their future practice?

Before discussing my research design, process, analysis and results, I provide a review of relevant literature to present both a justification for studies regarding analyses of White PSTs' attitudes toward concepts such as diversity and CRP and the ways Whiteness as a force of normalization has been addressed in educational research.

Literature Review

The 2014–2015 school year was the first during which multiple districts reported White students constituting less than 50% of the student body in schools across the United States (Wells, 2015). Juxtaposed against these changes, current data from the U.S. Department of Education (2016) show 82% of the teacher population in elementary and secondary schools is White. These demographics are reflected within teacher education programs (TEPs) as well. In relation to this study, participants attended a TEP in which 72% of the student population was White.

Similar demographics are also seen in provinces throughout Canada. While many seem to recognize the need for a racially diverse teaching force, "various groups, including first-generation students, students with disabilities, students from Aboriginal descent, and other racialized minorities—are underrepresented in Ontario's colleges and universities" (Holden & Kitchen, 2018, p. 45). In terms of P–12 public education, Cardoza (2018) explained 30% of Canada's schoolchildren identify as having one parent who was born abroad or are immigrants themselves. While this population likely includes students who identify as White, living in Canada while holding cultural traits that differ from those held by some White Canadians can still be a marginalizing experience. Such immigrants can have visible effects on the perceptions of what it means to be "Canadian" as the recent rant by former sports commentator Don Cherry exposed. Mr. Cherry's tirade, during which he described his frustration with "you people" (i.e., immigrants), loving Canadian "milk and honey" but refusing to honor those who died fighting for the way of life they seemed to lackadaisically appreciate (McGran, 2019), can be understood as a diatribe of Whiteness.

Hayes et al. (2013) succinctly explained that, "Whiteness is not about White people, but is a mindset" (p. 3). Outcomes of such a mindset can be but are not limited to injustices such as being described as "Canadian" or "American" based on specific ways of acting and/or looking, or inequities related to the ways police often give certain individuals the "benefit of the doubt" based on dressing or acting certain ways. These outcomes also influence the design of structural policies (i.e., laws) that differentially affect individuals based on such characteristics. Understanding such definitions of Whiteness has been argued to be an essential element in developing truly culturally responsive White teachers who can meaningfully support students of color (Matias, 2016). To do so within teacher education, Duncan-Andrade (2011) and Milner (2010) both recommended a complete transformation of the way teacher educators instruct PSTs to navigate concepts such as race, racism and oppression.

Duncan-Andrade (2011) recommended using an interdisciplinary approach to inform design in teacher education programs. He argued scholarship published in fields such as public health, community psychology, social epidemiology and medical sociology should inform work in the field of teacher education. Specifically, such fields could provide information about the increasing importance of teachers becoming aware of the conditions of students' lives outside of school. He explained that, "each area that someone's identity falls outside of the dominant cultural norms of this country (White-heterosexual-male middle class or wealthy-English-speaking able bodied), they will experience forms of institutional violence" (Duncan-Andrade, 2011, p. 314). He went on to explain such power-dynamics should be considered when teacher educators develop curricula to inform PSTs about topics of race, oppression and inequity.

Milner (2010) described preparing PSTs for, "diversity, equity, and social justice" as one of the most daunting tasks facing the field (p. 119). He explained that teacher educators themselves must acknowledge PST, "mindsets, thinking, belief systems, attitudes, and overall understanding of the teaching and learning exchange" based on the fact that such perceptions will inevitably shape the sort of practices these teachers will deem necessary to develop as in-service teachers (Milner, 2010, p. 118). Similar recommendations have also been made in the Canadian context.

Kerr and Andreotti (2019) analyzed how teacher education candidates engaged with multiple forms of diversity and inequity in their TEPs. Specifically, the authors hoped to understand, "the processes through which societal inequity becomes reconstituted through teacher education" (Kerr & Andreotti, 2019, p. 647). Results of their work revealed that even when PSTs showed greater awareness of the systemic nature of inequity as they moved through their TEP, such awareness was not centered on dismantling but rather, "affirmed, supported or normalized these inequitable structures" (Kerr & Andreotti, 2019, p. 660). Based on this result, the authors "tempered their perspectives" regarding the common perception that education can be a place for emancipation. While they expressed a belief in teacher education's potential to "disrupt current educational and societal practices," they also described that rather than, "seek[ing] an illusive form as equity as an achievement, [they hoped to] engage different possibilities of knowing, being, and relating to the world" (Kerr & Andreotti, 2019, p. 661). Such a goal aligns well with conceptualizations of CRP, as presented next.

Current Study

The following criteria were listed on the TEP's website where this study took place regarding "diversity." They were the only references I found that came close to describing the commitment of faculty and staff in the program to supporting students in developing the mindsets described earlier:

- [T]ransform the curriculum so that every student will be exposed to critical aspects of diversity and equity;
- Encourage and support collaborative research that addresses the needs of culturally and linguistically diverse students/clients.

Although faculty in the TEP would likely be familiar with these goals, my review of the data revealed the majority of PST participants did not fully understand the concept of CRP, defined by Ladson-Billings (1995) as reflecting three main criteria:

1. Believing students must experience academic success
2. Believing students must develop and/or maintain cultural competence
3. Believing students must develop a critical consciousness through which they challenge the status quo of the current social order

I now present my theoretical and analytical frameworks used to anchor my interpretation of this result.

Theoretical Frame

When White individuals show emotions such as sadness or frustration when talking about topics related to racialized oppression, these displays redirect the emphasis of pain from the experience of those who are oppressed (i.e., persons of color) back onto the oppressors (i.e., White people). Matias (2016) labeled this "White emotionality." Outcomes of my analyses are discussed and interpreted using this concept. In short, by becoming frustrated with ideas such as CRP, the White PSTs in my study re-centered their beliefs by normalizing their perspectives.

Analytical Framework

Along with my theoretical frame, I utilized Engeström and Sannino's (2010) concept of expansive learning in an effort to better explain why the White PSTs in my study were not able to fully realize the concept of CRP. Engeström and Sannino (2010) explained expansive learning takes place when individuals formulate a theoretical concept of a new activity that gives rise to new concrete manifestations (i.e., actions). The authors provided a cyclical, recursive diagram adapted from Engeström (1999) to show how expansive learning takes place. Readers can find the diagram online.

In relation to the model, the first action is questioning. Engeström and Sannino (2010) explained this process involves criticizing or rejecting aspects of "existing wisdom." Next, the action of analysis involves, "mental, discursive or practical transformation of the situation in order to find out causes or explanatory mechanisms" (Engeström & Sannino, 2010, p. 7). Third, individuals go through the action of modeling during which solutions are developed for a "problematic situation." The fourth action is an examination of the model through experimentation to understand limitations. Fifth, implementation of the model takes place through "practical applications." Finally, the sixth and seventh actions are reflections based on evaluation and consolidation of outcomes into a "stable form of practice" (Engeström & Sannino, 2010, p. 7). This model provided a useful framework to operationalize Matias's (2016) concept of White emotionality as it related to developing an understanding of CRP.

Methods

Site and Participants

Site

The TEP under analysis is located in the Mid-Atlantic United States and housed within a large public university. As of writing, the program offers 23 areas of study and degrees ranging from but not limited to Bachelor of Science in Education (BSEd), Master of Education (MEd), Educational Doctorates (EdDs) and Doctorates of Philosophy (PhDs). The demographics of the TEP are overwhelmingly White and female, with 80% of the student population being reported as such. There are no required "diversity" or multicultural education courses to obtain credentials in any of the degree programs offered. All participants reported in this study were completing a BSEd.

Participant Selection

Using the university's participation pool, I disseminated the Quick Discrimination Index (QDI; Ponterotto et al., 1995) as a gateway for possible participation in my study. The participant pool is used by faculty and staff to select possible participants for numerous research studies within the TEP. Students are required to obtain a certain number of department-mandated "lab" hours for graduation, and I offered the QDI as one credit toward this requirement.

I selected only White individuals because I was interested in understanding the ways the majority White student body conceptualized concepts such as diversity and CRP. I contacted 35 students and stopped after eight participants agreed based on my goal of possibly following each into their classrooms in subsequent years. I present data in this chapter from Charles Purse (male), Victoria Welby (female) and Erin Markie (female). All names are pseudonyms. I provide only these data based on each participants' in-depth descriptions of their views toward diversity and CRP.

Researcher Positionality

My experience as a White male from a Jewish background situates my perspective related to understanding diversity and CRP. For the majority of my youth, I adhered to a racial ideology of indifference and felt the best form of interracial interaction was by "ignoring" a person's race. I believed this allowed me to treat everyone as "equals." In my mid-20s, I went through a process of racialized awareness based, in part, on a continued discussion with a biracial female colleague at the high school where I taught (Bennett, 2019). This conversation, along with my research regarding the concept of White privilege for my MA thesis (Bennett, 2012), shifted my views toward race, oppression and privilege. I began to acknowledge the fallacy of racial indifference and realized such a mindset inherently marginalizes experiences of persons of color and perpetuates a normalization of White perspectives. While I can never fully disconnect from Whiteness, my continued journey toward racial awareness was highly influential in my reasoning for developing this study.

Data Collection

Participant Interviews

Each participant took part in four approximately 45-minute interviews stag-gered between two semesters of an academic year (2015–2016). Interviews took place in a private office within the TEP. Each subsequent interview was designed around the following topics: (1) participants' backgrounds; (2) perceptions of the definition of knowledge; (3) perceptions of systemic inequities, race-based privilege and power; and (4) a discussion of how beliefs in the previous interview might affect future praxis. It was in this fourth interview that the topic of CRP was discussed.

I personally audio-recorded and transcribed each interview and then shared the personal transcripts with each participant. After interview data were shared, I developed analytical memos that I also shared with participants. These memos were used to find "themes" related to participant interpretations of CRP. I asked participants if my interpretation of their perceptions of CRP were correct to further the member checking process.

Reflexive Journals

Before our first interview, I asked participants if they would be willing to keep reflexive journals during the yearlong study. I described the journals as a place to write thoughts regarding diversity and oppression. All agreed, and I pro-vided each with bound composition notebooks that I collected at the end of the study. My analysis of these documents centered on searching for common themes within and between entries related to diversity and CRP through ana-lytic induction.

Data Analysis

Analytic induction is a strategy that allows researchers to develop explanations of interactional processes through which individuals develop distinct forms of social action (Katz, 2001). Furthermore, "initial cases are inspected to locate com-mon factors and provisional explanations. As new cases are examined and initial hypotheses are contradicted, the explanation is reworked" (Katz, 2001, p. 480). Therefore, this technique was useful for my needs based on my goal of develop-ing empirical assertions (Erickson, 1985).

Generating assertions from analysis rather than using a priori codes allowed me to test and strengthen each based on possible changing perceptions of my participants toward diversity and CRP. During analysis, key linkages between CRP and White emotionality were searched for throughout the data to identify possible patterns. Being flexible and adapting assertions to the generated data allowed for more accuracy in interpretation.

Results

Data show the expansive nature of learning about the topic of CRP was hampered within this TEP by the participants in this study. The majority of participants were unable to move past the first and second action phases of "questioning" and "analysis" and into the latter portion of the cycle through development of new beliefs leading to action, consolidation and revision.

Charles Purse

Background

Charles grew up in a suburban southern town. He described his father as an engineer who "worked his way up" at his job (Interview 1, October 15, 2015). His mother was a retired nurse, of whom he did not speak of much in the interview process. He described his household growing up as "chaotic," with little amounts of respect given to anyone. In terms of extended family, he explained there was a falling out with his father's parents because his father chose to raise Charles and his older brother in a secular, rather than Catholic, household.

In his reflexive journal, Charles included multiple entries regarding his perceptions of diversity and experiences as a student teacher in a middle school social studies classroom. In his first entry, he described his views toward the Black Lives Matter movement by explaining, "[I]t's not like a don't value the work of this group, it's just that I feel it's furthering the racial divide in this country. Shouldn't the slogan be 'All Lives Matter?' Like what about Hispanics, Asians and Whites too?" (Journal Entry, October 22, 2015). He went on to explain he would be the "first to admit" White privilege exists because of the lasting effects of discrimination throughout the history of the United States, but implored "that does not mean we should solve this problem by treating African Americans/Blacks differently than any other race."

The experiences described above affected the way Charles perceived the need to be culturally responsive in his future classroom. While he acknowledged the bigoted history of the United States, he seemed to believe these problems were in the past and therefore should be moved on from. As such, his views regarding CRP were incomplete and problematic.

Expansive Learning of CRP

Charles was in the second stage of Engeström and Sannino's (2010) cycle: analysis. He seemed to question the need for CRP in general, but did not begin to "model new solutions" in relation to stage three. His definition of CRP was also limited to the second criterion: cultural competence.

Charles reported his teacher education faculty talked "too much" about concepts such as CRP. He explained:

> It [culturally responsive pedagogy] was just harped on too many times, it was like, OK, I'm really sick of this idea … . I get the importance of it, I think there are some really defining qualities to that, but at the end of the day it's not what you're doing so why are you putting so much emphasis on that?
>
> *(Interview 4, April 1, 2016)*

Charles's argument that "at the end of the day it's not what you're doing" was in relation to his observations that his teacher educators as well as the supervising teacher in his field placement were not modeling culturally relevant practices.

Another reason for Charles's disenchantment with CRP was oversaturation. I asked Charles if there were multiple courses during which he discussed strategies such as CRP to inform his teaching practice. He explained it was discussed "in every single one [course]." He interpreted these discussions, however, as "add-ons" to the central curriculum. He explained there were, "certain classes [at the school of education] you can take on [CRP], and some people do, but, I feel like it was like, 'oh and remember to do this,' in addition to like the other like 100 things you have to do" (Interview 4, April 1, 2016).

The main critique Charles had about his experience with CRP was that many of the conversations he had within his TEP and student teaching experience about "difficult topics" such as race were "surface level." He described wanting to have more conversations about complex issues, however, he explained,

> I'd like to do it right … . I don't like the little cultural fairs, and all the bullshit basically, and like let's make things on the wall and post it and we're culturally responsive, we feel good about ourselves.
>
> *(Interview 4, April 1, 2016)*

He continued to say he did not think these sorts of activities benefited students and believed many of the conversations were merely about making "people" feel better about themselves, rather than truly becoming empathetic to the experiences of people from different racial groups.

Victoria Welby

Background

Victoria grew up in the suburbs of a large metropolitan center in the south. She described the area as being a "pretty average suburban neighborhood" without much racial diversity (Interview 1, October 27, 2015). Until middle school, Victoria was homeschooled by her parents. She described the experience as "relatively expensive, but worth it" (Interview 1, October 27, 2015). After this, she attended two Christian private schools until graduating high school.

She was a part of numerous Christian missionary trips throughout her youth. She explained the experiences were about

> … going down and meeting these people, and loving them and really learning from them because they had so much to teach us. So much more to teach us than we had to give them, about just like what it really means to live a Christian life and love G-d, when you have what would seem to us no reason, because you're just in constant, need, and pain lots of times.
> *(Interview 1, October 27, 2015)*

Based on her experiences working with impoverished families on her mission trips, Victoria felt she learned a lot about being happy while experiencing poverty.

In her reflexive journal, Victoria reflected on her previous work as a missionary in Guatemala as her younger sister was returning from the same experience. She wrote:

> I remember walking through the streets [of Guatemala] and having children run up to touch our skin and pet our hair. I think at the time I was flattered, but looking back the memory makes me anxious. They were in awe not because of curiosity, but because of a standard of beauty they'd been fed … . I think now, if put back in those same streets, I would feel sad and uncomfortable with all the attention.
> *(Journal Entry, February 28, 2016)*

Along with her experience as a missionary, Victoria also used her reflexive journal to discuss, in all but two entries, how "diverse" her home church was.

Multiple times, Victoria compared her experiences in her college town to that of her home town. She described becoming "gradually more aware" of how separated races (i.e., Black and White people) were in her college community. Juxtaposed against this experience, Victoria wrote about a service at her home church where songs were sung in "three different languages and passages read in 12 languages," she exclaimed:

> It is extremely encouraging to see [this] kind of diversity and varying cultural backgrounds join together. In a country [the US] still struggling to heal from decades of racism, it is beautiful to see not only successful but natural communities such as this one!
> *(Journal Entry, December 24, 2015)*

These experiences provided Victoria a different perspective from Charles related to CRP and diversity, however, did not produce the sort of expansive learning necessary to truly conceptualize CRP in a meaningful way that led to concrete manifestations.

Expansive Learning of CRP

Victoria was also in the "analysis" stage of Engeström and Sannino's (2010) cycle. She was open to questioning power and oppression in society, however, never expressed a desire to develop new models of practice in relation to expanding privileges to marginalized groups (i.e., entering the "modeling new solutions" phase). She did, however, describe taking a course outside her TEP that allowed her to think more about White privilege:

> This [question about what is White privilege] is actually super interesting, because I am taking a class on spirituality and religion, so we cover a lot of great topics … I think for a while there was this colorblind push but now we're like, 'oh no just kidding that was a terrible idea,' and now I think there's almost guilt on both sides now, it's a little bit overcompensated.
>
> *(Interview 3, February 1, 2016)*

Such a perception seemed to inform her perspective about diversity in her TEP and contributed to her lack of progress in relation to the expansive cycle of learning toward CRP.

Victoria explained her perception of "diversity pushes" within her TEP based on a "common read" program. A book was chosen annually by the faculty "Diversity Action Committee" to be incorporated in all classes. To augment class discussions, volunteer graduate students, faculty and staff led monthly book talks for anyone interested in exploring the common read topics in more depth. Victoria did not feel her professors created an environment where these topics were seen as important to discuss during or outside of class:

> [This school] has a lot of 'diversity pushes' … but I haven't attended any of the seminars or read any of the books, because, in a way it's put on my mind, like, yes diversity is extremely important, but the atmosphere [at this school] is already like go, go, go, so it's another thing to do, and it falls to the wayside because it's presented as extra.
>
> *(Interview 4, March 23, 2016)*

Similar to Charles, Victoria's comment that the school was already "go, go, go" and the idea that topics of diversity were "presented as extra" showed her perception that TEP faculty viewed topics of diversity as add-ons to the central curriculum and did not use CRP to inform their instruction.

Erin Markie

Background

The final participant, Erin Markie, explained that before kindergarten, her family already moved twice. From kindergarten to second grade, she lived in a large suburban town that she referred to as the most memorable part of her schooling. There, she attended a, "super-diverse elementary school" (Interview 1, September 22, 2015). After this, her family moved again. She recalled the move being a "really big shift" because the diversity she had become familiar with was not a part of her new town. In her previous school, she recalled learning about a lot of things from her classmates, such as reasons for the celebration of Hanukkah and Kwanza. She also explained a part of her experience within the diverse elementary school was being taught how to, "feel comfortable" in a classroom helping students learn how to read English (Interview 1, September 22, 2015). Her family moved a final time during her fifth-grade year to a small but affluent southern town.

In her reflexive journal, Erin described being excited when the topic of culturally responsive teaching came up in one of her courses. During the discussion, one of her peers asked if it would be wise to look up information about a foreign student to understand more about them. The teacher educator responded that it would "probably be a good idea" and Erin explained her uneasiness with this recommendation:

> [T]his [idea] has the potential to perpetuate stereotypes. If we do 'research' on our students, the source of information should be the students themselves. I think it's really important to know about our students ... but we should not be looking for general information on the internet.
>
> *(Journal Entry, February 20, 2016)*

She concluded by explaining her belief that when she explained this in class, her response was perceived as "unnecessary and confrontational" by her peers.

Expansive Learning of CRP

Erin seemed to have moved further along Engeström and Sannino's (2010) cycle than the previous participants. She described being willing to implement what she referred to as the, "theory of CRT (culturally responsive teaching)" in her future classroom (Interview 4, August 31, 2016). Therefore, I place her closer to the third and fourth levels of expansive learning (i.e., willing to go through the action of developing a model that uses CRP to generate supports for students and a willingness to experiment with CRP to understand its limitations related to her practice). Reasons for her arrival at this point, however, were complex.

When asked to describe how CRP was presented in her TEP, she explained:

> We had a conversation about culturally responsive teaching in the class that I just came out of. We spent a long time talking about like, basic [components], which is fine because most people hadn't encountered most of the theories we were talking about.
>
> *(Interview 4, August 31, 2016)*

Erin went on to explain that concepts such as systemic inequity and White privilege were important for a teacher to reflect on related to informing practice because

> … who you are as a person, your identity and your background, are automatically going to affect how you interact with others. And in addition to your students backgrounds and their life experiences, and especially as a privileged person trying to teach students who don't have the same life experiences.
>
> *(Interview 4, August 1, 2016)*

When asked how she came to believe that teachers should reflect on topics of systemic inequity and privilege, she described taking courses outside of her TEP. The most important aspect of these courses to Erin was not the content, but the lessons they taught her about how to "question things." She explained,

> [I]t wasn't like I learned great content in those classes … but I think the biggest thing I learned in those classes was how to question stuff. Because we would read one thing one week and then we'd constantly be encouraged to question each other [in our discussions].
>
> *(Interview 2, November 10, 2015)*

Such an interpretation directly aligned with Engeström and Sannino's (2010) model of expansive learning. Erin was motivated to begin questioning "stuff." This can be interpreted as the beginning development of the sort of critical consciousness Ladson-Billings (1995) explained was necessary when using CRP to inform teaching practice.

Based on the search for disconfirming evidence within the data presented earlier within this section, I generated the following assertion:

- *White preservice teachers in this study perceived their teacher educators did not position CRP as synonymous with effective teaching and rather saw the strategy as an "add-on." This impeded the expansive learning of participants who held a rudimentary grasp of CRP, resulting in frustration toward the concept and a re-centering of Whiteness through disbelief in the need to adopt such strategies to influence future teaching practice.*

Discussion

The majority of participants in this study found "diversity" to be important, however, did not believe incorporating CRP in their teaching praxis was necessary to develop supports for their future students. Moreover, common definitions used by the PSTs were based on knowing students' backgrounds and cultures to build "better relationships," rather than understanding CRP as a strategy to develop critical consciousness and challenge status quos. Matias's (2016) concept of White emotionality provides a possible explanation for why this occurred. White PSTs unwillingness to adopt CRP redirects emphasis from the importance of understanding strategies to support the needs of students of color (as encouraged by scholars of color) back on White PSTs perceptions of those needs.

For instance, in relation to Charles, his perception of the unnecessary role of using CRP to inform his future practice can be connected to White emotionality in that he seemed to believe he knew more about how to implement CRP to inform practice than his teacher educators and mentor teachers. This was exhibited in his explanation that he thought both groups were misusing CRP. As Matias (2016) explained, this confidence is connected to White emotionality in that it shows a sort of narcissism that many White individuals embody: they believe their experiences are "normal" and therefore portray an inability to understand a person from another race/ethnicity's perspective. Charles's confidence in his understanding of CRP, however, was misplaced in that his references to the topic were based on "building empathy" and understanding students' "cultures." Even though Charles "thought there were some defining qualities" to CRP, he was not willing to use it to inform his future practice.

In relation to Victoria, she seemed able to question "existing wisdom" within the first stage of expansive learning. Her journal entries reflected an ability to critique how she felt while in Guatemala when people were in "awe" of her skin color and hair. This also revealed, however, how White emotionality can lead to a sort of blindness about experiences with and saviorism toward impoverished populations. Victoria seemed to believed individuals with whom she worked in Guatemala should have been miserable based on their monetary impoverishment. These views show how a White savior mentality can engulf well-intentioned White preservice teachers. As Aronson (2017) explained, White saviorism manifests when, "[u]ltimately, people are rewarded from "saving" those less fortunate and are able to completely disregard the policies they have supported that have created/maintained systems of oppression" (p. 36). In our interactions with one another, Victoria seemed sincere in her desire to support all her future students, however, Matias's (2016) work shows how problematic these intentions can become if PSTs are not supported in understanding connections between structural oppression and Whiteness.

The final participant, Erin Markie, was the only PST who showed a willingness to possibly use CRP to inform her future teaching practice. It is important to note, however, that her positive views toward the usefulness of CRP did not come from her experience within the TEP. Rather, she explained teacher education faculty were not effective in designing coursework that allowed for the critical reflection necessary to use CRP to inform teaching practice. Therefore, she sought out courses within other departments that could live up to her standards. If students enter TEPs with a lack of experience in diverse settings similar to Charles, however, or believe they already understand the complexities of marginalization like Victoria, they may not seek out courses about topics related to power and racialized oppression as Erin did. Based on this, these students might remain in the "questioning" phase of Engeström and Sannino's (2010) cycle by discussing the importance of holding conversations about topics such as diversity and CRP, while simultaneously never becoming motivated to develop applicable strategies to inform either. Implications can be discerned from this chapter as they relate to future programmatic designs of TEPs in Canada and the United States.

Implications: New Directions in TEPs Toward Expansive Learning

To possibly find better results related to having PSTs make connections between power, oppression, race and the usefulness of CRP to inform teaching practice, the model of expansive learning could be used as a useful and practical curriculum and programmatic design tool. Table 4.1 shows how CRP could be addressed in TEPs through expansive learning based on analyses of racialized power dynamics in schools and society. This table could be applied to programmatic reform in that multiple courses could be developed with goals related to each stage of the expansive learning cycle to inform PSTs understanding of CRP.

Following the chart left to right—teacher educators could design activities within early-program courses that direct PSTs to question the reason for needing or not needing to utilize CRP in their classrooms. Teacher educators could then design subsequent courses or activities to bring PSTs into the analysis stage of expansive learning. For instance, specific policies could be analyzed through document analyses to provide context for students related to power, racialization, culture and oppression. Next, activities could be designed to push PSTs toward modeling by developing new definitions of academic success and including multiple perspectives within course curriculum to increase the power of marginalized groups through expanded representation.

In the final stages of the program or course, after PSTs have been guided through the previous stages of expansive learning and seem to hold a solid grasp of the concepts being addressed, the model developed in stage three could be disseminated to local teachers, students and/or administrators. Here, PSTs could move into the examining stage working alongside these stakeholders in P–12 schools to determine if the models meet the needs of their particular context.

TABLE 4.1 Possible Road Map for Expansive Learning of CRP

	Questioning	Analysis	Modeling	Examining	Implementing	Reflecting/Consolidating
Academic Success	PSTs question what the meaning of "academic success" is for specific students	PSTs research how academic success is defined through analysis of state/federal policies	PSTs create a model of interpretation of academic success and include expanded view of possible limited definitions	PSTs examine the model created to determine possible limitations	PSTs apply the model to the development of supports to allow students to reach full potential (i.e., academic success)	PSTs reflect on application of model to make necessary adjustments to supporting students
Cultural Competence	PSTs question how cultural and ethnic backgrounds of students might affect their perceptions of schooling	PSTs analyze how student cultural and ethnic identities are represented in school, state, federal policies	PSTs create a model of specific cultural and ethnic identities represented in policies and include expanded view	PSTs examine the model created to determine possible limitations	PSTs apply the model to the development of supports to include multiple perspectives within class curriculum	PSTs reflect on application of model to make necessary adjustments to including multiple perspectives
Critical Consciousness	PSTs question power representation within school, state, federal curriculum (i.e., whose voice is being heard?)	PSTs analyze how power is displayed through representation in school, state, federal curriculum	PSTs create model of ways power is disseminated through representation in curriculum and include expanded view	PSTs examine the model created to determine possible limitations	PSTs apply the model to the development of action-based strategies to question status quos (e.g., letter writing campaigns, non-violent protests)	PSTs reflect on application of model to make necessary adjustments in developing strategies to questions and change status quos

After such reflection, the stage of implementation could include iterations of the model informed by the groups above applied to the development of lesson or unit plans in relation to supporting student conceptual development of certain topics. Finally, as is expansive learning, this process would be iterative and continuous, not concluding but beginning again with the "reflecting/consolidating" stage followed by reapplication.

In conclusion, this study showed a possible outcome of White PSTs not understanding the realities of systemic oppression: having White PSTs adhere to paradoxical views that simultaneously appreciate diversity while perpetuating Whiteness. Without programmatic change, expansive learning may continue to be hampered across teacher education contexts as it relates to CRP, Whiteness and emotionality.

References

Aronson, B. A. (2017). The White savior industrial complex: A cultural studies analysis of a teacher educator, savior film, and future teachers. *Journal of Critical Thought and Praxis*, 6(3), 36–54.

Bennett, J. S. (2012). *White privilege: A history of the concept [Master's thesis]*. Georgia State University. https://scholarworks.gsu.edu/history_theses/54

Bennett, J. S. (2019). Heritage not hate?: Crossroads between racial ideologies and teaching. In G. Samuels & A. Samuels (Eds.) *Democracy at a crossroads: Examining the past and facing the future* (pp. 135–158). Charlotte, NC: Information Age Publishing

Cardoza, K. (2018, February 28). In Canada's public schools, immigrant students are thriving. *Education Week*. https://www.edweek.org/ew/articles/2018/02/28/in-canadas-public-schools-immigrant-students-are.html

Duncan-Andrade, J. M. R. (2011). The principal facts: New directions for teacher education. In A. F. Ball & C. A. Tyson (Eds.) *Studying diversity in teacher education* (pp. 309–326). Lanham, MD: Rowman & Littlefield.

Engeström, Y. (1999). Activity theory and individual and social transformation. In Y. Engeström, R. Miettinen & R.J. Punamäki (Eds.) *Perspectives on Activity Theory* (pp. 19–28). Cambridge: Cambridge University Press.

Engeström, Y., & Sannino, A. (2010). Studies of expansive learning: Foundations, findings and future challenges. *Educational Research Review*, 5(1), 1–24.

Erickson, F. (1985). *Qualitative methods in research on teaching* (Occasional Paper No. 81). National Institute of Education.

Hayes, C., Juárez, B. G., Witt, M.T., & Hartlep, N. D. (2013). Toward a lesser shade of White: 12 steps towards more authentic race awareness. In C. Haynes & N. D. Hartlep (Eds.), *Unhooking from Whiteness: The key to dismantling racism in the United States* (pp. 1–16). Boston, MA: Sense Publishers

Holden, M., & Kitchen, J. (2018). Where are we now? Changing admission rates for underrepresented groups in Ontario Teacher Education. *Canadian Journal of Educational Administration and Policy*, (185) 45–60.

Katz, J. (2001). Analytic induction, in N.J. Smelser and P.B. Baltes (Eds.), *International Encyclopedia of the Social & Behavioral Sciences* (pp. 480–484). Oxford: Elsevier.

Kerr, J., & Andreotti, V. (2019). Crossing borders in initial teacher education: Mapping dispositions to diversity and inequity. *Race Ethnicity and Education*, 22(5), 647–665.

Ladson-Billings, G. (1995). But that's just good teaching! The case for culturally relevant pedagogy. *Theory Into Practice*, 34(30), 159–165.

Matias, C. E. (2016). *Feeling White: Whiteness, emotionality, and education*. Boston, MA: Sense Publishers.

McGran, K. (2019, November 11). 'I don't regret a thing.' *Don Cherry not backing down after being fired by Sportsnet. Toronto Star*. https://www.thestar.com/news/canada/2019/11/11/don-cherry-fired-from-sportsnet-following-toxic-rant.html

Milner IV, H. R. (2010). What does teacher education have to do with teaching? Implications for diversity studies. *Journal of Teacher Education*, 61(1–2), 118–131.

Ponterotto, J. G., Burkard, A., Rieger, B. P., Grieger, I., D'Onofrio, A., Dubuisson, A., Heenehan, M., Millstein, B., Parisi, M., Rath, J. F., & Sax, G. (1995). Development and initial validation of the quick discrimination index (QDI). *Educational and Psychological Measurement*, 55(6), 1016–1031.

U.S. Department of Education. (2016). *The state of racial diversity in the educator workforce*. Washington, DC: U.S. Department of Education, Office of Planning, Evaluation and Policy Development, Policy and Program Studies Service.

Wells, A. S. (2015). *Policy briefs: Diverse housing, diverse schooling: How policy can stabilize racial demographic change in cities and suburbs*. Boulder, CO: National Education Policy Center.

5

CONTEXTS AND COMPLEXITY

Promoting Racial and Linguistic Justice Through Bilingual Dual Language Teacher Education

Manka Varghese, Teddi Beam-Conroy, Renee Shank, and Rachel Snyder

The purpose of this chapter is to show how bilingual dual-language (DL) teacher education acts as a layer of context that influences teachers as well as multilingual classroom pedagogies and policies in superdiverse settings in the United States. The layers of the national and state contexts that this chapter first delves into are ones that have been the focus of scholarly work in the past (Hornberger, 2006; Snyder & Varghese, 2019; Wiley & García, 2016). What this chapter differently reveals and demonstrates is the importance of teacher education programs (TEPs) and their influence on how teachers may take up particular stances and pedagogies in relationship to language. In particular, we examine the increased focus on racial and linguistic justice in a major TEP in the city of Seattle in the state of Washington which in recent years added the preparation of bilingual DL elementary teacher candidates (TCs). Engaging in racial and linguistic justice take into account both how race and language have been historically used as ways to oppress people of color and those who engage in using nondominant forms of language as well as promoting the ways of being, speaking, living, and succeeding of these groups when recognizing the historical and current injustices in all forms that they have been subjected to.

Seattle can aptly be described as a superdiverse city due to its racial, ethnic, and linguistic diversity versus some other locales in the United States which have one or two predominant racial, ethnic and/or linguistic groups. In their recent report of DL learners in the United States, Park, Zong, and Batalova (2018) explain that although 51% of DL learners in the country are primarily Spanish speakers, DL learners as a larger category have more racial, ethnic, and linguistic diversity within states and within school districts than such a percentage would suggest. However, controversy around whether superdiversity as a concept is useful or particularly novel can be illuminated by the particular layers of context we are describing in this chapter. Although superdiversity has been intentionally adopted due to what scholars (in particular, sociolinguistics) have observed to be the insufficiency of the term *diversity* and because of the simple categorizations of linguistic practices that actually are not captured in contemporary processes of globalization, the concept and its usage also have its critiques. A significant critique that has been raised is the dearth of attention in the superdiversity scholarship to racialized linguistic minorities and the larger justice projects to challenge racial and neoliberal hierarchies that have always existed within particular language policies and practices (Flores & Lewis, 2016). A similar and what we could describe as a parallel tension is evident in the way bilingual education, and especially DL education, has played out in the United States and not only in superdiverse settings. Bilingual and DL education has been seen by some as a way to correct historic injustices towards racialized linguistic minorities while for others its goals of language learning have been to serve all students and could be characterized as instrumentalist and neoliberal. This chapter illuminates these tensions and shows how teacher education, especially through bilingual DL education, can promote racial and linguistic justice.

In this chapter, we first provide background to the sociopolitical context of bilingual and DL education with a focus on racialized linguistic minorities in the United States and Washington state, in particular, western Washington. We then provide a description and perspectives of the elementary TEP that all authors are involved in, especially our work to enhance what has already been a focus on racial and linguistic justice by building a more intentional set of experiences and pathways for bilingual DL teachers. Since this program for bilingual DL teachers has been embedded within the mainstream program, its effects have also permeated throughout the whole program. Last, we describe the experiences of TCs who were in our program to illustrate some of the affordances and challenges provided to them and as articulated by them of a bilingual/DL TEP. These experiences highlight in particular the complex nature of linguistic and racial justice in superdiverse contexts and the significance of explicit attention to race, power, language, and identity in TEPs in promoting critical multilingual pedagogies.

National and State Sociopolitical Contexts

In terms of the national context, the first issue to bear in mind is that federal policy in the United States does not actively prescribe any particular form of language programming nor programming for linguistic minority youth including explicit support for the maintenance of minority languages (Wiley & García, 2016). Although scholars such as Hornberger (2006) suggest that this has created openings for language programming, it has also been argued that the lack of institutionalization of bilingual education at the federal level has actually implicitly and explicitly promoted cultural assimilation and mastery of English (Flores, 2016; Sung, 2017). This trend was demonstrated in the name change of the Department of Education's Office of Bilingual Education and Minority Language Affairs to the Office of English Language Acquisition at the start of the second Bush administration (Cahnmann & Varghese, 2006; García, 2009). Numerous efforts at the state level have also been made, on one hand, toward anti-bilingual education bills and restrictive linguistic policies in some states and, on the other, in favor of DL programs (Johnson & Johnson, 2015; Miller & Katsiyannis, 2014). In the state of Washington, the default language education policy is that of Transitional Bilingual Education (TBE) programs, or programs that utilize students' native languages in instruction for some part of their schooling (Johnson & Johnson, 2015). Since the law permits districts to use ESL "In those cases in which the use of two languages is not practicable" (Dual Language Grant Program, 2017, RCW 28A.180.030, sub 4(b)), most programs in the state are transitional bilingual programs in name only. Moreover, the law mandates that subject matter testing be conducted only in English.

Washington state is part of the consortium of states that have adopted the Seal of Biliteracy, which on graduation from high school, grants a specialized diploma to students fluent in two or more languages (DeLeon, 2016). Most recently, Washington has passed a law providing grants for new DL programs. Although these adoptions demonstrate an encouragement of multilingual policies, programming, and funding in the state compared with the restrictive laws enacted in Arizona and other states, their existence does not guarantee results that center the needs and priorities of racialized linguistic minorities (Johnson, 2012). It is important to take into account that in terms of DL education in the country and especially in Washington state, although it is not exclusive, a neoliberal ideology that DL is beneficial to all students (including White, middle-class students) supersedes one that equates DL programs with advancing the rights of racialized linguistic minority communities. The neoliberal framing of bilingual education and DL programs has been significantly critiqued by various scholars (Flores, 2016; Valdés, 1997; Varghese & Park, 2010). Flores (2016), in particular, has argued that the racial justice project inherent in bilingual education in the United States has been eliminated by a framing of bilingual education that benefits and serves hegemonic Whiteness. Flores makes an explicit link between Whiteness and a language ideology in which bilingual education—especially when articulated as DL education—is promoted as beneficial to all students. Overall, the dominant language ideology promoted at the state level even in states promoting multiple languages seems very much aligned with interest convergence (an understanding that victories for racialized minorities only occur when it is in the interests of the White-dominant majority) and neoliberal agendas (Flores & García, 2017; Grinberg & Saavedra, 2000). Snyder (2019) shows this to be very much the case in her careful discursive analysis of language policies in Washington state.

National and state ideologies and policies and their relationship to racial hierarchies naturally influence TEPs, TCs, and practicum placement experiences. Since language education policy such as bilingual education becomes a way to promote, neutralize or actively suppress languages and their affiliated population (Fishman 1980; Ruiz, 1984), it has a direct effect on the daily experiences and structural affordances for racialized linguistic minority students and their families. However, teachers, administrators, and schools have always been identified as the most significant agents of language policy (Johnson & Johnson, 2015); in this vein, it is important to highlight the supportive or subtractive role of TEPs in determining what is taught, what preservice teachers are learning, and how TCs' understandings and interpretations of language policy and pedagogy is filtered through their experiences. Particularly for preservice bilingual teachers, but also for mainstream teachers, the linguistic and what we could call the raciolinguistic (Daniels & Varghese, 2020)—how understandings of race and language are intertwined—environments of the TEP can be significant in potentially forming counterhegemonic racial and linguistic ideologies and related practices. This was especially relevant in this elementary TEP that is the focus of this chapter because of its potential ability to challenge the mainly neoliberal ideology underpinning language education more generally and bilingual DL education in the state of Washington.

Elementary Teacher Education Program

Although this elementary TEP has maintained a strong commitment to social justice and to serving under-resourced schools, similarly to most TEPs in the United States, it has been subject to the "overwhelming presence of whiteness" (Sleeter, 2001), denoting the White privilege and dominant culture of the program or profession (Sleeter, 2001; Villegas & Davis, 2008). As in many TEPs, this program's coursework and content have aimed to prepare White teacher candidates for work with "diverse learners," even when more than 50% of teacher candidates were students of color. More broadly, critiques leveled at TEPs have been in terms of their failure to fully acknowledge racial injustice and recognize how Whiteness and standardized English work in concert to create White-dominant norms and a dominant culture, marginalizing faculty and TCs of color (Daniels & Varghese, 2020; Haddix, 2016; Varghese et al., 2019). Bilingual TEPs, on the other hand, have been overall more likely to focus on racial and linguistic justice but have been offered as separate programs from mainstream TEPs. Making multilingualism and bilingual teaching more intentional and embedding them within mainstream teacher preparation can be a way to address both racial and linguistic justice. The attention to racial and linguistic justice in this TEP was expanded by the support of a federally funded grant, Project BECA (Bilingual Educator CApacity) that included partial scholarships and a support mechanism for TCs who wanted to become bilingual/DL teachers. These teachers not only go through our mainstream TEP but are also provided DL practicum placements and specialized support. This included mainly those bilingual in Spanish but also Vietnamese and Mandarin. Prior to BECA, the TEP trained as many as nine TCs to work in bilingual classrooms each year. Through the grant, with a full-time staff member dedicated to recruitment and support for bilingual TCs as well as partial scholarships for those starting in 2018, the number of preservice bilingual teachers soon doubled, creating a critical mass of TCs that necessitated an infrastructure within the program to support bilingual teacher candidate learning.

Over the past three years of BECA in particular, we have all been collaboratively involved in interrogating and challenging Whiteness in concert with developing bilingual and DL teachers in our mainstream elementary TEP and centering multilingualism in different ways. Our efforts to center multilingualism stem also from a recognition and understanding that teacher identity—especially racial and linguistic identity—plays an important role in how an individual teaches (Achinstein & Ogawa, 2011; Monzó & Rueda, 2003; Riojas Clark et al., 2011; Varghese et al., 2005; Varghese et al. 2016). Unfortunately, Whitestream (Urrieta, 2007), monolingual English K–16 education has denied many TCs of color the chance to learn about their languages and cultures during their own schooling. Therefore, creating opportunities for TCs to recognize these kinds of experiences have made our program a primary location for self-discovery and critique of educational systems that perpetuate oppression.

Our efforts to center multilingualism in the overall program also utilize and legitimize the funds of knowledge (Moll et al., 1992) multilingual learners bring to the TEP. This focus helps make teacher candidate learning transformative (Monzó & Rueda, 2003). Through active recruitment of native and heritage speakers of DL target and other languages, we are able to train teachers that share the same background as their students. By accessing their own funds of knowledge, TCs are able to create curriculum and provide instruction that matches the contexts of students' lives. This recruitment has changed the demographic composition of the program in several ways. Table 5.1 shows the changing racial demographic of the whole elementary TEP cohort over the past several years, with the percentages denoting TCs of color. Additionally, at least 50% of the past three cohorts report speaking languages in addition to English fluently, many of these not represented in local DL programs.

In the following section, we describe the program's efforts and the perspectives of DL TCs who were in the elementary TEP before BECA and of TCs after we received the grant and instituted BECA, a program specifically for bilingual DL TCs within the mainstream program. We show that we were able to integrate multilingualism and focus more centrally on racial and linguistic justice since instituting BECA although a number of challenges remain.

TABLE 5.1 Percentage of Teacher Candidates of Color in Elementary TEP, 2012–2019

2012	2013	2014	2015	2016	2017	2018	2019
36%	44%	40%	47%	38%	54%	50%	65%

Bilingual/DL Teacher Preparation and Candidate Perspectives in Elementary TEP

Pre-BECA

Prior to the beginning of the BECA grant, TCs experienced significant marginalization within the program on a number of levels, the most salient being the lack of specific course work related to DL teaching. At the time, the TEP did not yet offer a bilingual/DL endorsement, and DL TCs took the mainstream methods course sequence with little differentiation. Linguistic preparation was relegated to a single course in the Differentiated Instruction sequence titled Culturally and Linguistically Responsive Teaching. Fernando, a student TC in the program at that time, stated, "I think personally, I didn't feel prepared from the university … there were a few classes that were helpful to us, but they were not enough … if I had known how little support we would receive I might have chosen a different program."

Elena and Sebastián were asked to apply and relate literacy course work to their placement experience, yet they worked in departmentalized Spanish math and science classrooms and did not teach literacy. Elena stated, "Literacy was really hard for me, we were asked to relate the material to our placement, and it really didn't relate at all." This indicates that the program's course work treated DL teaching as a simple translation of monolingual English methods or a set of skills to be learned in apprenticeship rather than a complex set of teaching methods necessitating additional preparation (Martínez & Baker, 2009).

The lack of DL specific preparation was reinforced through evaluations and feedback provided to TCs. The DL TCs were evaluated through course work, observation of their teaching, and a formal standardized assessment, again with no differentiation. Jennifer stated that "no professor gave me any feedback on anything I did that related to DL or EL teaching." These TCs did receive feedback related to DL teaching from their instructional coaches and their mentor teachers, but these sets of feedback were related to specific teaching moments rather than general teaching methods. One of the coaches stated, "Despite their fluency in Spanish, the TCs might not have the vocabulary or know about how to teach Spanish Literacy … they need more than just the practicum." Also, mentor teachers frequently gave feedback related to behavior management, structures, and routines but less frequently gave DL-specific feedback. Although TCs did make efforts to develop needed content-specific vocabulary in Spanish, the lack of space for such development in the TEP studied made it necessary for TCs to use their own personal time to do this.

Compounding this treatment of their teaching work, Elena, Fernando, and Sebastián experienced racial microaggressions in class. As Latinx students, Elena, Fernando, and Sebastián related DL teaching to their racialized identities and experienced the marginalization of language in the program as a form of discrimination related to their racial identity. Elena described a class in which the topic of DL was being discussed. Many of the White TCs sitting with her dismissed the topic stating that they felt it was not relevant. She said, "I don't know where you want to teach, but that you said that? That hurt me, and made me feel super uncomfortable. And there were a couple times where things like that happened." Fernando and Sebastián similarly suggested that there were a set of White TCs that purposefully avoided topics of race and language in classwork and that they both began to tire of speaking up in these conversations.

Another layer underlying the marginalization experienced by racialized DL TCs were prevailing language ideologies, both of the program and of society more generally, of linguistic purity and an ideal of linguistic fluency. All the TCs questioned their linguistic abilities, either in relation to English, Spanish, or both. Because of their own educational histories, both Sebastián and Elena felt that they may have been lacking certain linguistic abilities in Spanish, while Fernando intuited that his "English accent" might be judged by White parents. Elena described her first meeting with her mentor teacher, who was originally from Spain:

> When we went to check out the school, she (the mentor teacher) asked us to speak Spanish to her immediately because she said "if your Spanish isn't good enough you shouldn't be doing this." And we were both really afraid about that, because we didn't grow up speaking in school. I knew that she was going to have a different Spanish from me because she's from Spain! And I worried, is that going to invalidate my Spanish language?

Jennifer similarly felt that, although Spanish was her first language, she should not teach DL classes higher than third grade because of the language loss she had experienced in elementary school.

The mainly monoglossic orientation of the TEP studied reinforced this view of language where languages should be kept apart and pure. Fernando stated that most of the classes were oriented towards "English speakers, or for students who were learning English, not for students who were learning Spanish or who are Spanish-speakers, continuing to build their language." A number of the TCs who struggled in the program during the year studied were TCs of color with multilingual linguistic repertoires. The environment and course content of the TEP did not provide space for TCs to grapple with their own language ideologies or language ideologies associated with bilingual education in the United States, including the intersections of race and power and immigrant rights with these ideologies. As Sebastián stated, "I just wish there could … have been one class that we had, that would just focus on teaching in Spanish and developing the language."

At the tail end of these TCs' experiences (after Elena, Fernando, Sebastián, and Jennifer finished) in the program and as BECA was starting, hiring and intentional scheduling/pairing meant that DL TCs started to be placed in literacy methods courses with faculty with teaching experience in DL and multilingual settings as well as pedagogical orientations that supported their teaching in these programs. The program expanded its partnerships with DL schools from three to seven and to include Mandarin. Program evaluation materials shifted to require *all* TCs to explicitly plan for their multilingual students in their instruction while DL teachers had additional requirements to consider bridging opportunities between the languages of instruction and other languages that might be spoken among their students.

BECA has allowed the university and our program to partially fund the education of multiple multilingual students (15 out of 60 in the 2018/2019 program year), many of whom are teachers of color. The first cohort of BECA fellows graduated in August 2019. The design of the BECA program ensures that the bilingual TCs are still part of the Elementary TEP cohort while also receiving additional support throughout the program, as well as course work following the TEP in the form of a bilingual endorsement. BECA TCs spend the academic year student teaching in Vietnamese, Spanish, or Mandarin DL classrooms.

Post- BECA

The design of the BECA program has started to transform the experience of bilingual TCs within the program and the overall TEP. For example, the bilingual TCs now engage in explicit practice in multiple languages and discussion of bilingual teaching throughout the program. Also, pushed by the needs of the BECA TCs, multiple instructors in the TEP have embraced multilingual pedagogies for all students, allowing course work to be completed heteroglossically. In many cases, the experience and practice of using multiple languages flexibly in class assignments allowed TCs to develop a commitment to such work in their own classrooms. For example, in a dialogue journal written in the bilingual methods class, Jimena articulated that "Por consiguiente, translanguaging pedagogy allow us as teachers respect the full repertoire in which a student has been immersed in life, and I feel the duty to honor that."

Understanding that our bilingual TCs need to develop more flexibility, and an ability to teach in multiple languages and modes than those teaching in monolingual settings, the second cohort of TCs has been participating in a practicum seminar that meets weekly with the goal of creating connections between TCs' teaching experiences and methods courses along with conversations about the varying DL program models, language policy, and critical conversations regarding dialectical hierarchies. These conversations have been complemented by guided methodological practice in the target language including focused metalinguistic connections between English and the target language. BECA fellows also have the opportunity to practice numeracy lessons with peers and teach lessons in the two languages to third- and fifth-grade DL students.

Attention to identity, race, and language throughout the TEP (including in course work and racial caucusing), which had started pre-BECA, as well as their bilingual endorsement program after TEP has supported BECA TCs to develop a critical consciousness regarding their role as language teachers. Jimena wrote in her bilingual endorsement biliteracy methods class the following reflection on the meaning of critical consciousness:

> Tener y desarrollar una conciencia crítica y problematizar la política opresiva detrás del uso establecido de los idiomas ayudando al individuo a desarrollar más libremente su identidad poniéndolo en una situación de ventaja dónde se pone en duda la disparidad en el uso del poder con respecto al lenguaje haciendo reflexionar a todas las partes acerca de su posicionalidad y privilegios.
>
> (Having and developing a critical conscience and problematizing the oppressive policy behind the established use of languages helping the individual to develop his identity more freely by putting him in a situation of advantage where the disparity in the use of power with respect to language is questioned by making all parties reflect on their positionality and privileges.)

This reflection illustrates the connection Jimena made in her course work between liberation and linguistic justice.

Course work, especially in literacy, foundations classes, and their integrated seminar assigned over the year also encouraged TCs to explore their identities and histories and make connections between their educational histories, linguistic, and racial identities and persistent inequities in U.S. schools. These connections enable TCs to critically approach language use in their future classrooms and navigate racial inequities in current DL programs. In her final presentation in her bilingual endorsement biliteracy methods class, Cindy discussed the ways in which her identities shaped her teaching choices, particularly the way in which she planned to use language in her future classroom. She immigrated from Vietnam to the United States as a teenager and said, "[I]t was a really lonely experience," because she felt unable to connect with others through language. Now, as a mother of a multiracial child, she wants her daughter to learn Vietnamese and English and to use both. She explained, "I know that feeling of showing up at school and not knowing what is happening, and I don't want her to feel that way." Cindy extended this to her philosophy of language use in the classroom, arguing that her future classroom would be open to translanguaging and responsive teaching through linguistic flexibility. Currently, Cindy practices this by offering translations, engaging students in language brokering, and differentiating material for students with varying language backgrounds in her Vietnamese class.

These positive developments are also accompanied by related tensions and challenges. Although we have been training TCs for work in bilingual contexts, the common language for all University classes remains English. While understandable, this does not allow the TCs to complete any courses exclusively in the target language as in other bilingual TEPs. With a critical mass of Spanish-speaking TCs, the TCs are encouraged to and often use Spanish to discuss readings and course content. However, because of the structure and demands of the program, the Mandarin and Vietnamese speakers have not always been paired together, leaving them without a partner with whom they can practice and an environment where whole-group discussions are in English rather than a target language.

Some existing course work and related required assessments do not speak to the unique experiences of bilingual teachers of color and, in some cases, create barriers to their success in the TEP. Additionally, some recently graduated BECA TCs have expressed that they have still felt underprepared by the program (particularly for teaching literacy in bilingual settings). The question of what course work to include within the constraints of a yearlong program is a challenging one. For example, Anita (a Mexicana teacher) explains in a reflection on the program in her second month of teaching full-time:

> It's just like now having to translate, to work in two languages, to figure all this out, and having taken methods courses in English … it just feels hard. It did not feel like the courses (in the program) were for us.

Last, although the TEP as a whole and BECA has attempted to address racism and racial injustice there has been a sense among the TCs of color, especially in the first cohort, of the differential commitments between them and their White BECA counterparts. The three TCs who did not choose to work in DL classrooms after the program was over were White. In an interview with Anita after the program, she opened up in the following way:

> I think it's a general feeling but I'll speak for myself … there is definitely an upset about people who joined BECA and who then decided to not take a DL job. And further decided to not do any of the work afterwards. Cause then it straight up feels racist. It really does, because it comes down to being White, taking, in this case money and opportunity, and then not giving anything back. And I know that there is the idea that you can be a DL teacher without actually being a DL teacher. That's true. But I would push back and say that while that's true, you don't actually have to put in the actual physical work and hours that we do. And it just feels like it's frustrating that even in spaces that are supposed to be for people like me, who look like me and people who want to become allies then at the end they decide that being an ally is too much work.

Anita's words illustrate that even in the context of a program that is committed to serving multilingual students of color, power, privilege, and Whiteness continue to impact students' daily experiences. Thus, conversations regarding racial and linguistic (in)justice in program contexts do not necessarily translate to material manifestations of such justice. Also, for privileged White teacher candidates who have not been materially impacted by racism and linguicism over the course of their lives, more identity work remains to be done to translate understanding to action.

At the same time, the quote indicates Anita's critical consciousness, or ability to see power, and her commitment to use her voice to draw attention to this injustice. Anita's willingness to share this critique with program staff indicates that ongoing conversations on racial and linguistic justice have created a necessary platform for teachers of color to share their experiences and connect their ongoing marginalization to systemic injustice. As this scenario indicates, programs that are committed to increasing attention to racial and linguistic (in)justice must also be open to critical feedback from students who experience such injustices reproduced in the programmatic environment. This example shows the significance of explicit attention to power, race, language, and identity in the context of TEPs that serve multilingual TCs of color, especially those preparing to teach in dual language schools.

Discussion and Conclusion

This chapter argues that focusing on bilingual DL education in terms of policies, ideologies, and pedagogies at the national and state levels and within TEPs can clarify and enhance a community and a program's commitment toward racial and linguistic justice. This is also the case in superdiverse contexts and when taking into account linguistic practices and communities that are rooted in what may be characterized as superdiversity. The particular national and state contexts presented in this chapter as well as the shifts within the elementary TEP showcased here are a useful illustration of this.

Although the tension between bilingual education in terms of neoliberal goals and its historical project for racial and linguistic justice is evident throughout the country, various states seem to be more oriented towards one or the other of these stances. Washington state's neoliberal and race erasure emphases in bilingual education have been documented (Snyder, 2019) while its openings in and support of bilingualism and multilingualism are also evident. Both of these stances and their coexistence and entanglements have made it possible for an increase in DL schools and investments in such programs in the area since they have had the support of privileged communities.

In its commitment to preparing teachers for DL teaching and programs, the TEP we have all been involved in has helped increase recruitment and support of multilingual teachers of color as well as encouraging and integrating multilingualism in all class content and assignments, especially through the BECA program. The stance that the TEP takes toward bilingual education is aligned, or could even be described as intersecting in terms of its general mission, with that of centering racial and linguistic justice. This chapter emphasizes how critical TEPs are as spaces for the mediation of language policy/multilingual pedagogies while it is important to acknowledge that this work is only part of what is needed to decenter Whiteness. In the context of TEPs and schools in superdiverse contexts, it is also important that we not only invite and value multilingualism but that we have explicit political conversations regarding power/identity and the role of language in schools. Bilingual DL education provides a sociopolitical and pedagogical foundation for this. As such, TEPs should offer the opportunity for TCs to delve into course work and experiences that focus on developing critical consciousness; have them reflect on their own racial, linguistic, and intersectional identities; and understand the important political role they can play in their communities in being change agents. The program featured in this chapter, especially with its bilingual DL program being embedded in its regular program and its attention on racial and linguistic justice, provides an initial step forward in helping to make this possible.

References

Achinstein, B., & Ogawa, Rodney T. (2011). *Change(d) agents: New teachers of color in urban schools*. New York, NY: Teachers College Press.

Cahnmann, M., & Varghese, M. (2006). Critical advocacy and bilingual education in the United States. *Linguistics and Education*, 16(1), 59–73.

Daniels, J., & Varghese, M. (2020). Troubling Practice: Exploring the relationship between Whiteness and practice-based teacher education in considering a raciolinguicized teacher subjectivity. *Educational Researcher* 49(1), 56–63.

DeLeon, T. M. (2016). *The new ecology of biliteracy in California: An exploratory study of the early implementation of the state seal of biliteracy*. Los Angeles, CA: Loyola Marymount University.

Fisher D., & Frey N. (2014). *Better learning through structured teaching: A framework for gradual release of responsibility*. Alexandria, VA: ASCD.

Fishman, J. A. (1980). Bilingual education, language planning and English. *English World-Wide*, 1(1), 11–24.

Flores, N. (2016). Why we need to re-think race and ethnicity in educational research. *Educational Policy*, 30(1), 13–38. doi:10.3102/0013189X032005003.

Flores, N., & García, O. (2017). A critical review of bilingual education in the United States: From basements and pride to boutiques and profit. *Annual Review of Applied Linguistics*, 37, 14–29. doi:10.1017/S0267190517000162

Flores, N., & Lewis, M. (2016). From truncated to sociopolitical emergence: A critique of super-diversity in sociolinguistics. *International Journal of the Sociology of Language*, 2016(241), 97–124. doi:10.1515/ijsl-2016-0024

García, O. (2009). *Bilingual education in the 21st century: A global perspective*. West Sussex, England: Wiley.

Grinberg, J., & Saavedra, E. R. (2000). The constitution of bilingual/ESL education as a disciplinary practice: Genealogical explorations. *American Educational Research Journal*, 70(4), 419–441.

Haddix, M. M. (2016). *Cultivating racial and linguistic diversity in literacy teacher education: Teachers like me*. New York, NY: Routledge and NCTE.

Hornberger, N. H. (2006). Nichols to NCLB: Local and global perspectives on U.S. language education policy. In O. Garcia, T. Skutnabb-Kangas, & M. Torres Guzman (Eds.), *Imagining multilingual schools: Languages in education* (pp. 223–237). Clevedon, England: Multilingual Matters.

Johnson, E. J. (2012). Arbitrating repression: Language policy and education in Arizona. *Language and Education*, 26(1), 53–76. doi:10.1080/09500782.2011.615936

Johnson, E. J., & Johnson, D. C. (2015). Language policy and bilingual education in Arizona and Washington state. *International Journal of Bilingual Education and Bilingualism*, 18(1), 92–112. doi:10.1080/13670050.2014.882288.

Kazemi, E., Ghousseini, H., Cunard, A., & Turrou, A. C. (2016). Getting inside rehearsals: Insights from teacher educators to support work on complex practice. *Journal of Teacher Education*, 67(1), 18–31. doi:10.1177/0022487115615191

Martínez, R., & Baker, S. (2009). Preparing teachers of bilingual students. *Teachers College Record*, 109(2), 319–350. Retrieved from http://files.pressible.org/10/files/2010/10/Martinez-and-Baker.pdf

Miller, R. D., & Katsiyannis, A. (2014). Students with limited English proficiency. *Intervention in School and Clinic*, 50(2), 121–124. doi:10.1177/1053451213496161

Moll, L. C., Amanti, C., Neff, D., & Gonzalez, N. (1992). Funds of knowledge for teaching: Using a qualitative approach to connect homes and classrooms. *Theory Into Practice*, 31(2), 132–141.

Monzó, L. D., & Rueda, R. (2003). Shaping education through diverse funds of knowledge: A look at one Latina paraeducator's lived experiences, beliefs, and teaching practice. *Anthropology & Education Quarterly*, 34(1), 72–95.

Park, M., Zong, J., & Batalova, J. (2018). *Growing superdiversity among young U.S. dual language learners and its implications*. Washington, DC: Migration Policy Institute.

Ricento, T. K., & Hornberger, N. H. (1996). Unpeeling the onion: Language planning and policy and the ELT professional. *TESOL Quarterly*, 104(3), 401–427.

Riojas Clark, E., Guardia Jackson, L., & Prieto, L. (2011) Identity: A central facet of culturally efficacious bilingual education teachers. In M. Bustos Flores, R. Hernández Sheets, & E. Riojas Clark (Eds.), *Teacher preparation for bilingual student populations: Educar para transformar* (pp. 27–39). New York, NY: Routledge.

Ruiz, R. (1984). Orientations in language planning. *NABE Journal*, 8(3), 15–34.

Sleeter, C. E. (2001). Preparing teachers for culturally diverse schools: Research and the overwhelming presence of Whiteness. *Journal of Teacher Education*, 52(2), 9–106.

Snyder, R. (2019). The right to define: Analyzing Whiteness as a form of property in Washington state bilingual education law. *Language Policy*. doi:10.1007/s10993-019-09509-0

Snyder, R., & Varghese, M. (2019). Language Diversity and Schooling. In J. A. Banks & C. M. Banks, Eds. *Multicultural Education: Issues and Perspectives*, pp. 174–197.

Sung, K. (2017). "Accentuate the positive; eliminate the negative": Hegemonic interest convergence, racialization of Latino poverty, and the 1968 Bilingual Education Act. *Peabody Journal of Education*, 92(3), 302–321. doi:10.1080/0161956X.2017.1324657

Transitional Bilingual Instruction Act (TBIA), 28A.180 RCW, c 548 § 704, c 72 § 301, 2nd sp.s c 9 § 3 (2009, 2013, 2016, 2017).

Urrieta, L. (2007). Identity production in figured worlds: How some Mexican Americans become Chicana/o activist educators. *The Urban Review*, 39(2), 117–144.

Valdés, G. (1997). Dual language immersion programs: A cautionary note concerning the education of language minority students. *Harvard Educational Review*, 67, 391–429.

Varghese, M., Daniels, J., & Park, C. (2019). Structuring disruption: Race-based caucuses in teacher education programs: : Possibilities and challenges of race-based caucuses. *Teachers College Record*, 121(6), 1–34.

Varghese, M., Morgan, B., Johnston, B., & Johnson, K. (2005). Theorizing language teacher identity: Three perspectives and beyond. *Journal of Language, Identity, and Education*, 4(1), 21–44.

Varghese, M., Motha, S, Park, G., Reeves, J., & Trent, J. (2016). In this issue. *TESOL Quarterly* 50(3), 545–571. doi:10.1002/tesq.333

Varghese, M. M., & Park, C. (2010). Going global: Can dual-language programs save bilingual education? *Journal of Latinos and Education*, 9(1), 72–80. doi:10.1080/15348430903253092

Villegas, A. M., & Davis, D. (2008). Preparing teachers of color to confront racial/ethnic disparities in educational outcomes. In M. Cochran-Smith, S. Feiman-Nemser, & J. McIntyre (Eds.), *Handbook of research in teacher education: Enduring issues in changing contexts* (pp. 583–605). Mahwah, NJ: Earlbaum.

Washington State Transitional Bilingual Instruction Act (2009, 2013, 2016, 2017) Retrieved October 29, 2020: https://apps.leg.wa.gov/rcw/default.aspx?cite=28A.180&full=true

Wiley, T. G., & García, O. (2016). Language policy and planning in language education: Legacies, consequences, and possibilities. *Modern Language Journal*, 100, 48–63. doi:10.1111/modl.12303

SECTION II

Research on Teacher Education in a Time of Superdiversity

6

TEACHER EDUCATION FOR DIVERSITY THROUGH AN AUTOETHNOGRAPHIC LENS

Antoinette Gagné

The increasing diversity of our student population around the world has led to multiple calls to action to improve teacher education in recent years (e.g., Senyshyn, 2018; UNESCO, 2016). The fact that most teacher candidates have been educated by elementary and secondary school teachers who may not have had a diversity mindset or been responsive to their diverse students makes the need to prepare teachers for today's and tomorrow's schools urgent. We need to support new teachers to thrive on shifting landscapes of policitized transnationalism and immigration in superdiverse classrooms and schools. In this chapter, I provide some insight into how one graduate teacher education program in Ontario has evolved to prepare teachers for this new world.

As the province of Ontario has undergone dramatic demographic shifts in the last three decades, it reflects the diversification in the population in many countries. The 2016 census reveals that 29.3 percent of Ontario's approximately 14 million people identify as visible minorities. In addition, in 2016, 29.1 percent of Ontarians were born outside of Canada and 27.9 percent have a mother tongue other than French or English (Statistics Canada, 2016). Other important milestones include the release of *Ontario's Education Equity Plan* in 2017 and Ontario Institute for Studies in Education's (OISE's) updated *Guiding Principles on Equity and Diversity* in 2018. In 2017, the Ontario College of Teachers also published its initial teacher education *Accreditation Resource Guide* with an explanation of its intention which matches many of the calls to action for teacher education:

> The guide is predicated on the principle that students of programs of professional education and teachers need a strong body of foundational professional knowledge that is evidence-based and practice-informed in order

to begin to develop professional judgment and skills in pedagogical decision-making. The guide presumes that all teachers view themselves as learners and understand that the student/learner must be the centre of their work in teaching and learning. The concept that teachers are life-long learners who are beginning the continuum of professional learning underpins the guide. The guide expects that all teachers hold a growth mindset and work from an asset-based approach for their students and themselves.

(p. 5)

Finally, there are about 2 million students in elementary and secondary schools in Ontario, with a quarter either currently or formerly identified as English learners (ELs). In Toronto, the number of ELs is much higher as 46.1 percent of the population is from an immigrant background (People for Education, 2015).

In the next section, I begin by explaining autoethnographic methodology and go on to narrate parts of my 30-year journey as a teacher educator at the University of Toronto. I then propose two conceptual lenses that help to make sense of my deconstruction of one graduate teacher education program that has evolved over several years to prepare teachers for diversity and provide intercultural learning opportunities. In particular, I examine the sociopolitical context and the collaborative efforts of faculty, staff, school and community partners through the overlapping lenses of the *Teaching for Equity* framework (Grudnoff et al., 2017) and Dimitrov and Haque's model for *Intercultural Teaching Competence* (2016), as well as the lens of my own experiences as a teacher educator in this program. Finally, I discuss the complexity involved in preparing teachers for diversity and providing intercultural learning opportunities for future teachers and readers are encouraged to consider how to prepare teachers with a diversity mindset and responsiveness in their unique contexts.

Analytic Autoethnography

Analytic autoethnography is one of several strands which are part of the broader autoethnographic research tradition. Autoethnography is a type of qualitative research methodology where the researcher/author writes reflexively, explores personal/professional experiences and connects these to sociopolitical issues to make sense of them.

I have adopted an analytical autoethnographic approach to critically examine the genesis and evolution of a graduate teacher education for equity and diversity. Anderson (2006) and Marechal (2010) explain that in analytic autoethnography, the researcher is a "full" member of the group in a particular setting. In addition, the autoethnographer is "visible" to the reader as a fully embedded member in the setting. Finally, a commitment to the development of theoretical understandings of broader social phenomena also characterizes analytic autoethnographers. Marechal (2010) highlights that analytic autoethnography includes an analytic agenda: "Developing theoretical understanding of broader social phenomena, grounded in self-experience, analytic autoethnography remains framed by empirical data and aims to generalize its insights to a wider field of social relations than the data alone contain" (p. 4).

As an autoethnographer, I am aware of my dual roles as a social actor in my own context and a researcher who hopes to evoke strong responses in the reader. I attempt to frame my data in such a way as to allow for a deeper understanding of teacher education for diversity and equity as it is operationalized in one graduate teacher education program.

My Journey in Teacher Education in Ontario

As a teacher educator at the University of Toronto since 1989, I have had multiple opportunities to be involved in rethinking how we prepare teachers to work with diverse learners. During these more than 30 years, I have seen the impact of ever-changing local, provincial and federal policies, as well as the power of the demographic shift in the Greater Toronto Area, where in 1991, 13 percent of the population identified as visible minorities while in 2016 nearly 30 percent did. In the 1990s, I felt marginalized because of my interest in addressing issues of diversity in teacher education. Starting in the early 2000s, my interest in linguistic and cultural diversity among teachers and in schools was beginning to garner more support among colleagues and policy makers alike. In the last 10 years, it has become clear to many policy makers and teacher educators that the preparation of teachers for diversity has to be taken up as a mainstream pursuit and can no longer be ignored or placed on the margins of teacher education. To illustrate these changes over time, I describe some of the initiatives I instigated or played a central role in Figure 6.1.

My involvement in various teacher education initiatives since the early 1990s has afforded me opportunities to see the complex scaffolding required for teacher education to begin to touch the surface of preparing all teachers to work effectively with the superdiversity of students in elementary and secondary schools in Ontario.

Conceptual Frames

I have chosen two frameworks, as well as my own direct experiences, to make sense of the sociopolitical context and the collaborative efforts of faculty, staff, school and community partners as well as teacher candidates. These include the overlapping lenses of the Teaching for Equity framework (Grudnoff et al., 2017) and Dimitrov and Haque's model for Intercultural Teaching Competence (2016).

Time Frame	Initiative	Context & Rationale
Early 1990s to 2000s	I proposed and implemented **a cohort-based program for future teachers of English, French and other international languages.** This cohort existed for a dozen years as it was reinvented by successive teams of teacher educators working collaboratively.	This new program grew from the need to break down the barriers between approaches to teaching first, second and additional language and literacy and ultimately to better meet the needs of multilingual learners in classrooms.
1994 to 1996	I took part in a **pilot for a 2-year teacher education program** prior to which the standard length of B.Ed. programs in Ontario had been 8 months. The pilot involved the further exploration of cohorts in teacher education and the benefits of close partnerships with selected schools whose staff worked collaboratively with teacher educators and teacher candidates to bridge the theory-practice gap.	Our dissatisfaction with the 8-month time frame to prepare teachers to work with diverse learners led to the exploration of a longer period of time to do this challenging work. The theory-practice gap continued to plague teacher education in general and more specifically in teacher education for diversity.
1996 to 2001	I took part in **the redesign process** which involved **extending our 8-month program to a 10-month program with an internship opportunity** that would allow our teacher candidates to explore teaching opportunities with diverse learners in a wide variety of learning spaces locally, nationally or internationally. I created an **internship** for teacher candidates **to gain experience working with English learners** as well as internship opportunities to support internationally educated teacher candidates who sought opportunities to learn about schools and working with diverse learners in Ontario, beyond what was available in the mainstream program.	The government of Ontario refused to fund an extended teacher education program. A focus on ELs had only been allowed within the realm of Additional Qualifications courses taken after completing initial teacher education in the B.Ed. program. Many teachers had begun to immigrate to Canada and expressed a need to learn more about Canadian schools within the framework of the B.Ed. program
Early 2000s	The teacher education design and redesign activities culminated in a Social Sciences and Humanities Research Council funded **project focused on infusing issues related to English learners across the teacher education curriculum known as the ESL Infusion Initiative** Additional infusion initiatives including *Equity Infusion* and the development of several new stand-alone courses such as *ESL Across the Curriculum* and the *Language and Culture in the Classroom* grew from the *ESL Infusion Initiative*.	Several years of the *ESL Infusion Initiative* at OISE led to an understanding that our focus needed to expand beyond helping teacher candidates to consider the needs of linguistically and culturally diverse students to a more complex and intersectional understanding of diversity among students and future teachers.

FIGURE 6.1 My Journey in Teacher Education in Ontario

2004 to 2007	I was invited to facilitate **the development of a dual degree program** that would bring seven academic units across the University of Toronto together in preparing future teachers in high demand areas over a 5-year period.	A range of different faculties at the University of Toronto had expressed an interest in becoming involved in teacher education. Ontario was experiencing a shortage of teachers in a number of areas.
	For 3 years, three representatives from each unit including an academic administrator, a professor and a member of the registrarial staff committed to the preparation of teachers, worked collaboratively to learn about promising teacher education practices and to develop programming tailored to a 5-year dual degree teacher education program to meet the needs of the highly diverse student population in Ontario schools.	The University of Toronto supported this program development process because they wanted to create the necessary conditions for cross-faculty collaboration at the program level.
2007 to 2012	During this development period and the subsequent 5-year roll out of the program, we were engaged in a **design, implementation, documentation and reflection cycle**.	
	This concurrent teacher education program included several novel elements including **three courses** offered in Years 1, 2 and 3 of the 5-year Concurrent Education program - *Child & Adolescent Development, Equity & Diversity in Education* and *Teaching ESL & Special Education* that each included a 20-hour field experience, as well as a third year 100-hour **internship** which could be completed locally or internationally.	These three courses and internship were embedded in the discipline-based undergraduate degree programs in the partner units.
2013	I was asked to **design a new course called** *Supporting English Learners* and **contribute to the development of our new 20-month Master of Teaching (MT)**.	New guidelines for teacher education in Ontario were released and specified that, as of 2015, all teachers should be prepared over a 2-year period and learn to work with linguistically, culturally, and racially diverse students as well as learners with special needs.
2015 to 2020	I have been the **course lead for the** *Supporting English Learners* **course as well as the Associate Chair for Student Experience** in the Department of Curriculum, Teaching and Learning.	The MT is a large cohort-based program requiring several layers of leadership to ensure consistency across cohorts.
	I have been one of the principal investigators of a **multi-stranded study focussed on the** *Supporting English Learners* course mandated in the *Ontario Enhanced Teacher Education* policy.	Learning about how one of the mandatory courses in our programs supports TC learning has provided insights into TC development across the MT.

FIGURE 6.1 *Continued*

Teaching for Equity

Grudnoff et al. (2017) derived their Teaching for Equity framework from a meta-analysis of multiple, international studies of teaching practices that have a positive influence on the learning of diverse students. From the common elements identified, Grudnoff et al. derived six general teaching principles for equity which they built into a framework conceived as a lens to consider equity-centred teacher education curriculum aiming to prepare teachers who can work effectively with diverse learners by creating learning opportunities leading to positive outcomes for all students and particularly students who have been disadvantaged in schools.

The Teaching for Equity conceptual framework (Grudnoff et al., 2017) is a helpful heuristic in the deconstruction of the scaffolding required to prepare teachers to work with all students regardless of their background and other identity markers including race, language, and culture. Grudnoff et al. (2017) define their conceptual framework as a "coherent set of interrelated understandings about teaching, learning, and learning to teach situated within local and larger political and social contexts" (p. 322). As such, the Teaching for Equity framework allows me to consider curriculum design, review and renewal processes related to teaching within the Master of Teaching (MT) program while keeping in mind the vision for the program and the nature of the diverse learners in the context of Ontario.

Figure 6.2 is adapted from Grudnoff et al.'s conceptual framework for equity-centred teacher education and shows that teacher candidates learn to teach in complex and often stratified sociopolitical contexts. Intersectionality Theory (Crenshaw, 1989; Hankivsky, 2014) underpins this framework with the understanding that social inequities and learners' experiences of discrimination are often related to particular aspects of their multiple identities including race, legal status, language, religion, socioeconomic status and more. As learning to teach is tied to local schools, the distinct culture of each school influences what teacher candidates learn during their practicum experiences. Another assumption reflected in Figure 6.2 is that all educators share the responsibility to address inequities by working alone or together to operationalize practices that will lead to better outcomes for all students while challenging the status quo and working as change agents with a social justice orientation.

By reviewing the literature, Grudnoff et al. (2017) identified six facets of practice for equity, which reflect what teachers and their students and student teachers do in classrooms. Teacher candidates learn to be educators for equity by learning new ways to reflect on their practice which mirror particular values and attitudes. Figure 6.2 illustrates how teacher candidates' beliefs, attitudes, values, knowledge, interpretive frames, sense of efficacy and agency interact with the six facets of practice as they learn to teach for diversity and equity.

This figure attempts to show how teacher candidates learn to operationalize these six facets of practice for equity by working collaboratively with members of the school and community while engaging in a cycle of critical reflection. At the

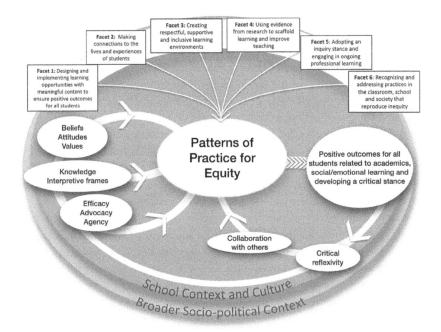

FIGURE 6.2   The Teaching for Equity Conceptual Framework (adapted from Grudnoff et al., 2017)

core of the Teaching for Equity framework is the notion that all the elements interact to form patterns of practice for equity resulting from the particularities of the teacher candidates, schools and communities connected to the teacher education program. It also means that the enactment of the principles may appear somewhat different depending on the context.

Grudnoff et al. (2017) explain that

> [p]utting equity at the centre of initial teacher education requires that teacher candidates learn how to construct patterns of practice that are consistent with the six general facets and are appropriate to particular content, tailored to particular local contexts and histories, linked to the culture of a particular school as well as the knowledge traditions of particular cultural communities, and embedded in the relationships of particular teachers and students.
>
> *(p. 322)*

Model for Intercultural Teaching Competence

Dimitrov and Haque's (2016) model for Intercultural Teaching Competence (ITC) was developed for use as a reflection and development tool with university instructors working with diverse students across a variety of disciplines. Dimitrov and Haque mention that the foundational, facilitation and curriculum design competencies in their model are of particular benefit to instructors who include intercultural and Indigenous perspectives or explore global or social justice issues in their courses. Dimitrov and Haque are clear in saying that their model should not be understood as a recipe for developing intercultural teaching competence nor should it be used to assess an educator's intercultural teaching competence. I therefore use it to consider the opportunities for intercultural learning created across the MT program and in one course in particular focused on learning to support English learners in elementary and secondary classrooms and schools.

In the ITC model, there are five foundational competencies that focus on the educator's intercultural awareness and capacity to model intercultural skills for their students. There are also 10 facilitation competencies which refer to an educator's ability to determine the needs of the learners, develop a sense of community among the students, co-construct clear academic expectations and create opportunities for active learning. There are also five curriculum design competencies aligned around connecting learning and assessment activities to ensure students achieve the desired outcomes, ensuring that multiple perspectives, intercultural skills and various ways for students to show their learning are woven into the curriculum. Figure 6.3 includes all twenty competencies described in detail in Dimitrov and Haque's 2016 article.

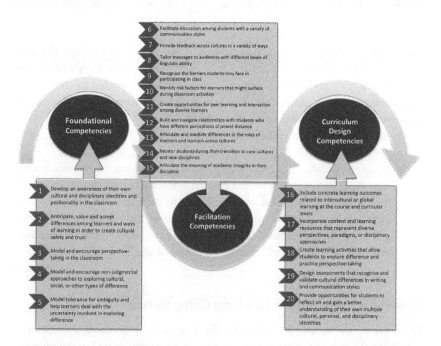

FIGURE 6.3 Foundational, Facilitation and Curriculum Design Competencies for Intercultural Teaching Competence (adapted from Dimitrov & Haque, 2016)

The Evolution of Teacher Education for Equity and Diversity in the Master of Teaching Program

In this section, as an active participant on the landscape of the MT program, I consider the socio-political context in Ontario as well as the collaborative efforts of faculty, staff, school and community partners to understand how the MT evolved into a program that prepares teachers for equity and diversity.

The MT Program is a 20-month graduate teacher education program that combines the study of educational theories, evidence-based teaching practices for equity, opportunities to conduct and use research, four practicum placements in local schools as well as an optional internship in Canada or abroad at the end of the program. Figure 6.4 shows how I understand the socio-political landscape at various levels as it relates to the evolution of the MT as a teacher education program for equity and diversity.

Ontario College of Teacher Accreditation Resource Guide 2017

As mentioned previously, in 2017, the Ontario College of Teachers published the *Accreditation Resource Guide* for the "enhanced" teacher education plan first introduced in 2013 with a mandated implementation in 2015. The enhanced program requirements included a new focus on equity and diversity as reflected in the section titles where various program components are described including (1) theories of learning and teaching and differentiated instruction, (2) supporting English-language learners, (3) supporting students with special education needs, (4) mental health, addictions and well-being and (5) Indigenous perspectives, cultures, histories and ways of knowing.

This excerpt from the *Accreditation Resource Guide* is illustrative of how these guidelines are aligned with the Teaching for Equity framework:

FIGURE 6.4 The Context of the MT Program

The intention is that graduates are able to work with all students, using student strengths and interests to promote their learning and development. Capacities to work with families and other professionals in support of students are also needed.

(Ontario College of Teachers, 2017, p. 21)

The *Accreditation Resource Guide* (Ontario College of Teachers, 2017) is also very specific in terms of what should be included in particular courses along with suggested teaching, learning and assessment strategies. Figures 6.5 and 6.6 specify this information for the course on supporting ELs.

Like all teacher education programs in Ontario, the MT is reviewed on a cyclical basis and must demonstrate how it adheres to the *Accreditation Resource Guide* (Ontario College of Teachers, 2017). In my various leadership roles over the past 30 years, I have become very familiar with the accreditation process and how it has evolved to support equity- and diversity-focused teacher education. In 2014, during the collaborative development of the Supporting English Learners course, my colleagues and I frequently referred to the list of suggested content as well as teaching and assessment strategies in the *2013 Enhanced Teacher Education* guidelines (renamed the *Accreditation Resource Guide* in 2017) as these resonated for us. In fact, I rejoiced when I saw the specificity of the guidelines provided because I had struggled to find effective ways to put ELs on the landscape in teacher education. Initially, attempts to infuse English as a Second Language (ESL) across the teacher education curriculum were not successful for many reasons including the high turnaround of seconded and sessional instructors in the program, the belief of many of my colleagues that the needs of ELs did not need to be addressed in mainstream teacher education as well as the overcrowded

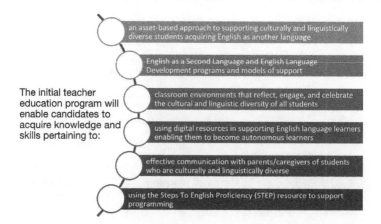

FIGURE 6.5 Suggested Content for the Course on Supporting English Language Learners (adapted from the *Accreditation Resource Guide*; Ontario College of Teachers, 2017)

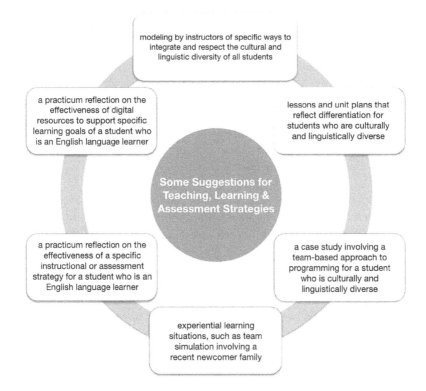

FIGURE 6.6 Suggested Learning, Teaching and Assessment Strategies for the Course on Supporting English Language Learners (adapted from the *Accreditation Resource Guide*; Ontario College of Teachers, 2017)

curriculum in our then 10-month teacher education program. The introduction of a stand-alone elective course called ESL Across the Curriculum was also ineffective because only about 70 teacher candidates from a pool of 1,000 had the opportunity to take this elective during their busy program.

Ontario's Education Equity Action Plan 2017

As a teacher educator, I am always keeping my eye on initiatives of the Ontario Ministry of Education. As such, I was pleased when the *Education Equity Action Plan* (2017), which builds on the previous 10 years of equity work in Ontario, clearly stated the need to remove systemic barriers to ensure that school and classroom practices reflect and respond to the diversity of students and staff. The "School & Classroom Practices" section of the plan goes on to highlight how current structures, policies, programs and practices may place certain students at a disadvantage and provides a list of the most vulnerable students which includes "racialized students, students experiencing poverty, Indigenous students, new-comers to Canada, students who identify as LGBTQ or Two-Spirited, children and youth in care, religious minorities, French language minorities, students with disabilities, and students with special education needs" (p. 14).

It is heartening to see that systemic barriers are clearly identified in the *Education Equity Action Plan* (Ontario Ministry of Education, 2017) and that there are specific indicators for educators, school administrators and the public to look for as the action plan is operationalized one year at a time. However, this excerpt from the plan illustrates that it would be difficult to identify the locus for a complaint regarding its implementation:

> Responsibility and accountability for completing the action items rests with the Ministry of Education and its component divisions, branches and offices, including the Education Equity Secretariat, as appropriate for each item and activity.
>
> *(Ontario Ministry of Education, 2017, p. 21)*

As a new premier with a more conservative education agenda was elected in 2018 and the pandemic closed schools in March 2020, it remains to be seen if the action items delineated in the plan for 2020 will be realized. In fact, the pandemic has increased the visibility of inequities in the education system at every level while making it very challenging to mitigate these.

University Level—University of Toronto

There are several initiatives at the University of Toronto that have directly or indirectly supported the evolution of the MT program in preparing teachers for equity and diversity. I describe each of these initiatives in the following and highlight how each is connected to the MT program. Employment Equity policies (University of Toronto, n.d.-a) are slowly leading to a more diverse pool of teacher educators who bring new perspectives to the MT program. Although there are workshops on unconscious bias offered to faculty and staff on hiring committees (University of Toronto, n.d.-b), these are optional. As I have been on dozens of hiring teams, I have experienced and witnessed the pull of bias in our work and the need to keep my senses heightened to the dangers of hiring that reproduce whiteness and middle-class attitudes in the academy. As such, there should be clear requirements for professional development related to equity for anyone involved in hiring new faculty.

A renewed focus on teaching and curriculum development across the University of Toronto has led to the development of resources related to writing learning outcomes (Centre for Teaching Support and Innovation [CTSI], 2014) which supported our efforts to create clear statements about the MT program and make transparent the learning goals of the program for teacher candidates. The CTSI (n.d.) has also developed resources related to the Universal Design for

Learning (UDL) which "aims to change the design of the environment rather than to change the learner. When environments are intentionally designed to reduce barriers, all learners can engage in rigorous, meaningful learning" (Centre for Assisted Special Technology, n.d.). In 2019, MT faculty were invited to a hands-on professional development session to learn about how to operationalize UDL in teacher education. Having taken part in this workshop, I discovered the alignment of the core UDL principles and practices and those described in the Teaching for Equity framework (Grudnoff et al., 2017). Although I was pleased to see this synergy, I am concerned about the proliferation of acronyms and parallel paradigms leading to more equity and diversity-oriented programming. The field is getting increasingly crowded with complementary ideas which are sometimes lost because educators cannot see how they align with other frameworks and practices they are committed to. As MT faculty, we are encouraged to operationalize UDL principles in our courses as an important way to model inclusive teaching practices. However, UDL is not taken up equally across the teacher education curriculum which sometimes causes teacher candidates to raise concerns about some faculty who may not be "walking the talk" when it comes to inclusive design in teacher education. Some faculty resist implementing UDL because they simply don't know what it is and are not interested in learning about it while other instructors, who may be teaching just one course, may not have had the luxury to attend an unpaid professional development (PD) leading to additional unpaid time spent on revamping the one course they teach in the program.

An expansion of the Accessibility Services and the renewal of the university's commitment to the mental health and well-being of its students, has made it easier to adopt an equity and diversity orientation in the MT program. It makes a difference for MT teacher candidates to see more inclusive and responsive policies and practices in their university when they are learning about their responsibilities as educators to work to break down systemic barriers and respond to needs of their diverse learners and create inclusive learning spaces. However, as Associate Chair for Student Experience, I see the frustration that some students experience because their instructors do not know how to accommodate them within the framework of their courses or practicum experiences. Although we are making progress in terms of creating a safe and inclusive environment for our teacher candidates, we need to increase the PD provided to teacher educators to understand the complex intersections between mental health and various forms of discrimination faced by teacher candidates in the program.

Faculty Level—Ontario Institute for Studies in Education

OISE Guiding Principles on Equity and Diversity

In 2018 the *OISE Guiding Principles on Equity and Diversity* were updated and strongly support the MT Program in preparing teachers for equity and diversity.

The following excerpt highlights three principles that align directly with the Grudnoff et al. (2017) framework:

To further ensure that social justice prevails in our programs we will aim to:

- enrol and support a student body that reflects the diversity of the communities we serve through, for example, processes for student recruitment, selection, admission and subsequent support and accommodations;
- ensure that social justice is promoted in all areas of our curriculum, in our pedagogy, in the climate of our classrooms, and in all aspects of the OISE environment;
- hire and support individuals who have a demonstrated commitment and capacity to realize our social justice goals through their work and community involvement.

Having been a member or the chair of the admissions committee for several of our initial teacher education programs since 2006 when OISE first published its guiding principles for equity and diversity in education, I can attest to OISE's commitment to a more diverse and representative student body. In fact, several colleagues (e.g. Childs & Ferguson, 2015; Childs et al., 2011, 2017) have researched and published on the effectiveness of different admissions initiatives since 2005. Their research has highlighted the need for creating space for applicants to write about how they understand the connection between their multiple identities and the kind of teacher they want to. Ruth Childs and her colleagues also point to the need for a proactive stance in attracting a more diverse pool of applicants and collecting demographic data on applicants to teacher education programs.

Master of Teaching Curriculum Review Process

A multiphase MT curriculum review process began in 2017 which included (1) the development of the MT Program Vision, (2) the development of program expectations, (3) curriculum mapping to identity connections between program expectations and requirements such as courses and field experiences and (4) the creation of an action plan for the renewal of the MT program with ongoing assessment that would lead eventually lead us to revisioning.

Master of Teaching Vision Statement

During 2016–2017, the OISE community began a visioning process to explore ways to enhance teacher education in the MT program. This culminated in a vision statement that reflects a commitment to equity, diversity and accessibility:

Teaching excellence and scholarly research are the mutually reinforcing pillars of the Master of Teaching program. The program prepares candidates to become outstanding teachers and leaders who consult, critique, create, and mobilize educational research. As a community, our faculty, students and graduates share a deep commitment to all learners and the building of a more just, equitable and sustainable world.

(Ontario Institute for Studies in Education, n.d.)

My involvement in the collaborative development of the MT vision statement was mostly energizing because the process reflected the elements that I had learned were important through my participation in the design and implementation of various teacher education programs and courses over several years. The process was also frustrating at times because of the heightened tensions around the choice of words to include in the final sentence of the vision statement. The divisions between teacher educators along the critical to conservative continuum were evident in the many long discussions that finally led to a vision statement we could all live with and that incorporated multiple elements of the Teaching for Equity framework (Grudnoff et al., 2017).

Master of Teaching Admissions Statement

The Master of Teaching Admissions Statement is aligned with the MT Mission Statement and flows from *OISE's Guiding Principles on Equity and Diversity* as this excerpt reveals:

At the University of Toronto, we strive to be an equitable, diverse and inclusive community … . OISE is dedicated to admitting qualified candidates who reflect the ethnic, cultural and social diversity of Toronto's schools.

(OISE, 2018)

In fact, the Master of Teaching Race and Inclusion Committee has been working to develop more diverse recruitment pathways, particularly with respect to Black and Indigenous applicants as these groups are underrepresented in our student body. These include outreach to middle and secondary schools and extracurricular programming to help minority students to begin to imagine teaching as a possible career.

It has been exciting to witness the gradual shift in the composition of the student body in initial teacher education at the University of Toronto from 1989 to today. Although we still have some underrepresented groups, the MT class of 2020 is among the most diverse group of teacher candidates we have ever had in terms of all types of diversity. For example, about one third of our teacher candidate (TC) population is composed of visible minorities which is reflective of the trends in Ontario captured in the 2016 census indicating that 29.3 percent of Ontario's approximately 14 million people identified as visible minorities.

Master of Teaching Program Expectations

A working group composed of program leaders and course leads, in consultation with all MT instructors and field partners such as school district leaders and representatives from the Ontario Teachers Federation, met multiple times for more than a year to identify 23 core program expectations. These expectations are aligned with the mandatory content stipulated by the Ontario College of Teachers and also reflect the graduate nature of the MT program as well as the program vision. The expectations include knowledge, competencies and values the MT candidates will develop and display following the successful completion of the MT program. I have selected a few of the expectations that connect particularly well to elements of the Teaching for Equity framework (Grudnoff et al., 2017):

- Engage in data collection, analysis and the mobilization of research in respectful ways that consider communities and context
- Recognize and investigate their own social locations, biases, (dis)advantages, and predispositions in relationship to their teaching and research
- Understand that teaching requires ongoing learning and engagement with current issues and the different perspectives and worldviews of local and global communities
- Demonstrate pedagogies and actions that support well-being, equity, social justice, cultural responsiveness and environmental sustainability to promote the transformative purposes of education
- Demonstrate an understanding of the ways systemic and institutional practices impact learners and groups, and b) identify ways to address inequities and inequalities (Ontario Institute for Studies in Education, 2020, pages 8 and 9)

It is important to note that these expectations will continue to evolve as the curriculum renewal process is ongoing. As the program structure changes and new courses or initiatives are rolled out, it will be necessary to revisit the program expectations to ensure coherence between these and the experiences of TCs in the MT programs. Once again, I had mixed emotions as I took part in our regular meetings spread over 2 years because there continued to be some tension between the committee members who espoused neoliberal values and those wanted to infuse criticality across the teacher education curriculum. I found it difficult to listen to the repeated call of a small number of committee members to treat teacher candidates equally with little understanding of the concept of equity in teacher education.

Master of Teaching Curriculum Mapping

The Curriculum Mapping process has been invaluable for me as a course lead for one of the mandatory courses in our program. It allowed me to get a clear sense of how the program expectations map onto the various courses and which teaching/learning/assessment strategies are preferred. It has made strengths, gaps and areas in need of attention visible through maps and charts from many perspectives.

Curriculum Mapping also helped me to see the interconnections between courses in terms of content and preferred teaching and assessment strategies. Although all MT courses touch in one way or another on aspects of equity and diversity, there are several mandatory courses where these topics are central:

- Introduction to Special Education and Mental Health
- Anti-Discriminatory Education
- Supporting English Learners
- Curriculum and Teaching in Social Studies and Aboriginal Education
- Indigenous Experiences of Racism and Settler Colonialism in Canada: An Introduction
- Educational Research 1 and 2

For each of the mandatory courses in the MT program, there is a course lead to ensure consistency in terms of the core content as well as teaching, learning and assessment strategies across the multiple sections of each course. As a course lead for the Supporting English Learners course, my role has included (1) the design of the course in keeping with the guidelines for core content as well as teaching, learning and assessment strategies, (2) the hiring of the instructional team to teach about 14 sections of this course a year and (3) working collaboratively with the course instructors to refine the course. My work as a course lead is supported by the Teaching and Learning Coordinator who convenes regular meetings to ensure good communication across course leads and other curriculum leaders in the MT program.

Although I have worked closely with other teacher educators for several decades and am convinced of the power of collaboration within and across cohorts of teacher candidates, it is not until joining the MT community that I experienced such a complexly interwoven set of collaborative opportunities to ensure the operationalization of the principles set out in the Teaching for Equity framework (Grudnoff et al., 2017).

The Supporting English Learners Course

To illustrate how the broader context of education at the provincial level, along with University of Toronto– and OISE-level initiatives, has guided the constant refinement and renewal of one mandatory course within the MT program, I focus on the Supporting English Learners course which is offered in the second year of the MT program once teacher candidates have completed at least eight courses and two practicum experiences in two settings. Since 2016, 60 cohorts of teacher candidates, that is, about 1,800 teacher candidates have completed this course.

Learning and Assessment Strategies in the Supporting English Learners Course

The core content as well as the main learning/assessment strategies that appeared in the original course outline in 2016 have evolved thanks to the input and experimentation and collaboration of 14 different instructors. As a course lead, I have met with instructors on a regular basis to find out about their experiences with different cohorts of TCs preparing to teach different grades and subjects. Our discussions can be mapped onto Dimitrov and Haque's 2016 model for Intercultural Teaching Competence as the topics we explored were for the most part related to the foundational, facilitation and curriculum design competencies of this model. In fact, we have considered how the core topics and teaching, learning and assessment strategies in the Supporting English Learners course help TCs develop the intercultural teaching competencies required to work effectively with diverse students learning English. The activities we have gradually added to the course have sought to create learning opportunities involving the exploration of self, an increased awareness of the varied life experiences of newcomer students and their families and critical reflexivity. Figure 6.7 provides a brief description of five of the core strategies in the Supporting ELs course and shows how these are embedded in the Intercultural Teaching Competence model. Each of these five core activities supports teacher candidates in developing several of the foundational, facilitation and curriculum design competencies included in Dimitrov and Haque's 2016 model for Intercultural Teaching Competence.

As an instructional team, we have also discussed how our own personal and professional identities impact on the way we approach teaching this course and what topics we may emphasize as a result of our complex identities. As such, although we are mindful of the core content and strategies, we have become aware of how our unique identities influence how we relate to teacher candidates in preparing them to work with diverse learners in schools.

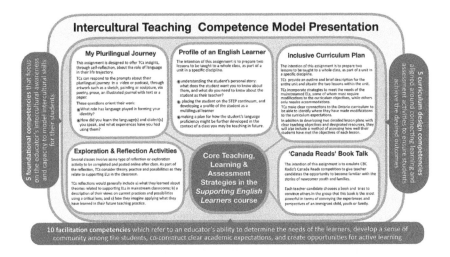

FIGURE 6.7 Core Teaching, Learning and Assessment Strategies in the Supporting English Learners Course

Conclusion

Although the socio-political landscape continues to shift in Ontario, the rise of transnationalism and the high level of immigration that have led to the diversification of the population, have proved to be positive forces for change in teacher education. In particular, education and teacher education policies at the provincial level, along with university and faculty level initiatives have finally aligned in support of the development of teacher education for equity and diversity within the framework of the Master of Teaching Program at the University of Toronto.

Using an autoethnographic lens, I have attempted to give a glimpse into how the forces have aligned in support of a more equity- and diversity-oriented graduate teacher education program. However, as I continue to work with my colleagues to create and sustain a strong program where teachers can learn to work effectively with diverse learners, I worry about a number of issues that plague most teacher education programs in Canada. These include (1) an over-reliance on sessional instructors who are precariously employed, (2) tensions that arise as we strive to be respectful of the academic freedom of instructors while also being accountable in terms of the content requirements of professional programs leading to certification and (3) the locus of decision making as many decisions about teacher education programs are made by continuing faculty because of the high turnover of sessional faculty who, often, are not remunerated for work beyond teaching.

As I have not been able to deconstruct every aspect of the evolution of the program, it may seem that the transformation process is straightforward.

However, it is only through intensive and continuing collaboration at many levels that teacher education for equity and diversity can grow. Safe spaces for faculty, teacher candidates and school partners to disclose concerns related to equity and diversity must exist and structures to support redress in these situations must be put into place as well. In addition, the systemic inequities in universities must be addressed by creating more permanent positions in faculties of education and recognizing the need to compensate sessional faculty for their labour which goes beyond teaching particular courses. It is definitely not enough to have courses with clear expectations aligned with frameworks such as Teaching for Equity (Grudnoff et al., 2017) or models such Intercultural Teaching Competence (Dimitrov & Haque, 2016) to claim that a teacher education program is truly preparing teacher candidates to be inclusive practitioners working with their diverse students in a socially just manner. Moving toward teacher education for equity and diversity is a multidimensional process which demands time, commitment and high levels of collaboration, continuing professional development opportunities related to equity and diversity as well as systemic change that recognizes the many inequities in university-based teacher education programs.

References

Anderson, L. (2006). Analytic autoethnography. *Journal of Contemporary Ethnography*, 35(4), 373–395. doi: 10.1177/0891241605280449

Centre for Assisted Special Technology. (n.d.) *UDL guidelines*. http://udlguidelines.cast.org/

Centre for Teaching Support and Innovation. (2014). *Developing learning outcomes: A guide for University of Toronto Faculty*. University of Toronto. https://teaching.utoronto.ca/wp-content/uploads/2015/08/Developing-Learning-Outcomes-Guide-Aug-2014.pdf

Centre for Teaching Support and Innovation. (n.d.) *Universal Design for Learning*. Retrieved from https://teaching.utoronto.ca/teaching-support/udl/

Childs, R. A., Broad, K., Gallagher-Mackay, K., Sher, Y., Escayg, K.-A., & McGrath, C. (2011). Pursuing equity in and through teacher education program admissions. *Education Policy Analysis Archives*, 19(24), 1–16.

Childs, R. A., & Ferguson, A. K. (2015). Changes in, to, and through the initial teacher education program admission process. In L. Thomas & M. Hirschkorn (Eds.), *Change and progress in Canadian teacher education: Research on recent innovations in teacher preparation in Canada* (pp. 420–440). Ottawa, Canada: Canadian Association for Teacher Education.

Childs, R. A., Hanson, M. D., Carnegie-Douglas, S., & Archbold, A. (2017). Investigating the effects of access initiatives for underrepresented groups. *Perspectives: Policy and Practice in Higher Education*, 21(2–3), 73–80. doi:10.1080/13603108.2016.1231720

Crenshaw, K. (1989). Demarginalizing the intersection of race and sex: A Black feminist critique of antidiscrimination doctrine, feminist theory and antiracist politics. *University of Chicago Legal Forum*, 1989(1). https://chicagounbound.uchicago.edu/cgi/viewcontent.cgi?article=1052&context=uclf

Dimitrov, N. & Haque, A. (2016). Intercultural teaching competence: A multi-disciplinary model for instructor reflection. *Intercultural Education*, 27(5), 1–20. doi:10.1080/14675986.2016.1240502

Grudnoff, L., Haigh, M., Hill, M., Cochran-Smith, M., Ell, F., & Ludlow, L. (2017). Teaching for equity: Insights from international evidence with implications for a teacher education curriculum. *The Curriculum Journal*, 28(3), 305–326. doi:10.1080/09585176.2017.1292934

Hankivsky, O. (2014). *Intersectionality 101.* The Institute for Intersectionality Research & Policy, Simon Fraser University.

Marechal, G. (2010). Autoethnography. In A. J. Mills, G. Durepos, & E. Wiebe (Eds.), *Encyclopaedia of case study research* (pp. 43–45). Sage Publications.

Ontario College of Teachers. (2017). *Accreditation resource guide.* https://www.oct.ca/-/media/PDF/Accreditation%20Resource%20Guide/Accreditation_Resource_Guide_EN_WEB.pdf

Ontario Institute for Studies in Education. (2018). *OISE guidin\g principles on equity and diversity.* https://www.oise.utoronto.ca/oise/UserFiles/File/OISE_Council_General/policy_equity_apr2005_rev.Nov.2018_FINAL.pdf

Ontario Institute for Studies in Education (2020). *Master of Teaching Graduate Program Handbook 2020-2021.* University of Toronto.

Ontario Institute for Studies in Education. (n.d.). *Why choose the Master of Teaching Program?* https://oise.utoronto.ca/mt/Why_Choose_MT_.html

Ontario Ministry of Education. (2017). *Ontario's education equity action plan.* Queen's Printer for Ontario. http://www.edu.gov.on.ca/eng/about/education_equity_plan_en.pdf

People for Education. (2015). *2015 annual report on schools: The gap between policy and reality.* https://peopleforeducation.ca/wp-content/uploads/2017/10/P4E-Annual-Report-2015.pdf

Senyshyn, R. (2018). Teaching for transformation: converting the intercultural experience of preservice teachers into intercultural learning. *Intercultural Education*, 29(2), 163–184. https://doi.org/10.1080/14675986.2018.1429791

Statistics Canada. (2016). *Data products, 2016 Census.* https://www12.statcan.gc.ca/census-recensement/2016/dp-pd/index-eng.cfm

UNESCO. (2016). *Education 2030: Incheon Declaration and Framework for Action for the implementation of Sustainable Development Goal 4: Ensure inclusive and equitable quality education and promote lifelong learning.* https://unesdoc.unesco.org/ark:/48223/pf0000245656

University of Toronto. (n.d.-a) *Employment equity.* http://equity.hrandequity.utoronto.ca/employment-equity/

University of Toronto. (n.d.-b). *Unconscious bias education.* https://faculty.utoronto.ca/resources/enhancing-diversity/unconscious-bias-education/

7

PRE-SERVICE TEACHERS' CRITICAL DISPOSITIONS TOWARDS LANGUAGE

Transforming Taken-for-Granted Assumptions About Racially, Culturally, and Linguistically Diverse Learners through Teacher Education

Andrea Sterzuk

While Canadian classrooms are made up of children from a broad range of linguistic, racial, and religious backgrounds, Canadian teachers are predominantly English monolingual and white settler (Ryan et al., 2009; Dandala, 2018). Current educational programs also do not have equitable representation of preservice teachers (Childs & Ferguson, 2016; Holden & Kitchen, 2018; Marom, 2019). This mismatch between teacher and student identity has implications for teacher practices and student experiences. While schools are sites of linguistic pluralism, taken-for-granted assumptions about what constitutes legitimate academic English can lead teachers to see English-language variation and multilingualism as something that gets in the way of acquiring literacy skills and mastering subject material (Delpit & Dowdy, 2008; Pettit, 2011; Baecher, 2012; Polat & Mahalingappa, 2013; Ennser-Kanane & Leider, 2018). Teacher education programs require a readjustment in terms of problematizing deficit views of language and reinforcing critical dispositions towards language (Sterzuk, in press; Stille & Cummins, 2013; Ennser-Kanane & Leider, 2018).

This chapter shares findings from a 3-year, mixed-methods study exploring 24 white, settler, preservice educators' dispositions towards racially, culturally and linguistically diverse learners. As a teacher educator in the area of language and literacy education, my ultimate goal is to support preservice teachers in pluralistic understandings of language (Canagarajah, 2007); critical multilingual language awareness (García, 2016) and assets-based pedagogical practices (Ennser-Kanane & Leider, 2018).Yet, teacher preparation programs are unlikely to influence preservice teachers' critical understandings of language and eventual practice as fully as intended because of preservice teachers' K–12 learning experiences (Britzman, 1991) and field experiences which include the influence of the cooperating teacher (Rozelle & Wilson, 2012; Clarke et al., 2014). In light of these potential constraints, it is important to investigate influences on preservice educators' views of language to better understand how teacher education can support preservice teachers in addressing the needs of culturally, linguistically and racially diverse students and their families.

Critical Understandings of Language and School

This chapter investigates preservice teachers views of language—or socially constructed views about languages, in terms of how, where, when, and with whom they should and should not be spoken and written—and implications for education.These types of views about what constitutes legitimate language, particularly when held by teachers and other educators including administrators, curriculum designers, teachers, and speech and language pathologists, can negatively impact speakers of "illegitimate" languages and language varieties (Bourdieu, 1991). In schools, English-language variation can often be viewed as a detriment, as something that gets in the way of acquiring literacy skills and mastering subject material (Nero, 2006). Biased language beliefs legitimatize discriminatory school practices and traditional teaching practices in culturally and linguistically diverse classrooms can consign linguistically and culturally diverse students to failure. Educational research links teacher expectations of students who are speakers of English-language varieties not sanctioned by schools to lower levels of literacy development as well as academic failure (see Labov, 1972; Delpit & Dowdy, 2008; Prendergast, 2003; Lee, 2006; Nero, 2006; Sterzuk, 2011). When teachers view English language variation as evidence of deficiency or delays in language development, it is important to examine the nature of teacher views of language.

Literature in the area of preservice to in-school teacher transition also informs this research. This period is sometimes referred to as "the induction years" and includes the final practicum or internship in a teacher education program, as well as the early years of full-time in-service teaching. This literature includes inquiry into beginning teachers' beliefs during socialization into the school systems. Teacher preparation programs may be unlikely to influence preservice teachers' eventual practice as fully as intended (Britzman, 1991; Frykholm, 1996; Ball, 1997) for two reasons: preservice teachers' K–12 learning experiences and the influences of field experiences (Zeichner & Tabachnick, 1981; Guyton & McIntyre, 1990; Guyton & Wesche, 1996; Odell & Huling, 2000). Blankenship and Coleman (2009) explain that isolated from their teacher education programs and working closely with their mentor teachers, "the beliefs and skills beginning teachers have learned from their teacher education program are actually 'washed out'" by the circumstances they encounter during their teaching internship (p. 97). The first year of teaching brings about other changes and influences for preservice educators. In addition to the necessary reorientation of their roles (from student teacher to teacher) this transition also requires the development of a teacher identity (Alsup, 2006) and professional practice (Wanzare, 2007). School influences during this transition phase include beliefs of school administrators as well as those of other teachers.

Methodology

Teacher education program design varies across Canada. Some are *consecutive*, meaning students complete a 4-year degree in a field of their choice followed by a 2-year Bachelor of Education program. *Concurrent* models see students completing teacher education courses while they take other academic courses. The teacher education program in this study is organized in this way. Students take education courses and academic courses while also completing multiple mentored, short-term field experiences in each year of their program. The field experience in year three is called *pre-internship* and extends over two semesters. It consists of eight Wednesdays teaching in an elementary or secondary school in the fall semester and a 3-week block of teaching during the winter semester. To transition to the fourth year, 16-week field experience, or *internship*, students must be successful in their pre-internship. The research participants in this study were all part of this 4-year teacher education program. Sixteen were in elementary education programs, and eight were in secondary. A key difference between these two groups of students is that all the elementary students would have taken at least one mandatory class in multilingual education. This class includes a school placement where preservice teachers work with English-language learners. Only some of the secondary students (depending on their major) would have had this multilingual education course.

This study asks, (1) What do preservice teachers believe about English-language variation, multilingualism and communication? (2) Do preservice teachers' views on language and communication change as they transition to full-time teaching? and (3) What influences preservice teachers' views of language and communication? Both qualitative and quantitative phases of the research were undertaken concurrently and findings from the quantitative phases informed the qualitative phases of the study (Johnson & Onwuegbuzie, 2004). The quantitative phase of the study included the design and piloting (to assess the appropriateness of the instrument scale items) of the Views of English Variation (VELV) questionnaire that was distributed to, and collected from, 24 participants at three times during the study: the end of the pre-internship year, after their internships and at the end of their first year of in-service teaching. Three theoretical perspectives (multiliteracies theory, language and symbolic power and postcolonial theory) informed the initial pool of approximately 50 items for the VELV questionnaire. Items were both positively and negatively worded (reverse-worded). Content validity was established by sending the VELV questionnaire to educational researchers in languages and literacies in western Canadian universities, and items were both added and deleted based on this feedback. A pilot study was conducted and this preliminary questionnaire was administered to in-service teachers. Based on these results, some items were reworded or deleted but no other changes were made. Thirty items were included in the final questionnaire (see Appendix 7.1).

At three points in the study (pre-internship, during internship and in the first year of in-service teaching), the 24 participants were asked to indicate on a Likert-type scale how strongly they agreed or disagreed with each statement on the questionnaire and each item was scored on a scale of 1 (*strongly disagree*) to 5 (*strongly agree*). This questionnaire was administered throughout the research project and data was analysed using a repeated-measures analysis of variance (ANOVA; using SPSS software) to determine how their views of English-language variation would change over the 3 years of the study. Because the inductive thematic analysis and generation and questionnaire items were guided by the same theoretical perspectives, triangulation of qualitative and quantitative data is used to respond to the three research questions.

The qualitative phase of the study consisted of a case study analysis (Yin, 2002). This phase focused on 10 pre-service teachers, selected through analysis of their questionnaires. Participants whose responses were most likely to contribute to answering the research questions were selected. Semi-structured interviews with participants were conducted separately and were based on questions related to views of language and literacy in schools. Content analysis (Holsti, 1969); discourse analysis of the participants' ideas, messages, values, beliefs, and ideological systems; and inductive thematic analysis (Coffey & Atkinson, 1996) were used to examine the qualitative research data.

Findings ad Discussion

The questionnaire data were analysed to determine if there was a change in the participants' scores before, after internship, and during their first year of teaching. The null hypothesis was that there was no significant change in the participants' VELV scores before, after internship and during their first year of teaching (Q1 was after pre-internship, Q2 was at the end of internship and Q3 was during the first year of teaching). The dependent variable was the VELV score (the highest score was 5). The independent variable in this study was *Time* (Table 7.1).

The result of this analysis was failure to reject the null hypothesis. There was not a significant change in the group's mean score on the survey as the transition from teacher education to the field, at least not in the time frame tested. Most of the students remained consistent in their views as they transitioned. This finding

TABLE 7.1 Group Mean Scores on VELV Questionnaire

	Mean	Standard Deviation	N
Q1	3.523750000	.3485225025	24
Q2	3.484166667	.4001729698	24
Q3	3.488333333	.3319332917	24

indicates that the field was not a significant influence on the mean scores of the students, neither in deficit or pluralistic orientations.

While transitioning into schools was not a significant influence on the group's mean score, group mean scores are lower (more deficit) than hoped. There are also some items on which the group mean score is lower than anticipated. On an item developed to understand student understandings of language variation (*Item 27: As a teacher, one aspect of my job will be to teach students to speak proper English*), the group mean scores began low (Q1 = 2.25) and dropped as they began to transition to the field (Q2 = 1.91; Q3 = 1.93). Another item on the topic of students acquiring English as an additional language (*Item 11: Students learning English as an additional language [EAL] will learn English more quickly if they speak English at home*) showed evidence of deficit understandings of bilingualism (Q1 = 2.45; Q2 = 2.25; Q3 = 2.38). Finally, on another item designed to delve into preservice teachers understanding of supportive classroom practices for emerging bilingual students (*Item 15: Teachers need help from the speech and language pathologist when English as an Additional Language [EAL] students arrive in class*), the group mean score once again shows evidence of deficit understandings of language learning (Q1 = 2.83; Q2 = 2.83; Q3 = 2.58). These results point to a need to refocus energy on the topic of language variation, bilingualism, and language acquisition in this program. These relatively low scores are troubling for newly graduated teachers, entering schools at a time of increasing cultural and linguistic diversity, and suggest a need for knowledge of how to teach in contextually responsive ways.

The questionnaire data also raise the question of whether teacher education programs can, indeed, influence students' views towards language. There were some participants who remained unchanged from start to finish (see Student 15 in Table 7.2). This finding evokes other questions: Are their ideas so stable that they can't be influenced? What role does the participants' dominant settler identity play in this unchanging pattern? How might differences in student academic programs influence these students' lack of change? Some individuals changed more than others (see the highlighted students in Table 7.2). Seven of the 24 participants' mean scores changed between the first two test times by .4 or more (more pluralistic or more deficit); five of the seven students became more deficit in their views and two became more pluralistic. These changes may tell us something about the influence of internship on these participants' views.

TABLE 7.2 Individual Questionnaire Scores

	Gender	Program	L1	L2?	Q1	Q2	Q3
1	W	ELEM	ENG		3.9	4.2	4.08
2	W	ELEM	ENG		3.3	3.46	3.13
3	W	ELEM	ENG		3.7	3.6	3.56
4	W	ELEM	ENG		4	3.66	3.56
5	W	ELEM	ENG		4.03	4.4	3.93
6	W	ELEM	ENG		3	3.06	2.86
7	W	ELEM	ENG		3.7	3.96	3.3
8	W	ELEM	ENG		3.06	3.1	3.53
9	W	ELEM	ENG		3.86	3.26	3.43
10	W	SEC	ENG		3.6	3.2	3.6
11	W	SEC	ENG		3.8	3.16	3.8
12	W	SEC	ENG	YES	3.4	3.3	3.23
13							
14	W	ELEM	ENG		3.4	3	3.3
15	M	SEC	ENG		3.5	3.56	3.6
16	W	ELEM	ENG	FRENCH	3.56	3.3	3.43
17	W	ELEM	ENG	GERMAN	3.4	2.9	3.2
18	W	SEC	ENG		3.3	3.2	3.3
19	W	ELEM	ENG	FRENCH	3.36	3.3	3.06
20	W	ELEM	ENG		2.5	3.86	3.7
21	W	ELEM	ENG		3.8	3.96	3.96
22	W	SEC	ENG		3.4	3.06	2.9
23	W	SEC	ENG	FRENCH	3.8	3.86	3.56
24	W	ELEM	ENG		3.7	3.6	3.9
25	W	SEC	ENG		3.5	3.66	3.8

Two of these seven preservice teachers were part of the group of ten students who were interviewed at three points in the study: Megan (Student 5) and Lesley (Student 17). Both names are pseudonyms. Megan became more pluralistic in her views (Q1 = 4:03 to Q2 = 4.4) and Lesley became more deficit in hers (Q1 = 3.4 to Q2 = 2.9). Lesley's scores on the questionnaire were also below the group average and Megan's were above, almost the most pluralistic of the group on all three questionnaires. It is valuable to consider why and the participants' interview data is useful for this purpose. The interviews give insight into participants' views of language, and they provide us with information about the influences on their views. The primary focus of the discussion that follows is on understanding the influences on their views of language.

Lesley and Megan shared some similarities. Both were from white set-tler backgrounds, first-language speakers of English and elementary education majors, meaning they had each taken the required course in multilingual educa-tion. Another commonality was that they both had parents who had experienced mother tongue language loss. They also had many differences. Lesley grew up in rural Saskatchewan. She was a mother, a mature student, and had worked as an educational assistant in rural Saskatchewan prior to beginning her BEd. While not a fluent speaker, Lesley had some comprehension of German because she grew up hearing English and German around her as a child. Both her parents spoke German when they were children. Of the two, Lesley's mother retained more German-language fluency and it is from her mother and her maternal grand-parents that Leslie remembers hearing some German throughout her childhood. Lesley completed her internship in rural Saskatchewan, close to her hometown. All of Lesley's students were white settler and English-speaking, as was her coop-erating teacher. Megan was from urban Saskatchewan. She had several years of work experience prior to beginning her teacher education studies, but none of it was in a school environment. Megan came from a "family of teachers," and her father's first language was French. She did not speak or understand French but had first cousins who were French–English bilinguals and had grown up hearing French spoken around her at family gatherings. She interned in urban Regina in a downtown core neighbourhood. Her students came from a broad range of linguistic, racial, and cultural backgrounds. Her cooperating teacher was Métis.

Excerpts from interviews with both Megan and Leslie highlight influences from the internship experience. In fact, across all 10 interviewed participants, the influence of the mentor teacher was apparent in terms of instruction, views of language and understandings of education systems. In the following exchanges, I asked both Leslie and Megan to talk to me about their cooperating teachers.

LESLEY: We're very similar in all the ways that we run the classroom and orga-nize stuff and planning, so it was really easy to work with her

MEGAN: Yeah, my co-op was great and ah … any ideas that I had towards helping the children in that sort of way was received really really well. We worked together a lot.

Both women described positive exchanges with their cooperating teachers and highlight the ability to work together. Lesley also mentioned her cooperating teacher's similarity to herself in terms of management, instruction and organiza-tion. Megan emphasized the receptiveness of her teacher to Megan's ideas. Given what we know about Lesley and Megan's scores on the VELV questionnaire, as well as the way they described their ease with working with their assigned teach-ers, it is possible to infer that these mentor teachers share similar perspectives on language to those of their respective interns. In this way, we can start to under-stand the reinforcement of Megan and Lesley's views of language during intern-ship and the resulting increase in their respective increasing deficit and pluralistic orientations towards language.

Throughout most of our conversation, Lesley presented her perspectives on language and literacy education in ways that tend to mirror dominant orienta-tions and practices. For example, in the following excerpt, Lesley discussed a student's difficulty with reading:

LESLEY: I don't think there is a whole lot of support at home, so the reading practice, the word practice, none of them was happening at home. She had [the student], she was pulled out for some RTI [Response to Intervention], the sounds and phonics and that sort of stuff, uh …

Literacy development requires time and energy. I empathize with the efforts of teachers in supporting students as they learn to read and write. It also would not be fair for me to read too much into Lesley's description of the student. Here, I wish to use Lesley's excerpt to draw attention to some of her possible beliefs about student performance in reading. Her depiction of the student's troubles contains a familiar message about reading and the role of parents in student success (or failure). In Lesley's comment, we see evidence that could suggest that Lesley is taking up and reproducing meta-educational discourses about literacy development.

Turning now to Megan, we see evidence for the value of reinforcement of pluralistic views of language through field experiences. Prior to this 6-month internship placement, Megan had previous interactions with a pluralistically oriented language educator mentor during a second-year course on the topic of multilingualism and schools. The previous experience seems to reinforce Megan's pluralistic orientation:

MEGAN: I think ever since I had your class [on multilingualism and schools] that I got to go with Cathy [EAL field experience teacher from Year 2 of program] and see the differences that allowing languages in the class and things like that. The comfort, the safety they feel…I saw the passion she [Cathy] has and the benefits the students were experiencing, the confidence they had to talk to her, the light way they came into the classroom, their giggles in conversations in their first languages with each other and they weren't doing it out of silliness. It was just ok there. They were safe.

From her own perspective, Megan's pluralistic language views didn't simply emerge during her internship. Her VELV questionnaire results also mirror this early orientation. She traces her perspective back to the second-year required multilingual education course I mentioned in the description of the elementary education program earlier in this chapter. Cathy, Megan's mentor in her placement, completed her master's in education with a research focus on integrating student languages and multilingual repertoires in the English as an additional language (EAL) classroom. Through her experience of working with this particular mentor teacher, Megan was introduced to pluralistic perspectives and practices of language education in the second year of her program. As an elementary program major, Leslie also took this course and had a school placement working with children acquiring English as an additional language. Like Megan, Leslie also mentioned this second-year field placement during one of her interviews. She explained that experience helped her to understand that English-language fluency doesn't have to be something that holds English-language learners back from academic progress. The key difference between Megan's and Lesley's placements was the mentor teacher. In Megan's case, she was placed with someone who was particularly knowledgeable in the area of multilingual education and who encouraged children to use their home languages in the classroom. This was not a practice in Lesley's placement. This early and meaningful influence helped to orient Megan in a way that addressed the needs of culturally, linguistically, and racially diverse students and their families.

In her post-internship interview, Megan discussed a moment of confronting another teacher at the school about somewhat deficit views of language learners. In our exchange, I probed to understand the reason Megan felt able to stand up for her own critical views:

ANDREA: What made you feel you could engage in that conversation? What was it that made you think that 'oh, I have something to say!'?

MEGAN: My co-op was a really good listener. She always made me feel that my opinion mattered. I think that's a lot of it.

What this excerpt, as well as her previous statements suggest, is that in cases where the mentor teacher possesses a critical disposition towards language, this pairing seems effective in terms of bolstering the student teacher's own criticality. Throughout our post-internship interview, Megan identified her cooperating teacher as supportive of her views around language and literacy.

In my conversations with Leslie, there were moments where she demonstrated pluralistic views of language and students. She shared her ideas about accepting language variation so students can focus on academic learning as they acquire English ("as long as you can still understand it") and the importance of focusing on content in writing and not just "whether they use proper grammar." These types of comments point to a willingness to be pluralistically oriented to language use in her classroom. In my conversations with Megan, I found no evidence of normative educational practices around language. In some ways, Megan seems remarkably insulated from deficit thinking around language despite having grown up in the prairies as a white settler and all that entails in terms of exposure to dominant societal and school-based understandings of language. In the following excerpt about an experience during her internship, Megan shared an instance of disrupting a pullout approach to language pathology exercises:

MEGAN: … Sometimes because 'th' isn't in Tagalog, the sound, it was interesting to do the spelling test. Some of them didn't ever hear the sound because it's not in their language. So it would be like 'f' or 'd' rather than 'th'. Actually I had the speech pathologist come and show them where the tongue goes for the 'th' in words that have it at the end of a word or in the beginning or in the middle. And after she did, there was actually an improvement. So the kids know where to put it. I know that's just challenging blend to do but I mean overall English language arts with that multicultural classroom, it's interesting.

ANDREA: How did you get the idea to do that? To have the speech pathologist come and help students with that sound.

MEGAN: Well, we actually got one of the girls that was going to the speech pathologist. She had 'th' words sheet and put it up by the door. She was supposed to say them before she left the classroom every day. And I thought that the other kids would benefit

In this instance, she drew on a sophisticated understanding of how phonological differences between first and target languages can affect literacy development in the target language and determined a way to avoid singling out a student that could have potentially resulted in the child feeling negatively targeted. As a teacher educator, what I find most promising about Megan's classroom practices is that the pluralistic orientation she demonstrated in her VELV questionnaire scores translates to her instructional decision-making. What Megan's anecdote suggests is that in addition to focusing on teaching skills and instructional strategies, teacher education programs need to imbue the program with critical perspectives. If we can introduce preservice teachers to critical understandings of language, provide them with supportive mentor teachers and valuable field experiences, their pluralistic orientations towards language can emerge.

Conclusion

As a group, preservice teachers in this Saskatchewan-based teacher education program do not have a particularly strong pluralistic orientation towards racially, culturally, and linguistically diverse learners. In fact, group mean scores on some of the VELV items suggest that there is still much work to do in terms of supporting preservice teachers in the development of critical orientations towards language. Next, the transition from teacher education to internship doesn't affect students' views in a statistically significant way. Transition to internship/school community does not automatically lead to deficit thinking about language. This is good news in terms of what is often described as a divide between theory and practice. This finding suggests that schools and teacher education programs can work together. Field experiences did, however, influence language views of seven students (two became more pluralistic and five became more deficit). Qualitative data suggest that cooperating teacher and type of school may influence some interns' views.

In terms of influences on preservice teachers' views, findings suggest that factors such as teacher identity, enrollment in critical language education courses, field placements in racially, culturally and linguistically diverse classrooms, and the mentor teacher relationship interact and influence preservice teachers' perspectives differentially. Critical experiences and critical mentors do appear to help participants question dominant school discourses around language. Because of differences in student majors, several participants in secondary programs received little or no critical language teaching content (no multilingual education courses or placements in EAL classrooms) during their teacher education program. This absence may constrain the development of a critical orientation towards language variation. Some students align themselves with their cooperating teacher and dismiss teacher education course content as *theory* or something that is not relevant to classroom practicalities. This dismissal is potentially dangerous because it can provide interns/new teachers with a professionally accepted way to reject social justice–oriented ideas. The finding of the mentor teacher influence on Megan's criticality, in particular, demonstrates the importance of both careful selection of mentor teachers as well as the significance of the relationship between teacher education and the practitioner community in terms of long-term transformation of taken-for-granted assumptions about racially, culturally, and linguistically diverse learners. Teacher education engagement with the field is crucial if teacher education communities are to foster effective communication and social justice–oriented teaching in future teachers. This particular finding may entail systemic reform in teacher education programs.

The research described in this chapter offers several possible directions in terms of future research. Data from this study suggest that mentor teacher and school experience may be factors influencing some interns' views. Future research might explore mentor teacher views of language to better understand this influence on preservice teachers or shadow preservice teachers in their field placements. VELV scores on some items were low, indicating the presence of deficit thinking in relation to language variation and multilingualism. More research is necessary to determine how to shift thinking of preservice teachers. Finally, it's also not clear whether the teacher education program influenced student views in first place. To understand this, it would necessary to test student views prior to beginning their degree programs. Research on this topic might also help us to understand factors that shape student teachers' dispositions prior to becoming educators.

Appendix 7.1

Views of English Language Questionnaire

Where one (1) is the lowest and five (5) is the highest, please respond to the following statements by indicating whether you:

1. Strongly disagree
2. Disagree
3. (Are) undecided
4. Agree
5. Strongly agree

1. Saskatchewan elementary and high school students need to speak proper English.
2. The Saskatchewan Curriculum mandates teachers to teach students to write proper English.
3. As a teacher, one aspect of my job will be to teach students to speak proper English.
4. When students read slang in books and novels used in school, it makes them think that this type of language is acceptable for them to use themselves.
5. Saskatchewan elementary and high school students should learn to write grammatically correct English.
6. Teachers should model the use of proper English
7. As a teacher, all types of English will be welcomed in my classroom
8. As a teacher, inviting English as an Additional Language (EAL) parents to my class will be difficult.
9. As a teacher, it will be my responsibility to correct all spelling, vocabulary, grammatical and sentence structure mistakes when I mark students' writing.
10. As a teacher, I will use poems, novels, and/or other texts with different types of English, including different accents, different English dialects and different registers of English.
11. As a teacher, I will teach my students that there are different types of English, including different accents, different English dialects and different registers of English.
12. Differences between students' home and school Englishes slow down their reading and writing development.
13. Students learning English as an Additional Language (EAL) will learn English more quickly if they speak English at home
14. Kindergarten students who do not speak proper English should be assessed by the speech and language pathologist when they begin school
15. Teachers need help from the speech and language pathologist when English as an Additional Language (EAL) students arrive in class.
16. If English as an Additional Language (EAL) students speak their first languages in class, this will interfere with their English language development.
17. Children with English language delays and impairments live in environments with insufficient language.
18. Speaking more than one language negatively interferes with students' intellectual development within schools.
19. Multilingualism is a positive social and personal resource for learning in Saskatchewan schools.
20. Immigrant students should not use their first languages in English as an Additional Language classroom
21. Younger generations' use of online writing (acronyms like lol; slang; phonetic spelling, and emoticons) has a negative impact on their offline writing development

22. Speech and language assessment tests are an effective way of determining whether a student's language development is typical
23. English as an Additional Language (EAL) students should not take elective classes like French or Music until their English language and literacy skills have been developed to an intermediate level.
24. In classrooms where there are English as an Additional (EAL) students present, teachers should include EAL adaptions in their lesson-planning.
25. Teachers with English as an Additional Language (EAL) students in their classes should make adjustments to the way they speak to the class.
26. Teachers with foreign accents are not ideal language models for Saskatchewan students.
27. Teachers with "native accents" are not ideal language models for Saskatchewan students
28. Grouping immigrant children with the same first language in English as an Additional Language (EAL) classrooms has a positive effect on their English learning.
29. Using a first language while learning English may inhibit immigrant students' English language development.
30. When bilingual students mix languages when they speak, this demonstrates a lack of control over their languages.

References

Alsup, J. (2006). *Teacher identity discourses: Negotiating personal and professional spaces.* Mahwah, NJ: Lawrence Erlbaum Associates, Inc.

Baecher, L. (2012). Examining the place of English language learners across the teacher education curriculum. *Journal of Curriculum and Teaching*, 1(2), 8.

Bakhtin, M. M. (1981). The dialogic imagination: Four essays, ed. Michael Holquist, trans. *Caryl Emerson and Michael Holquist* (Austin: University of Texas Press, 1981), 84(8), 80–2.

Ball, D. L. (1997). Developing mathematics reform: What we don't know about teacher learning—but would make good working hypotheses. In S. N. Friel & G.W. Bright (Eds.), *Reflecting on our work* (pp. 77–111). Lanham, MD: University Press of America.

Blankenship, B. T., & Coleman, M. M. (2009). An examination of "wash-out" and workplace conditions of beginning physical education teachers. *Physical Educator*, 66(2), 97.

Britzman, D. P. 1991. *Practice makes practice: A critical study of learning to teach.* Series. Albany: State University of New York Press.

Brown, C. G., & Scott, J. A. (2014). Who are we choosing for school leaders? A review of university admissions practices. *International Journal of Educational Leadership Preparation*, 9(2), 1–9.

Bourdieu, P. (1991). *Language and symbolic power.* Harvard University Press.

Canagarajah, A. S. (2007). After disinvention: Possibilities for communication, community and competence. In S. Makoni & A. Pennycook (Eds.), *Disinventing and reconstituting languages* (pp. 233–239). Clevedon, England: Multilingual Matters.

Clarke, A., Triggs, V., & Nielsen, W. (2014). Cooperating teacher participation in teacher education: A review of the literature. *Review of Educational Research*, 84(2), 163–202.

Coffey, A., & Atkinson, P. (1996) *Making sense of qualitative data: Complementary research strategies.* Thousand Oaks, CA: Sage Publications.

Childs, R., & Ferguson, A. K. (2016). Changes in, to, and through the initial teacher education program admission process. In L. Thomas, & M. Hirschkorn (Eds.), *Change and progress in Canadian teacher education: Research on recent innovations in teacher preparation in Canada* (pp. 420–440). Ottawa, ON: Canadian Association for Teacher Education.

Dandala, S. (2018). Public accountability and workforce diversity in Canadian public education sector. *Educational Review*, 72(5), 1–13.

Delpit, L., & Dowdy, J. K. (Eds.). (2008). *The skin that we speak: Thoughts on language and culture in the classroom.* The New Press.

Ennser-Kananen, J., & Leider, C. M. (2018). Stop the deficit: Preparing pre-service teachers to work with bilingual students in the United States. In P. Romanowski, & M. Jedynak (Eds.), *Current research in bilingualism and bilingual education* (pp. 173–189). Cham: Springer.

Feagin, J., Orum, A., & Sjoberg, G. (Eds.). (1991). *A case for case study.* Chapel Hill, NC: University of North Carolina Press.

Frykholm, J. A. (1996). Pre-service teachers in mathematics: Struggling with the standards. *Teaching and Teacher Education*, 12(6), 665–681.

García, O. (2016). Critical multilingual language awareness and teacher education. In J. Cenoz, D. Gorter, & S. May (Eds.), *Language awareness and multilingualism* (pp. 1–17). Cham: Springer International Publishing.

Guyton, E., & McIntyre, D. J. (1990). Student teaching and school experience. In W. R. Houston (Ed.), *Handbook of research on teacher education* (pp. 514–534). Thousand Oaks, CA: Corwin.

Guyton, E., & Wesche, M. (1996). Relationships among school context and student teachers' attitudes and performance. In J. McIntyre & D. Byrd (Eds.), *Preparing tomorrow's teachers: The field experience* (pp. 9–25). Thousand Oaks, CA: Corwin.

Harris, L. R., & Brown, G. T. (2010). Mixing interview and questionnaire methods: Practical problems in aligning data. *Practical Assessment, Research, and Evaluation*, 15(1), 1. doi:10.7275/959j-ky83

Holden, M., & Kitchen, J. (2018). Where are we now? Changing admission rates for underrepresented groups in Ontario teacher education. *Canadian Journal of Educational Administration and Policy*, (185). https://journalhosting.ucalgary.ca/index.php/cjeap/issue/view/2999

Holsti, O. R. (1969). *Content analysis for the social sciences and humanities.* Reading, MA: Addison-Wesley.

Johnson, R. B., & Onwuegbuzie, A. J. (2004). Mixed methods research: A research paradigm whose time has come. *Educational Researcher*, 33(7), 14–26.

Labov, W. (1972), *Language in the inner city: Studies in Black English vernacular.* Philadelphia: University of Pennsylvania Press.

Lee, C. D. (2006). Every good-bye ain't gone: Analyzing the cultural underpinnings of classroom talk. *Qualitative Studies in Education*, 19(3), 305–327.

Mackey, W. (2010). History and origins of language policies in Canada. In M. Morris (Ed.), *Canadian language policies in comparative perspective* (pp. 18–66). Montreal & Kingston: McGill–Queen's University Press.

Marom, L. (2019). Under the cloak of professionalism: Covert racism in teacher education. *Race Ethnicity and Education*, 22(3), 319–337.

Nero, S. (Ed.) (2006). *Dialects, Englishes, Creoles, and education.* Mahwah, NJ: Lawrence Erlbaum Associates, Publishers.

Odell, S. J., & Huling, L. (Eds.). (2000). *Quality mentoring for novice teachers*. Indianapolis, IN: Kappa Delta Pi.

Oei, T. I., & Zwart, F. M. (1986). The assessment of life events: Self-administered questionnaire versus interview. *Journal of Affective Disorders*, 10(3), 185–190.

Pettit, S. K. (2011). Teachers' beliefs about English language learners in the mainstream classroom: A review of the literature. *International Multilingual Research Journal*, 5(2), 123–147.

Polat, N., & Mahalingappa, L. (2013). Pre-and in-service teachers' beliefs about ELLs in content area classes: A case for inclusion, responsibility, and instructional support. *Teaching Education*, 24(1), 58–83.

Prendergast, C. (2003) *Literacy and racial justice: The politics of learning after Brown v.* Carbondale: Board of Education, Southern Illinois.

Ryan, J., Pollock, K., & Antonelli, F. (2009). Teacher diversity in Canada: Leaky pipelines, bottlenecks and glass ceilings. *Canadian Journal of Education*, 32(3), 591–617.

Rozelle, J. J., & Wilson, S. M. (2012). Opening the black box of field experiences: How cooperating teachers' beliefs and practices shape student teachers' beliefs and practices. *Teaching and Teacher Education*, 28(8), 1196–1205.

Sterzuk, A. (2010). Indigenous English and standard language ideology: Towards a postcolonial view of English in teacher education. *Canadian Journal of Native Education*, 32, 100–113.

Sterzuk, A. (2011). *The struggle for legitimacy: Indigenized Englishes in settler schools*. Multilingual Matters.

Sterzuk, A. (In press). Building language teacher awareness of colonial histories and imperialistic oppression through the linguistic landscape. In S. Dubreil, D. Malinowski, & H. Maxim (Eds.), *Language teaching in the linguistic landscape*. Springer.

Stille, S., & Cummins, J. (2013). Foundation for learning: Engaging plurilingual students' linguistic repertoires in the elementary classroom. *TESOL Quarterly*, 47(3), 630–638.

von Staden, A. & Sterzuk, A. (2017). Un-frenching des Canadiennes-françaises: Histoires des Fransaskoises en situation linguistique minoritaire. *La revue Canadienne de Linguistique Appliquée*, 20(1), 98–114. https://journals.lib.unb.ca/index.php/CJAL/article/view/24593/29680

Wanzare, Z. (2007). The transition process: The early years of being a teacher. In T. Towsend & R. Bates (Eds.), *Handbook of teacher education: Globalization, standards and professionalism in times of change* (pp. 343–363). Dordrecht: Springer.

Yin, R. (2002). *Case study research. Design and methods* (3rd ed, Applied Social Research Method Series, Vol. 5). *Sage Publications California*.

Zeichner, K., & Tabachnick, B. R. (1981). Are the effects of university teacher education 'washed out' by school experience? *Journal of Teacher Education*, 32(3), 2–6.

8

PRISM OF PROMISE

Towards Responsive Tools for Diverse Classrooms

Patriann Smith and Sara Hajek

A compelling body of evidence focuses on teachers' ability to use culturally and linguistically responsive pedagogy to respond to the diverse needs of learners (e.g., Banks, 2017; Krakouer, 2015; Ladson-Billings, 2014; Lehtomaki et al., 2017; Li, 2017; Lucas & Villegas, 2013). Yet, research continues to highlight teacher unpreparedness as an obstacle for addressing the needs of this increasing culturally and linguistically diverse (CLD) student population (Durgunoğlu & Hughes, 2010; Gay, 2014; Li, 2017). The continued documentation of teacher unpreparedness is likely due to observations that "standardized curricula and pedagogy have supplanted … approaches [to diversity], marginalizing [these approaches] in the greater educational discourse as neoliberal reforms have risen" (Aronson & Laughter, 2016, p. 164; Sleeter, 2012). It is also possible that indications regarding teacher unpreparedness are related to the continued absence of sufficient evidence about student outcomes based on culturally and linguistically responsive practices leveraged in classrooms (Aronson & Laughter, 2016; Sleeter, 2012).

Emerging research suggests that in determining the progress made with teacher responsiveness to CLDs, the focus has been largely on *what* constitutes teacher unpreparedness (Durgunoğlu & Hughes, 2010; Maxwell, 2014; Gay, 2014; Haddix, 2017; Li, 2017; de Oliveira & Athanases, 2007) and less on K–12 *student outcomes* associated with this process, despite the influence of teacher responsiveness to CLDs on these outcomes (Aronson & Laughter, 2016; Dee & Penner, 2016). Across these foci, the *extent to which* teachers demonstrate preparedness or a lack thereof in their responsiveness to CLDs remains unexplored. Many teachers do use generalized pedagogical approaches to address the needs of CLDs (see Aronson & Laughter, 2016; Gay, 2014), and progress thus far with responsiveness to CLDs has been laudable and critical to fulfilling the goals of multicultural education in schools (Risko et al., 2017; Sleeter, 2012). Yet, if teachers lack mechanisms to themselves independently determine and address their responsiveness, they will continue to struggle with the enactment of this responsiveness and rely on teacher educators to do so.

To address this concern, the purpose of this study was to identify the extent to which elements of culturally responsive literacy pedagogy (CRLP) and linguistically responsive literacy pedagogy (LRLP) were visible in self-reports of in-service teachers' literacy practices as they assessed and instructed K–12 learners within the context of an online literacy course. We were also concerned with describing the ways in which in-service teachers' self-reports reflected *varying degrees* of CRLP and LRLP. We asked the questions:

1. To what extent do in-service teachers' self-reports reflect elements of CRLP and LRLP based on their literacy instruction and assessment within the context of an online literacy assessment course?
2. In what ways are varying degrees of CRLP and LRLP represented in the in-service teacher self-reports?

Culturally and Linguistically Responsive Pedagogy

Culturally relevant pedagogy, "the ability to link principles of learning with deep understanding of (and appreciation for) culture" (Ladson-Billings, 2014, p. 77), provided a lens in this study to view diversity in the literate practices of teachers. Its extension, *culturally sustaining pedagogy*, the "multiplicities of identities and cultures that help formulate today's youth culture" (Ladson-Billings, 2014, p. 82), also served as a way to consider how teachers addressed linguistic diversity based on interactions across monocultural and multicultural populations. We were interested in how literacy teachers enhanced students' literacy success, cultural competence and sociopolitical consciousness (Ladson-Billings, 2014) while, at the same time, helped CLDs transculturally to support the literacies of their *majority* student peers in ways that empowered all students to better relate to difference in the literacy classroom (Smith et al., 2017).

Linguistically responsive pedagogy (LRP) also functioned as a lens given the increasing linguistic diversity in and beyond U.S. schools. LRP allowed us to identify and describe teachers' responses to the needs of learners across a wide range of linguistic groups (e.g., Li, 2017; Lucas & Villegas, 2013) given that teachers who make a significant change in students' literacies must have social and academic language proficiency, knowledge of students' cultural and linguistic diversity; multilingual awareness; knowledge of linguistic components; create comfortable learning environments; and engender translingualism (Au, 2000; Cummins, 2008; García, 2008; Jessner, 2006; Krashen, 2003; Pennycook, 2008; Wright, 2002).

Critical Multilingual and Multicultural Awareness

Without awareness of language and culture, teachers may struggle to reflect the tenets of CRP and LRP described earlier (see Smith et al., 2020). As such, pedagogy could be influenced by the degree to which multilingual and multicultural awareness is reflected by literacy teachers (García, 2008; Nieto, 2000; Smith et al., 2020). "Multilingual awareness" refers to a knowledge of the subject matter of the language an educator uses to support literacy, social and pragmatic norms and to the teacher's ability to create opportunities for learning language through literacy in the classroom (García, 2015). And "multicultural awareness" represents a person's ability to note predispositions such as biased views, a tendency to adopt a worldview that incorporates varying perspectives and knowledge about people and events unfamiliar to them (see Nieto, 2000).

The extensions of these constructs, critical multilingual and critical multicultural awareness (García, 2015; Nieto & Bode, 2008) have also been shown to help literacy teachers move beyond static ways of responding to students' languages and cultures. Such forms of awareness draw from plurilingualism for democratic citizenship, determine how literacy reinforces or challenges colonial histories and identify how literacy uses language to reflect its unending social creation and change (García, 2015) while also alerting educators to norms that reinforce or challenge various forms of oppression, their role in contributing to or deconstructing these norms and how their actions contribute to or reenact the power structures that adversely affect nondominant populations (Nieto & Bode, 2008; Roxas et al., 2017).

Exploring Responsiveness and Awareness in an Online Literacy Community

Guided by the aforementioned conceptions of awareness and responsiveness, we used an exploratory interpretive qualitative design (Neuman, 2004) to inform our examinations of the research questions in this "comparatively small [course] community" (p. 15). As course instructor, I (Author 1) taught a community of in-service teachers to approach diversity within an online instructional setting regarding a specific content area—literacy—the research setting of which was particularly new to us.

The research was conducted at a large public university in the southwestern United States for a duration of 16 weeks each, within the context of a graduate online reading assessment course held in the Fall semesters of (2015) and (2017) and upon receiving permission from the university's institutional review board. During this period, I taught the course via asynchronous and synchronous methods focusing on perspectives, instructional strategies and assessments in reading/literacy, readings on diversity in reading/literacy, practical applications of literacy, assessment and intervention. Students (i.e., in-service teachers) enrolled in the course were expected to prepare a case study for dissemination to stakeholders (i.e., teachers, administrators, parents) based on materials developed and activities in which they engaged throughout each semester (see Appendix 8.1).

The In-Service Teachers

In addition to my participation as instructor, the study included 14 participants (i.e., in-service teachers) in the Fall of 2015 and 15 participants in the Fall of 2017, totaling 29 participants. Most participants were master's (22) and the rest were doctoral students (7). Students were all women between the ages of 25 to 55 years old seeking degrees in language and literacy education (27) or bilingual education (2). A majority were Caucasian and monolingual, and four were bilingual-speaking students (i.e., Arabic, German, Korean, Spanish). The in-service teachers had each taught for at least one year and, throughout the course, worked with K–12 learners who presented cultural, geographical, linguistic, racial, national, class, religious or other differences in relation to teachers' personal backgrounds.

Approach to Diversity in the Course

To emphasize diversity within the context of the course, I included specific guidelines within the syllabus that helped in-service teachers to identify K–12 learners with whom they would work based on the notion of diversity as situated within an interaction between the teacher and student as opposed to being located *within a specific population* (see Smith et al., 2017). I also provided readings from books and articles regarding diversity (e.g., Herrera et al., 2012; Risko, 2012), prompting students, on an ongoing basis, to draw on and use these readings in their synopses (described later) as they critiqued assessment and instruction practices in their support of K–12 learners. I modeled to students how to engage in these processes through my ongoing qualitative feedback and followed guidelines regarding social presence, cognitive presence and teaching presence, as well as an appreciation of students' individuality and cultures, connections to each other, conflict resolution and awareness of culture (e.g., Grant & Lee, 2014; Kumi-Yeboah et al., 2017).

Teacher Synopses and Responses as a Basis for Inquiry

Data for this study accrued naturally from the course and took the form of in-service teachers' weekly synopses as well as asynchronous responses to these synopses based on their assessment and instruction of K–12 learners in relation to assigned readings over 16 weeks *each* for the Fall of 2015 and 2017. Each synopsis contained students' reactions and responses, summaries of assessment or instructional processes, recommendations and connections between instructional processes and assigned readings. Altogether, student synopses and their corresponding asynchronous discussions were downloaded from the Blackboard course at the end of the course, de-identified and then compiled into a total of approximately 1,000 Microsoft Word pages of single-spaced, Times New Roman–font content in preparation for analysis.

Making Sense of Teacher Synopses and Responses

Qualitative analysis involved procedures for open coding using the QDA Miner analysis tool. First, we (Authors 1 and 2) iteratively and collaboratively coded participants' synopses and asynchronous discussions from the first module of Fall (2015) using QDA Miner to determine the depictions of CRLP and LRLP as well as initiate a ranking system for these elements that would serve as an initial guide for coding and classifying remaining modules along a continuum. The identified codes allowed for a six-level ranking system and were labeled from *least responsive* (i.e., Levels 0, 1 and 2) to *more responsive* (i.e., Levels 3, 4, 5) in relation to both CRLP and LRLP. In this way, the codes (i.e., levels) depicted the degree to which teachers were responsive to students along a spectrum (see Figures 8.1 and 8.2 for operational definitions of CRLP and LRLP levels). Second, Author 2 generated frequency analyses using QDA Miner to indicate the number of occurrences of CRLP and LRLP reflected by participants across all modules from the Fall of (2015) and (2017).

Understanding Teacher Awareness and Responsiveness across a Spectrum

Findings from our analyses revealed degrees of representativeness of CRLP and LRLP elements, reflected across a wide range of literacy practices, including motivation, word recognition, comprehension, biliteracy, bilingualism, literature, fluency and writing.

Culturally Responsive Literacy Pedagogy

The degree of representativeness of CRLP is reflected in Table 8.1. Most participants operated at "Level 0" of CRLP, demonstrating unawareness of culturally responsive and sustaining pedagogies and fewer participants operating at "Levels 2, 3, 4 and 5".

Level 0. Participants operating at a CRLP Level 0 reflected statements that suggested unawareness of their students' cultural backgrounds, experiences, or viewpoints. Not only were these participants unaware of their own positionality in the classroom, but they also did not understand how or why their students viewed the classroom differently than themselves. Some comments reflected frustration on the part of the participants toward their students without recognizing

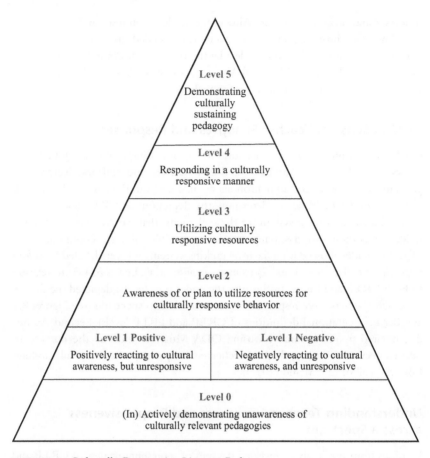

FIGURE 8.1   Culturally Responsive Literacy Pedagogy

the bigger picture of students' unique cultural backgrounds. One participant wrote, "He was having a bad day, so it felt like we were back to square one", reflecting her frustration with the literary task at hand but unwilling to acknowledge the unique challenges that the student faced. In response, a participant's cultural unawareness was reflected in the following statement: "I can't wait for the day when S can spell illiterate and say, 'That is not me!'" With this statement, the participant suggests that this student presents no literacies in the classroom, a notion that provides support for the view that CLDs' "invisible literacies" are often overlooked in classrooms (Dyson, 2015).

Level 1 "Negative" and "Positive." Participants operating at a CRLP Level 1 "Negative" and Level 1 "Positive" reflected an awareness of their students' unique cultural backgrounds and saw these backgrounds as different from that

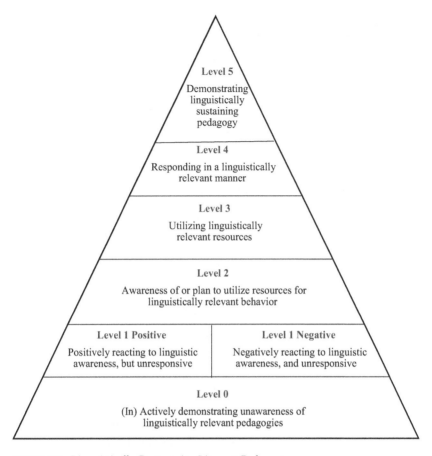

FIGURE 8.2 Linguistically Responsive Literacy Pedagogy

of participants. However, certain participants viewed these cultural backgrounds as problematic in some way while others viewed them as a positive element. We coded instances of the former as "Level 1 Negative" and instances of the latter as "Level 1 Positive".

Level 1 "Negative". Many participants operating at a CRLP Level 1 "Negative" seemed to react in significantly negative ways towards students, making assumptions about students' background knowledge when they recognized difference. For instance, there were statements such as, "I have found in working with our 3rd grade ELL [English language learner] population that they were not aware that [they] needed to be thinking as they were reading." Although this statement was not exactly clear and while it may have been the case that there was a positive orientation based on the usefulness of thinking during reading – metacognition (Afflerbach et al., 2008), this participant, as with other participants in Year 1, made

TABLE 8.1 Culturally Responsive Frequencies

Category	Code	Description	Count	Codes (%)
Cultural	Zero	Actively demonstrating unawareness of culturally relevant pedagogy	126	31.8%
Cultural	One Positive	Positively reacting to cultural awareness, but unresponsive	123	31%
Cultural	One Negative	Negatively reacting to cultural unawareness and unresponsive	53	13.38%
Cultural	Two	Awareness of or plan to utilize resources for culturally relevant behavior	30	7.57%
Cultural	Three	Utilizing culturally relevant resources	24	6%
Cultural	Four	Responding in a culturally relevant manner	30	7.57%
Cultural	Five	Demonstrating culturally sustaining pedagogy	10	2.52%
			396	100%

a blanket statement that inadvertently appeared to essentialize all ELL students within the school context, reflecting stereotypical norms (Nieto, 2000).

Level 1 "Positive". On the other end of this level of CRLP were teachers operating at a Level 1 "Positive". At this level, participants made various comments about cultural differences with regard to their students and attached positive associations to these differences. However, these participants did not go to the extent of talking about resources available to support students who they identified as different from themselves upon embarking on the case study. In her description, one participant made it clear that her student's scores on state standards were not the fault of the student herself but rather from something yet unknown, reflecting that she recognized the student's capacity for success even while wanting to address the challenge (Ladson-Billings, 2014). She stated:

> I am thankful that she is so willing to participate in class... . I am also glad that she is so confident in her abilities in class. This is just another example of why I am so confused as to why she isn't meeting the state standards on her reading and writing tests.

Level 2. Participants operating at a CRLP Level 2 not only demonstrated an awareness of students' cultural backgrounds, experiences and viewpoints (Nieto, 2000), but they were also aware of resources available to address the unique needs of serving these students in the classroom. However, they did not rise to the level of cultural responsiveness where they described their use of these (i.e., Level 3) despite having opportunities to do so based on iterative feedback provided during the course. One participant wrote, "This [technology app] is especially helpful for those struggling students. Something happens to them when they are using technology apps". In this example, the participant was aware of her student's struggles but did not blame the student for these struggles. Instead, she recognized that a change was necessary and was aware of resources available to address in the student's struggles. However, this participant did not go so far as to discuss the implementation of the technology apps or discuss specifically how the apps might assist the student who was struggling (Cahill & McGill-Franzen, 2013). Although seemingly reflecting awareness of the need for knowledge about the student and technology that seemed unfamiliar (Nieto, 2000), and therefore, a shift towards higher tiers of CRLP, this participant did not work to identify how she would foster cultural competence regarding this technology to enhance the student's academic (i.e., literacy) success (Ladson-Billings, 2014).

Level 3. Participants operating at a CRLP Level 3 appeared to go beyond recognizing the need for cultural relevance (Nieto, 2000). As with Level 2, participants operating at this level demonstrated their awareness of students' varied cultural background, experiences and viewpoints, their awareness of resources available to help these students in the classroom and mentioned the ways in which they would utilize these resources in the present and/or future. Despite significantly referencing resources in Level 2, the reported *use* of these resources in participants' classrooms was a far less frequently documented occurrence—the second-lowest CRLP-coded frequency.

Operating at a Level 3 was one participant who discussed specifically how she would change her own behavior or the way she managed her classroom in order to serve the needs of her student. She wrote, "I'm going to try a different approach when I see J tomorrow… I have located some leveled readers from the Reading Interventionist and I am going to use those". Not only was this participant aware of her student's needs, but she was also cognizant of the resources necessary for changing her behavior to fit the needs of her struggling student. Admittedly, the presence of a specific plan to utilize the resource did not necessarily translate into a Level 4 because there was no mention of additionally relevant information about the use of culturally responsive considerations to guide choices made about this literature while also keeping the specific student's difference in mind (Harris, 2008). In a sense, the participant was aware of her student's needs, aware of resources, had a plan to use said resources in a specific way but did not indicate that when using leveled readers, there was the potential for these texts to overlook literacy that draws from plurilingualism (García, 2015) in ways that could inadvertently reinforce various forms of oppression (Nieto & Bode, 2008; Roxas et al., 2017) and omit a worldview that incorporated varying perspectives (see Nieto, 2000).

Level 4. Participants operating at a CRLP Level 4 also met the criterion of operating at Level 2 and 3 on CRLP and demonstrated their willingness to change as well as adapt *themselves* in response to student needs. Many of the instances of this type of cultural responsiveness were related to participants' recognition of the student as presenting legitimate differences and the potential for elements in the environment to be adjusted in responding to the needs of the student (i.e., student as a *constant* and everything else as the *variable*). For example, one of the most moving and poignant examples of cultural responsiveness at the CRLP Level 4 came in the form of a suggestion from a participant towards another peer in the course when the observation was made that a K–12 student was always "off-topic" during intervention and assessment sessions by talking about her own family. In response to this observation, the responding peer operating at CRLP Level 4 suggested that the participant try to first recognize patterns when this 'off-topic' behavior is occurring, assess factors impacting the behavior, reflect and then try to pull materials which would lead the student into the lesson by utilizing her desire to talk about her own family in the lesson. This peer concluded her feedback by stating that following the steps above would "seem more organic to [the student] and less frustrating". Such an example appears to indicate that participants operating at CRLP Level 4 reflected a willingness to understand and sustain the various cultures in which youth's literacies practices are embedded (Ladson-Billings, 2014, p. 82). The participants in these cases appeared to consider themselves *but a variable* in each student's learning journey and made changes to their views of what it typically means to be compliant in the classroom through awareness of their roles in deconstructing such a norm that could become oppressive to the "multiple identities and cultures of students" even as they worked to address diversity and enhance academic (i.e., literacy) success (Ladson-Billings, 2014, p. 82).

Level 5. Participants operating at a CRLP Level 5 demonstrated culturally sustaining pedagogy, indicating that they were not only willing to change *themselves* to reflect students' needs, as with Level 4–coded interactions, but that they also reflected sustained and constant change in response to the differences presented by CLDs. At this level, participants seemed to embody self-awareness that extended beyond recognizing difference in others. Participants (a) viewed their students in a positive way, (b) were aware of and planned to use resources to support culturally responsive pedagogy, (c) used said resources and (d) most significantly, consistently and seamlessly adhered to the elements of CRLP Levels 2, 3, 4 and 5 throughout their work with the student throughout the course. These examples ranged from a clearly adaptive participant who changed according to his or her students' needs to a participant who found it important to discuss what was on his or her student's mind before addressing the day's lesson. The teacher in the latter example wrote, "Z's background knowledge about magazine advertisements… seems to be limited… . This leads me to believe she is 'uninterested' in this text… Would a [low-]SES background student [*sic*] struggle to read this text? Yes! … Again, educators must be sensitive to the needs of our students". She also went on to describe, in detail, the resources she would use as she progressed through the project with this student.

Another participant at Level 5 stated, "We are all subconsciously primed to perceive things in a certain way because of predetermined labels". With this recognition of perception, the participant appeared to truly understand what it meant to be diverse as she was aware that all interactions reflected some elements of diversity. She recognized that everyone possesses bias and therefore operated from the position that students are labeled in certain ways that create bias (Nieto, 2000). From there, she described how labels were merely a contrived notion of how a student should act and explained how she consistently and individually treated her students based on their specific cultural or linguistic backgrounds. By merely recognizing that these contrived labels existed, this participant automatically operated from a position of critical awareness about how power structures can adversely affect nondominant populations and seemed constantly primed to recognize when she needed to change to fit the needs of her students and to enhance their sociopolitical consciousness (Ladson-Billings, 2014; Roxas et al., 2017).

Linguistically Responsive Pedagogy

The degree of representativeness of LRLP is reflected in Table 8.2, reflecting that most participants operated at "Level 0" of LRLP and very few participants operating "Levels 1, 2, 3, 4 and 5".

Level 0. Participants operating at an LRLP Level 0 seemed unaware of linguistically relevant pedagogy. For instance, a participant wrote, "How are we as secondary teachers supposed to meet their language needs if we have to build

TABLE 8.2 Linguistically Responsive Frequencies

Category	Code	Description	Count	% Codes
Linguistic	Zero	Actively demonstrating unawareness of linguistically relevant pedagogy	22	44.89%
Linguistic	One Positive	Positively reacting to linguistic awareness, but unresponsive	14	28.57
Linguistic	One Negative	Negatively reacting to linguistic unawareness and unresponsive	5	12.24
Linguistic	Two	Awareness of or plan to utilize resources for linguistically relevant behavior	6	10.20
Linguistic	Three	Utilizing linguistically relevant resources	0	0.0
Linguistic	Four	Responding in a linguistically relevant manner	2	4.08
Linguistic	Five	Demonstrating linguistically sustaining pedagogy	0	0.0
			49	100

their entire English foundation, while also teaching on-grade level text?" The assumption here was that the student arrived to the class completely devoid of an English-language foundation. Based on the tenets of both culturally and linguistically responsive pedagogy where students have a knowledge of, draw from, and sustain students' cultures and languages (Ladson-Billings, 2014; Lucas & Villegas, 2013), this assumption appears to not only be incorrect but also damaging to the future relationship between teacher and student. Another participant echoed similar sentiments stating, "It's incredibly difficult to have students learn new words when they can't even pronounce them". These participants judged students based solely on the notion that having a linguistic background different from that of the dominant population meant that the *students* reflected a deficit, which, in turn, posed a hindrance to instruction. They insinuated that the lesson would be much easier if the students were to arrive in the instructional setting with a linguistic background that was based on the monolingual standardized English norm (Flores, 2013). In turn, negative assumptions ensued about the students' ability to learn, which were, in turn, associated with the student's linguistic background when mechanisms could have been put in place to support vocabulary learning across languages. Such examples suggest that there was learning to be gained about social and academic language proficiency (Cummins, 2008) as well as developing a plurilingual perspective (García, 2015) in addressing students' language differences.

Level 1 "Negative". Participants operating at an LRLP Level 1 "Negative" were aware of their students' diverse experience with language but viewed this experience in a negative way. Teachers at this level negatively reacted to their own linguistic awareness and were unresponsive to their students' needs. During instances where LRLP Level 1 "Negative" appeared to be reflected, one participant in Year 1 stated,

> She only has less than two years of formal education left at this point before she will either enter the work force [*sic*] as an adult or attempt to pursue higher education. With her current set of limitations in her understanding of the English language, I am afraid for her prospects of getting an education beyond high school.

This participant seemed to view her student from a deficit perspective. Similarly, another participant wrote, "My student was an ELL who was almost at grade level but parents only spoke Spanish at home. Language was an evident hurdle in his learning". The preceding excerpt reflected an unawareness of linguistic differences. The participant, at first reading seemed to be making a simple observation about her selected student. At close glance, despite being aware of this student's linguistic difference, this difference was viewed in a negative way.

Level 1 "Positive". Participants operating at an LRLP Level 1 "Positive" reflected a positively reaction to linguistic awareness but were unresponsive. For instance, one participant stated:

My hypothesis on the "th" and the "y" are that these may stem from her native language being Spanish and coming from a Spanish speaking home. There is no equivalent to the "th" sound in the Spanish language and it seems she has missed this piece of phonics instruction in formal education. In observing what she tried to do with y's as she encountered them in words, I thought her pronunciation of them seemed to be coming from what they would do in Spanish rather than the rules the y follows in English. Similarly, two vowels next to each other in Spanish usually stand for two distinct sounds, whereas many adjacent vowels in English are vowel teams making only one sound, the rules of which change depending on the individual word. On the names test in particular I noticed that if she did not know a name, she seemed to try Spanish sounds just as often as she tried English sounds to decode the name.

We coded this commentary as "Positive" because the teacher demonstrated a clear acknowledgment about the student's difference in linguistic background. She demonstrated her personal knowledge of both Spanish and English based on plurilingualism (García, 2015) and did not use a deficit lens to approach the student's misunderstanding. This teacher, however, did not act to engage with the difference in language and instead, merely stated that it existed.

Level 2. Participants operating at an LRLP Level 2 demonstrated an awareness of resources available to them which could help to support students' unique language needs in the classroom but did not go so far as to indicate plans for implementation. For instance, one participant operating at Level 2 mentioned her awareness of resources or of knowledge that could affect the way she interacted with students of various linguistic backgrounds. Another wrote about a piece of technology that would assist her non-native English speakers, sharing, "Yes, it was a digital voice. . . . A little strange and I wish the pronunciation was better and I would use it with new English learners. You type and it talks and you can give it different accents. I could see students getting a kick out of it".

The preceding comment was coded at a Level 2 because the participants not only recognized that the students had a linguistic background different from their own, but they also reflected plurilingualism, a knowledge of linguistic components of the subject matter of the language an educator uses to support literacy, as well as the ability to create opportunities for learning language through literacy in the classroom (García, 2015; Wright, 2002).

Level 4. The participant operating at a LRLP Level 4 demonstrated an awareness of her student's unique linguistic needs in the classroom, but she also discussed resources available to meet this student's needs *as well as* described how she had used these resources or knowledge in the past and/or planned to use them in the future. The participant wrote:

It wasn't until I taught Pre–K, and I learned about the foundations of literacy, that I began to teach the students to recognize patterns and I thought about spelling rules. Furthermore, since many of my Pre–K students were ELLs, I approached their learning from a different perspective because many of my students didn't understand me at all. Therefore, I had to develop different strategies for getting the students to understand classroom routines and activities. The way that I taught spelling as a 4th grade teacher did not help these students with English language acquisition because it didn't take into consideration anything regarding the student's native language. Strict, rote memorization was how spelling was implemented.

This example of operating at a LRLP Level 4 represented the participant who was actively responding to her linguistically diverse students in a way where she positioned herself and the curriculum as the variable—capable of undergoing continuous change—in relation to the student for whom she was responsible. Not only did this participant recognize that linguistic differences between herself and her students existed, but she also did not attach a negative perspective to those differences (Lucas & Villegas, 2013). Additionally, she viewed her literacy curriculum in relation to her students rather than viewing her students as peripheral to the curriculum. In other words, instead of blaming students for their failure, she viewed both herself and the district-mandated curriculum as reinforcing oppressive norms that were detrimental to her students (Roxas et al., 2017).

Towards Informal Tools for Responsiveness and a Prism of Promise

We embarked on this study to examine the ways in which in-service teachers reflected certain elements of CRLP and LRLP in their literacy practice and the varying degrees along which CRLP and LRLP were reflected in this practice. Findings suggest that operating at the higher end of CRLP seemed to be represented by a change in behavior and pedagogical responsiveness based on and in response to the evolving evidence regarding student diversity while also seeking a positive explanation for students' differences by working actively to address and deconstruct oppressive norms (Ladson-Billings, 2014; Lucas & Villegas, 2013; Roxas et al., 2017). Indications of self-reflection (Tschannen-Moran & Woolfolk Hoy, 2001) also seemed visible as teachers appeared to recognize self as the most malleable variable—the ones who supposedly held the power to engage students as they adapted to the cultural ebb and flow of students' literacy journeys.

The CRLP and LRLP gradations generated in this study revealed how responsiveness functioned along a continuum. This provided a basis for our creation of corresponding informal CRLP and LRLP tools, which literacy teachers can use to develop responsiveness. These informal tools (see Tables 8.3 and 8.4), developed based on our findings reflect: (a) descriptors of participants' culturally

TABLE 8.3 Informal Tool for Culturally Responsive Literacy Pedagogy

Level	Definition	Example 1	Explanation	Reflexive Questions
Zero	Participants who were coded at this level operate in a way that lends them to make statements which reflect their complete unawareness of their students' cultural backgrounds, experiences, or viewpoints. These participants are blatantly unaware of how or why their students might view the classroom differently than themselves.	"It's weird to think about students in fourth and fifth grade needing this assistance. I sure am glad to discover their needs while I can address them and not farther down in their education when I will not be able to help them" (Level 0, Module 4, Year 2).	This participant seems unable to understand why her students might have difficulty in reading and does not attempt to associate any other cause for the difficulty (i.e., background experience, cultural difference, negative previous educational encounters) and therefore comes to the conclusion that the students will indefinitely need reading assistance if she does not step in now to intervene. In addition to a lack of knowledge about cultural background as a factor affecting literacy, this participant also acts with a "savior complex" indicating that she does not believe her students can be successful without her.	How do I reflect an awareness of my students' cultural backgrounds, experiences, or viewpoints? How and why might my students' cultural backgrounds, experiences, or viewpoints differ from my own?

Continued

TABLE 8.3 Informal Tool for Culturally Responsive Literacy Pedagogy (*Continued*)

Level	Definition	Example 1	Explanation	Reflexive Questions
One Negative	Participants who were coded at this level have an awareness of their students' varied cultural backgrounds, experiences, and viewpoints but view this as problematic in some way	"For example, I have a diverse group of students. Out of my 125 students, approximately one-third of them are labeled as 'at-risk' and did not meet the state passing standard on their 7th grade reading STAAR test. These students come from many different backgrounds and have a wide array of interests. It would be very difficult to complete IRI's, use the data, and plan an intervention for each of these students with the time constraints and curriculum requirements that are placed on me in the general education classroom; however, this may work for a reading enrichment or resource class. These classes are typically much smaller and students could be grouped by interests and/or targeted areas from their IRI's. The teacher would be able to put them in small groups and provide more one- on-one attention" (Level One Negative, Module 6, Year 1).	In this excerpt, the teacher admits her awareness of students' diverse background. She is clearly aware of their economic diversity and "different backgrounds", but rather than view this diversity through the lens of an educator determined to do what she can for students' literacy journey, she writes about her own difficulties in helping this third of her students and goes so far as to associate a resource classroom as the best place for utilizing a tool that she discusses. Rather than view the tool as an option to help her diverse students, she views it as something that could not be of benefit to her student.	How do I view students when I have an awareness of their varied cultural backgrounds, experiences, or viewpoints? Do I reflect a deficit perspective to the varied cultural backgrounds, experiences, or viewpoints of which I am aware? Do I believe or feel that these varied cultural backgrounds, experiences, or viewpoints are problematic for literacy learning in the classroom?

| One Positive | Participants who were coded at this level have an awareness of their students' varied cultural backgrounds, experiences, and viewpoints, and view them in a positive way. At this level, participants show awareness, but do not mention an effort to respond to these students in a culturally relevant way | "I completely understand because reading out loud in an 11th grade English class, students feel they shouldn't struggle with many words and their peers like to point it out when they say a word wrong which leads to embarrassment and fear of ever reading again" (Level 1 Positive, Module 3, Year 1). | This participant operates with a small bit of background knowledge that has helped her to make better decisions as a teacher. She is aware of her students' feelings and emotions when reading out loud. Even though this feeling of embarrassment is most likely not felt by this participant now, she understands what it is like for a struggling reader to read out loud in class. If she were to mention resources to curb this embarrassment, she would be operating at a Level 3. | How do I view students when I have an awareness of their varied cultural backgrounds, experiences, or viewpoints? How do I reflect a positive perspective to these elements? How do I believe or feel that these varied cultural backgrounds, experiences, or viewpoints present assets for literacy learning in the classroom? |

Continued

TABLE 8.3 Informal Tool for Culturally Responsive Literacy Pedagogy (*Continued*)

Level	Definition	Example 1	Explanation	Reflexive Questions
Two	Participants at this level are aware of their students' varied cultural backgrounds, experiences, and viewpoints *and* are aware of resources to help students of varied cultural backgrounds become successful in their classrooms. These participants, however, do not allude to utilizing these resources in any way in the future.	"I have to admit, when I started this assessment with my Fifth Grader, I assumed it would be too simplistic. However, after assessing 'Z', I learned my lesson" (Level 2, Module 4, Year 2).	In this example, the participant used a resource available to her in one situation. She is therefore aware of at least one resource available to her. She is also aware that her own biases were disbanded because of this resource. However, she does not mention future resources available to her that would further her student's literacy journey. In other words, this participant used one resource available to her, but did not make plans based on this exchange for utilization of further resources in the future.	How do I acknowledge the resources that support my ability to address the varied cultural backgrounds, experiences, or viewpoints of students? Do I identify the ways that I can use these resources to facilitate students' literacies in the future?
	At this level, participants are aware of their students' varied cultural backgrounds, experiences, and viewpoints, are also aware of resources to help them work with students of said cultural diversity, *and* mention the ways in which they will utilize the resources with students.	"When we conducted the surveys with our case study students, I noticed that mine didn't have any reading role models. I suspect this is the case with many of our struggling readers. So by implementing this and reading with them, I am modeling good reading for them" (Level 3, Module 6, Year 1).	At this level, this participant utilized a resource available to her (reading surveys) and found information based on that resource. She then also discusses how she used this information to respond in a way that does not blame students for their lack of reading role models, but rather talks about how she will now implement new ideas in the future in order to support her struggling readers	How do I acknowledge the resources that support my ability to address the varied cultural backgrounds, experiences, or viewpoints of students? In what ways do I consider a variety of diverse needs as I use resources to support students' literacies?

| Four | Participants who were coded at this level operate with all of the intentions of a level 3 participant, but *also* repeated past, present, and future instances where they have, are, or will utilize relevant resources to aid students in the classroom. These participants operate in a way that is culturally responsive which *also* means that they are willing to change *themselves* to respond to students' needs. | "I had a word wall for the first couple of years I taught and was shocked to discover that my kids were completely oblivious to it! When we started interacting with the words via different activities and hands-on materials, the world wall became an actual resource for my kids. I've also learned that your word walls should be fluid. They should change depending on the words your students encounter and/or struggle with" (Level 4, Module 8, Year 1). | This participant wrote about her willingness to change in response to her students' literacy needs. She wrote about a past experience that has shaped her current view on literacy. Rather than simply keep her resource static and expect her students to adapt, she changed the way she utilized the resource and responded to students' classroom behavior in a way that brought the information to them. Additionally, she discussed that the word wall should be based on words that "students encounter and/or struggle with", meaning that she is also aware of students' background knowledge and is willing to incorporate it into the classroom in an obvious and supportive way. | How do I rethink how I respond to the varied cultural backgrounds, experiences, or viewpoints of students? How am I being open to new ways of viewing, learning, and envisioning the world, the texts with which I work, the way my students interpret various texts, the languages and dialects my students bring? How can I use these assets to help students develop confidence and success in their literacy learning in classrooms? |

Continued

TABLE 8.3 Informal Tool for Culturally Responsive Literacy Pedagogy (*Continued*)

Level	Definition	Example 1	Explanation	Reflexive Questions
Five	Participants operating at the highest level of the hierarchy operate at the level of culturally sustainment. This means that the participants indicate their core values are aligned with a cultural awareness in a way that *every* interaction with their students reflects a belief that students are at the core of learning and are therefore are continuously changing *themselves* to reflect students' needs.	"I have worked out a strategy with J where he will spell a word that he is struggling with three different ways. Then, he brings it to me or his teacher, and we will help guide him towards the correct spelling. This strategy is really helping him because he is using his knowledge of letter association but there have been several instances where one of the words he has practiced with is correct. By doing this, J is manipulating the letters, and this strategy is really helping him to understand the letter-sounds association. In addition, J is pretty proud of himself when he gets one of the spellings correct, so this is also helping to boost his confidence" (Level 5, Module 5, Year 1).	Operating at the highest level on the cultural awareness hierarchy, this participant recognizes that her student struggled in the area of letter association but does not blame him for it. Instead, she utilizes a self-constructed strategy in order to target specific literacy needs that are unique to her student. Additionally, this participant recognizes that it is not simply a skill that the student needs to work on, but also that he needs to build confidence in himself. By recognizing that she must work in the classroom on her student's literacy confidence, this participant is operating on the premise that she must not only work with the student to help him with his letter–association but also with foundational confidence to lead a life of successful literacy. In this way, she is extending her influence beyond her own interactions with the student but also setting him up for success well into his future.	How do I rethink who I am, what I think, and how I see the world as I respond to the varied cultural backgrounds, experiences, or viewpoints of students? In what ways are my responses to students' differences consistent with the value that I place on diversity regardless of where I am? How am I working as an advocate for students' literacy needs on a consistent basis by considering the differences, they present in my classroom? How am I consistently rethinking the

resources I use and my interactions with students in ways that challenge me to maintain a welcoming approach to students' cultural differences?

In short, this participant recognizes the student's needs, utilizes a strategy that will help him to be successful, ensures that this strategy is utilized often, and considers the student's future in literacy by working indirectly on his confidence. She has adapted both herself and the curriculum to meet the student's needs.

TABLE 8.4 Informal Tool for Linguistically Responsive Literacy Pedagogy

Level	Definition	Example 1	Explanation	Reflexive Questions
Zero	Participants at this level make statements that demonstrate their complete unawareness of linguistic diversity and how it functions.	"I have found in my time as an instructional coach that many of our 'dual teachers' can speak English 'fluently' but even they do not have a handle on the grammar, and vocabulary that is needed in STAAR" (Module 5, Year 1, Level 0).	This participant goes on to attack the dual-language teachers that she coaches, starting with certainty that they are essentially unqualified to teach because of their own linguistic backgrounds.	How do I reflect an awareness of my students' varied linguistic backgrounds, experiences, or viewpoints? How and why might my students' varied linguistic backgrounds, experiences, or viewpoints differ from my own?
One Negative	Participants are aware of their students' diverse experiences with language but view these experiences with a negative outlook.	"My student was an ELL who was almost at grade level but parents only spoke Spanish at home. Language was an evident hurdle in his learning" (Module 4, Year 2, Level 1 Negative).	This participant associates the student's literacy achievement negatively with his home language, then goes on to talk about his first language as a 'hurdle in his learning' rather than viewing it as simply the way in which the student communicates at home.	How do I view students when I have an awareness of their varied linguistic backgrounds, experiences, or viewpoints? If I do, why might I reflect a deficit perspective to the varied linguistic backgrounds, experiences, or viewpoints of which I am aware? What do I believe or feel about these varied linguistic backgrounds, experiences, or viewpoints? Do I feel like they are problematic for literacy learning in the classroom?

| One Positive | Participants are aware of their students' diverse experiences with language and view them with a positive outlook. | "I am certain moving between two languages can be difficult" (Module 5, Year 1, Level 1 Positive). | This participant is both aware of the students' background language and has the realization that it must be difficult for them to move between the two. She does not view the bilingualism of her students in negative terms. | How do I view students when I have an awareness of their varied linguistic backgrounds, experiences, or viewpoints? How do I reflect a positive perspective to these elements? How do I believe or feel that these varied cultural backgrounds, experiences, or viewpoints present assets for literacy learning in the classroom? |

Continued

TABLE 8.4 Informal Tool for Linguistically Responsive Literacy Pedagogy (*Continued*)

Level	Definition	Example 1	Explanation	Reflexive Questions
Two	At this level, participants are aware of resources available to them which will assist students of linguistic diversity. They do not yet discuss specific plans for implementation.	"The sounds of each letter, syllable and phonemes are much different in English than in Spanish. T has been in a Bilingual and now Dual Language Classroom since he began school. Spanish is a phonetic language and therefore, I can say that T may be confused in the sounds that a word can make when reading. A 'struggling reader' in light of phonological awareness is very possible if there are deficiencies like in T's case. Not knowing which letters make what sounds may affect comprehension because of the focus is to sound out the word out" [*sic*] (Module 4, Year 2, Level 2).	The participant was coded as a Level 2 because there is a connection between the phenomenon she is seeing with her student and a clear connection to a deep understanding of linguistic background knowledge. Rather than become frustrated with her student, she relies on her background knowledge of linguistics to explain the phenomenon.	How do I acknowledge the resources that support my ability to address the varied linguistic backgrounds, experiences, or viewpoints of students? Do I identify the ways that I can use these resources to facilitate students' literacies in the future?

Participants at this level should be aware of resources available to assist them with their students of diverse linguistic backgrounds and discuss how the have used that knowledge in the past or present.	None recorded at this level.	How do I acknowledge the resources that support my ability to address the varied linguistic backgrounds, experiences, or viewpoints of students? In what ways do I consider a variety of diverse needs as I use linguistic resources to support students' literacies?

Continued

TABLE 8.4 Informal Tool for Linguistically Responsive Literacy Pedagogy (*Continued*)

Level	Definition	Example 1	Explanation	Reflexive Questions
Four	Participants at this level are aware of resources available to them, discuss how they have used that knowledge in the past, and plan to use that knowledge in the future.	"It wasn't until I taught Pre–K, and I learned about the foundations of literacy, that I began to teach the students to recognize patterns and I thought about spelling rules. Furthermore, since many of my Pre–K students were ELLs [English language learners], I approached their learning from a different perspective because many of my students didn't understand me at all. Therefore, I had to develop different strategies for getting students to understand classroom routines and activities. The way that I taught spelling as a 4th grade teacher did not help these students with English language acquisition because it did not take into consideration anything regarding the student's native language. Strict, rote memorization was how spelling was implemented. When I ask my 6th graders how spelling was taught to them, they tell me that they have a pre-test on Monday, they memorize the words, and then they have their final test on Friday. This continues to be the way spelling is handled in my district. Because of this approach to the spelling curriculum, the best needs of the ELL students aren't being met" (Module 5, Year 1, Level 4).	This participant discusses her experience reflecting on the resources available and concludes that they are not sufficient for her student learning goals. She then "approached their learning from a different perspective" which then lead to further change that seems to have affected her philosophy on literacy. At her core, she disagrees with mandated methods of teaching because she knows that this is not helping her ELL students become successful. In essence, this teacher recognizes that changes must occur in order to have her students become successful. This realization shows that she is operating at a higher level of linguistic awareness.	How do I rethink how I respond to the varied linguistic backgrounds, experiences, or viewpoints of students? How am I being open to new ways of viewing, learning, and envisioning the world, the texts with which I work, the way my students interpret various texts, and the languages and dialects my students bring? How can I use these linguistics assets to help students develop confidence and success in their literacy learning in classrooms?

| Five | Participants at this level should demonstrate consistently that they are aware of students' diverse linguistic backgrounds and consistently react in positive ways to facilitate learning. | None recorded at this level. | How do I rethink who I am, what I think, and how I see the world as I respond to the varied linguistic backgrounds, experiences, or viewpoints of students? In what ways are my responses to students' language differences consistent with the value that I place on diversity regardless of where I am? How am I working as an advocate for students' literacy needs on a consistent basis by considering the linguistic differences they present in my classroom? How am I consistently rethinking the resources I use and my interactions with students in ways that challenge me to maintain a welcoming approach to students' linguistic differences? |

and linguistically responsiveness practices across levels of CRLP and LRLP, (b) examples of teacher responsive practices, (c) factors such as reflection on self and on content that influenced their responsiveness and (d) questions that allow teachers to reflect on the extent to which their literacy practices align with various degrees of CRLP and LRLP.

By focusing equally on four dimensions—*degrees of CRLP, degrees of LRLP, reflection on self as a teacher, reflection on wide range of literacy content*—while also highlighting the student as central to the process of responsiveness, these tools based on our findings point to the need for (re)envisioning responsiveness to literacy from multiple angles. Considering these multiple entry points from which literacy teachers can operate to maximize learning instruction in diverse classrooms, we use a *prism* to represent these elements critical to literacy responsiveness (see Figure 8.3).

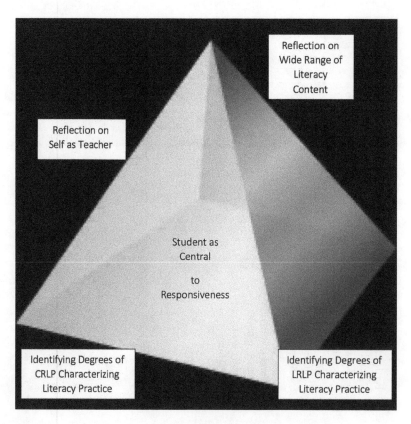

FIGURE 8.3   Culturally and Linguistically Responsive Literacy Prism

Beyond Dichotomies

This study finds significance in the promise that the culturally and linguistically responsive prism and its corresponding informal tools, hold for teachers and literacy teacher educators. Extending previous research that focuses on the unpreparedness of teachers for CLDs, responding to the need to dismantle dichotomies inherent in this process and illustrating the elements of teachers' responsiveness that create a basis for enhanced student academic outcomes (Aronson & Laughter, 2016; Ladson-Billings, 2014), the study fills a much-needed gap with regards to *the extent to which* literacy teachers and educators can be attuned to responsiveness to CLDs as demonstrated by literacy teachers. Being able to identify their progress along a continuum is especially crucial given that teachers must use these pedagogies in ways that vary within the specific content areas in which they work (e.g., literacy) (Aronson & Laughter, 2016; Cruz et al., 2014). Literacy educators and administrators, too, in conjunction with teachers, will find the prism presented, as well as its corresponding tools, useful for reflection as the field moves beyond dichotomies that often label teachers as "responsive or "nonresponsive," "prepared" or "unprepared," "effective" or "ineffective" in their work with CLDs.

Appendix 8.1

Fall (2015)

Apply and Evaluate (A&E) Assignment (30 points)

Description of the A&E Assignment:
This Phase 1 course is based primarily on helping you become proficient with reading assessment. Therefore, shared participation is important to expose you to various perspectives and viewpoints concerning reading assessment materials and procedures. To facilitate this goal, you are required to conduct a Case Study that will span the entire duration of the course where you individually and collaboratively observe, administer, score and analyze a number of reading assessments, based on which you will design student instruction. This project may differ for each graduate student in the course and therefore individual consultation with me throughout the stages of this process is critical. Based on analysis and interpretation of these results, you will make instructional recommendations for the Grade 2–12 learner with whom you have interacted. These recommendations will be shared with parents and teachers via the Case Study that you create as a result of this process. As you engage in the assessment and instruction process, be sure to maintain a record of all assessment results, associated artifacts and instructional plans. You will be guided carefully every week about uploading these artifacts from your assessment process to our Blackboard course site. To accomplish this goal, follow the steps below:

- *Obtain permission* to observe and administer reading assessments to a learner in grades 2-12 in his/her classroom setting in a school of your choice. This permission should be obtained as soon as possible using the appropriate consent forms (templates to be provided in Blackboard). Upon obtaining the parent's, principal's and teacher's signatures, you are responsible for returning the signed forms to me by uploading these in the appropriate area on Blackboard. Place hard copies of the original form with your personal EDLL 5346 files and provide copies of the relevant signed forms to the parents, teachers and principals of each of the students with whom you will work. Under no condition should assessments be administered prior to securing signed permission forms from parents, principals and teachers.

- *Observe and administer assessments* to the learner you have chosen at least once every week. You may choose a student in a classroom or school in which you teach (or not). The student may *or* may not be a "struggling reader." The student chosen should reflect some form of diversity, with diversity defined as a point of difference that you have not engaged with based on your own characteristics and backgrounds (e.g., lower socio-economic background, immigrant – these may be students of any ethnicity, including Caucasians, bi/multilingual, cross-cultural background – lived across multiple cultural settings, reading disabled, learning disabled, non-mainstream ethnic background – these may students such as Latino/a, African-American, African, Native American Indian, Caribbean (Mixed) students). So, for example, an African-American teacher working with a Caucasian student would reflect his/her engagement with diversity and therefore this match would be fine for this course. Similarly, a multilingual teacher working with a monolingual student would reflect diversity and the match would be acceptable for this course. I will review your basis for diversity carefully and guide you as to whether you have met this requirement for choosing a student when you present your choices for a student in our brainstorming forum on Blackboard.

- *Complete a weekly summary and analysis* of your assessment process and findings as well as areas identified for instruction. This summary will constitute part "2" of each Weekly Post and will eventually inform your A&E Case Study. Specifically refer to:
    a. the process used when conducting your reading assessment for that week
    b. findings and analyses from assessment results
    c. questions and concerns you have about the process and your findings
    d. if and how your student appears to be a "struggling reader" as you identify the ways in which responsive instruction and differentiated instruction can function as tools for increasing the reading proficiency of your learner
    e. underlying factors (i.e., sociocultural, motivational, linguistic, historical) that affect the student's response to the particular assessment being administered
    f. areas where you believe your student will benefit from instruction.

g. how consideration of these factors can be used to identify instructional measures that can improve the needs of your learner.

Be sure to summarize in detail and to use specific examples from your assessment artifacts indicating exactly how the K–12 learner performed on all areas of the assessment. The specific titles for your weekly summaries and analyses are as follows:

a. Preliminary Assessments – Anecdotal Notes, Interest Inventories, Interviews (upload artifacts to BB; include summary of process and instructional recommendations in Weekly Post)

b. Reading Motivation Assessments – Anecdotal Notes, Surveys, Interest Inventories (upload artifacts to BB; include summary of process and instructional recommendations Weekly Post)

c. Phonics and Phonological Awareness Assessments – Anecdotal Notes, Checklists (upload artifacts to BB; include summary of process and instructional recommendations in WP)

d. Spelling Assessments – Anecdotal Notes, Spelling Inventories, Formal Assessments in District (upload artifacts to BB; include summary of process and instructional recommendations in WP)

e. Decoding and Comprehension Assessments – Anecdotal Notes, Running Records, Miscue Analyses (upload artifacts to BB; include summary of process and instructional recommendations in WP)

f. Comprehension and Vocabulary Assessments – Anecdotal Notes, Retellings, Cloze Procedures, Formal Assessments in District (upload artifacts to BB; include summary of process and instructional recommendations in WP)

g. Fluency Assessments – Anecdotal Notes, Checklists, Formal Assessments in District (upload artifacts to BB; include summary of process and instructional recommendations in WP)

h. Formal assessments used by school district (upload artifacts to BB; include summary of process and instructional recommendations in WP)

Note that I, along with your peers will provide feedback on your process each week.

- *Create the Apply and Evaluate (A&E) Case Study Narrative* towards the end of the semester using information and feedback from all weekly individual assessments and corresponding summaries of results, analyses, interpretations, and instructional recommendations you have made in your Weekly Posts throughout the course. This narrative will be a professionally written academic document that organizes your information gathered about student to provide guidance to teachers and parents and administrators. In all written work, you will assign the student(s) a pseudonym to protect his or her identity in all your written work. Your Case Study narrative/paper will be submitted on Blackboard and will be due towards the end of the course. Note that the content of the Case Study may differ for each graduate student in this course and therefore individual consultation with me before and during the stages of this process is critical.

- *Organize your Apply and Evaluate (A&E) Case Study Narrative* using the following headings:
- Cover Page
  - Assignment Title, Name of Student, Date, Name of Professor
- Introduction
  - Introduce the Grade 2–12 student
  - Describe his/her social, cultural, academic, language, literacy, geographic and other backgrounds as necessary using findings from informal student interview
  - Describe perspectives of parents and teachers of the student using findings from informal parent and teacher interviews
  - Summarize who the student appears to be in the final paragraph and what you hope to achieve as a result of the Case Study
- Preliminary Assessments Summary
- Reading Motivation Assessments Summary (if/as needed)
- Phonics and Phonological Awareness Assessments Summary (if/as needed)
- Spelling Assessments Summary (if/as needed)
- Decoding and Comprehension Assessments Summary (if/as needed)
- Comprehension and Vocabulary Assessments Summary (if/as needed)
- Fluency Assessments Summary (if/as needed)
- Other Formal Assessments Summary (if/as needed)
- Summary of Student's Strengths
  - Create 2–3 paragraphs that summarize the student's focal areas of strengths based on all the findings listed in the above assessments
- Summary of Student's Areas of Need
  - Create 2–3 paragraphs that indicate areas where the student most needs instruction based on all the findings listed in the above assessments
- Instructional Recommendations
  - Identify the specific Texas Essential Knowledge and Skills (TEKS) to be targeted for this student in English Language Arts and Reading based on the areas of need identified above?
  - Beneath each TEKS, identify and describe strategies from our professional readings/articles/books (with specific citations) aligned with the TEKS that you would recommend to help the student?
- Professional and Personal Reflection
  - Describe how the process of observing and assessing this K–12 learner has caused you to think about your personal and professional perspectives concerning reading assessment and the various diverse perspectives

(student focused, motivation, sociocultural, constructivist, linguistic, historical, diagnostic) needed to approach instruction for these learners. Use as many citations from our readings as possible to support your reflection.

- Conclusion
  - ○ Describe how the assessments and recommended instructional strategies target student focused, motivation, sociocultural, constructivist, diagnostic/assessment, and instructional needs of your K–12 learner.
  - ○ Describe how the process of observing and assessing this K–12 learner has caused you to think professionally about your student's reading as a process of meaning construction represented by the interaction between and among the reader's existing knowledge, the information suggested by the written language, and the context of the reading situation. Use as many citations from our readings as possible to develop your conclusion.
  - ○ End with personal implications for your current classroom and/or plans for classroom implementation.
- References
  - ○ List all references cited in the A&E Case Study in alphabetical order in APA style (6th edition). See OWL Purdue.

Note that you are expected to use feedback obtained from your weekly Discussion Board submissions to guide the creation of your A&E Case Study Draft. Failure to neglect this feedback will result in points deducted from your Case Study assignment grade. I will review Case Study drafts prior to your final submission to allow you a final opportunity for revision. The Final Case Study will be graded based on a rubric. The tentative rubric for this project is provided below and is subject to change. You will begin the course with **30 points** for the Case Study. Points will be deducted as necessary based on your performance.

Weekly Posts (20 points)

Active participation and a pluralistic perspective require an engagement of each student and as indicated previously, a sharing of individual perspectives. You will prepare 8 weekly posts based on assigned and chosen weekly readings and the assessments you administer weekly. Each post will constitute your personal notes based on the weekly readings that are central to the chapter or article, have caught your attention, need further clarification, and are based on ideas you wish to use to "push" our thinking further. These notes will all be connected to the assessments identified and administered in this course and will also relate to how your student responds to these assessments. Your post may be formatted as a table, diagram, narrative, a multimodal assignment, or otherwise. Your response is not meant to be a "book" or "article report" or an extensive summary of what you have read, but rather, should contain citations or references from the readings that refer to key concepts followed by reactions, comparisons of the ideas of various authors, linkages between and among ideas from your reading, your experiences, and classroom practices as relates to assessment. Your response may further serve as a means of developing questions about what you have read, and a forum through which you may add notes from class discussions to supplement your thinking. Use this interaction with the readings as an opportunity to explore your own thoughts as you contemplate new ideas in the readings and as a basis for supporting conversations in our learning community.

Include the following components in each Weekly Post:

1. *A reaction or a response to the readings assigned/chosen.* Be honest in your response. Explain what you found interesting about the readings assigned and whether they examine students' needs from the following lenses: student focused/individual, motivation, sociocultural, constructivist, diagnostic/ assessment, and instructional. Point out concerns and explore them. What is new information for you? What are you thinking after reading the articles? Have the articles/chapters changed your view? Refer specifically to your choice text for this course in your reaction and say how it relates to your thinking about the module.

2. *A summary of the process used for your assessment for that week, your findings from the assessments, questions and concerns you have about the process and your findings, and the areas where you believe your student will benefit from instruction.* Be sure to summarize in detail and to use specific examples from your assessment artifacts indicating exactly how the K–12 learner performed on all areas of the assessment. More detail about this is provided under the A&E Case Study Assignment.

3. *Connections between the assessment results and class readings/discussions.* Be sure to use appropriate citations from our course articles, books and other materials (e.g., online or otherwise) as you make these connections. (For instance: Risko (2012) describes the ways in which students' cultural backgrounds can affect the prior knowledge they bring to the text in much the same way that I saw Isaiah (student pseudonym) use his familiarity with war to understand what the author meant in the text …). Please do not include long quotes from the articles/chapters in your Weekly Posts. Instead, paraphrase quotes and refer to them by page number.

For doctoral students only. Select a text of choice based on reading assessment or linking reading assessment to instruction. You may choose these from the supplementary texts in this course syllabus or decide to choose elsewhere. Refer specifically to your choice text for this course in your connections (# 3 above) and say how the information in this text helps you think about the instruction you would like to recommend for your student from one or more of the following perspectives: student focused/individual, motivation, sociocultural, constructivist, diagnostic/assessment, and instructional. Also, write about what you agree or disagree with in the article. Question points of the articles/chapters assigned for the module based on your philosophy for teaching and assessing reading. Make sure you say exactly why you are posing these questions by referring specifically (using citations) to part of the choice text you chose to read for this course to help you identify why you agree or disagree. Feel free to refer to other texts in other courses in which you are enrolled to extend connects further and support your argument(s).

These are the types of reflective opportunities important for your professional growth and development and pivotal to distinguishing yourself as a literacy leader. You will begin the course with a total of **20 points** for all weekly posts. Evidence that you have failed to complete at least one Weekly Post will result in the loss of 2 points. For every subsequent absence of a Weekly Post, 2 points will be deducted. Note that the Weekly Post is time-sensitive, meaning that the it is significant only when you have used its content to support your own meaning construction and that of your peers on a weekly basis. **As such, late weekly posts will not be accepted.**

Course Specific Student Learning Outcomes and Methods of Assessment

The conceptual framework, program goals, and course emphases lead to a set of expected student learning outcomes and related assessment measures. These expectations are featured in the following table.

Graduate Student Learning Outcomes	Course Assignments	Methods of Assessment
By the conclusion of the course, the student will:	Students will complete the following assignments to address the student learning outcomes:	Student learning outcomes will be assessed by the following methods:
Students will demonstrate a critical stance in utilizing the term "struggling reader" as they identify the ways in which responsive instruction and differentiated instruction function as tools for increasing the reading proficiency of all learners	• Weekly Posts that each include: ○ A summary of the readings ○ A summary of assessments administered ○ Instructional recommendations based on these assessments ○ Connections between summaries of readings, assessments, and instructional recommendations	• Qualitative feedback from Instructor • Qualitative feedback from Peers • Extent to which feedback is integrated into the Apply and Evaluate (A&E) Case Study Assignment

Graduate Student Learning Outcomes	Course Assignments	Methods of Assessment
Students will highlight, critique and evaluate the multiple underlying factors that affect students who are "struggling readers" (e.g., sociocultural, motivational, linguistic, historical) in their assessment of learners and their identification of instructional measures designed to meet learners' needs	• Weekly Posts that each include: o A summary of the readings o A summary of assessments administered o Instructional recommendations based on these assessments o Connections between summaries of readings, assessments, and instructional recommendations	• Qualitative feedback from Instructor • Qualitative feedback from Peers • Extent to which feedback is integrated into the Apply and Evaluate (A&E) Case Study Assignment
Students will analyze multiple reading assessment results to design and implement effective literacy instruction that is responsive to individual strengths, needs, and interests	• Weekly Posts that each include: o A summary of the readings o A summary of assessments administered o Instructional recommendations based on these assessments o Connections between summaries of readings, assessments, and instructional recommendations • Apply and Evaluate (A&E) Case Study	• Qualitative feedback from Instructor • Qualitative feedback from Peers • Extent to which feedback is integrated into the Apply and Evaluate (A&E) Case Study Assignment • Qualitative feedback from Instructor • A&E Case Study Grading Rubric

Graduate Student Learning Outcomes	Course Assignments	Methods of Assessment

Students will discuss and design effective literacy instruction relative to phonemic awareness, phonics, word identification, fluency, comprehension, and vocabulary	• Weekly Posts that each include:
	  ○ A summary of the readings
	  ○ A summary of assessments administered
	  ○ Instructional recommendations based on these assessments
	  ○ Connections between summaries of readings, assessments, and instructional recommendations
	• Apply and Evaluate (A&E) Case Study
		• Qualitative feedback from Instructor
		• Qualitative feedback from Peers
		• Extent to which feedback is integrated into the Apply and Evaluate (A&E) Case Study Assignment
		• Qualitative feedback from Instructor
		• A&E Case Study Grading Rubric

Students will synthesize knowledge of convergent research about literacy practices and how this knowledge can be applied in providing effective literacy instruction to students with reading difficulties	• Reading Instruction Project/Research Paper	• Completion Points • Qualitative feedback from Peers • Grading Rubric
Students will discuss the importance of strategic reading and becoming a strategic reader	• Article Inquiry	• Completion Points • Qualitative feedback from Peers

Graduate Student Learning Outcomes	Course Assignments	Methods of Assessment
Students will analyze reading as the process of constructing meaning through the interaction of the reader's existing knowledge, the information suggested by the written language, and the context of the reading situation	• Apply and Evaluate (A&E) Case Study	• Qualitative feedback from Instructor • A&E Case Study Grading Rubric

Fall (2017)

Comprehensive Case Study

This Phase 2 master's Course is based primarily on helping you become proficient with reading assessment, designing instruction and implementing the instruction based on assessment results. Therefore, shared participation is important to expose you to various perspectives and viewpoints concerning reading assessment materials and procedures. To facilitate this goal, you are required to use the module synopses and synopsis discussions that you engaged in throughout the semester to develop a Comprehensive Case Study of your 2–12 learner based on your assessments and instruction of the learner for duration of the course. You will follow these steps to work with the 2–12 learner before and while you complete the synopses that will be used to develop the Comprehensive Case Study:

• Obtain permission to observe and administer reading assessments to a learner in grades 2–12 in his/her classroom setting in a school of your choice or in another instructional context. This permission should be obtained as soon as possible using the appropriate consent forms (templates to be provided in Blackboard). Upon obtaining the parent's, principal's and teacher's signatures, you are responsible for returning the signed forms to me by uploading these in the appropriate area of the Discussion forum on Blackboard. Keep "hard" copies of the original signed forms with your personal EDLL 5346 files and provide copies of the relevant signed forms to the parents, teachers and principals of each of the students with whom you will work. Under no condition should assessments be administered prior to securing signed permission forms from parents, principals and teachers.
• Observe and administer assessments to the learner you have chosen based on guidelines in our four modules on Blackboard. You may choose a student in a classroom or school in which you teach (or not). You may choose a student

in another instructional context that does not necessarily reflect the parameters of "school". The student may or may not be a "struggling reader." The student chosen should reflect some form of diversity, with diversity defined as "a point of difference that you have not engaged with based on your own characteristics and backgrounds" (e.g., lower socio-economic background, immigrant – these may be students of any ethnicity, including Caucasians, bi/multilingual, cross-cultural background – lived across multiple cultural settings, reading disabled, learning disabled, non-mainstream ethnic background – these may students such as Latino/a, African-American, African, Native American Indian, Caribbean (Mixed) students). Basically, you need to confirm that the student is different from you in three specific and different ways. So, for example, an African-American teacher working with a Caucasian student would reflect his/her engagement with diversity and therefore this match would be fine for this course. Similarly, a multilingual teacher working with a monolingual student would reflect diversity and the match would be acceptable for this course. I will review your basis for diversity carefully and guide you as to whether you have met this requirement for choosing a student when you present your choices for a student in our brainstorming forum on Blackboard.

This project may differ for each graduate student in the course and therefore individual consultation with me throughout the stages of this process is critical. Based on analysis and interpretation of these results, you will make instructional recommendations for the Grade 2–12 learner with whom you have interacted. An outline of these recommendations will be shared with parents and teachers to help improve the child's reading after you are finished with the course. As you engage in the assessment and instruction process, be sure to maintain a record of all assessment results, associated artifacts and instructional plans. You will be guided carefully during each module about uploading these artifacts from your assessment process to our Blackboard course site. Your Comprehensive Case Study will include the following sections:

- Cover Page
  - Assignment Title, Name of Student, Date, Name of Professor
- Introduction
  - Introduce the grade 2–12 student
  - Describe his/her social, cultural, academic, language, literacy, geographic and other backgrounds using findings from informal student interview
  - Describe perspectives of parents and teachers of the student using findings from informal parent and teacher interviews
  - Summarize who the student appears to be in the final paragraph and what you hope to achieve as a result of the Case Study

- Description of Results from Background, Motivation, and Foundational Reading Assessments
- Description of Results from Fluency and Vocabulary Assessments
- Description of Results from Comprehension Assessments
- Description of Results from Writing Assessments
- Summary of Student's Strengths based on All Assessments
    ○ Create 2–3 paragraphs that summarize the student's focal areas of strengths based on all the findings listed in the above assessments
- Summary of Student's Areas of Need based on All Assessments
    ○ Create 2–3 paragraphs that indicate areas where the student most needs instruction based on all the findings listed in the above assessments
- Instructional Recommendations
    ○ Identify the specific Texas Essential Knowledge and Skills (TEKS) (or other standards) to be targeted for this student in English Language Arts and Reading based on the areas of need identified above
    ○ Beneath each TEKS (or other type of standard), identify and describe strategies from our professional readings/articles/books (with specific citations) aligned with the TEKS (or other standards) that you would recommend to help the student
- Professional and Personal Reflection
    ○ Describe how the process of observing and assessing this 2–12 learner for the semester has caused you to think about your personal and professional perspectives concerning reading assessment and the various perspectives (diversity, student-focused vs. teacher-directed, motivation, sociocultural, constructivist, linguistic, historical, diagnostic) needed to approach instruction for these learners. Use as many citations from our readings as possible to support your reflection.
- Conclusion
    ○ Describe how your assessments and recommended instructional strategies target diversity, student-focused, motivation, sociocultural, constructivist, diagnostic/assessment, and instructional needs of your 2–12 learner
    ○ Describe how the process of observing and assessing this 2–12 learner has caused you to think professionally about your student's reading as a process of meaning construction represented by the interaction between and among the reader's existing knowledge, the information suggested by the written language, and the context of the reading situation. Use as many citations from our readings as possible to develop your conclusion.
    ○ End with personal implications for your current classroom and/or plans for classroom implementation.
- References
    ○ List all in-text citations in the Comprehensive Case Study in alphabetical order in APA style (6th edition) at the end of the paper. See OWL Purdue.

The rubric for assessing your Comprehensive Case Study is available in Appendix C at the end of this syllabus.

Module Synopses and Synopsis-Based Discussion *[45%|18%]*

During the course, you are *required* to participate in *nine* (9) (asynchronous) synopsis-based discussions; *invited* to participate in *four* (4) (asynchronous) brainstorming discussions; and *invited* to participate in **seven (7)** synchronous discussions on Blackboard.

I.   Nine (9) Required Module Synopses and Nine (9) Required Synopsis-based Discussions

Each module synopsis will be based on your work with assessment and instruction of the 2–12 learner. Each synopsis-based discussion will be based on the module synopses posted to the discussion forum on Blackboard. The synopses and discussions include two steps:

- In the first part of this process, you are required to prepare and post your synopsis for a relevant module in the designated place by the deadline. Use the guidelines for developing the synopsis and relevant questions in the applicable learning module as a guide before you post.
  - Be honest in your response. Explain what you found interesting about the readings assigned and whether they examine students' needs from the following lenses: student focused/individual, motivation, sociocultural, constructivist, diagnostic/assessment, and instructional. Point out concerns and explore them. What is new information for you? What are you thinking after reading the articles? Have the articles/chapters changed your view?
  - Be sure to summarize in detail and to use specific examples from your assessment or instruction artifacts indicating exactly how the 2–12 learner performed on all areas of the assessment or instruction. Include the following in your summary from work with the 2–12 learner:
    a. the specific assessments or instructional strategies that you use and the citations for each assessment or strategy
    b. the process used when conducting your reading assessment or instruction for a particular module
    c. the findings and descriptions of analyses from assessment results
    d. questions and concerns you have about the process you used for assessment or instruction and your findings
    e. if and how your student appears to be a "struggling reader" as you identify the ways in which responsive instruction and differentiated instruction can function as tools for increasing the reading proficiency of your learner

     f. underlying factors (i.e., diversity, sociocultural, motivational, historical) that affect the student's response to the particular assessment being administered or instruction being provided

     g. areas where you believe your student will benefit from further instruction and/or assessment

- Be sure to use appropriate citations from our course articles, books and other materials (e.g., online or otherwise) as you make these connections. (For instance: Risko (2012) describes the ways in which students' cultural backgrounds can affect the prior knowledge they bring to the text in much the same way that I saw Isaiah (student pseudonym) use his familiarity with war to understand what the author meant in the text …). Please do not include long quotes from the articles/chapters in your Weekly Posts. Instead, paraphrase quotes and refer to them by page number.
- These types of reflective opportunities are important for your professional growth and development and pivotal to distinguishing yourself as a literacy leader.

- In the second part of this process, you are required to respond to the synopses of two of your peers for a given module in the designated place by the deadline. Develop two responses to different posts of your peers with one *that you will agree* and with the other that *you do not agree or at least partially disagree*. State why you agree or disagree using citations from our readings.

Points will be lost after the second module synopsis if feedback from the instructor concerning the first module is not addressed in the second and/or subsequent module synopses. Points will be lost if students consistently fail to respond to peers' synopses <u>or</u> provide only superficial responses. A substantive response may do one or more than one of the following:

a. make a thoughtful connection between and among readings as relates to your peers' synopses;

b. question your peers' perspectives and supply additional references to support or refute arguments;

c. reference readings from other classes in which you are enrolled to guide your peers;

d. use your literacy teaching and leadership experiences as examples and models to guide your peers;

e. be sensitive in your *ways of being*, willing to *disagree respectfully* with peers and to allow views to which you do not subscribe to be aired comfortably as you learn from and share with others.

II. Four Optional Brainstorming Discussions

Each brainstorming session will help with your thinking about completing tasks for each module. Brainstorming posts and responses are optional (not required) and will <u>not</u> be graded.

III. Eight Optional Synchronous Discussions

Each discussion will occur via Blackboard Collaborate in our class shell at 6:00–7:30 P.M. CST and will be recorded. Synchronous sessions are scheduled on the following dates, all of which are Mondays: *August 28th; September 18th, 25th; October 16th, 23rd; November 13th, 20th.* Our synchronous discussions will help with your understanding of the syllabus, your thinking about completing module-based synopses and activities for each module, and will provide opportunities to discuss our readings and the findings from your instruction and assessment of the 2–12 learners. Online synchronous discussions are optional (not required) and will <u>not</u> be graded. *You will need a microphone and a computer to be able to attend and participate.*

Course Specific Student Learning Outcomes and Methods of Assessment

Graduate Student Learning Outcomes	*Course Assignments*	*Methods of Assessment*
By the conclusion of the course, the student will:	Students will complete the following assignments to address the student learning outcomes:	Student learning outcomes will be assessed by the following methods:

Students will demonstrate a critical stance in utilizing the term "struggling reader" as they identify the ways in which responsive instruction and differentiated instruction function as tools for increasing the reading proficiency of all learners	• Module synopses that each include:
	  o A summary of the readings
	  o A summary of assessments administered
	  o Instructional recommendations based on these assessments
	  o Connections between summaries of readings, assessments, and instructional recommendations
		• Qualitative feedback from Instructor
		• Qualitative feedback from Peers
		• Extent to which feedback is integrated into the Comprehensive Case Study Assignment

Graduate Student Learning Outcomes	Course Assignments	Methods of Assessment

Students will highlight, critique and evaluate the multiple underlying factors that affect students who are "struggling readers" (e.g., sociocultural, motivational, linguistic, historical) in their assessment of learners and their identification of instructional measures designed to meet learners' needs	• Module synopses that each include:
	  o A summary of the readings
	  o A summary of assessments administered
	  o Instructional recommendations based on these assessments
	• Connections between summaries of readings, assessments, and instructional recommendations
		• Qualitative feedback from Instructor
		• Qualitative feedback from Peers
		• Extent to which feedback is integrated into the Comprehensive Case Study Assignment

Students will analyze multiple reading assessment results to design and implement effective literacy instruction that is responsive to individual strengths, needs, and interests	• Module synopses that each include:
	  o A summary of the readings
	  o A summary of assessments administered
	  o Instructional recommendations based on these assessments
	• Connections between summaries of readings, assessments, and instructional recommendations
	• Comprehensive Case Study
		• Qualitative feedback from Instructor
		• Qualitative feedback from Peers
		• Extent to which feedback is integrated into the Comprehensive Case Study
		• Qualitative feedback from Instructor
		• Comprehensive Case Study Grading Rubric

Graduate Student Learning Outcomes	Course Assignments	Methods of Assessment

Students will discuss and design effective literacy instruction relative to phonemic awareness, phonics, word identification, fluency, comprehension, and vocabulary	• Weekly Posts that each include:
	  o A summary of the readings
	  o A summary of assessments administered
	  o Instructional recommendations based on these assessments
	  o Connections between summaries of readings, assessments, and instructional recommendations
	• Comprehensive Case Study
		• Qualitative feedback from Instructor
		• Qualitative feedback from Peers
		• Extent to which feedback is integrated into the Comprehensive Case Study Assignment
		• Qualitative feedback from Instructor
		• Comprehensive Case Study Grading Rubric

Students will synthesize knowledge of convergent research about literacy practices and how this knowledge can be applied in providing effective literacy instruction to students with reading difficulties	• Article Inquiry or Research Paper	• Completion Points • Qualitative feedback from Peers • Grading Rubric
Students will discuss the importance of strategic reading and becoming a strategic reader	• Article Inquiry or Research Paper	• Completion Points • Qualitative feedback from Peers
Students will analyze reading as the process of constructing meaning through the interaction of the reader's existing knowledge, the information suggested by the written language, and the context of the reading situation	• Comprehensive Case Study	• Qualitative feedback from Instructor • Comprehensive Case Study Grading Rubric

References

Afflerbach, P., Pearson, P. D., & Paris, S. G. (2008). Clarifying differences between reading skills and reading strategies. *The Reading Teacher*, 61(5), 364–373.

Aronson, B., & Laughter, J. (2016). The theory and practice of culturally relevant education: A synthesis of research across content areas. *Review of Educational Research*, 86(1), 163–206.

Au, K. (2000). *Literacy instruction in multicultural settings*. Fort Worth, TX: Harcourt Brace.

Banks, J. A. (2017). Diversity and citizenship education in multicultural nations. *Multicultural Education Review*, 1(1), 1–28.

Cahill, M., & McGill-Franzen, A. (2013). Selecting "app"ealing and "app"ropriate book apps for beginning readers. *The Reading Teacher*, 67(1), 30–39.

Cruz, B. C., Ellerbrock, C. R., Vásquez, A., & Howes, E. V. (Eds.). (2014). *Talking diversity with teachers and teacher educators: Exercises and critical conversations across the curriculum*. New York, NY: Teachers College Press.

Cummins, J. (2008). BICS and CALP: Empirical and theoretical status of the distinction. In B. Street & N. H. Hornberger, (Eds.), *Encyclopedia of language and education* (2nd Ed., Vol. 2, pp. 71–83). New York, NY: Springer.

Dee, T. S., & Penner, E. K. (2016). The causal effects of cultural relevance: Evidence from an ethnic studies curriculum. *American Educational Research Journal*, 54(1), 127–166.

de Oliveira, L. C., & Athanases, S. Z. (2007). Graduates' reports of advocating for English language learners. *Journal of Teacher Education*, 58(3), 202–215.

Durgunoğlu, A. Y., & Hughes, T. (2010). How prepared are U.S. preservice teachers to teach English language learners? *International Journal of Teaching and Learning in Higher Education*, 22(1), 32–41.

Dyson, A. H. (2015). The search for inclusion: Deficit discourse and the erasure of childhoods. *Language Arts*, 92(3), 199–207.

Flores, N. (2013). Silencing the subaltern: Nation-state/colonial governmentality and bilingual education in the United States. *Critical Inquiry in Language Studies*, 10(4), 263–287.

García, O. (2008). Multilingual language awareness and teacher education. In J. Cenoz & N. H. Hornberger (Eds.), *Encyclopedia of language and education* (2nd ed., vol. 6, pp. 385–400). Berlin: Springer.

García, O. (2015). Critical multilingual language awareness and teacher education. In J. Cenoz et al. (eds.), *Language awareness and multilingualism* (pp. 1–17). Springer International Publishing.

Gay, G. (2014). Foreword. In B. Cruz, C. Ellerbrock, A. Vasquez, & E. Howes (Eds.), *Talking diversity with teachers and teacher educators: Exercises and critical conversations across the curriculum* (pp. x–xiv). New York, NY: Teachers College Press.

Grant, K. S. L., & Lee, V. J. (2014). Teacher educators wrestling with issues of diversity in online courses. *The Qualitative Report*, 19(6), 1–25.

Haddix, M. (2017). Diversifying teaching and teacher education. *Journal of Literacy Research*, 49(1), 141–149.

Harris, V. J. (2008). Selecting books that children will want to read. *The Reading Teacher*, 61(5), 426–430.

Herrera, S. G., Murry, K. G., & Cabral, R. M. (2012). *Assessment accommodations for classroom teachers of culturally and linguistically diverse students*. Boston, MA: Pearson Higher Education.

Jessner, U. (2006). *Linguistic awareness in multilinguals: English as a third language: English as a third language*. Edinburgh: Edinburgh University Press.

Krakouer, J. (2015). *Literature review relating to the current context and discourse on Indigenous cultural awareness in the teaching space: Critical pedagogies and improving Indigenous learning outcomes through cultural responsiveness. Australian Council for Educational Research.* Retrieved from https://research.acer.edu.au/indigenous_education/42/

Krashen, S. D. (2003). *Explorations in language acquisition and use.* Portsmouth, NH: Heinemann.

Kumi-Yeboah, A., Yuan, G., & Dogbey, J. (2017). Online collaborative learning activities: The perceptions of culturally diverse graduate students. *Online Learning*, 21(4), 5–28.

Ladson-Billings, G. (1995). Toward a theory of culturally relevant pedagogy. *American Educational Research Journal*, 32(3), 465–491.

Ladson-Billings, G. (2014). Culturally relevant pedagogy 2.0: Aka the remix. *Harvard Educational Review*, 84(1), 74–84.

Lehtomaki, E., Janhonen-Abruquah, H., & Kahangwa, G. L. (2017). *Culturally responsive education: Reflections from the global South and North.* New York, NY: Routledge.

Li, G. (2017). Preparing culturally and linguistically competent teachers for English as an international language education. *TESOL Journal*, 8(2), 250–276.

Lucas, T., & Villegas, A. M. (2013). Preparing linguistically responsive teachers: Laying the foundation in preservice teacher education. *Theory Into Practice*, 52(2), 98–109.

Maxwell, L. A. (2014), June 17. *Most teacher preparation falls short on strategies for ELLs.* National Council on Teacher Quality. Retrieved from http://blogs.edweek.org/edweek/learning-the-language/2014/06/most_teacher_prep_falls_short_.html

Nieto, S. (2000). *Affirming diversity: The sociopolitical context of multicultural education.* New York, NY: Longman.

Nieto, S., & Bode, P. (2008). *Affirming diversity: The sociopolitical context of multicultural education* (5th ed.). Boston, MA: Pearson.

Neuman, W. I. (2004). *Basics of social research: Qualitative and quantitative approaches.* Boston, MA: Pearson.

Pennycook, A. (2008). Translingual English. *Australian Review of Applied Linguistics International Forum on English as an International Language*, 31(3), 30.1–30.9.

Risko, V. (2012). *Be that teacher!: Breaking the cycle for struggling readers.* New York, NY: Teachers College Press.

Risko, V., Reid, L., Hoffman, J., Rodesiler, L., Skerrett, A., Teale, W., & Shoffner, M. (2017). *Literacy teacher preparation [Research advisory].* International Literacy Association and National Council of Teachers of English. Newark, DE; Urbana, IL: Authors.

Roxas, K., Dade, K. B. M., & Rios, F. (2017). Institutionalizing internationalization within a college of education: Toward a more critical multicultural and glocal education perspective. In Y. K. Cha, J. Gundura, S. H. Ham, & M. Lee (Eds.), *Multicultural education in glocal perspectives* (pp. 201–213). Singapore: Springer.

Sleeter, C. E. (2012). Confronting the marginalization of culturally responsive pedagogy. *Urban Education*, 47(3), 562–584.

Smith, P., Karkar, T., Varner, J., Nigam, A., & Finch, B. (2020). Making visible awareness in practice: Literacy educators in diverse classrooms. *Review of Education*, 8(2), 380-415.

Smith, P., Richards, J., Gutierrez, S., Schaffer-Rose, J., & Kumi-Yeboah, A. (2017). Shifting from diversity in multicultural populations to teacher/student interactions within transcultural spaces in an online literacy teacher education course. *Literacy Practice and Research*, 42(3), 7–15.

Tschannen-Moran, M., & Woolfolk Hoy, A. (2001). Teacher efficacy: Capturing an elusive construct. *Teaching and Teacher Education*, 17, 783–805.

Wright, T. (2002). Doing language awareness: Issues for language study in language teacher education. In H. Trappes-Lomax & G. Ferguson (Eds.), *Language in language teacher education* (pp. 113–130). Amsterdam, PA: John Benjamins.

9

CONNECTING EDUCATORS, FAMILIES AND COMMUNITIES THROUGH PASTEL (PLURILINGUALISM, ART, SCIENCE, TECHNOLOGY AND LITERACIES) APPROACHES IN AND AROUND FRENCH IMMERSION

Danièle Moore

School classes are more linguistically and culturally diverse than ever, and teachers and educators are more aware of, and better equipped to address, the complex sociolinguistic fabric of their social environments. In Canada, as in other parts of the world, there is increasing educational emphasis on the need to recognize and value the various languages and multiple forms of knowledge and resources that learners bring with them. The value of such resources not only lies in accommodating children's languages and cultures. It is also anchored in the knowledge and practices of families as a resource and bridge to connect teachers, learners, families and communities (Gonzalez et al., 2005). Raising awareness is pivotal in encouraging teachers and learners, as well as parents, to collaborate and become researchers in their daily lives and experiences.

This plurilingual and pluricultural stance on knowledge production draws on the entire language repertoire, multiple worldviews, and transfer of skills and knowledge, disrupting boundaries and challenging monolingual ideologies and practices in education (Le Nevez et al., 2010). This change is based on the acknowledgment that plurilingualism and plurilingual practices are both normal and inevitable in classrooms around the world (Vallejo & Dooley, 2019) and that plurilingualism is valuable in curriculum design (Piccardo, 2013). Plurilingual pedagogies offer an *asset-oriented perspective* in terms of the plurality of the experiences, skills, and competencies that learners possess, in and around class-rooms. As Coste et al. (2009) state,

> [a]ssets represent more than their economic or fiduciary connotations. If, in the relationship with plurality, the school directly or indirectly promotes attitudes of tolerance, of curiosity about things new and different, of inter-cultural perception and of identity awareness and affirmation in a world where levels and degrees of belonging display multiple and complex aspects, it will play a full role in civic and ethical education which today, in widely differing contexts (not unaccompanied by renewed debate) is at the centre of much reflection about schools.
>
> *(p. 25)*

While teacher education in Canada is currently experiencing a profound shift in how to meet the needs of diverse learners, many educators, like elsewhere in the world, remain inexpert in implementing practical approaches to promote plu-rilingual awareness and multiperspectivity in their classroom routine (Moore et al. 2020). For example, Li et al., (2018) report that studies among Canadian educators emphasize their feeling of remaining untrained and inexperienced to effectively empower children's linguistic and cultural experiences and to work as partners with their parents and communities (see also Campbell, 2017; Li et al., 2018). Teachers remain mostly unaware of plurilingual practices in everyday lives and in classrooms; they also tend to be unversed in plurilingual theory, and their profes-sional knowledge rarely includes awareness and proficiency in the practice, goals and benefits of plurilingual education (Galante, 2016; Lau & Van Viegen, 2020). This is even more true in French immersion classrooms in Canada, where teachers are focused on teaching disciplines through a minority language while they need to adapt to ever-changing classroom landscapes (Fortune & Tedick, 2008; Nikula et al., 2016) and are expected to infuse Indigenous learning principles within their daily practice (Kerr & Parent, 2016; Côté, 2019).

Within this gap in teacher training, this chapter describes curriculum devel-opment and the development of pedagogical material within a model of teacher education based on professional learning communities working together towards the development of pedagogical scenarios to support, develop, and infuse pluri-lingualism, intercultural awareness and Indigenous worldviews within the disci-plines in the second-language immersive contexts in which they teach. I focus on one pedagogical scenario, described later, as illustrative of a modelling frame-work for promoting and building school, home, and community relations. It exemplifies the many ways that integrating multilingual literacies, storytelling and art, and content knowledge can create transformative learning environments designed to harness cultural and linguistic diversity as a vital resource to develop literacy and disciplinary knowledge (Cenoz & Gorter, 2015; Conteh & Meier, 2015). The present work is positioned at the intersection of CLIL (content and

language integrated learning) and plurilingualism studies, within which researchers have called for the development of strategic language awareness in teacher
education (Cammarata & Tedick, 2012; Marsh et al., 2019; Troyan, 2014). It is also
profoundly anchored in a core belief that

> [t]o accept the notion that the educational curriculum is not limited to
> school and does not end with it is also to accept that plurilingual and plu-
> ricultural competence may begin before school, and proceed parallel with
> it: through family experience and learning, history and contacts between
> generations, travel, expatriation, emigration, and more generally belonging
> to a multilingual and multicultural environment or moving from one envi-
> ronment to another, but also through reading, and through the media.
>
> *(Coste et al., 2009, p. 32)*

Intersecting Science Learning and Plurilingual Education: Creating Spaces for Contact with Diversity

Although science is omnipresent around us, and important in education, not
many studies focus on the value of family–school partnerships in science education and teacher training (McCollough & Ramirez, 2012; McCollough et al.,
2019). Even fewer studies focus on science education in its relations to plurilingualism and multiperspectivity to expand learning experiences. While many
scholars have highlighted the importance of building continuity between home,
community and school practices (Ishimaru et al., 2015) and the importance
of working with families and communities when preparing teachers to teach
(Zeichner et al., 2016), we still lack research that investigates why and how families' and communities' cultural and linguistic practices and ways of knowing can
be leveraged as resources in education (Bottoms et al., 2017).

A plurilingual lens in teaching and learning can open the space to explore what
diverse learners believe and how they talk about STEM (science, technology, engineering, mathematics)–related content and experience science in different social
environments and cultural spheres. Cooperative inquiry-based science prompts
learners to attend to and to share a common objective to investigate a problem, to
explore alternative solutions from multiple angles, to compare their respective perspectives, and to reconcile divergent thinking so as to construct new understandings:

> Perspective problems thus present children with conflicting perspectives
> about an objective situation that must be somehow resolved or coordi-
> nated, sometimes by constructing new concepts… . resolution requires a
> flexible coordination of the differing perspectives involved, including an
> objective perspective with which all others must somehow be compatible.
>
> *(Tomasello, 2018, n.p.)*

The intersecting of science learning with plurilingualism expands on previous research that demonstrated the many ways plurilingualism can foster, deepen and challenge conceptual understandings in content learning (Gajo, 2007; Gajo & Berthoud, 2018). To encourage learning in several languages has been shown to also promote multiple perspectival agency (Moore et al. 2020; Moore, 2018). This body of research explores how learners, in different learning contexts (school, families, and communities), weave their languages and complex transgenerational experiences as leverage for their learning (Castellotti & Moore, 2010; Bottoms et al., 2017). Plurilingualism contributes to language awareness, and a deepened understanding of the cultural components instantiated in the content, metaphors, use and embodiment of language(s) (Sharifian, 2017).

Hence, learning is dynamic and multi-situated and language is not only an instrument for communication; it also plays "a central role in the discovery, identification and storage of new knowledge ... (it) is often itself the space where knowledge is created" (Beacco et al., 2016, p. 19). As Beacco et al. (2016) further state, the relation between language and knowledge is very complex, and combines at least four interrelated functions: of representation, mediation, interaction and creativity. The approach to plurilingual education in plurilingual science inquiries presented here builds on, redefines, and expands these four functions as defined in Beacco et al. (See Moore et al. (2020), for a detailed discussion):

- **Representation:** understanding the social and situated nature of knowledge building, expounding and disseminating knowledge; *Valorizing plurilingualism expands learners' repertoire of perspectives on science entities.*
- **Mediation:** transposing, verbalising, making it possible to shuttle between languages, semiotic resources and multiple modalities of representation: *Intergenerational approaches to science inquiry support perspective-taking within and among generations.*
- **Interaction:** transforming, allowing exchanges (discussion, debate, disputes) between diversely situated producers of knowledge, and coordinating diverse perspectives to cooperatively resolve tensions: *Perspective taking in science inquiry requires that learners be given opportunities to coordinate their own beliefs with those of others and with an objective perspective (reality) on science phenomena.*
- **Creativity:** creating new knowledge: *Infusing a diversity of worldviews and perspectives into the design of social spaces in science inquiry provides new ways of knowing.*

As Coste (2014) argues, plurilingual education acknowledges the plurality of populations, cultural references, knowledge and know-how, values and principles, and visions and goals of different actors within education settings. Plurilingual approaches to education focus on the linkages across languages and cultural experiences. They support a vision that learners' multiple language resources and knowledge systems, their connections to the land, and their communities nurture and support learning (Ignace, 2016).

In this vein, the following section presents key principles to guide the development of pedagogical scenarios and unit plans that embrace plurilingualism and Indigenous perspectives and knowledge as key components of the learning process. They are embedded in a very long and strong tradition of socially anchored educational research in bilingualism and second-language acquisition that offer a holistic view of language and learners, and which have influenced plurilingual theories and the development and practice of plurilingual and intercultural education (Cummins, 2009; Hornberger, 2009; Grommes, & Hu, 2014; Ntelioglou et al., 2014; Sarkar & Lavoie, 2014; Cenoz & Gorter, 2015; McIvor & McCarty, 2017). These views support an understanding of (pluri)languaging as a dynamic process of meaning-making, using and meshing semiotic resources in creative, entwined, interrelated, unbalanced, and ever-changeable complex ways (Coste et al., 2009; Lau & Van Viegen, 2020; Lüdi, 2014; Piccardo, 2016; García et al., 2017). As Piccardo and Puozzo (2015) write,

> [p]lurilingualism is a unique, overarching notion, implying a subtle but profound shift in perspective, both horizontally, toward the use of multiple languages, and vertically, toward valuing even the most partial knowledge of a language (and other para- and extralinguistic resources) as tools for facilitating communication.
>
> *(p. 319)*

A Plurilingual Pedagogical Scenario for Science Learning in French Immersive Contexts and Beyond

General Structure of a Scenario Plan in the Context of French as a Second-Language Teaching in North America

A scenario plan approach is the backbone of the strategy proposed. "A learning scenario (or "script,", as in film studies) [*un scénario pédagogique*] can be described as "a sequence of learning, its teaching objectives and the means to implement these goals (as, for example, the identification of the didactic resources needed" (Egli Cuenat et al., 2011, n.p.). The nature and order of the objectives on which language learning are focused can vary greatly depending on the local context and the targeted learners, irrespective of the weight of school traditions and systems. Designing a general structure for a scenario plan offers the possibility for local diversification, transposition, and adaptation, and the development of activities that support and sustain learning within a particular educational ecology:

"one of the aims of curriculum design, whatever the particular curriculum, is to make learners aware of the diversity of ways of constructing a plurilingual and pluricultural repertoire, and of their own capacity to handle this repertoire" (Coste et al., 2009, p. 33).

The teachers who participate in the collaborative development of scenario plans all teach French in a North American context, at the primary or secondary level, in immersive contexts, CLIL contexts, or the contexts of bilingual education in international French schools. The co-designing of a general scenario that could fit in with different circumstances and experiences allows teachers to share their experiences and enhance their reflective practice through collaborative dialogue. All participating teachers are engaged in research action. They all teach in urban areas that are highly multilingual and multicultural but where French is very much minoritized and not very present in the learners' homes and communities (see, e.g., Beaumont & Moore, 2020).

Two global curricular frameworks orient and support educators in defining target competencies related to the development of linguistic, intercultural, plurilingual and educational learning in highly diverse contexts: the *FREPA – Framework of Reference for Pluralistic Approaches to Languages and Cultures* (Candelier et al., 2012), and the *Common European Framework of Reference for Languages (CEFR), Companion Volume with New Descriptors* (2018). The FREPA lists different aspects of plurilingual and intercultural competences in a hypertextual structure independent of language level, organised according to three broad areas: Knowledge (*savoir*), Attitudes (*savoir-être*) and Skills (*savoir-faire*; see Candelier et al., 2012). The 2018 CEFR provides progression scales and assessment grids defining areas of competence in plurilingual and intercultural education (North & Piccardo, 2018) Combined, they provide useful descriptors and illustrative learning activities to support plurilingual education. These tools, which are easily available through their related websites, are consulted and adapted within scenario plans that align with each local curricular framework and teaching context. In the case of British Columbia, the conceptualisation of scenario plans is also embedded in the First Peoples Principles of Learning, a set of educational principles articulated by Indigenous Elders, scholars and knowledge-keepers to guide the development of curriculum and teaching to better reflect First Nations epistemologies, experiences, values, and lived realities (Ignace, 2016; Kerr & Parent, 2016). The intersection of these three educational guides provides the overarching structure to the conceptualisation of cross-curricular learning scenarios.

Guiding Principles to Develop Cross-Curricular Scenarios for Unit Plans

Learning language(s), learning through language, and learning about language constitute the three-fold, integrated perspective of immersive CLIL (Coyle et al.,

2010). Within this context, and anchored in the theoretical key points highlighted earlier, five principles guide the co-development of experiential and investigative learning that (1) makes meaningful connections to learners and their lives, (2) incorporates family and community knowledge, and (3) builds upon transferable skills in multiple disciplinary contexts and across experiences and learning contexts (families–schools–communities):

1. **Continuum of learning:** Students learn more effectively when they draw from their entire repertoire, experience, and funds of knowledge (Gonzalez et al., 2005) and are active participants in their own learning.
2. **Participation** is achieved when concepts and procedures are introduced through an investigative approach and are connected in meaningful ways to learners' prior knowledge and experience, across place, time, and space.
3. **Plurilingualism** (here, the capacity to navigate multiple languages and/or to learn through more than one) is a tool and an asset for knowledge construction.
4. **Multiperspectivity** and **reflexivity** can be achieved through the critical and respectful integration of different worldviews, ways of knowing and relating to the world, and of storying knowledge.
5. **Plurilingual Interaction and translanguaging** create favourable relational frameworks to bring in learners' multiple semiotic resources for the construction and problematization of knowledge.

This plurilingual lens implies shared access to knowledge building, empowering the learners as critical citizens and participants in socio-scientific discourse and affording them transgenerational and intercultural experiences of diversity. The following example builds from a large body of stimulating material that already exists and aims to complement what teachers and educators already do in their classroom to address diversity and plurality and encourage further exploration.

Mapping out a Unit Based on a Cross-Curricular Theme: a Plurilingual Exploration of Symmetry Through Light and Shadow

The theme presented here focuses on a plurilingual exploration of symmetry through light and shadow. The unit was first developed in collaboration with science educators within a larger research project investigating plurilingualism and science literacy (Moore et al., 2018). The original activities were designed to develop science literacy through experiential learning in a variety of languages and through diverse cultural lenses and to build learning bridges between families, schools, and a local community centre. The unit was then further developed as a reflective template for collaborative unit planning with groups of teachers, all engaged in action research in their classrooms in various French immersive contexts in North America (French immersion and French international schools in Canada and the United States; see, e.g., Beaumont & Moore, 2020).

Using the five guiding principles presented earlier, teachers worked together across contexts to develop various pathways within a common pedagogical scenario design. The design infused plurilingualism throughout the co-planning of activities in environmental science and biology, technology and social sciences using (Indigenous) art and stories and cross-curricular topics, using a multisensory learning approach (Do, Touch, See, Listen, Speak) in multiple languages. Because plurilingualism, art, and multilingual and multimodal literacies stand as core components throughout this CLIL approach to STEM-based teaching and learning, this pedagogical approach is named here under the umbrella term of PASTEL (Plurilingualism, Art, Science, Technologies and Literacies; Moore, 2018).

Learning Beyond the Classroom

Integrating disciplinary core ideas, crosscutting concepts, and real-world practices, the lesson unit invites learners to explore what happens when light is filtered through various materials, for a direct experience of scientific concepts, through observation, investigation, storytelling, and play. Each aspect of the unit is designed to relate to different elements of the curriculum—life stories, natural sciences, art, cultural knowledge, and learners' varied language abilities to provide a connective structure, using language(s), stories, and imagination. Lesson plans support multiple understandings and multi-situated perspectives. The unit planning template is organized as a web (Ignace, 2016) to allow more flexibility to develop and order activities within the general PASTEL framework, build on disciplinary areas, and navigate languages depending on available resources, timeframes, and learning goals.

This PASTEL approach places storytelling and multilingual books (Armand & Maraillet, 2013; Moore & Sabatier, 2014) at the heart of unit planning. Storytelling is intrinsically linked to plurilingualism and learners' language stories and language biographies. Stories relate to their families' life trajectories, their social networks, and are deeply embedded in the local landscapes they navigate. Storytelling constitutes a key knot to invite families' engagement, rely on their expertise, honour their stories and identities, invite collaborative inquiry, and inspire creativity (Cummins & Early, 2011). Figure 9.1 illustrates a unit plan scenario using a PASTEL approach. It can be used as a trigger for the collaborative development of more elaborate pedagogical scenarios and lesson plans in various teaching and learning contexts.

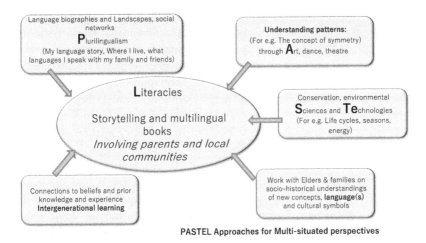

FIGURE 9.1   Unit Plan Template Using a PASTEL Approach

Learning in Class: The Power of Reflective Dialogues in Teacher Training

The collaborative development of lessons plans with museal institutions and the importance of developing cross-curricular scenarios that extend beyond the classroom to include families and communities is further discussed in Moore (2015, 2018), Moore et al. (2018), and Araújo e Sá et al. (2020).

In those experiences, teachers use reflective journaling, artefacts, and video clips of their classrooms as part of their individual and collective inquiry during the co-development of pedagogical resources, which teachers share with each other. Honouring all learners' languages in the French classroom is the first step in a plurilingual approach to learning. Teachers use language portraits, language biographies, and other similar activities to invite students to voice their experiences with plurilingualism. For example, using an activity based on "*La fleur des langues*" (elodil.com; Armand & Maraillet, 2013), each student is invited to write the language or languages known and/or spoken in their family on a petal fixed around a flower bud. The flower is then assembled to represent all the languages of the students in the class. In one example shared in a French immersion classroom (Grade 4) in British Columbia, the languages included Arabic, Punjabi, Hindi, Gujarati, Mandarin, Tagalog, Japanese, and Somali to Spanish, Italian, French, and English. Other participating teachers shared pictures drawn by students in their classrooms, comparing the flowers produced in various classes to discuss differences in language configurations. They encouraged students to show the flowers to their parents so they could also inquire about why some spoke different languages and which ones while others did not. This learning experience "for all" aims to honour children's family languages, connect school and home experiences, and raise awareness of plurilingualism. The activities also encouraged teachers and learners to explore together current theories that frame language use and language planning (what is a mother tongue, a second language, a dominant language, an official language, etc.) and to investigate language power within the language ecology of local neighbourhoods, communities, families, and schools. In another activity, teachers and learners use an investigative approach to explore languages practices in their locality (e.g., by taking pictures of languages present on signage in their neighbourhood and in their school) and to read documents to understand the politics around language planning (see Dagenais et al., 2009). Learners are also encouraged to develop interview guides to inquire about parents, grandparents, and elders' language use and their learning stories (of migration, language learning, language loss) and to inquire about science vocabulary in their families' languages or languages they are interested in (using Google Translate or other online tools). They gather stories around the themes investigated in the classroom (e.g., the stories around the sun and the moon in various cultures) and are invited to discuss the communalities and dissonances these various perspectives offer and how they can enrich their learning. For example, a visit to a science centre where children experienced what happens when air moves using an air cannon to "see" what air can do with objects within a blast zone triggered science learning about sustainable energy and wind power.

French, English, Family, and Indigenous languages and stories can easily be woven into classroom discussions to encourage provoking dialogues around the complex relationships and connections between peoples, places, languages, and concepts. Specific use of vocabulary and metaphors in various languages can invoke different cultural stories and engage children's imagination; for example, students discovered that the French word *éolienne* (turbine) comes from *Éole*, the keeper of the winds in Greek mythology and the king of the island of Aeolia whom Ulysses visits during his Odyssey. Participants decided to explore their own stories in relation to other stories that relate to the wind in other languages and cultures, including in local Indigenous stories. In British Columbia, for example, the word *SK̲wx̲wú7mesh* means "Mother of wind" in SK̲wx̲wú7mesh sníchim (Squamish), a local Indigenous language.

In British Columbia, assimilationist and colonialist policies and practices led to the near eradication of many Indigenous languages and cultures. For example, Indigenous children were removed from their homes and communities and placed in residential schools where they were forbidden to speak their own language. Currently, there are efforts to revitalize Indigenous languages and incorporate culture and knowledge in the curriculum. For example, local stories such as "The Raven Steals the Light" (by Bill Reid & Robert Bringhurst, 1984) were chosen to stand at the core of teachers' science unit plans. The story allowed embedding the lesson in the local space to deepen learners' understanding of science connections to Indigenous art and perspectives. Teachers' reflective dialogues revealed their efforts to honour Indigenous ways of knowing as crucial ways to explore multiperspectival connections to the (science) curriculum, a land-based approach to science learning, and community members' participation. Infusing Indigenous ways of knowing into the content of daily lessons and into teachers' practice is not without challenges. The lack of legitimacy, fear of cultural appropriation, and ignorance of proper protocols are amongst the recurrent themes raised by teachers throughout their reflective journaling and their comments during discussions with their peers.

While teachers wanted to honour the contemporary and historical contributions of learners' families, and strived to teach through and with, rather than *about*, Indigenous knowledge and ways of knowing (Kerr & Parent, 2016), they felt unprepared to ensure that Indigenous knowledge systems are also recognized as legitimate forms of knowledge. Nevertheless, most were ready to take the risk as they saw their philosophy of teaching as strongly anchored in the complementarity and interconnectedness between Indigenous knowledge systems and other Western knowledge forms. Integrating children's, families', and local communities' experiences and knowledge was for all teachers engaged in the co-development of lesson plans profoundly embedded in their belief that all these resources complement and enrich the school curriculum and students' learning.

Conclusion

This chapter aimed to highlight the importance of plurilingual education to encourage educators to engage with the rich linguistic resources present in and beyond multicultural and multilingual classrooms, children's imagination, and "funds of knowledge in the home" (Ntelioglou et al., 2014, n.p.). Revisiting STEAM (Sciences, Technology, Art, Mathematics) approaches to include plurilingual PASTEL (Plurilingualism, Art, Science, Technology and Literacies) pedagogies, the chapter proposed key guiding principles to design learning activities that sustain transferable skills in multiple disciplinary contexts and make meaningful connections to learners and their lives. In contexts in which French is absent or minoritized Indigenous languages are seriously endangered, and English is ever present in the daily multilingual lives of students, connecting professionals and families through reflective dialogue represents in itself an experience of alterity. It opens a collaborative space where families and educators can invest together in the co-development of language-rich inquiries, in science (Buxton et al., 2012) or other disciplines (Araújo e Sá et al., 2020).

While the contribution primarily addressed curriculum development, the development of pedagogical material and teacher education, it can also offer some guiding support to education policy makers and professionals in their efforts to assist practicing teachers' experience in collaborating with families and communities in the context of science.

Plurilingualism weaves the fabric of today's classrooms and needs to become a central component of every school's mission and culture (Castellotti & Moore, 2010). As Li and colleagues (2018) state, it is vital for teachers, alongside parents and community educators, to be afforded the collaborative space needed to co-construct learning environments that can benefit all children and their families (see also Edwards & White, 2018). Professional development experiences need to be designed so as to enhance educators' (and learners') awareness of language and plurilingualism (Bernaus et al., 2007; Pomphrey & Burley, 2009; Troyan, 2014; Melo-Pfeifer, 2015) and to harness their professional knowledge and abilities to teach in diverse contexts and engage with learners' families. Plurilingual education has the potential to provoke new, imaginative and transformative experiences, to support reflective inquiry and lifelong learning through the constant disturbance and provocation of beliefs and practices (Gear, 2018), and the weaving together of new stories (Kerr & Parent, 2016).

References

Armand, F., & Maraillet, E. (2013). *Éducation interculturelle et diversité linguistique (ELODIL)*. http://www.elodil.umontreal.ca/guides/education-interculturelle-et-diversite-linguistique/

Araújo e Sá, H., Moore, D., & Carinhas, R. (2020). Le partenariat comme déclencheur de la recherche participative: un narratif (auto)ethnographique sur la création d'un projet école-musée-famille pour/par le plurilinguisme. Recherches en Didactique Des Langues. *Les Cahiers de l'Acedle*, 17(2), 1–17.

Beacco, J. C., Byram, M. Cavalli, M., Cuenat Egli, M. Goullier, F., & Panthier, J. (2016). *Guide for the development and implementation of plurilingual and intercultural education*. Strasbourg: Council of Europe. https://rm.coe.int/16806ae621

Beaumont, S., & Moore, D. (2020). Plurilinguisme et formation des enseignants de l'éducation nationale en Amérique du Nord. Une recherche-action-formation pour le développement d'outils et pratiques innovantes. *Recherches et Applications/Le Français dans le Monde*, 67, 30–40.

Bernaus, M., Andrade, A. I., Kervran, M., Murkowska, A., & Trujillo Sáez, F. (2007). *Plurilingual and pluricultural awareness in language teacher education: A training kit*. Graz: Council of Europe Publishing European Centre for Languages.

Bottoms, S. I., Ciechanowski, K., Jones, K., de la Hoz, J., & Fonseca, A. L. (2017). Leveraging the community context of Family Math and Science Nights to develop culturally responsive teaching practices. *Teaching and Teacher Education*, 61, 1–15.

Buxton, C. A., Allexsaht-Snider, M., & Rivera, C. (2012). Science, language, and families: Constructing a model of steps to college through language-rich science inquiry. In J. Bianchini, V. Akerson, A. Calabrese Barton, O. Lee, & A. Rodriguez (Eds.), *Moving the equity agenda forward: Equity research, practice, and policy in science education* (pp. 241–250). New York: Springer.

Cammarata, L., & Tedick, D. (2012). Balancing content and language in instruction: The Experience of Immersion Teachers. *The Modern Language Journal*, 96(2), 251–269.

Campbell, C. (2017). Developing teachers' professional learning: Canadian evidence and experiences in a world of educational improvement. *Canadian Journal of Education*, 40(2), 1–33.

Candelier, M., Camilleri-Grima, A., Castellotti, V., de Pietro, J.-F., Lörincz, I., Meissner, F.-J., Noguerol, A., & Shröder-Sura, A., Molinié, M. (2012). *A framework of reference for pluralistic approaches (FREPA)*. Graz: Council of Europe Publishing. http://carap.ecml.at

Castellotti, V. & Moore, D. (2010). *Capitalising on, activating and developing plurilingual and pluricultural repertoires for better school integration (Studies and Resources no. 4)*. Strasbourg: Council of Europe Language Policy Division.

Cenoz, J., & Gorter, D. (2015). Towards a holistic approach in the study of multilingual education. In J. Cenoz & D. Gorter (Eds.), *Multilingual education: Between language learning and translanguaging* (pp. 1–15). Cambridge: Cambridge University Press.

Conteh, J., & Meier, G. (Eds.). (2015). *The multilingual turn in languages education. Opportunities and challenges*. Clevedon: Multilingual Matters.

Coste, D. (2014). Plurilingualism and the challenge of education. In P. Grommes & A. Hu (Eds.), *Plurilingual education: Policies, practices, language development* (pp. 15–32). Amsterdam/Philadelphia: John Benjamins.

Coste, D., Moore, D., & Zarate, G. (2009). *Plurilingual and pluricultural competence*. Strasbourg: Council of Europe.

Côté, I. (2019). Les défis et les réussites de l'intégration des perspectives autochtones en éducation: synthèse des connaissances dans les recherches menées au Canada. *Journal of Belonging, Identity, Language, and Diversity (J-BILD)/Revue de langage, d'identité, de diversité et d'appartenance (R-LIDA)*, 3(1), 23–45.

Coyle, D., Hood, P., & Marsh, D. (2010). *CLIL. Content and language integrated learning*. Cambridge: Cambridge University Press.

Cummins, J. (2009). Fundamental psychological and sociological principles underlying educational success for linguistic minority students. In A. K. Mohanty, M. Panda, R. Phillipson, & T. Skuttnabb-Kangas (Eds.), *Multilingual education for social justice: Globalising the local* (pp. 21–35). New Delhi: Orient Blackswan.

Cummins, J., & Early, M. (2011). *Identity texts. The collaborative creation of power in multilingual schools*. Stoke-on-Trent (UK): Trentam Books.

Dagenais, D., Moore, D., Sabatier, C., Lamarre, P., & Armand, F. (2009). Linguistic landscape and language awareness. In E. Shohamy & D. Gorter (Eds.), *Linguistic landscape: Expanding the scenery* (pp. 253–269). New York: Routledge.

Edwards, P., & White, K. (2018). Working with racially, culturally, and linguistically diverse students, families, and communities: Strategies for preparing preservice teachers. *Journal of Family Diversity in Education*, 3(1), 1–22.

Egli Cuenat, M., Cole, J., Muller, C., Szczepanska, A., Bleichenbacher, L., & Wolfer, B. (2011). *Mobility for plurilingual and intercultural education: Tools for language teachers and teacher trainers [Draft version]*. Graz: European Centre for Modern Languages, Council of Europe Publishing. http://plurimobil.ecml.at/Portals/37/Documents/plurimobil_engl_1_rev260712.pdf

Fortune, T. W., & Tedick, D. J. (Eds.). (2008). *Pathways to multilingualism: Evolving perspectives on immersion education*. Clevedon, UK: Multilingual Matters.

Gajo, L. (2007). Linguistic knowledge and subject knowledge: How does bilingualism contribute to subject development?. *International Journal of Bilingual Education and Bilingualism*, 10(5), 563–581. doi:10.2167/beb460.0

Gajo, L., & Berthoud, A.-C. (2018). Multilingual interaction and construction of knowledge in higher education. *International Journal of Bilingual Education and Bilingualism*, 21(7), 853–866. doi:10.1080/13670050.2018.1540537

Galante A. (2016). Linguistic and cultural diversity in Language education through plurilingualism: Linking the theory into practice. In P. Trifonas & T. Aravossitas (Eds.).

Handbook of research and practice in heritage language education (Springer International Handbooks of Education, pp. 1–17)., Cham: Springer.

García, O., Ibarra Johnson, S., & Seltzer, K. (2017). *The Translanguaging classroom. Leveraging student bilingualism for learning.* Philadelphia: Caslon.

Gear, A. (2018). *Powerful understanding: Helping students explore, question, and transform their thinking about … themselves and the world around them.* Markham: Pembroke.

Gonzalez, N., Moll, L., & Amanti, C. (Eds.). (2005). *Funds of knowledge: Theorizing practices in households, communities, and classrooms.* New York: Routledge.

Gorter, D., & Cenoz, J. (2017). Language education policy and multilingual assessment. *Language and Education,* 31(3), 231–248. doi:10.1080/09500782.2016.1261892

Grommes, P., & Hu, A. (Eds.). (2014). *Plurilingual education: Policies, practices, language development.* Amsterdam/Philadelphia: John Benjamins.

Hornberger, N. (2009). Multilingual education policy and practice: Ten certainties (grounded in Indigenous experience). *Language Teaching,* 42(2), 197–211.

Ignace, M. (2016). *First Nations language curriculum building guide.* First Nations Education Steering Committee/First Nations Schools Association of British Columbia. http://www.fnsa.ca/portfolio-item/first-nations-language-curriculum-building-guide

Ishimaru, A.M., Barajas-López, F., & Bang, M. (2015). Centering family knowledge to develop children's empowered mathematics identities. *Journal of Family Diversity in Education,* 1(4), 1–21.

Kerr, J., & Parent, A. (2016). Being taught by Raven: A story of knowledges in teacher education. *Canadian Journal of Native Education,* 38(1), 62–79.

Lau, S. & Van Viegen, S. (Eds.). (2020). *Plurilingual pedagogies: Critical and creative endeavors for equitable language (in) Education.* Cham, Switzerland: Springer.

Le Nevez, A., Hélot, C., & Ehrahrt, S. (2010). Negotiating plurilingualism in the classroom. In A. Le Nevez, C. Hélot, & S. Ehrahrt (Eds.), *Plurilinguisme et formation des enseignants: Une approche critique/Plurilingualism and teacher education: A critical approach* (pp. 5–21). Berlin: Peter Lang.

Li, G., Anderson, J., Carr, W., & Hare, J. (2018). Supporting teachers with diversity-plus competencies for working with culturally, linguistically, and racially diverse students, families and communities. *Journal of Family Diversity Education,* 3(1), 1–91.

Li, G., Hinojosa, D., & Wexler, L. (2018). Beliefs and perceptions about their preparation to teach English language learners: Voices of mainstream pre-service teachers. *International Journal of TESOL and Learning,* 7(1-2), 1–21.

Lüdi, G. (2014). Dynamics and management of linguistic diversity in companies and institutes of higher education: Results from the DYLAN project. In P. Grommes, & A. Hu (Eds.), *Plurilingual education: Policies, practices, language development.* (pp. 113–138). Amsterdam/Philadelphia: John Benjamins.

Marsh D., Díaz Pérez, W., & Escárzaga Morales, M. (2019). Enhancing language awareness and competence-building through a fusion of phenomenon-based learning and Content and Language Integration. *Journal of e-Learning and Knowledge Society (Je-LKS),* 15(1), 55–65. doi:10.20368/1971-8829/1617

McCollough, C. & Ramirez, O. (2012). Cultivating culture: Preparing future teachers for diversity through family learning events. *School Science and Mathematics,* 112(7), 443–451.

McCollough, C., Wolff-Murphy, S., & Blalock, G. (2019). Reforming science teacher education with cultural reflection and practice. *International Journal of Learning, Teaching and Educational Research,* 18(1), 31–49. doi:10.26803/ijlter.18.1.3.

McIvor, O. & McCarty, T. (2017). Indigenous bilingual and revitalization-immersion education in Canada and the USA. In O. García et al. (Eds.). *Bilingual and multilingual education, Encyclopedia of language and education* (pp. 1–17). Switzerland: Springer International Publishing.

Melo-Pfeifer, S. (2015). Multilingual awareness and heritage language education: children's multimodal representations of their multilingualism. *Language Awareness*, 24(3), 197–215.

Moore, D. (2018). PASTeL au musée: Plurilinguismes, AST (Art, Sciences, Technologie) et Littératies, quelles contributions pour la didactique du plurilinguisme? *Mélanges CRAPEL*, 38(1), 59–81. http://www.atilf.fr/IMG/pdf/5_moore.pdf.

Moore, D., Hoskyn, M., & Mayo, J. (2018). Thinking language awareness at a science centre: iPads, science and early literacy development with multilingual, kindergarten children in Canada. *International Journal of Bias, Identity and Diversities in Education (IJBIDE)*, 3(1), 40–63. doi:10.4018/IJBIDE.2018010104

Moore, D., & Sabatier, C. (2014). Les approches plurielles et les livres plurilingues. De nouvelles ouvertures pour l'entrée dans l'écrit et pour favoriser le lien famille-école en milieu multilingue et multiculturel. *Les Nouveaux C@hiers de la recherche en éducation (NCRÉ)*, 17(2), 32–65.

Moore, D., Oyama, M., Pearce, D. & Kitano, Y. (2020). Plurilingual education and pedagogical plurilanguaging in an elementary school in Japan: A perspectival origami for better learning. *Journal of Multilingual Theories and Practices*, 1(2), 243–265.

Nikula, T., Dafouz, E., Moore, P., & Smit, U. (Eds.). (2016). *Conceptualisation and integration in CLIL and multilingual education*. Bristol/Buffalo/Toronto: Multilingual Matters.

North, B., & Piccardo, E. (2018). *Aligning the Canadian Language Benchmark (CLB) to the Common European Framework of Reference (CEFR)* (Research Report). https://www.language.ca/wp-content/uploads/2019/01/Aligning-the-CLB-and-CEFR.pdf

Ntelioglou, Y., Fannin, J., Montarena, M., & Cummins, J. (2014). A multilingual and multimodal approach to literacy teaching and learning in urban education. A collaborative inquiry project in an inner city elementary school. *Frontiers in Psychology*, 5. https://www.ncbi.nlm.nih.gov/pmc/articles/PMC4062072/

Piccardo, E. (2013). Plurilingualism and curriculum design: Towards a synergic vision. *TESOL Quarterly*, 47(3), 600–614.

Piccardo, E. (2016). Plurilingualism: Vision, conceptualization, and practices. In P. Trifonas & T. Aravossitas (Eds.), *Handbook of research and practice in heritage language education* (Springer International Handbooks of Education). Cham: Springer.

Piccardo, E., & Puozzo, C. I., (Eds.). (2015). It is the entire special issue of *The Canadian Modern Journal*. Toronto: Toronto Press.

Pomphrey, C., & Burley, S. (2009). Language awareness as methodology: Implications for teachers and teacher training. *Language Awareness*, 18, 422–433. doi:10.1080/09658410903197314

Sarkar, M., & Lavoie, C. (2014). Language education and Canada's Indigenous peoples. In D. Gorter, V. Zenotz, & J. Cenoz (Eds.), *Minority languages and multilingual education* (pp. 85–103). New York: Springer.

Sharifian, F. (2017). *Cultural linguistics: Cultural conceptualisations and language*. Amsterdam/Philadelphia: John Benjamins.

Tomasello, M., (2018). How children come to understand false beliefs: A shared intentionality account. *Proceedings of the National Academy of Sciences*, 115(34), 8491–8498. doi:10.1073/pnas.1804761115

Troyan, F. (2014). Preparing teachers for plurilingualism through language awareness. *Tréma*, 42, 86–101.

Vallejo, C., & Dooley, M. (2019). Plurilingualism and translanguaging: Emergent approaches and shared concerns. *International Journal of Bilingual Education and Bilingualism*, 23(1), 1–16. doi:10.1080/13670050.2019.1600469.

Zeichner, K., Bowman, M., Guillen, L., & Napolitan, K. (2016). Engaging and working in solidarity with local communities in preparing the teachers of their children. *Journal of Teacher Education*, 67, 1–14.

10

INFUSING ELL PREPARATION INTO INITIAL TEACHER PREPARATION

(How) Does it Work?

Ester de Jong

Background

There is an urgent mandate to better prepare grade level or mainstream teachers to work with culturally and linguistically diverse (CLD) students. This is true for educational systems in countries around the world trying to address the increased linguistic and cultural diversity that have followed global trends in migration. In the United States, increased attention to English language learners (ELLs) and teacher preparation was fueled in part by a federal policy, the 2001 No Child Left Behind (NCLB) Act. NCLB required schools and districts to report achievement and growth by subgroup (including ELLs), which challenged educational leaders to view ELLs as the responsibility of all teachers, not just specialist language teachers, such as English as a second language (ESL) or bilingual education teachers. Although NCLB had many negative consequences for ELLs and their schooling (e.g., Menken, 2008, 2010), teachers also reported that the policy led to more awareness of ELLs and their needs and the allocation of new resources to support mainstream, grade-level teachers, ELL students, and their families (e.g., de Cohen & Clewell, 2007; Wright & Choi, 2006).

In addition, the lack of state and national capacity to provide the rapidly growing group of ELLs access to qualified specialist language teachers and the increased placement of ELLs in mainstream classrooms further contribute to the urgent call for better mainstream teacher preparation. In 2003, nearly 50% of all ELLs received minimal (fewer than 10 hours) or no special services, compared to 32% a decade earlier (Center on Education Policy, 2005). Furthermore, continued demographic mismatch between teachers' (predominantly white) and students' lived experiences (predominantly students of color) raise deep questions about how to best prepare teachers (Garcia et al., 2010; Ingersoll & May, 2011; G. Li, 2018).

Despite the growing acknowledgment of the need for better mainstream teacher preparation, state requirements for preparing all teachers to work with CLD students and ELLs are sorely lagging behind U.S. classroom realities (Education Commission of the States, 2014; Quintero & Hansen, 2017). To date, only a handful of states have formal CLD/ELL-related requirements for mainstream teacher preparation, in addition to specialist ESL or bilingual teacher certification requirements (Arizona, California, Florida, Massachusetts, Minnesota, New York, Pennsylvania). Teacher certification assessments rarely include ELL-specific items (Sampson & Collins, 2012) and fewer than a quarter of colleges offering pre-service teacher preparation include training on working with ELLs (Ballantyne et al., 2008; Wixom, 2015). Not surprisingly, practicing teachers consistently report a lack of foundational knowledge and efficacy for working with ELLs (Ballantyne et al., 2008; Coady et al., 2011).

A closer examination of how mainstream teachers are prepared to work with ELLs in K–12 settings is warranted. Despite a long-standing call to better prepare teachers for working with linguistically and culturally diverse students (e.g., Lucas & Grinberg 2008; Lucas et al., 2008; Walker & Stone, 2011) and multiple frameworks that outline the knowledge and skills needed for addressing this need (e.g., Faltis & Valdés, 2016; de Jong & Harper, 2005; de Jong et al., 2013; Lucas, 2011; Lucas & Villegas, 2013), research on how teacher preparation programs are approaching mainstream teacher preparation for ELLs is still in its beginning stages. Recent reviews of the literature (G. Li, 2018; Villegas et al., 2018) have shown that scholarship on mainstream teacher preparation for ELLs is relatively recent and has primarily focused on teachers' beliefs and attitudes.

The purpose of this chapter is to address this gap by focusing on one specific dimension of mainstream teacher preparation, namely, the notion of "infusion" as one approach to preparing mainstream teachers to work with ELLs. It considers this issue in the context of Florida as one of the first states to develop a comprehensive framework for mandatory mainstream teacher preparation for ELLs for practicing teachers (since 1990) and for preservice teacher candidates (since 2003). Although the studies included are thus context-specific, the lessons learned may be helpful for teacher education programs in other settings. After an introduction to the Florida context, this chapter addresses the following two questions:

1. What is "Infusion" and what does it look like in initial teacher preparation programs for elementary teachers in Florida?
2. What impact does the inclusion of ELL-specific knowledge and skills have on elementary teacher candidates and K–5 ELLs?

To respond to these two questions, a literature review was conducted identifying empirical and conceptual studies that took place within the Florida context and examined different dimensions of the ESL-Infused Model since it emerged as a proposed policy in 2001.

The Florida Context

The Migrant Policy Institute indicates that 21% of Florida's residents were for-eign-born and 34% of school-age children have at least one foreign-born parent (Sugarman & Geary, 2018). The Florida Department of Education (2001) reports that about 10% of the total student population is identified as ELL, with most ELLs enrolled in school districts in South Florida. As a major destination for immigration, Florida has a long tradition of policy and programming for ELLs in the United States and is one of the few states with clear requirements for professional development (PD) for mainstream teachers working with ELLs. The mandate for this PD originated in a 1990 federal court order (referred to as the Florida Consent Decree) mandating the preparation of all in-service teachers to work with ELLs. The amount of PD required by the Consent Decree was based on a teacher's instructional assignment. For example, elementary and secondary English language arts teachers needed 300 hours of training, while math, science, and social studies teachers needed 60 hours and teachers of other subject areas such as music, art, and physical education needed 18 hours of PD in what is called in Florida, English to Speakers of Other Languages (ESOL). The 300 hours consisted of five 60-hour courses: applied linguistics, cross-cultural communica-tion, ESOL methods, ESOL Curriculum and Materials, and ESOL Testing and Evaluation designed to meet a set of 25 ESOL Performance Standards.

The state of Florida has required that elementary preservice teachers from state-approved initial teacher preparation programs graduate with an ESOL endorsement since 2003 (Nutta et al., 2012). A guiding document, *Preparing Florida Teachers to Work with Limited English Proficient Students* (Florida Department of Education), explains that this requirement can be met by offering five stand-alone courses with each course counting for 60 of the 300 hours of ESOL training or through an ESOL Infusion model with a minimum of two stand-alone ESOL courses with additional ELL-related content infused into general education courses (Florida Department of Education, 2001). The latter approach thus reduces the number of specialized, stand-alone ESOL courses, "by incor-porating content from the 5 ESOL courses into other classes and field experi-ences" (Nutta & Stoddard, 2005, p. 21). No more specifics are provided in the document regarding the infused model. It merely notes that "[t]he manner and extent of infusion will vary based on a variety of factors, particularly the number of courses available for infusion" (Florida Department of Education, 2001, p. 9). To prepare instructors for the infusion of ELL-specific content into their general education courses, the state requires that instructors complete 45-hours of ESOL

PD, which can take many different forms, ranging from individual readings to workshops to taking a course.

To date, the Florida ESOL Infusion model has gone through two cycles of implementation due to changes in teacher preparation standards that needed to be met. The initial implementation used the original 25 ESOL performance standards and their indicators that were developed for the in-service ESOL endorsement requirements. A second round of implementation occurred in 2010, after a revision of the teacher preparation requirements. At that time, the Florida Department of Education approved a new set of standards, modelled after TESOL International Association's P–12 standards for initial teacher preparation (TESOL, 2010). The current framework still aligns with the titles of the original five courses but significantly reduced the number of indicators and standards to be addressed. This framework still informs current efforts in initial mainstream teacher preparation programs in Florida.

Infusion Model as a Curricular Model

Nancy Hooyman distinguishes between three curricular approaches to the inclusion of specialized knowledge and skills within a degree program. When programs create a new stand-alone specialized course or certificate, she refers to this as *specialization. Integration* refers to embedding or bringing expertise into existing courses, for example, through lectures and readings. Integration could result in an add-on approach but also be more systematic throughout a course. She defines *infusion* as the process of "identifying cross-cutting themes to present across the entire curriculum, communicating these themes in program materials, updating the objectives of existing courses to reflect these themes, and/or using assignments to assess learning of novel content related to these themes" (Hooyman, 2006, cited in Shapiro et al., 2015, p. 3).

The Florida model is thus probably best described as including elements of both specialization (the requirement of two stand-alone ESOL courses) and integration (embedding content in existing courses). Indeed, the original designers of the model referred to it as an "integrated Elementary/ESOL teacher preparation program" (Bristor et al., 2000). In the remainder of this chapter, "ESOL Infusion Model" is used when referring to Florida's formal teacher preparation model. Following Hooyman, "embedding" and "integrating" ELL-specific knowledge and skills are used to refer to actual practices.

Integrating ELL Expertise in Elementary Teacher Preparation

When the ESOL Infusion model was initially proposed, Govoni (2011) warned, "the ESOL infused model requires extensive curricular changes to teacher education programs and highly qualified faculty teaching both the stand-alone and ESOL infused courses" (p. 2). This section focuses first on curricular, course-level changes related to infusion and then addresses experiences with faculty development (see also Meskill, 2005; Nutta et al., 2012).

Course-Level Changes

Readings and Class Discussions. Personal accounts show that including different readings, class discussions, and adjustments in assignments to make ELLs more visible emerge as initial steps toward the integration of ELL-expertise (Hutchinson, 2011; de Jong & Naranjo, 2019; McHatton et al., 2009; Nutta & Stoddard, 2005; de Oliveira & Shoffner, 2009; Verkler, 2003, 2007). A recent study by de Jong and Naranjo (2019) found that syllabi explicitly reflected the ESOL teacher standards through readings and assignments. Faculty recognized the importance of including linguistic diversity in their courses and demonstrated awareness of cultural differences and the importance of differentiated instruction for ELLs' proficiency levels.

When general teacher education faculty gain more experience and collaborate directly with ESOL faculty, they realize that this level of integration may not be sufficient. At this juncture, studies suggest that collaborative, cross-disciplinary discussions are needed (Nutta & Stoddard, 2005; Verkler & Hutchinson, 2002; see also Gort & Glenn, 2010; Gort et al., 2011; de Oliveira & Shoffner, 2009), for non-Florida examples. Nutta and Stoddard (2005) use a dialogue format to describe how Nutta, as a junior ESL faculty member, and Stoddard, as a seasoned special education faculty, worked together to change a course traditionally focused on students with special needs. They insightfully reflect the tensions, confusions, and ongoing negotiations that emerged as they tried to revise the course to be more reflective of ELLs. An example of the need for open and explicit dialogue occurred when they realized the differential meanings and instructional implications of common terms in both fields, such as "accommodations" and "modifications". Once clarified, efforts toward deeper integration became possible.

Ideologies. More (language) ideologically driven shifts are also needed. Literacy courses that take monolingualism as their starting point and native speakers as the accepted norm may perpetuate deficit perspectives of bilingual learners (see also Gort & Glenn, 2010; de Oliveira & Shoffner, 2009). Hutchinson (2011), for example, notes that it was not till she received specifically designed case studies of ELLs with different backgrounds and English proficiency levels from her ESL colleague that she was able to transform her general methods course's micro-teaching experience.

Using syllabus analysis and interviews with six general education faculty, de Jong and Naranjo (2019) found that lesson plans (a) considered ELL accommodations after a generic lesson was already developed and (b) often conflated different student groups when it came to thinking about instructional changes. Specifically, ELLs tended to be grouped with struggling readers, students with disabilities, and so forth as though the same strategy would meet the needs of each of these groups of students. As a result, teacher educators inadvertently reinforced a "just good teaching" perspective (de Jong & Harper, 2005), while failing to recognize ELLs' strengths and differences from students with special needs.

Field Experiences. Another dimension of the ESOL Infusion model is required field experiences with ELLs. Several studies (e.g., Coady et al., 2011; Hancock, 2010; Shamon, 2015) confirm the importance attached to direct interaction with ELLs: program graduates wished they had had more field experiences as part of their teacher preparation program leading to an ESOL endorsement. Although field experiences are viewed as a crucial component in the preparation of mainstream teachers (National Council of Accreditation for Teacher Education (NCATE) Blue Ribbon Panel, 2010), few studies have documented experiences in Florida. Ariza (2003) describes an after-school tutoring effort that brought parents, ELLs, and teacher candidates together as part of a stand-alone ESOL course. A similar tutoring effort with a focus on reading skills through the *American Reads* tutoring program is presented by Al Otaiba (2005). In the latter effort, teacher candidates received specific training as tutors prior to working with ELLs. Lee et al. (2018) describe teacher candidates' experiences with two 10-hour practica. One takes place at the beginning of the program in a rural district with a focus on observation and getting to know ELLs and their families. The other takes place towards the end of the program prior to a full-year internship and takes place in specialized language classrooms with an expectation of working directly with ELLs.

Govoni (2011) notes that multiple opportunities for direct contact with ELLs can be particularly challenging for teacher preparation programs in areas with few ELLs. Some universities have experimented with virtual learning environments (Regalla et al., 2016) and/or micro-teaching as alternative structures to create opportunities for teacher candidates' practice and application (Lee, 2018).

Preparing General Teacher Educators

General teacher educator preparation plays a significant role in successful ELL expertise integration in a teacher preparation program (Baecher, 2012; Brisk, 2008; Levine et al., 2014; Roy-Campbell, 2013). In recognition of this prerequisite, faculty teaching formally identified "ESOL infused" courses must complete 45 hours of PD in Florida. Verkler (2003) describes the content of, and one college of education faculty's experiences with, a set of five PD modules aligned with the five domains outlined in the Florida Consent Decree. Supported through external grant funding, Project Jericho allowed for course design and faculty support, and Verkler reports positive initial responses from faculty. In a follow-up study (Verkler, 2007), general education faculty reported that they felt supported and prepared to integrate ELL-related standards into their courses. They also indicate that the various ESOL requirements can be confusing and difficult to meet.

In another study, de Jong et al. (2018) surveyed ESL faculty in 15 Florida colleges and universities regarding their faculty PD. They found that PD tended to include traditional concepts of second language acquisition (Krashen's theories, proficiency stages, social vs academic language), in addition to demographics and policies. At most institutions, ESL faculty had moved from conducting in-person workshops to online delivery of the content in order to maximize flexibility for faculty to complete the 45 hours. The study reported that barriers to successful implementation included a compliance mentality (i.e., a box to be checked rather than something being valued), lack of administrative support, and differing visions of the ESOL Infusion model. General education faculty's own experiences with linguistic diversity facilitated participation and implementation (de Jong & Naranjo, in press). Another factor was the ELL content itself. Faculty reported being more comfortable integrating culture-related content than the more specialized linguistics content (Mihai & Pappamihiel, 2012).

The Impact of ESOL-Infused Model on Elementary Teacher Preparation

With fifteen years of implementation, a reasonable question is what impact Florida's framework for preparing mainstream teachers through initial teacher preparation has had (see also Coady et al., 2018). Following the general trend in the research (G. Li, 2018; Li & Peters, 2016; Villegas et al., 2018), this question has received little attention. This section reviews studies that examined the impact on teacher candidates' knowledge and beliefs, the impact on instructional decision-making, and on student learning.

Impact on Teacher Candidates. ELL-infused course work can have a positive impact on students' beliefs and attitudes. Smith (2011) reported on an online survey administered in two stand-alone ESOL courses at the beginning and at the end of teacher candidates' participation in an ESOL Infused program. The survey addressed teacher candidates' perceived knowledge and skills and their attitudes towards having ELLs placed in mainstream classrooms. His study showed a positive effect for candidates' perceived knowledge and skills across the two courses. They indicated feeling most knowledgeable in the area of cultural diversity. No significant differences were noted for attitudes towards the inclusion of ELLs. Teacher candidates indicated they thought ELLs with higher English proficiency would be appropriate in a mainstream classroom but did not share this belief for ELLs at lower English proficiency levels. In a similar vein, de Jong and Harper (2011), who surveyed 180 elementary teacher candidates about their knowledge, skills, and confidence in working with ELLs, found that cultural issues were more comfortable to address pedagogically and more visible for the teacher candidates. A survey of special education, elementary, and secondary English language arts teacher candidates indicated that they felt prepared to work with ELLs during their internship (Verkler, 2007). Positive results were also found in a study by Shamon (2015) in which teacher candidates felt confident in their knowledge base related to ELLs. She also notes, however, that teacher candidates' ability to respond pedagogically to linguistic differences and assessment data was still emerging.

Research confirms the important role of field experiences where teacher candidates work directly with ELLs (Bodur, 2012; Lee et al., 2018). Ariza (2003) noted the positive impact of an after-school tutoring program on relationships among students, parents, and teacher candidates and on opportunities for teacher candidates to translate theory taught in the stand-alone ESOL course into practice. Looking at formal reading measures and preservice teachers' reflections, Al Otaiba (2005) found that tutoring training and experience enhanced teacher candidates' awareness of the structure of English at the word and phoneme level. Lee et al. (2018) used student reflections and focus interviews with teacher candidates to better understand the impact of two field experiences. Their work highlights the impact of field experiences on teacher candidates' empathy and ability to understand how theory shapes practice. Finally, Pappamihiel (2007) examined the impact of a community-based service-learning project, an assignment that was part of a survey ESOL course, on a diverse group of teacher candidates, including elementary and secondary preservice teachers. The course was designed to address components of each of the five courses that make up the 300 hours. She noted that the experience had a differential impact on the teacher candidates but included shifts in attitudes, questioning of prior beliefs and misconceptions, and a better understanding of the role of ELLs in schools.

Postgraduation. Two studies considered Florida initial teacher preparation program graduates, their attitudes, and their sense of preparedness. Overall, these studies reported positive experiences with their teacher preparation program. Vázquez-Montilla et al. (2014) surveyed 487 teachers in Southwest Florida using a modified version of the Language Attitude Scale, 50 of whom had graduated from a Florida institute of higher education. Although responses reflected aspects of a culture of care, respondents also expressed support for English-only practices and assigned a lack of motivation to ELLs as a reason for not doing well in school. The study did not find any statistically significant difference between the Florida and non-Florida graduates in terms of attitudes and beliefs.

Coady et al. (2011, 2016) and de Jong et al. (2013) reported on the results of another post-training study. Their mixed-method study, Project DELTA (Developing English Language and Literacy Through Teacher Achievement), found that graduates from a Florida ESOL Infused Program overwhelmingly reported they felt well-prepared and efficacious to work with ELLs. They felt most confident in creating a welcoming environment and incorporating students' cultural experiences. Using students' native languages as a resource for teaching and language-specific instruction were identified as the areas in which they felt least confident.

Impact on instructional decision-making. Teachers' instructional decision-making for ELLs (actual practices) is an area in need of more research. Based on analyses of teacher candidates' responses to scenarios involving instructional decision-making for ELLs at different proficiency levels in mathematics, Turkan & de Jong (2018) concluded that instructional decision-making drew from an awareness of vocabulary difficulty and the role of cultural experiences in interpreting content. Wheeler and Govoni (2014) reported that teacher candidates in their ESOL-Infused program were able to apply a wide range of ESOL strategies aligned with ELLs' proficiency levels in their lesson planning in math, science, social studies, and language arts.

In the classroom, decision-making is more complex than writing a lesson plan and is embedded in broader school cultures and contexts. Follow-up interviews and observations in focal teachers' classrooms in Project DELTA showed that, although graduates of the ESOL-Infused program felt positive toward the ELLs in their classrooms, instructional decision-making in the classroom reflected in-the-moment responses rather than a planned consideration of their ELLs' needs. In-depth cases of two focal teachers showed that individual attention was the go-to strategy for ensuring access to instruction. Missed opportunities for language development and cultural connections were common, leading the researchers to distinguish between inclusion (placing ELLs in mainstream classrooms) and creating inclusive classrooms (Coady et al., 2016).

Impact on student learning. The impact of an integrated ELL teacher preparation model on ELL learning and achievement is the least researched area. Ariza (2003) showed student growth in the course of an after-school tutoring experience as documented by one of the teacher candidates' reflection journals. Al Otaiba (2005) found a positive impact of the one-on-one tutoring program on formal measures of word attack, word identification, and passage comprehension. Examining the achievement of ELLs taught by program graduates as part of Project DELTA, de Jong and colleagues reported that ELLs taught by graduates with the ESOL endorsement scored higher on the standardized state achievement test in reading and math than graduates without this preparation (de Jong et al., 2007).

When considering ELL achievement trends in Florida, however, little progress can be noted. Recent data show that Florida ELLs' fourth- and eighth-grade reading and math scores decreased between 2009 and 2017 on the National Assessment of Educational Progress tests (U.S. Department of Education, 2018b). Moreover, the academic achievement gap between ELLs and non-ELLs on Florida's state tests has not narrowed since the implementation of NCLB in 2001 (Coady et al., 2018). These findings raise important questions regarding the intended and actual impact of Florida's approach.

Looking Ahead: The Place of Infusion

What can we learn from the experiences of a state with 15 years of experience with a policy requiring the equivalent of 300 hours of PD for elementary teacher candidates through an integrated ESOL approach and 45 hours of general teacher education faculty PD? Although more research is clearly needed, Florida's teacher preparation program faculty and students report several positive experiences. ELL expertise is included through syllabus redesign, through the inclusion of ELL-specific readings and assignments, and particularly through structured field experiences that encourage direct interactions with ELLs. There also emerges a cautionary note, however, from the Florida story.

The ELL-specific knowledge and skills as they pertain to the role of culture in school are perceived as easier to be integrated. Moreover, teacher candidates indicate they are most comfortable with making their classrooms a welcoming environment and instruction comprehensible. Most challenging appears the paradigm shift that requires general education faculty to view ELLs from an asset-based, multilingual perspective and systematically challenge the monolingual norm that dominates mainstream teacher preparation (de Jong, 2013). The latter becomes even more challenging when general education faculty themselves have not had many personal or professional experiences with cultural and linguistic diversity. These findings point, first, to the need for course work for teacher candidates in which in-depth and specialized ELL expertise can be developed by experts in the field of ELL teaching and learning. The combination of specialization and integration seems to allow for a teacher preparation program that is more inclusive of ELL-related considerations while acknowledging the professional expertise base of working with ELLs. Second, these findings underscore a key challenge in achieving curricular ELL-related infusion because it in many cases requires a shift in positioning and ideologies. As efforts in infusing diversity in general or multicultural perspectives have shown, this paradigm shift allows for actual program *transformation*, is the hardest to achieve, and requires significant whole-program faculty development (e.g., Gay, 1997; Levine et al., 2014).

Finally, it must be noted that, despite positive experiences, there is limited understanding of the impact of the Florida framework for ELL teacher preparation on teaching practices and ELL learning. The few studies that do exist raise important questions about the ability of the ESOL Infused model to improve learning opportunities for ELLs. It is important to reiterate here that the Florida infused approach was not intended to replace the need for specialist ESL teachers. Govoni (2011) notes,

> It was imperative for all educators to bear in mind that the curricular goal of the EICM [Elementary Integrated Curriculum Model] was designed to prepare preservice teachers to work effectively with students from diverse linguistic and cultural backgrounds and that it was not designed to transform every teacher into an ESL specialist.
>
> *(p. 2)*

In reality, the candidate who graduated with an elementary teacher certification with an ESOL endorsement and the candidate who graduated with a certification in ESOL are indistinguishable when it comes to hiring. Florida policy considers both equally qualified when teaching ELLs. This would suggest that the ESOL Infusion model approach to mainstream teacher preparation may not be the problem. Rather, the equation of being prepared through an ESL infused program and being prepared as an ESL specialist teacher and the resulting diminishing expertise based in schools may be more at the heart of the continued achievement gap. Recent work by López and Santibañez (2018) again underscores the importance of specialist preparation. Comparing teacher preparation policy impact on ELLs (or emergent bilinguals, EBs) in Arizona, California, and Texas, they conclude

> it makes sense to ensure all teachers have some knowledge about the particular needs of EBs.... This approach, however, cannot replace more rigorous training that does require more time and resources.
>
> *(p. 32)*

In short, ELL-expertise infusion in the context of mainstream teacher preparation is a must and should be imperative for all teacher preparation programs with the goal of enhancing mainstream teacher preparation for linguistically and culturally inclusive classrooms. It is simultaneously crucial to avoid losing the deep specialized knowledge and skill competencies of the specialist teacher. In addition to requirements for mainstream teachers, states should thus maintain high standards for those responsible for the education of ELLs to demonstrate this discipline-based professional expertise.

References

Al Otaiba, S. (2005). How effective is code-based reading tutoring in English for English learners and preservice teacher-tutors? *Remedial and Special Education*, 26(4), 245–254. doi:10.1177/07419325050260040701

Ariza, E. W. (2003). TESOL tutor time homework center: A collaboration of volunteer preservice teachers in the public elementary schools. *Urban Education*, 38(6), 708–724. doi:10.1177/0042085903257316.

Baecher, L. (2012). Examining the place of English language learners within the teacher education curriculum. *Journal of Curriculum and Teaching*, 1(2), 8–20.

Ballantyne, K. G., Sanderman, A. R., & Levy, J. (2008). *Educating English language learners: Building teacher capacity*. Washington, DC: National Clearinghouse for English Language Acquisition.

Bodur, Y. (2012). Impact of course and fieldwork on multicultural beliefs and attitudes. *The Educational Forum*, 76(1), 41–56.

Brisk, M. E. (2008). Program and faculty transformation: Enhancing teacher preparation. In M. E. Brisk (Ed.), *Language, culture and community in teacher education* (pp. 249–265). New York: Lawrence Erlbaum Associates.

Bristor, V. J., Pelaez, G. M., & Crawley, S. (2000). An integrated elementary education/ESOL teacher preparation program. *Action in Teacher Education (Association of Teacher Educators)*, 22(2), 25–32.

Center on Education Policy. (2005). *State high school exit exams: States try hard, but gaps persist.* Washington, DC: Author.

Coady, M., de Jong, E. J., & Harper, C. (2011). Preservice to practice: Mainstream teacher beliefs of preparation and efficacy with English language learners in the state of Florida. *Bilingual Research Journal, 34*(2), 223–239.

Coady, M., Harper, C., & de Jong, E. (2016). Aiming for equity: Preparing mainstream teachers for inclusion or inclusive classrooms? *TESOL Quarterly, 50*(2), 340–368. doi:10.1002/tesq.223

Coady, M. R., Li, S., & Lopez, M. (2018). Twenty-five years after the Florida ESOL Consent Decree: FL DOE's preparing all teacher for English Learners work? *FATE Journal 3*(1), 26–55.

de Cohen, C. C., & Clewell, B. C. (2007). *Putting english language learners on the educational map: The no child left behind act implemented.* Washington, DC: The Urban Institute. Retrieved from https://www.urban.org/research/publication/putting-english-language-learners-educational-map

de Jong, E. J. (2013). Preparing mainstream teachers for multilingual classrooms, *Association of Mexican American Educators Journal, 7*(2), 40–49.

de Jong, E. J., Coady, M. R., & Harper, C. A. (2007). *Project DELTA [Developing English Language and Literacy through Teacher Achievement]. Project Overview.* https://education.ufl.edu/project-delta/project-overview/

de Jong, E. J., & Harper, C. A. (2005). Preparing mainstream teachers for English language learners: Is being a good teacher good enough? *Teacher Education Quarterly, 32*(2), 101–124.

de Jong, E. J., & Harper, C. A. (2011). "Accommodating diversity": Preservice teachers' views on effective practices for English language learners. In T. Lucas (Ed.), *Teacher preparation for linguistically diverse classrooms: A resource for teacher educators* (pp. 73–90). New York: Routledge.

de Jong, E. J., Harper, C. A., & Coady, M. (2013). Enhanced knowledge and skills for elementary mainstream teachers of English language learners. *Theory Into Practice, 52*(2), 89–97.

de Jong, E. J., Naranjo, C., Li, S., & Ouzia, A. (2018). Beyond compliance: ESL faculty's perspectives on preparing general education faculty for ESL infusion. *The Educational Forum, 82*(2), 174–190.

de Jong, E. J., & Naranjo, C. (2019). *General education teacher educators and English language learner teacher preparation: Infusion as curricular change. The New Educator, 15*(4), 331–354.

de Oliveira, L. & Shoffner, M. (2009). Addressing the needs of English language learners in an English education methods course. *English Education, 42*, 91–111.

Education Commission of States. (2014). *What training, if any, is required of general classroom teachers?* Retrieved from http://ecs.force.com/mbdata/mbquestNB2?rep=ELL1415

Faltis, C. J., & Valdés, G. (2016). Preparing teachers for teaching in and advocating for linguistically diverse classrooms: A vade mecum for teacher educators. In D. H. Gitomer & C. A. Bell (Eds.), *Handbook of research on teaching* (5th ed., pp. 549–592). Washington, DC: American Educational Research Association.

Florida Department of Education (2001). *Preparing Florida teachers to work with limited English proficient students.* Tallahassee, FL: Bureau of Educator Recruitment and Professional Development.

Garcia, E., Arias, M. B., Murri, N. J. H., & Serna, C. (2010). Developing responsive teachers: A challenge for a demographic reality. *Journal of Teacher Education, 61*, 132–144.

Gay, G. (1997). Multicultural infusion in teacher education: Foundations and applications. *Peabody Journal of Education, 72*(1), 150–177.

Gort, M., & Glenn, W. J. (2010). Navigating tensions in the process of change: An English educator's dilemma management in the revision and implementation of a diversity-infused method's course. *Research in the Teaching of English*, 45, 59–86.

Gort, M., Glenn, W. J., & Settlage, J. (2011). Toward culturally and linguistically responsive teacher education: The impact of a faculty learning community on two teacher educators. In T. Lucas (Ed.), *Teacher preparation for linguistically diverse classrooms: A resource for teacher educators* (pp. 179–194). New York, NY: Routledge.

Govoni, J. (2011). The evolution, evaluation, and lessons learned with ESOL infusion in Florida. *Tapestry Journal*, 3(2), 1–6. Retrieved from http://tapestry.usf.edu/journal/documents/v03n02-Govoni.pdf

Hancock, S. J. (2010). *Perceptions of teaching and learning to teach English language learners in elementary classrooms* [Unpublished doctoral dissertation]. Gainesville, FL: University of Florida.

Hutchinson, C. J. (2011). Infusing content into a foundation course. *TAPESTRY*, 3(2), Article 4. Available at: https://stars.library.ucf.edu/tapestry/vol3/iss2/4

Ingersoll, R. M., & May, H. (2011). *Recruitment, retention, and the minority teacher shortage*. Philadelphia, PA: Consortium for Policy Research in Education.

Lee, Y. (2018). *An exploratory study of preservice teachers and their self-efficacy as teachers of English language learners using micro teaching experiences* [Unpublished dissertation]. University of Florida.

Lee, Y., Kim, H., & de Jong, E. J. (2018). Becoming a teacher of culturally and linguistically diverse students: Elementary pre-service teachers' ESL field experiences working with English language learners. *Sunshine State TESOL Journal*, 12(1), 29–40.

Levine, T., Howard, E., & Moss, D. (2014). *Preparing classroom teachers to succeed with second language learners: Lessons from a faculty learning community*. New York, NY: Routledge.

Li, G. (2018). Moving toward a diversity plus teacher education: Approaches, challenges, and possibilities in preparing teachers for English language learners. In D. Polly, M. Putnam, T. M. Petty, & A. J. Good (Eds.), *Innovative practices in teacher preparation and graduate-level teacher education programs* (pp. 215–236). Hershey, PA: IGI Global.

Li, N., & Peters, A. W. (2016). Preparing K–12 teachers for ELLs: Improving teachers' L2 knowledge and strategies through innovative professional development. *Urban Education*, 1–18. Advanced online publication. doi:10.1177/0042085916656902

López, F., & Santibañez, L. (2018). Teacher preparation for emergent bilingual students: Implications of evidence for policy. *Education Policy Analysis Archives*, 26(36). doi:10.14507/epaa.26.2866

Lucas, T. (Ed.). (2011). *Teacher preparation for linguistically diverse classrooms: A resource for teacher educators*. New York: Routledge.

Lucas, T., & Grinberg, J. (2008). Responding to the linguistic reality of mainstream classrooms: Preparing all teachers to teach English language learners. In M. Cochran-Smith, S. Feiman-Nemser, & D. J. McIntyre (Eds.), *Handbook of research on teacher education: Enduring questions in changing contexts* (3rd ed., pp. 606–636). New York, NY: Routledge.

Lucas, T., & Villegas, A. M. (2013). Preparing linguistically responsive teachers: Laying the foundation in preservice teacher education. *Theory Into Practice*, 52(2), 98–109. doi:10.1080/00405841.2013.770327.

Lucas, T., Villegas, A. M., & Freedson-Gonzalez, M. (2008). Linguistically responsive teacher education: Preparing classroom teachers to teach English language learners. *Journal of Teacher Education*, 59, 361–373. doi:10.1177/0022487108322110.

McHatton, P. A., Keller, H., Shircliffe, B., & Zalaquett, C. (2009). Examining efforts to infuse diversity within one college of education. *Journal of Diversity in Higher Education*, 2(3), 127–135.

Menken, K. (2008). *English learners left behind: Standardized testing as language policy.* Clevedon, UK: Multilingual Matters.

Menken, K. (2010). NCLB and English language learners: Challenges and consequences. *Theory Into Practice,* 49(2), 121–128. doi:10.1080/00405841003626619.

Meskill, C. (2005). Infusing English language learner issues throughout professional educator curriculum: The training all teachers project. *Teachers College Record,* 107, 739–756.

Mihai, F. M., & Pappamihiel, N. E. (2012). Strengthening the curriculum by adding EL-specific coursework and related field experiences. In J. Nutta, K. Mokhtari, & C. Strebel (Eds.), *Preparing every teacher to reach English learners: A practical guide for teacher educators,* (pp. 253–270). Cambridge, MA: Harvard Education Press.

National Council of Accreditation for Teacher Education (NCATE) Blue Ribbon Panel (2010). *Transforming teacher education through clinical practice: A national strategy to prepare effective teachers.* Washington, DC: National Council for Accreditation of Teacher Education

Nutta, J., & Stoddard, K. (2005). Reducing confusion about infusion: A collaborative process of infusing ESOL into special education teacher preparation. *Florida Journal of Teacher Education,* 8, 21–32.

Nutta, J., Mokhtari, K., & Strebel, C. (2012). *Preparing every teacher to reach ELs: A practical guide for teacher educators.* Cambridge, MA: Harvard Education Press.

Pappamihiel, E. (2007). Helping preservice content-area teachers relate to English language learners: An investigation of attitudes and beliefs. *TESL Canada Journal/Revue TESL du Canada,* 24(2), 41–60.

Quintero, D., & Hansen, M. (2017). *English learners and the growing need for qualified teachers. Brookings Institution.* Retrieved December 17, 2019 from https://www.brookings.edu/blog/brown-center-chalkboard/2017/06/02/english-learners-and-the-growing-need-for-qualified-teachers/

Regalla, M., Hutchinson, C., Nutta, J. & Ashtari, N. (2016). Examining the impact of a simulation classroom experience on teacher candidates' sense of efficacy in communicating with English learners. *Journal of Technology and Teacher Education,* 24(3), 337–367. Retrieved December 17, 2019 from https://www.learntechlib.org/primary/p/171498/

Roy-Campbell, Z. M. (2013). Who educates teacher educators about English language learners? *Reading Horizons,* 52(3), 255–280. Retrieved from http://scholarworks.wmich.edu/reading_horizons/vol52/iss3/4/

Sampson, J., & Collins, B. (2012). *Preparing all teachers to meet the needs of English language learners.* Washington, DC: Center for American Progress. Retrieved December 17, 2019 from http://files.eric.ed.gov/fulltext/ED535608.pdf.

Shamon, C. (2015). *Responding to the Florida teacher standards for the English as a second language endorsement: A study of elementary preservice teachers' perceptions* [Unpublished doctoral dissertation]. Boca Raton, FL: Florida Atlantic University.

Shapiro, V. B., Hudson, K. D., Moylan, C. A., & Derr, A. S. (2015). Changing organisational routines in doctoral education: an intervention to infuse social justice into a social welfare curriculum. *Arbor: Ciencia, pensamiento y cultura,* 771(A202), 1–15.

Smith, P. (2011). Teaching inclusivity: Preservice teachers' perceptions of their knowledge, skills and attitudes towards working with English language learners in mainstream classrooms. *Tapestry Journal,* 3(1), 1–21.

Sugarman, J., & Geary, C. (2018). *English learners in Florida: Demographics, outcomes, and state accountability policies.* Washington, DC: Migration Policy Institute.

TESOL (Teachers of English to Speakers of Other Languages) International Association. (2010). *Standards for the recognition of initial tesol programs in p–12 esl teacher education.* Arlington, VA: Author.

Turkan, S., & de Jong, E. J. (2018). An exploration of preservice teachers' reasoning about teaching mathematics to English language learners. *Teacher Education Quarterly*, 45(2), 37–60.

U.S. Department of Education. (2018a). *Our nation's English learners.* Retrieved from https://www2.ed.gov/datastory/el-characteristics/index.html#intro

U.S. Department of Education. (2018b). *Academic performance and outcomes for English learner. Performance on national assessments and on-time graduation rate.* Retrieved from https://www2.ed.gov/datastory/el-outcomes/index.html

Vázquez-Montilla, E., Just, M, & Triscari, R. (2014). Teachers' dispositions and beliefs about cultural and linguistic diversity. *Universal Journal of Educational Research*, 2(8), 577–587.

Verkler, K. (2003). Teacher Educators as students: A university shares its faculty ESOL professional development model. *Foreign Language Annals*, 36(2), 208–222.

Verkler, K. (2007). A university's college of education reflects on its faculty and student ESOL endorsement Infusion Model. *Journal of Educational Media & Literacy Sciences*, 45(1), 75–97.

Verkler, K. W., & Hutchinson, C. (2002). You can lead a horse to water but … ESOL faculty mentors reflect on their experiences. *SRATE Journal*, 11(1), 16–28.

Villegas, A. M., SaizdeLaMora, K., Martin, A. D., & Mills, T. (2018). Preparing future mainstream teachers to teach English language learners: A review of the empirical literature. *The Educational Forum*, 82(2), 138–155.

Walker, C. L. & Stone, K. (2011). Preparing teachers to reach English language learners: Pre service and in-service initiatives. In T. Lucas (Ed.), *Teacher preparation for linguistically diverse classrooms: A resource for teacher educators* (pp. 127–141). New York, NY: Routledge.

Wheeler, D. L., & Govoni, J. M. (2014). An ESOL curricular model: Infusing ESOL standards in teacher education. *The Tapestry Journal*, 6(2), 10–35.

Wixom, M. A. (2015). *ECS and national experts examine: State-level English language learner policies.* Washington, DC: Education Commission of the States. Retrieved August 8, 2019 from https://www.ecs.org/clearinghouse/01/17/92/11792.pdf

Wright, W. E., & Choi, D. (2006). The impact of language and high-stakes testing policies on elementary school English language learners in Arizona. *Education Policy Analysis Archives*, 14(13). Retrieved from https://epaa.asu.edu/ojs/article/view/84

SECTION III

Engaging Practices for Educators for Superdiversity

11

ACADEMIC SUPPORT FOR REFUGEE STUDENTS IN ELEMENTARY AND SECONDARY SCHOOLS AND TEACHERS' QUANDARIES ABOUT INCLUSIVITY

Hua Que and Xuemei Li

Background and Theoretical Framework

The move to inclusive education has changed the way of improving the educational outcomes of children with special needs. In the 1970s, children who used to study in separate classrooms for special education began to be placed in regular classrooms with their peers. At that time, a child's special needs generally related to disabilities. In recent decades, with the increase of immigrants and refugees coming to resettlement countries, special needs have been extended to the diverse educational, mental, and social needs of newcomer children (Taylor & Sidhu, 2012). In Canada, inclusive education has been embraced by provinces and territories to different extents (Bunch, 2015). In Newfoundland and Labrador (NL)—the most easterly province with a modest population, where the study took place, the Department of Education and Early Childhood Development (DEECD) defines inclusive education as "a philosophy that promotes the right of all students to attend school with their peers, and to receive appropriate and quality programming" (Collins et al., 2017, p. 7; DEECD, n.d., p. 1). However, it remains unknown if refugee students with a different set of special needs are included in the policy.

Between January 2016 and September 2018, 620 government-assisted refugees came to NL, of whom approximately 340 were younger than 18 years old upon arrival (Association for New Canadians, 2018a, 2018b, 2018c). Responding to this demographic change, two support programs, English as a Second Language (ESL) and Literacy Enrichment and Academic Readiness for Newcomers (LEARN), were designed to meet the educational needs of newcomer students (Collins et al., 2017). The ESL services "aim at supporting the student in the acquisition of English, including literacy skills and lifelong learning strategies, with the ultimate goal of successful social and academic integration" (DEECD, 2011a, p. 1). The LEARN Program "is developed to meet the academic needs of immigrant students with major gaps in literacy and numeracy achievement" caused by "a lack of formal schooling" (DEECD, 2011b, p. 2). The LEARN program consists of two levels. LEARN-1 aims to help refugee students improve their basic literacy and bring them up to a Grade 6 math level. LEARN-2 offers social studies and science in addition to language arts and mathematics, aiming to prepare refugee students for mainstream courses (DEECD, 2011b).

Researchers point out that smaller cities receiving a growing number of immigrants and refugees require more attention (Guo & Guo, 2016). This chapter focuses on the language and academic support for refugee students in elementary and secondary schools in a city in NL with a population of 219,207 (Statistics Canada, 2018). Using a framework for responsive practice, we particularly seek to investigate whether the programming for refugee students has adequately addressed their educational needs.

The framework for responsive practice is a whole-school approach that ensures the successful integration of refugee students in the school community (Ontario Ministry of Education, 2013, 2016). This framework focuses on enabling refugee students to acquire language and learn academic subjects simultaneously, building a welcoming learning environment, designing culturally responsive curriculum that takes an asset-based approach to incorporate refugee students' knowledge and life experience into the school curriculum, encouraging refugee students to voice their opinions, and setting goals with refugee students to choose appropriate career and academic pathways. In addition, because posttraumatic stress disorder is common among refugee children (Beiser & Korczak, 2018), educators need to become trauma-informed, preparing themselves for dealing with refugee students' traumas caused by pre-migration, transmigration, and post-migration life experiences. Culturally responsive policies and practices of school systems are a fundamental component of making school systems more culturally responsive (Richards et al., 2006).

Literature review
Educational Programming for Refugee Students

Mainstreaming refugee students through the provision of support programs has been a widely implemented approach to improving their educational outcomes. Ontario, Canada, for instance, offers the English Literacy Development (ELD) program to English language learners in Grades 3 through 12 with significant educational gaps (Ontario Ministry of Education, 2016). Similarly, in Alberta, a specialized program is offered to refugee children with limited or no literacy in English or in their mother tongue upon arrival, including subjects of English language, math, social studies, and an option (i.e., art or computer technology), for up to 20 months (Guo et al., 2019).

According to Asadi (2015), schools in which refugee students achieve high levels of academic performance pay equal attention to language instruction and content instruction and integrate refugee students into the mainstream classrooms as soon as students have gained basic literacy skills in English. However, determining the appropriate length of time that refugee students should spend in transitional programs is challenging for educators (Gunasekera et al., 2016). Students would be stigmatized as less intelligent if they stayed in the support programs for too long (Nilsson & Axelsson, 2013). Although support programs create safe and caring social and pedagogical settings for refugee students, they must be premised on a temporary basis (Nilsson & Axelsson, 2013).

In addition to the simultaneous provision of intensive English programs and basic content area instruction, spatial interactions between refugee students and their mainstream peers are another essential element of a successful transition (Pugh et al., 2012). African refugee students in Kanu's (2008) study in Manitoba, Canada, noted that they felt isolated, excluded, and lonely in school, as a result of spending a significant amount of time in segregated ESL classes. An urban secondary school in the United States in Hos (2016) study offered the newcomer program in a space that was separated from the main hallways and mainstream classrooms, which further marginalized refugee students. Similarly, the introductory classes for newly arrived refugee students in Nilsson and Axelsson's (2013) study were located in a separate building of the school, which inhibited refugee students' opportunities to interact with other students and classroom teachers.

Barriers to Achievement Faced by Refugee Students in Mainstream Classrooms

Refugee students tend to have a strong desire to transition to mainstream classrooms as they view it as "the opportunity to become like everyone else" (Nilsson & Axelsson, 2013, p. 159). However, mainstream classrooms may fail these students if additional support is not available. For example, Gunasekera et al. (2016) found that almost all the refugee students in the support programs set their career goals as becoming professionals such as doctors, teachers, and scientists, whereas many of them changed their career goals to those not requiring university degrees such as hairdressers, sports stars, and musicians after transitioning to mainstream classrooms. The authors further indicated that refugee students taking regular classes are likely to lose confidence in realizing their initial goals if additional support is not in place or ongoing support is not offered.

Without continuous support, the inclusion of refugee students in mainstream classrooms would also add extra challenges for classroom teachers. Classroom teachers tend to focus on the subject matter and are less inclined to provide specialized support for refugee students to address their language and literacy needs (Nilsson & Axelsson, 2013). In addition, some classroom teachers in Due et al.'s (2016) study struggled to identify, diagnose, and respond to refugee students' learning difficulties due to language barriers.

Modes of Ongoing Support in Mainstream Classrooms for Refugee Students

Tutoring is one of the modes that offer additional academic support, which has been shown to be effective in supporting refugee students in mainstream classrooms (Avery, 2017). For instance, previous research reported that tutors assisted refugee students in mainstream classrooms, withdrew them for additional support, or offered after-school tutoring (Naidoo, 2013; Weekes et al., 2011). In addition, co-teaching between ESL teachers and classroom teachers also could maximize the educational outcomes of newcomer students (Beninghof & Leensvaart, 2016). Ongoing support in mainstream classrooms thus places emphasis on the collaboration between support teachers and classroom teachers. For this reason, teacher preparation programs should encompass effective teacher collaboration to better prepare them for teaching newcomer students from diverse cultural backgrounds (Peercy & Martin-Beltran, 2012).

Methodology

The qualitative, multiple-case study (Stake, 2006) upon which this chapter is based was part of a larger project on the integration of refugee students in schools across Canada. A case study "investigates a contemporary phenomenon (the 'case') in depth and within its real-world context, especially when the boundaries between phenomenon and context may not be clearly evident" (Yin, 2014, p. 16). This project focused on three cases at different levels—one elementary school (School A), one middle school (School B), and one high school (School C), which enabled us to explore similarities and differences across cases. These schools had come to our attention because of their relatively large number of refugee students and accompanying language and academic support programs for them. In this chapter, we primarily focus on the inclusion of refugee children in elementary and middle schools, while the high school situations are mentioned only for comparison when needed. Educational issues specifically relating to refugee students in high schools are addressed in another article (Li & Que, 2020).

We obtained ethical clearance from our affiliating university and the local school district for accessing refugee students in the three schools and educational stakeholders in multiple sectors. Data were collected through one-on-one and semistructured interviews and two focus group discussions with educators, staff from community organizations, and refugee students. The interviews were centered on the educational needs of refugee students and the status quo of educational programming for them in the education system. All interviews lasted approximately one hour and were audio-recorded and transcribed by the research team. Of note, refugee students at School A were not interviewed, considering that they might not be able to share their insights due to their lack of English proficiency. After the initial analysis of the interview data, a focus group discussion was held to discuss useful resources for supporting refugee students. Twenty-four participants were split into five groups, whose discussions were recorded, transcribed, and analyzed. With the results from the previous stages, a follow-up focus group discussion was held to generate recommendations for policy and practice to improve academic outcomes for refugee students and their teachers. Table 11.1 summarizes the total number of participants and their engagement with the research process.

We used the constant comparative method of analysis (Glaser & Strauss, 1967) to code the data collected from each case and to identify within-case themes. The tenets of the framework for responsive practice helped us identify themes. We then conducted cross-case synthesis (Yin, 2014) to identify differences and similarities of themes across multiple cases. NVivo, a qualitative data analysis software, was used to organize and analyze the data. Triangulation and thick description were used to achieve qualitative credibility (Tracy, 2010). We achieved triangulation by using two methods of data collection (i.e., interviews and focus group discussions) and by collecting data from multiple groups of stakeholders with different perspectives. To ensure anonymity, we avoid mentioning the participants' personal identifying information when we cite them.

Findings

The study revealed an inverted pyramid structure with the language and academic support for refugee students. School A offered itinerant ESL services at the frequency of two instructional hours per 7-day cycle. Itinerant ESL services and a full-day LEARN program were available at School B. A comprehensive ESL program and a full-day LEARN program were provided at School C.

Inadequate ESL Instruction at Elementary and Secondary Schools

All of the administrators and teachers from School A and School B identified language learning as the most pressing need of refugee students, especially for the newly arrived. The educators were vocal about the inadequacy of the itinerant ESL service to meet the language learning needs of refugee students. For instance, School A shared one itinerant ESL teacher with several schools. Although the ESL teacher spent approximately 75% of her time working with refugee students at

TABLE 11.1 Participants and Data Sources

Affiliations	Participants	Interview	Focus group	Follow-up focus group
School A	1 Instructional Resource Teacher (special education)	X	X	X
	1 principal	X		
	1 vice-principal	X		
School B	1 LEARN teacher	X	X	
	1 LEARN intern teacher	X		
	7 refugee students	X		
School C	2 classroom teachers		X	
	1 LEARN teacher	X	X	
	ESL teacher A	X	X	X
	ESL teacher B	X	X	
	1 counsellor	X		
	1 principal	X		
	15 refugee students	X	6	
Local school board	1 itinerant ESL teacher		X	X
3 middle schools with the LEARN program	New LEARN teacher A	X	X	X
	New LEARN teacher B		X	
	New LEARN teacher C		X	
Government/ Department of Education	Senior education officer A	X		
	Senior education officer B		X	X
Community organization (resettlement)	3 settlement workers	X	X	
Community organization (cultural sharing)	1 staff member	X	X	
Community organization (Newcomer women & girls)	2 staff members		X	

School A as it has more refugee students than other elementary schools, the ESL instructional time was approximately 2 hours for each student in a 7-day cycle.

With the influx of 12 refugee children from Syria in the Easter week in 2016, a second Instructional Resource Teacher with a background in TESL was designated to work particularly with those newly arrived Syrian children at School A. The new teacher spent two or three afternoons in a 7-day cycle at School A. While administrators and teachers were grateful to have the extra support for Syrian refugee students, they were also concerned with the issue of educational equality of other refugee students. One of them indicated,

> It's just now the extra support has been given because these Syrian children are coming as a large group. You may have been getting children from other countries in a year, and they may need that support, not necessarily just Syrian families. It doesn't matter where you come from. Every refugee child needs that support.

Many refugee students from School B expressed their struggles with English learning and integration into mainstream classes. One said that he could handle Math but had trouble with reading. Another said that he didn't speak English well and counted on a friend to facilitate communication with the teacher. Yet another who already transitioned to mainstream classes found math difficult because no additional support was available anymore. Educators were in agreement that full-time ESL teachers should be assigned to elementary and middle schools that have significant numbers of refugee students rather than relying on itinerant ESL services.

The Missing LEARN Program at the Elementary Level

Adding to the gravity of inadequate language support for refugee students, no academic support programs like the LEARN are available at any elementary school in the province. The LEARN program is only offered at four middle schools and one high school. One administrator stated that "it could be beneficial to include the LEARN within the elementary programs" because when newcomer students came in and started "from scratch," it was difficult for them without any "foundation" in education. An experienced support teacher pointed out that having no academic bridging program for refugee students in elementary schools is "inexcusable." She further argued that some educators had little understanding of the language acquisition process and the educational gaps that some refugee children might have, and consequently they tended to be overly optimistic about refugee children's innate ability in learning. Similarly, another support teacher strongly argued that "it is a very high expectation" of the teachers for refugee students with wide educational gaps—"from no school to school"—"to do everything that everybody else is doing."

All the support teachers thought that the LEARN is an "essential" program for refugee children because "the earlier the intervention, the better." One support teacher explained, "The reason that we have kids in the LEARN at junior high is that they haven't done that in grade 6 or grade 4." Another support teacher argued, "Wouldn't it make more sense to catch these children at an earlier age, not waiting for them to go to junior high to figure it out?" Most support teachers agreed that the LEARN program should be offered to refugee students in fourth grade and above while K–3 refugee students would benefit more from learning with their peers in mainstream classrooms to improve their language and literacy skills.

As a matter of fact, the LEARN program was piloted at the elementary level in School A from 2006 to 2007, consisting of math, science, and vocabulary, which "was very successful" according to the teachers. However, the program was terminated. Insufficient funding was speculated as a reason by a support teacher. It also appeared that educators had different understandings of who should be responsible for implementing the LEARN program in schools. Some teachers believed that it was the school principals who should make the decisions, whereas some administrators considered LEARN "a district program" that they would not be able to implement without designated resources from the district.

The Achievements of the LEARN Program at the Secondary Level

School B used to be the only middle school offering the LEARN program, and in the fall of 2016, the LEARN program was expanded to three other middle schools to accommodate the sudden increase of refugee students from Syria. According to one educator, the rationality behind the expansion, to a large extent, was to ease the transportation difficulties encountered by some of the refugee students. Many of them who needed the LEARN program lived outside of School B's busing zones, having to rely on public transport, which took them at least an hour on each trip and cost about CN$60 for the bus pass per month. Going to school added an extra burden to their lives. After the expansion of the LEARN program, more refugee students were able to go to school close to home.

According to one support teacher, the LEARN classroom at School B was "diverse and inclusive," being a space for all the students of color. Not only refugee students but also immigrant students who were not taking the LEARN program felt, "this is the space where they feel they can come and relax." All the refugee students in School B noted that they felt close to the LEARN teacher and comfortable in the LEARN classroom.

More important, the LEARN program successfully prepared many refugee students for integration into mainstream classrooms. One support teacher gave us an example of a refugee girl who would have dropped out if not for the LEARN program. The student came to School B with a Grade 2 math level. Through intensive, one-on-one instruction given by the LEARN teacher, she improved significantly and was integrated into mainstream classes in grade 8. In addition, the LEARN teacher helped refugee students analyze academic English used in mainstream classes to facilitate understanding. Many high school refugee students also reported that they had caught up with peers academically through taking the LEARN class at School B so that they were able to be enrolled directly in mainstream classes in School C.

Improving the Allocation of LEARN Teachers and Promoting Teacher Collaboration

Many educators and refugee students indicated that there is a need to increase the number of LEARN teachers in School B, considering the growing number of refugee students. One support teacher noted that the LEARN program, to a large extent, "functioned due to volunteer help." For example, an 80-year-old lady used to read with the refugee students one-on-one; a gentleman in his seventies committed one afternoon per week to help refugee students with math. The support teacher was grateful to these volunteers. However, the teacher suggested School B should at least hire a teaching assistant from the newcomer community who speaks a language of the refugee students, such as Arabic, to team up with the LEARN teacher to facilitate communication between teachers and the students from this language background.

In addition, the support teacher indicated the need for closer collaboration with other educators, including school leaders. According to the teacher, placing refugee students in the regular classrooms is mere "exposure," not "education," and it is problematic to place all refugee students, regardless of the language they speak, in the English program. The support teacher stated, "There is some sort of weird karmic path unfolding that only English homerooms can work with the LEARN students." As a result, students from French-speaking countries were not able to take advantage of the French immersion program. The support teacher attributed the failure to integrate French-speaking refugee students into French immersion programs partially to "minimal collaboration or communication" with the French teachers.

Meanwhile, some refugee students who did not understand English or French upon arrival were overwhelmed with the core French class which is a mandatory subject of the English program curriculum. Furthermore, the support teacher and one of the school leaders appeared to have different pedagogical philosophies. The teacher believed that the refugee students who did not know English or French needed intensive English and academic support most. The teacher used to pull some refugee students from core French class to reteach them subject classes like social studies and science. However, the school leader believed that no student should be exempted from the French class and that refugee students can learn by osmosis.

The Muddled Assessment of Learning Disability and Mental Illness

Many educators reported that due to language barriers, it was difficult for them to identify whether the refugee students' difficulties were caused by educational gaps, learning disabilities, or mental distress. By policy, students younger than nine years old could receive IRT support without assessment, and School A had comparatively strong IRT support because of high demands. Older students would be required to take an assessment test and would be provided with IRT support if developmental delays were identified. However, few refugee students were on the lists of IRT teachers because "it's hard to assess students who don't speak English," one support teacher said.

A high school refugee student recalled that one of the teachers at her elementary school thought she had mental health issues and made her go through the tests. At that time, she had no idea of the nature of the tests. Five years later, when she was in middle school, she was shocked to know that she had been diagnosed with mental illness through those tests, of which she was unaware. The support teacher at her middle school knew her well and considered the test results inaccurate. The teacher believed that the student's language difficulty and knowledge gaps led to the wrong diagnosis of learning difficulties and mental illness.

Lack of Support and In-Service Training for Classroom Teachers

From the perspectives of educators, inadequate ESL instruction also made it challenging for classroom teachers to integrate refugee children into their classrooms. One administrator told us about a classroom teacher's frustration with being unable to communicate with the newly arrived refugee children. Of note, School A has more local students with special educational needs than other schools. A classroom teacher complained about her struggles to meet the needs of her students with autism and others with learning disabilities, as well as those of refugee students who were just beginning to learn the language of instruction. She said that "in a classroom with 20 kids, ... it's really hard to do what you would like to do because you just have so many kids." A support teacher at School A added, "Classroom teachers barely have enough support to be able to give to the children already in their classroom, and when new kids are coming in, it just adds more things for them to do."

Classroom teachers were also challenged in handling refugee students' behavior. A support teacher said, "If the child is grabbing things or making a mess of something and I am asking him to stop, ... they are not listening because they don't understand my language." A subject teacher added, "There have been some issues with students, like bullying each other in their own language ... it's hard to stop that when you don't know what they are saying." Very often, classroom teachers had to ask other refugee students who were fluent in their mother tongue and English to help with translation. Administrators and teachers at School A all felt "fortunate" to have a diverse population of students in their school helps them out. However, they thought it would be beneficial for their students and teachers to have a full-time, school-based settlement worker like School B and School C had to better facilitate the settlement and integration of refugee students, such as offering interpretation and translation services.

Through working with refugee students, many teachers have seen different types of trauma caused by pre-migration and resettlement experiences, such as "acute trauma, chronic trauma, and memory issues." Some traumas could be hidden, as one teacher said, "Someone may present very well-adjusted, but in fact, you don't know what's going on." Many teachers, especially classroom teachers, felt frustrated with the fact that they had not received training in dealing with war-affected, migration-related mental health problems of refugee students. An English teacher stated,

> A lot of time, I don't know where they come from. I don't know in terms of the trauma or PTSD what triggers may be. So as an English teacher, I teach poetry, I teach stories, visual media, and often I would probably choose not to do certain pieces because that might be the triggers.

Other teachers mentioned their inability to help refugee students due to language barriers. Even if interpretation services were provided, meaning could be lost in translation. One teacher said, "The counselling relationship is so sensitive and the compassion you want to transmit to your client—and the interpreter would kind of tarnish real message and real support there."

Teachers' Quandaries with Inclusive Education

According to educators at School A, the age-appropriate grade placement, as one of the key tenets of inclusive education in NL, makes it imperative to help refugee students bridge the gaps between their prior education and the requirements of their grade-level classes. Otherwise, they would only be physically but not academically included in the regular classrooms. One administrator said, "You get children that maybe never been to school in their lives, and we placed them with the same-age peers, which socially is wonderful, but the academic gap then is quite great."

However, without the academic bridging programs such as LEARN, classroom teachers had to try to close the gaps. The administrator explained, "When you are trying to teach the curriculum, your prescribed curriculum, and at the same time, you are trying to teach the alphabet to the child and trying to teach them some English. That's too much for classroom teachers." Another support teacher added, "I feel that a hundred percent inclusion, like leaving it on classroom teachers, is absolutely the wrong way to go about it. Inclusive classroom alone is the worst, in my opinion." The teachers all agreed that refugee students would benefit most by taking separate LEARN classes to catch up, complemented by learning with peers in mainstream classrooms. The age-based, inclusive education model did not work well for refugee students.

Discussion and Implications

Rhetorical Inclusion, Symbolic Anti-racism, and Culturally Responsive Approach

The inadequate support for refugee students in elementary and junior high schools indicates that policymakers in NL appear to have employed what George and colleagues call "symbolic anti-racism" (2020, p. 160) to achieve racial equity. The provincial government launched a Policy on Multiculturalism in 2008, aiming to "lead in developing, sustaining, and enhancing programs and services based on equality for all, notwithstanding racial, religious, ethnic, national, and social origin" (Government of Newfoundland and Labrador, n.d., p. 4). However, our findings suggested that the NL educational system failed to provide adequate programming to address the particular needs of young refugee students. Changes to the ESL program have been slow in the previous decade (Trahey, 2018). The reality that the policy remains strong on rhetoric but short on action is indicative of symbolic anti-racism in that "policy language that gestures toward a commitment to racial equity in line with the doctrine of Canadian multiculturalism …, but does not enact any targeted, substantive programming to identify, rectify, or prevent structural racism" (George et al., 2020, pp. 168–169).

Our top concern is that refugee children in elementary schools are probably most vulnerable to this symbolic anti-racism. Although the DEECD emphasizes that placing students with their peers in regular classrooms is one of the fundamental tenets of inclusive education policy (Collins et al., 2017), elementary-aged refugee students with gaps in their education are less likely to benefit from this age-appropriate placement due to inadequacy of ESL instruction and the absence of the LEARN program or one similar. Their diverse needs could not be addressed by classroom teachers and school administrators (Schroeter & James, 2015). Refugee children would have to wait until middle school to receive the instruction from the LEARN teacher and wait until high school to have access to the on-site ESL instruction. It should not have happened that some of our participants started their schooling from grade four in NL but still needed to take ESL classes and LEARN courses all the way up in high school. If they had received the LEARN support and intensive ESL instruction at the elementary level, they might have been able to integrate into the mainstream classes sooner. In view of the fact that primary-grade refugee students are being disadvantaged by age-appropriate placement intended for inclusion, we agree with Bryan's (2009) argument that "racial inequality is more likely to be reproduced—rather than contested or ameliorated—through national and educational policies and practices which are purported to have egalitarian and anti-racist aims" (p. 298).

The mental health needs of refugee students have not been reflected in the education policies in NL, which is of particular concern. As Richards et al. (2006) stressed, a culturally responsive institution (i.e., administration, policies, and values of school systems) is fundamental to culturally responsive pedagogy, and to make the institution more culturally responsive, school policies and procedures need reform. Previous research suggests that school administrators, especially principals, are viewed by teachers as the most important forces in the implementation of culturally responsive classroom approach (Wanless et al., 2013).

It is our view that refugee students in elementary schools whose academic abilities are behind the grade level should be provided with additional support, such as the LEARN program, to make them truly included in the school system. Better assessment methods should be adopted in placing refugee students in appropriate grades, taking into consideration their age and academic backgrounds.

Multilingual Teachers, Professional Learning, and Culturally Responsive Approach

The communication barriers between teachers and refugee students point to the need for hiring multilingual teachers from refugee or immigrant backgrounds in the school system to help accurately assess the mental health and educational needs of refugee students. A lack of diversity in the teaching profession needs to be addressed by educational authorities in the province. While students wish to see teachers of their own cultural background as role models and facilitators, current teachers also long for colleagues with whom they could consult when confronted with challenges while working with refugee students.

Teachers in NL have not been offered access to professional learning on dealing with refugee students with learning disabilities or mental health issues, nor have their needs for in-service training in this regard been addressed. A lack of professional development opportunities targeting refugee students' issues inhibits teachers in creating a culturally responsive classroom. In other parts of Canada where the newcomer population is larger, continuous professional development for teachers has been addressed to a greater extent. For example, in Ontario, teachers are advised to "engage in professional learning to understand the impact of traumatic experiences on student well-being" when working with refugee students and their families (Ontario Ministry of Education, 2016, p. 8). With the growing number of newcomers in NL, teachers' access to professional learning on mental health and other issues related to refugee students should be provided. It is imperative for teachers to adopt culturally responsive teaching to promote inclusivity in the classroom.

Our research offers implications for local educational authorities and school administrators in terms of provision of the LEARN program and allocation of full-time ESL teachers to elementary level refugee students, whose transition to secondary education will be greatly facilitated with such specialized programs at an early stage. For the same reason, the allocation of full-time ESL teachers to the four middle schools offering the LEARN program should be considered. Moreover, the current LEARN teachers' needs for assistance and collaboration should not be overlooked.

Refugee students' educational success is vital to their upward social mobility in the host countries (Portes & Rumbaut, 2001). We hope that through our project, educators and policymakers would gain a further understanding of how to foster truly inclusive school environments for refugee students. While the findings of this study are not intended to be generalizable to settings where support systems have been well established, they will provide insights for schools in smaller centers with similar concerns.

References

Asadi, N. (2015). Policies to make possible the integration. In A. A. Abdi, L. Shultz, & T. Pillay (Eds.), *Decolonizing global citizenship education* (pp. 189–205). Rotterdam, the Netherlands: SensePublishers.

Association for New Canadians. (2018a, December). *Government-assisted refugee (GAR) update: 2016 calendar year.* Retrieved from http://ancnl.ca/wp-content/uploads/2018/12/2016-GAR-Report.pdf

Association for New Canadians. (2018b, December). *Government-assisted refugee (GAR) update: 2017 calendar year.* Retrieved from http://ancnl.ca/wp-content/uploads/2018/12/GAR-Report-2017.pdf

Association for New Canadians. (2018c, December). *Government-assisted refugee (GAR) update: 2018 calendar year.* Retrieved from http://ancnl.ca/wp-content/uploads/2018/12/GAR-Report-Jan-to-Sep-2018.pdf

Avery, H. (2017). At the bridging point: Tutoring newly arrived students in Sweden. *International Journal of Inclusive Education,* 21(4), 404–415.

Beiser, M., & Korczak, D. (2018, April). *Post-traumatic stress disorder.* Retrieved from https://www.kidsnewtocanada.ca/mental-health/ptsd#:~:text=Post%2Dtraumatic%20stress%20disorder%20(PTSD,setting%20in%20which%20symptoms%20occur

Beninghof, A., & Leensvaart, M. (2016). Co-teaching to support ELLs. *Educational Leadership,* 73(4), 56–60.

Bryan, A. (2009). The intersectionality of nationalism and multiculturalism in the Irish curriculum: Teaching against racism? *Race Ethnicity and Education,* 12(3), 297–317.

Bunch, G. (2015). An analysis of the move to inclusive education in Canada. *What works. Revista Electrónica Interuniversitaria de Formación del Profesorado,* 18(1), 1–15.

Collins, A., Fushell, M., Philpott, D., Wakeham, M., Strong, C., & Tulk-Lane, S. (2017, July 21), *The Premier's Task Force on improving educational outcomes: Now is the time – The next chapter in education in Newfoundland and Labrador.* Retrieved from https://www.gov.nl.ca/education/files/task_force_report.pdf

Department of Education and Early Childhood Development. (2011a). *Guidelines for delivery of ESL services in K–6.* Retrieved from https://www.gov.nl.ca/education/files/k12_curriculum_guides_esl_esl_k-6_guidelines_for_delivery_of_esl_services_k-6.pdf

Department of Education and Early Childhood Development. (2011b). *Literacy Enrichment and Academic Readiness for Newcomers (LEARN)*. Retrieved from https://www.gov.nl.ca/education/files/k12_curriculum_guides_esl_learn_learn1_language_arts.pdf

Department of Education and Early Childhood Development. (n.d.). *Inclusive schools*. https://www.gov.nl.ca/education/k12/inclusion/

Due, C., Riggs, D., & Augoustinos, M. (2016). Diversity in intensive English language centres in South Australia: Sociocultural approaches to education for students with migrant or refugee backgrounds. *International Journal of Inclusive Education*, 20(12), 1286–1296.

George, R., Maier, R., & Robson, K. (2020). Ignoring race: A comparative analysis of education policy in British Columbia and Ontario. *Race Ethnicity and Education*, 23(2), 159–179.

Glaser, B., & Strauss, A. (1967). *The discovery of grounded theory: Strategies for qualitative research*. Chicago, IL: Aldine Publishing.

Government of Newfoundland and Labrador. (n.d.). *Our commitment to multiculturalism*. Retrieved from https://www.findnewfoundlandlabrador.com/live/why-nl/our-commitment-to-multiculturalism/

Gunasekera, S., Houghton, S., Glasgow, K., Carroll, A., & Hunter, S. (2016). A comparison of goal setting and reputational orientations of African adolescents from refugee backgrounds in intensive English centres and mainstream secondary school classrooms. *Journal of Cross-Cultural Psychology*, 47(473), 355–375.

Guo, S., & Guo, Y. (2016). Immigration, integration and welcoming communities: Neighbourhood-based initiative to facilitate the integration of newcomers in Calgary. *Canadian Ethnic Studies*, 48(3), 45–67.

Guo, Y., Maitra, S., & Guo, S. (2019). I belong to nowhere: Syrian refugee children's perspectives on school integration. *Journal of Contemporary Issues in Education*, 14(1), 89–105.

Hos, R. (2016). Caring is not enough: Teachers enactment of ethical care for adolescent students with limited or interrupted formal education (SLIFE) in a newcomer classroom. *Education and Urban Society*, 48(5), 479–503.

Kanu, Y. (2008). Educational needs and barriers for African refugee students in Manitoba. *Canadian Journal of Education*, 31(4), 915–940.

Li, X., & Que, H. (2020). Support for refugee students in a Newfoundland high school: Merits and ramifications. *Education in the North*, 27(1), 5–20.

Naidoo, L. (2013). Refugee Action Support: An interventionist pedagogy for supporting refugee students' learning in Greater Western Sydney secondary schools. *International Journal of Inclusive Education*, 17(5), 449–461.

Nilsson, J., & Axelsson, M. (2013). Welcome to Sweden: Newly arrived students' experiences of pedagogical and social provision in introductory and regular classes. *International Electronic Journal of Elementary Education*, 6(1), 137–164.

Ontario Ministry of Education. (2013, November). *Culturally responsive pedagogy: Towards equity and inclusivity in Ontario schools*. Retrieved from http://www.edu.gov.on.ca/eng/literacynumeracy/inspire/research/CBS_ResponsivePedagogy.pdf

Ontario Ministry of Education. (2016, July). *Capacity building K–12*. Retrieved from http://www.edu.gov.on.ca/eng/literacynumeracy/inspire/research/cbs_refugees.pdf

Peercy, M. M., & Martin-Beltran, M. (2012). Envisioning collaboration: Including ESOL students and teachers in the mainstream classroom. *International Journal of Inclusive Education*, 16(7), 657–673.

Portes, A., & Rumbaut, R. G. (2001). *Legacies: The story of the immigrant second generation.* Berkeley, CA: University of California Press.

Pugh, K., Every, D., & Hattam, R. (2012). Inclusive education for students with refugee experience: Whole school reform in a South Australian primary school. *Australian Educational Researcher,* 39(2), 125–141.

Richards, H., Brown, A., & Forde, T. (2006). Addressing diversity in schools: Culturally responsive pedagogy. *Teaching Exceptional Children,* 39(3), 64–68.

Schroeter, S., & James, C. E. (2015). We're here because we're Black: The schooling experiences of French-speaking African-Canadian students with refugee backgrounds. *Race Ethnicity and Education,* 18(1), 20–39.

Stake, R. E. (2006). *Multiple case study analysis.* New York, NY: The Guilford Press.

Statistics Canada. (2018, March 27). *Canada at a glance 2018: \Population.* Retrieved from https://www150.statcan.gc.ca/n1/pub/12-581-x/2018000/pop-eng.htm

Taylor, S., & Sidhu, R. L. (2012). Supporting refugee students in schools: What constitutes inclusive education? *International Journal of Inclusive Education,* 16(1), 39–56.

Tracy, S. J. (2010). Qualitative quality: Eight "big-tent" criteria for excellent qualitative research. *Qualitative Inquiry,* 16(10), 837–851.

Trahey, M. (2018). Reflections on 20 years of ESL teaching in St. John's: Changes and challenges. *The Morning Watch: Educational and Social Analysis,* 46(1–2). Retrieved from https://journals.library.mun.ca/ojs/index.php/mwatch/article/view/2043

Wanless, S., Patton, C., Rimm-Kaufman, S., & Deutsch, N. (2013). Setting-level influences on implementation of the responsive classroom approach. *Prevention Science,* 14(1), 40–51.

Weekes, T., Phelan, L., Macfarlane, S., Pinson, J., & Francis, V. (2011). Supporting successful learning for refugee students: The Classroom Connect Project. *Issues in Educational Research,* 21(3), 310–329.

Yin, R. (2014). *Case study research: Design and methods* (5th ed.). Los Angeles, CA: Sage Publications.

12

PARTNERING WITH AFRICAN AMERICAN PARENTS IN THE UNITED STATES

Implications for Educators

Patricia A. Edwards and Kristen L. White

This chapter explores how the racialized history of African Americans to obtain an education has impacted parent involvement in children's education before- and after-school desegregation in the United States. We first discuss how racism among the White teaching force has impacted parent–school relationships. Next, we describe some models of family–school engagement in the United States. We conclude by discussing the need for creating spaces in teacher preparation programs where preservice teachers can grapple with issues like race, equity, and Whiteness and niceness.

The Exclusion of African Americans in the Educational Landscape

Federal and state policies in the U.S. public schools have elevated parental involvement in schools as a national priority, in part due to the large number of failing schools and the increased achievement gap between White and African American students (as well as other ethnic minorities; Lewis et al., 2008). Parental involvement has been stressed for many reasons from better student performance in a multitude of areas to improved behavior and lower absenteeism and positive attitudes toward school; therefore, it is clear that parents play a vital role in the academic success of their children (Hayes, 2011).

Most of the general parental involvement literature fails to fully consider not only the role of race but also the role that social class plays when examining parenting practices within schools. Furthermore, when race and class were considered, rarely were upper-class African American families a part of the analysis. This is evidenced by studies that have focused on African American students and families, most of which reference data collected from underprivileged African Americans without consideration of the effects of parental involvement across various socioeconomic levels of African American families. Focusing entirely on African American families from low socioeconomic backgrounds can create incomplete findings on potential predictors of parental involvement and/or the influence of parental involvement and student outcomes (Hayes, 2011).

Thompson (2003) posits that it is critical for parents to be involved in the educational processes of their children. However, school personnel across the United States have found it challenging to reach parents of color. Many systems do not reach out to this group to gain their perspectives.

Teachers in public education have wide-ranging perceptions of Black parents. For example, some believe that Black parents are lazy, poor, and are not committed to education (G. Howard, 2007). According to statistics from the Department of Education, 83% of American teachers are White (U.S. Department of Education, National Center for Education Statistics, 2003). Leary (2005) argues that with widespread ideas of White supremacy, a significant gap and discord between racial and ethnic groups in American society is formed. This gap may skew how public schools view Black parents, and conversely, how Black parents view public schools.

Historical and Social Context for African American Parents' Experiences with Schooling

To understand issues that may affect African American parents' perceptions of public schools, one must first understand the plight of the African American people and their experiences with American institutions. African Americans have a long and challenging history in the United States, enduring trials such as the hideous brutality of chattel slavery, Jim Crow,[1] civil rights, school integration, and various levels of present-day racism. The argument can be made that the legacy of slavery may have left its fingerprints on both the struggles and the achievements of African American students in public schools (Mubenga, 2006).

Many African American parents of today's students are only one or two generations removed from Jim Crow laws and overt racism in America's public schools. After slavery officially ended in the United States in 1865, African American parents faced new challenges and hardships. American systems seemingly traded the overwhelming severity of chattel slavery with decisively unfair laws that further degraded Black communities and limited their growth. These actions were most intensified by Jim Crow laws which prevailed in the American South (DuRocher, 2011).

Through the Jim Crow era, segregation of Blacks from Whites became the primary focus of southern legislation. From the end of slavery until the civil rights movement, Jim Crow laws prevented Blacks from using the same public facilities as Whites, from riding in the front of public transportation buses, and from attending the same schools. As a result, Black facilities including schools—were viewed as inferior to White ones. Black schools were not given the same resources as White ones. Textbooks at Black schools were outdated or second-hand from White schools, school buildings were all but forgotten in terms of state budgets and funding, and achievement of Black students was not a concern of leaders in the Jim Crow south (Waugh, 2012).

Certainly, an effective method to slow the progress and growth of any demo-graphic is by denying them access to knowledge and education. As such, the relationship between Jim Crow, public education, and African American parents and students is significant in that it was the beginning of the creation of a legacy of disparity between the races in terms of education (Exum, 2012).

Although educational inequity persisted, not all African Americans remained idle. For example, Vivian Gadsden (1993) reported that

> [l]iteracy and education are valued possessions that African American fami-lies have respected, revered, and sought as a means to personal freedom and communal hope, from enslavement to the present
>
> *(p. 352)*

This quote reflects Pat's (the first author) family's view about education, and she is fairly sure that it reflects the views of other African American families. Other examples of Black families with high educational values are found in works such as *Maggie's American Dream: The Life and Times of a Black Family* (Comer, 1988) and *Gifted Hands: The Ben Carson Story* (Carson & Murphey, 1990). Pat often heard her parents, John and Annie Kate Edwards, say that education has always been an equalizer for the African American community.

Pat's own educational values were instilled by her parents, who always made school a top priority in her family. Her parents had their own parents as mod-els. For example, Pat's maternal grandfather, Tate Plummer, organized a school for colored children in the early 1900s who were sharecroppers' children and children who lived on plantations. The Plummer School was located in Albany, Georgia, the county seat for Dougherty County. In his classic book *The Soul of Black Folk,* renowned scholar Dr. W. E. B. Du bois (1903) portrayed Dougherty County as a place where vast ignorance festered untouched. Pat's grandfather recognized this and worked tirelessly to change it.

Pat's grandmother, Callie Robinson Plummer, shared this story with her that was later confirmed by her 92-year-old elementary school principal, Mr. Erasmus Dent, in a December 2012 interview. Mr. Dent had been Pat's mother's child-hood friend, and he had actually attended the Plummer School. He and Pat's grandmother indicated that her grandfather had asked the Albany mayor and the superintendent of schools to provide school transportation for sharecroppers' children and children who lived on various plantations. The answer was "no."

Pat's grandfather owned property and houses where 22 sharecropper families lived on his land. He, along with the help of two of his brothers, Elzee and Tucker, and Elzee's wife Ella, worked to make the Plummer School a success for colored children. Pat's grandfather and his close family members recognized, like John Dewey (1902) that "[w]hat the best and wisest parent wants for his child that must the community want for all its children" (p. 7). Even though things were not democratic during these times, Pat's grandfather simply wanted to make the best out of an unfair and unjust situation and to give colored children the opportunity to receive an education.

History of Parent Engagement Practices in African American Culture

Traditionally, parent engagement practices in the African American culture were passed down, as Pat's family story demonstrates, from one generation to the next by word of mouth (Federal Writers' Project, n.d.; Hauser Cram, 2009; Humes, 2016; Tobin & Snyman 2008). It is a form of knowledge sharing that utilizes oral stories that is also referred to as "legal storytelling" (Humes, 2016; Lynn et al., 2013; Tobin & Snyman 2008). Legal storytelling or counter storytelling is a form of sharing where "oral history" is a legitimate way to pass down family history, customs, traditions, and cultural stories, referred to as folklore (Tobin & Snyman, 2008). For instance, the African proverb reminds African American people and communities that "it takes a village to raise a child," meaning everyone in the community (i.e., all stakeholders) is a part of the upbringing of a child, not just the parents (Donahoo, 2013; Gordon et al., 2005; Tobin & Snyman, 2008). In essence, as Schönpflug (2008), pointed out, it is the belief that one and all were to be a gatekeeper for safety, shelter, nourishment, family values, and sharing of knowledge.

Schönpflug (2008) links cultural transmission from parents to child with multiple and repeated family interactions with language, traditions, customs, and exposure. In the spirit of this African proverb, local and national organizations have been created to support this ideology (Gordon et al., 2005). Over the years, educational scholars have reinforced this mantra and challenged one another to remember the (African and African American/Black) past and preserve the present so that there will be a future with a call to action for academic achievement (Bell, 1978, 1980, 1982, 1997; Bell & Edmonds, 1993; Bell et al., 2005; Berger, 1991; Delgado & Stefancic, 2012).

African American parents have been involved in parenting their children through parent engagement even though this topic has been unrepresented in the literature (Cotton & Wikelund, 1989; T. Howard & Reynolds, 2008). As part of the success of national and local organizations which encourage parent engagement on a national level, Jack and Jill of America is one of many premier organizations. It was founded in 1938 in Philadelphia, Pennsylvania, by 20 African American mothers who had a shared expectation; children should be happy and reared to have great expectations for the future by their families (Rankin & Quane, 2002). Under the tutelage of the late Marion Stubbs Thomas, the organization was founded to provide social, cultural, and educational opportunities for youth. Currently, this national organization has 245 chapters and represents over 40,000 African American family members.

According to the national organization Jack and Jill of America (2017), Tammy King, the immediate past president of Jack and Jill of America from 2011 to 2015, spearheaded a rigorous national theme, "Power to Make a Difference." To this date, the theme continues to empower the members and their mission: to have mothers advocate to enrich the lives of children 2 to 19 years old who were dedicated to nurturing future African American leaders by strengthening children through leadership development, volunteer service, philanthropic giving, and civic duty.

Researchers like Berger (1991), Bridglall and Gordon (2002), and Lubienski and Crane (2010) professed that the parents are the first and most important teacher alongside formal education. Gordon et al. (2005) led the way for uncovering the hidden curriculum of high achievement. They argue that while access to schools that enable and expect academic achievement is a necessary ingredient for the education of students, schools alone may not be sufficient to ensure universally high levels of academic development. In fact, Gordon et al. were globally distinguished for supplemental education, which refers to parents/guardians and community members creating opportunities for children in the aspects of education, culture, social involvement, and recreation (Bridglall & Gordon, 2002). This research stated that the learning can take the form of cultural events, history, tutoring, field trips, music, dance, and or any activity that would supplement the education a child receives in school. The research of Lubienski and Crane (2010) supported the work of Bridglall and Gordon (2002) and reported on the extensive impact of socioeconomic status (SES) and the number of books in the home that children were exposed to at an early age.

The research of Gordon et al. (2005) emphasized the importance of the role of the parents as supporters. For instance, the parents cannot expect everything to be taught in school and must advocate for special services (i.e., academic intervention services before, during, and after school), impart values and morals, as well as engage their children in educational, cultural, social, and civic experiences (Gordon et al., 2005; Mayfield & Garrison-Wade, 2015). As reported by Bridglall and Gordon (2002), Naomi's Program of Excellence (NPE) emerged in 2002 as an educational, cultural, and social enrichment program in the New York area that was developed by five African American families. According to Bourdeau-Oscar (NPE, 2017) in 2017, the program continued to thrive with its mission to uplift children (particularly of color) through parent engagement, along with family and friends. This program was founded to reinforce the belief that all children were naturally gifted and talented (Ford, 1994; Gordon et al., 2005). The life's work of Gordon et al. (2005) reiterated the importance of beliefs and behaviors from the parents'/guardians' perspective that impacted the exposure children have in their environment.

Barriers to African American Parent Engagement

Hauser Cram (2009) and Hallman (2008) both discussed the challenges that parents face in regard to parent engagement. Hauser Cram (2009) commented on the SES of parents that may impact the exposure parents impart to their children, meaning parents may be limited in their resources based on their past experiences. For instance, the SES of parents/guardians may be impacted by their level of education and/or adverse childhood experiences (Centers for Disease Control and Prevention, 2016). Hallman (2008) suggested that parents were to blame for not doing anything to remedy the situation of the educational lag for students of color. For example, he proposed that parents of color need to focus on intrinsic motivation to demonstrate valuing an education. By this he meant to encourage parents/guardians to focus on academic achievement by having high expectations, getting more involved in school matters, and supporting their students with strategies such as tutoring, more leisure reading, and other ways to expand their knowledge, so that students would intrinsically be more apt to accept the challenge of excelling (Bennett-Conroy, 2011; Fan & Williams, 2010; Swick & Williams, 2006).

Proponents of parent engagement like Shonkoff and Meisels (2000) and Wooden (2010) insist that parents need to spend time with their children, teaching them the importance of education and the proper behavior that is necessary for students to succeed in school.

According to Harris and Graves (2010) and T. Howard and Reynolds (2008), families in a higher SES have access to more opportunities like tutoring, organized sports and activities, and cultural arts (i.e., the theater, museum, zoo, library, dance lessons, music lessons, etc.). These families are more likely to engage their children in extracurricular activities and participate in local and national organizations that support their customs, traditions, expectations, and ideals. In contrast, as this research notes, families in the lower SES struggle with financial challenges and may not be able to afford extracurricular opportunities for their children (Desimone, 1999; Dotterer et al., 2009; Harris & Graves, 2010; Tamis-LeMonda et al., 2008). Moore and Lewis (2012) argued that education and economy were linked and yield encouraging outcomes. They contended that the level of education and the amount earned depict outcomes that result in more education yielding a higher income status. Other researchers reported that the reality of providing shelter, food, and clothing may be a struggle for families in the lower SES (DeNavas-Walt et al., 2004; Drake & Pandey, 1996; Garmezy, 1993; Yeung & Pfeiffer, 2009).

Hauser Cram (2009) and Henderson and Mapp (2002) had a different perspective. They contended that socioeconomic status has the same effects across all races. These researchers contended that it is the environmental factors that link to family and academic achievement; practices that parents pass on to their children, many of which were expectations that were ethnically centered. As such, they suggest these expectations affect the students' attitudes and success within the educational system. Other researchers agree that various factors contribute to the educational outcomes of students of color, including access to preschool and early childhood programs, quality of teachers, access to high-quality curriculum, school quality, socioeconomic status, and support systems (Amatea & West-Olatunji, 2007; Lee, 2005; Tamis-LeMonda, et al., 2008).

White Teachers' Perceptions of African American Parents

Despite the prevalence of discussions in the United States around parent involvement in their children's education, professional teacher preparation programs have not shown preservice teachers, who are mainly White and taught by White teacher educators, how to work with parents, particularly those who are culturally and linguistically diverse (Edwards & White, 2018). In addition, White teacher educators may avoid discussions about race and equity in order to be perceived as "kind" and "nice" (Castagno, 2019).

Similarly, Trent and Artiles (1995) expressed concerns about the instruction of African American students in integrated schools. In particular, they reported that

> [w]hen Black children entered integrated schools, they were met generally by White administrators and teachers who were unprepared to deal with their cognitive styles, social values, beliefs, customs, and traditions. Because of the discontinuity that developed overnight between home and school cultures, these personnel began teaching Black children with preconceived notions and stereotypical views about how they functioned.
>
> *(Trent & Artiles, 1995, p. 215)*

Integration did not necessarily impact the education of Black students positively. As indicated by Trent and Artiles, teachers were not prepared to teach Black children when integration was initially implemented. Edwards et al. (2010) posed a series of questions to teacher educators:

> Has anything changed? After being told that teachers are not prepared to teach Black children, have teacher education programs changed? Since integration has been in existence for several decades, can teacher education programs truthfully say that their teacher education graduates are well prepared to teach students and connect with families from diverse cultures? Have school curricula changed to reflect the changing demographics of the student population? Have teachers changed their instructional ideologies to adapt to the students in their classrooms? Or have teacher education

programs, school curricula, and teacher ideologies remained the same? If these changes have not occurred, should we be surprised that the enigma remains for African American students?

(p. 72)

Bissonnette (2016) argues that "teacher education classrooms are powerful spaces, and teacher educators are capable of working as agents of change" (p. 18). Henfield and Washington (2012) emphasize when discussing race and "Whiteness" with teachers, the dialogue further complicates the issues of race in the classroom. Discomfort and obliviousness are assurances of "Whiteness" within educational settings that are homogeneous. Defensiveness among White teachers is not uncommon when notions of "Whiteness" and White privilege are invoked. Teachers often exhibit confusion and frustration when they are forced to talk about race and the ways that it explicitly and implicitly impacts classroom instruction. Most often this is because they do not identify as members of a racial group, or they adopt the notion of unearned racial privileges (Henfield & Washington, 2012). Some White teachers have seldom considered the implications of racial privilege or what impact the dominant cultural perspective has on culturally diverse students (Henfield & Washington, 2012). White educators report that one of their greatest concerns is that many White teachers have limited personal and professional encounters with individuals who are racially, ethnically, linguistically and culturally different from themselves (Gay & Kirkland, 2003).

Niceness and Whiteness: Perpetuating Racism

Although Whiteness is prevalent among White classroom teachers and teacher educators, they are not a monolithic group. Kristen's (second author) presuppositions as a White, middle-class female stem from her 10 years of teaching in public schools in the United States. Her teaching career started in a mostly middle-class White community adjacent to a major midwestern city known as one of the most racially segregated cities in the country. When she began teaching in the district, it was experiencing a phenomenon known as "White flight." This means that when racially and linguistically diverse families, mostly from the city's inner ring, moved into the neighborhood on the city's outer ring, White families moved farther out into suburban areas to live with other White families. While the community where Kristen taught was becoming rapidly diverse, the district's staff remained predominantly White, middle class, and monolingual. As a result, racial and cultural tensions arose, although at the time she did not recognize them because of her Whiteness.

More African American families attended the district's schools. Nuanced tensions between the teachers and parents arose with, for example, declining enrollment in the school's Parent Teacher Organization (PTO), attendance at parent–teacher conferences, and students' test scores on standardized achievement tests. At the same time, the district also had an influx of students of Middle Eastern descent. The district was under-resourced in both school personnel and resources to service children whose first language was not English. She, like many of her colleagues, began to develop a deficit perspective of families, students, and the community because of the racial, cultural, and linguistic incongruence. When parents did not participate in events like ice cream socials or family picnics with live music, games, and a raffle, she assumed it was because they did not care about their children or their schooling. At other times, she became frustrated when some students, particularly those who were not White, did not adhere to the behavior "norms" of the school or her classroom.

Over time, she became frustrated with another issue the district was dealing with—student mobility. During one school year, she had around a dozen or so students enter and leave her first-grade classroom. She was not prepared to deal with families experiencing housing insecurity. Despite the fact that she was struggling as a classroom teacher to meet some of her students' social, emotional, and educational needs, she did not ask for help or complain. Her White culture, she believes, had ingrained in her that it was not nice to talk about race or class. Therefore, what she was not able to recognize was that her Whiteness and Niceness were sometimes perpetuating and, at other times, creating inequity for some students.

The collective "niceness" that permeated the school staff, according to Castagno (2019), "both enables avoidance and shields educators from doing the hard work of confronting inequity. The result is [the] perpetuation of educational inequity" (p. xix). The deficit views many teachers held, unknowingly and knowingly, were dangerous because they prevented them from interrogating their Whiteness and niceness. Deficit frameworks are destructive in that they are "tied to individualism in the sense that they locate issues or problems within individuals. This can be contrasted to a systems analysis or an institutional framework that locates issues and problems within systems, policies, and institutions" (p. xvii).

Thus far, we have described how Kristen's Whiteness and niceness intersect to create inequity in her classroom and school. While we do not seek to place blame for her own shortcomings as a person or educator on others, we do think it is important to recognize that professional teacher programs in universities often do not adequately prepare White teachers (like Kristen) to work with parents and families who are racially, culturally, and linguistically diverse. It is plausible that because so many teacher educators (like Kristen) are White, female, and monolingual, discussing diversity among families may foreground issues that many White people are not comfortable talking about, race, class, family composition, and religion.

Models of Family–School Community Engagement in the United States

As a result of desegregation, a mostly White teaching force is aware that teachers and parents must learn to work together. Despite that professional teacher preparation programs are still struggling to prepare preservice teachers to work with diverse families in diverse contexts, schools and districts around the country recognize that something has to change. There has been a national focus on parent involvement in their children's education. As a result, models for how to engage parents have evolved.

One model that is widely used throughout the United States for family, school, and community engagement was developed by Dr. Joyce Epstein (2001). The framework consists of six types of parent involvement (parenting, communicating, volunteering, learning at home, decision making, collaborating with community). Following , Dr. Karen Mapp (2013) introduced the four-part Dual Capacity Framework for Family-School Partnerships (the challenge, opportunity conditions, policy and program goals, family and staff capacity outcomes). Unique to this model is that it calls for school efforts to offer multiple groups of adult stakeholders, such as staff at the district and school levels as well as family members, opportunities to develop and sharpen their knowledge and skills for effectively engaging families. While these models have undoubtedly contributed to a growing knowledge base around parent, school, and community partnerships, they are a one-size-fits-all approach to building human relationships among diverse stakeholders, which is a complex endeavor. In addition, they have largely ignored the school curriculum.

In response to a one-size-fits-all approach to parent involvement, through her research, Pat introduced a more context-based model. The context-based model of parent engagement offers educators a five-part framework for establishing productive relationships and interactions with parents. In the fall of 1989, Pat joined the Michigan State University faculty, where she continued to expand her research agenda on creating a structure for families to be involved in the literacy development of their children. At Morton Professional Development School (a pseudonym) located in Lansing, Michigan, she coordinated the Home Literacy Project. The goals of the project were (1) to respect the multiple literacy environments the families represented; (2) to become knowledgeable of the family's capability, responsibility, and willingness to be involved in the school; (3) to help educators recognize that not *all* families are the same; (4) to help schools reach out to diverse families in new and different ways; (5) to help educators create a personalized learning environment among the teacher, student, and families that many expressed they had witnessed in years past; and (6) to develop a scope and sequence of family involvement activities coordinated around the grade level literacy curriculum. Figure 12.1 is what a Curriculum and Context-Based Model of Parent Involvement looks like. This model was created and implemented by Pat at Morton Professional Development School.

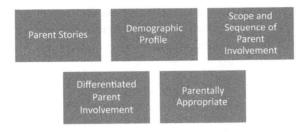

FIGURE 12.1 Curriculum and Context-Based Model of Parent Engagement

Parent Stories (Edwards et al., 1999) are windows into the lives of students. They can be seen as repositories of information about the literacies that exist within homes and communities. Teachers generate parent stories through thoughtful questioning and dialogue with caregivers.

Demographic Profile is a composite description of the parent community that exists in a school building, as well as in individual classrooms.

Scope and Sequence are grade-level family involvement activities that are developmentally based on shared decision-making and built around the elementary school literacy curriculum.

Differentiated Parenting recognizes that parents are different from one another in their perspectives, beliefs, and abilities to negotiate school.

Parentally Appropriate are activities or interactions that are designed to meet the specific needs of an individual parent or a group of parents.

Opening Up Space for Engagement with African American Parents

In this chapter, we argued that African American parents have historically been excluded from involvement in U.S. schooling. Now more than ever the student and family population in the United States and globally is increasingly diverse racially, culturally, and linguistically, yet the teaching force remains predominantly White and middle class. Therefore, it is imperative that professional teacher preparation programs equip teacher educators, preservice teachers, and in-service teachers with the skills and dispositions to engage families in their children's education in ways that honor, value, and respect their humanity. African American parents and families as well as White educators are not monolithic groups. Finally, we contend that educators in the United States must learn about and understand the social and historical context of African American parents' access to education and how that has affected involvement in their children's schooling. Although this chapter discusses African American families and parents, we believe that it supports the notion that teachers and parents, regardless of racial, cultural, and linguistic differences, must learn about each other's social and historical context with schooling to establish a relationship built on understanding. This first step enables a reciprocal relationship that may lead to increased parental involvement in children's schooling and ultimately raise student achievement.

Note

1 Jim Crow laws were a collection of state and local statutes that legalized racial segregation. Named after a Black minstrel show character, the laws—which existed for about 100 years, from the post–civil war era until 1968—were meant to marginalize African Americans by denying them the right to vote, hold jobs, get an education or other opportunities. Those who attempted to defy Jim Crow laws often faced arrest, fines, jail sentences, violence, and death. https://www.history.com/topics/early-20th-century-us/jim-crow-laws.

References

Amatea, E., & West-Olatunji, C. (2007). Joining the conversation about educating our poorest children: Emerging leadership roles for school counselors in high-poverty schools. *Professional School Counseling*, 11(2), 81–89.

Bell, D. A., Jr. (1978). The referendum: Democracy's barrier to racial equality. *Washington Law Review*, 54, 1.

Bell, D. A., Jr. (Ed.). (1980). *Shades of Brown: New perspectives on school desegregation.* New York, NY: Teachers College Press.

Bell, D. A., Jr. (1982). Preferential affirmative action. *Harvard Civil Rights: Civil Liberties Law Review*, 16(3), 855–873.

Bell, D. A., Jr. (1997). *Gospel choirs: Psalms of survival in an alien land called home.* New York, NY: Basic Books.

Bell, D. A., Delgado, R., & Stefancic, J. (2005). *The Derrick Bell reader.* New York, NY: NYU Press.

Bell, D. A., Jr., & Edmonds, E. (1993). Students as teachers, teachers as learners. *Michigan Law Review*, 91(8), 2025–2052.

Bennett-Conroy, W. (2011). Engaging parents of 8th grade students in parents/teacher bidirectional communication. *School Community Journal*, 22(2), 87–110.

Berger, E. H. (1991). Parents involvement: Yesterday and today. *The Elementary School Journal*, 91(3), 209–219.

Bissonnette, J. D. (2016). The trouble with niceness: How a preference for pleasantry sabotages culturally responsive teacher preparation. *Journal of Language and Literacy Education*, 12(2), 9–32.

Bridglall, B. L., & Gordon, E. W. (2002). The idea of supplementary education. *Pedagogical Inquiry and Praxis*, 3, 1–6.

Carson, B., with Murphey, C. (1990). *Gifted hands: The Ben Carson Story.* Grand Rapids, MI: Zondervan.

Castagno, A. E. (Ed.). (2019). *The price of nice: How good intentions maintain educational inequity.* Minnesota, MN: University of Minnesota Press.

Centers for Disease Control and Prevention. (2016). *Adverse childhood experiences. (ACEs).* Retrieved from https://www.cdc.gov/violenceprevention/acestudy/index.html

Comer, J. (1988). *Maggie's American dream: The life and times of a Black family.* New York, NY: Penguin Books.

Cotton, K., & Wikelund, K. R. (1989). Parents involvement in education. *School Improvement Research Series*, 6(3).

Delgado, R. (1992). The imperial scholar revisited: How to marginalize outsider writing, ten years later. *University of Pennsylvania Law Review*, 140(4), 1349–1372.

Delgado, R., & Stefancic, J. (2012). *Critical race theory: An introduction*. New York, NY: NYU Press.

DeNavas-Walt, C., Proctor, B. D., & Smith, J. C. (2004). *Income, poverty, and health insurance coverage in the United States: 2006. Current population reports: Consumer income.* U.S. Census Bureau: U.S. Department of Commerce, Economics and Statistics AdministrationRetrieved from https://www.census.gov/prod/2007pubs/p60-233.pdf

Dewey, J. (1902). *The child and the curriculum.* The University of Chicago Press.

Desimone, L. (1999). Linking parents' involvement with student achievement: Do race and income matter? *The Journal of Educational Research*, 93(1), 11–30.

Donahoo, D. (2013, August). The evolution of parent-school engagement. *The Huffington Post.* Retrieved from https://www.huffpost.com/entry/the-evolution-of-parentsc_b_3451576

Dotterer, A. M., McHale, S. M., & Crouter, A. C. (2009). Sociocultural factors and school engagement among African American youth: The roles of racial discrimination, racial socialization, and ethnic identity. *Applied Development Science*, 13(2), 61–73.

Drake, B., & Pandey, S. (1996). Understanding the relationship between neighborhood poverty and specific types of child maltreatment. *Child Abuse & Neglect*, 20(11), 1003–1018.

Du Bois, W. E. B. (1903). *The souls of Black folk.* Bantam Classic.

DuRocher, K. (2011). *Raising racists: The socialization of White children in the Jim Crow South.* The University Press of Kentucky.

Edwards, P. A., McMillon, G. M. T., & Turner, J. D., (2010). *Change is gonna come: Transforming literacy education for African American children.* Teachers College Press.

Edwards, P. A., Pleasants, H. M., & Franklin, S. H. (1999). *A path to follow: Learning to listen to parents.* Heinemann.

Edwards, P. A., & White, K. L. (2018). Working with racially, culturally, and linguistically diverse students, families, and communities: Strategies for preparing preservice teachers. *Journal of Family Diversity in Education*, 3(1), 1–22.

Epstein, J. L. (2001). *School, family, and community partnerships: Preparing educators and improving schools.* Boulder, C: Westview.

Exum, J. J. (2012). The influence of past racism on criminal injustice: A review of the New Jim Crow and the condemnation of Blackness. *American Studies*, 52(1), 143-152.

Fan, W., & Williams, C. M. (2010). The effects of parent involvement on students' academic self-efficacy, engagement and intrinsic motivation. *Educational Psychology*, 30, 53–74. doi:10.1080/01443410903353302

Federal Writers' Project. (n.d.). *African American slave testimonies and photographs.* Retrieved from http://www.paperlessarchives.com/african-american_slave_testimo.html

Ford, D.Y. (1994). Nurturing resilience in gifted Black youth. *Roeper Review*, 17(2), 80–85.

Gadsden, V. L. (1993). Literacy, education, and identity among African-Americans: The communal nature of learning. *Urban Education*, 27(4), 352–369.

Garmezy, N. (1993). Children in poverty: Resilience despite risk. *Psychiatry*, 56(1), 127–136.

Gay, G., & Kirkland, K. (2003). Developing cultural critical consciousness and self-reflection in preservice teacher education. *Theory Into Practice*, 42(3), 181–187.

Gordon, E. W., Bridglall, B. L., & Meroe, A. S. (Eds.). (2005). *Supplementary education: The hidden curriculum of high academic achievement.* Rowman & Littlefield.

Hallman, C. (2008, October 2). North High alumni call on Black parents to take action. *Sun Reporter*, pp. L4, L4A.

Harris, T. S., & Graves, S. L., Jr. (2010). The influence of cultural capital transmission on reading achievement in African American fifth grade boys. *The Journal of Negro Education*, 79(4), 447–457.

Hauser Cram, P. (2009). Education from one generation to the next: Mechanisms of mediation. *Merrill-Palmer Quarterly*, 55(3), 351–360.

Hayes, D. (2011). Predicting parental home and school involvement in high school African American adolescents. *High School Journal*, 94(4), 154–166.

Henderson, A. T., & Mapp, K. L. (2002). *A new wave of evidence: The impact of school, family, and community connections on student achievement. Annual synthesis 2002.* National Center for Family and Community Connections with Schools.

Henfield, M. S., & Washington, A. R. (2012). "I want to do the right thing but what is it?": White teachers' experiences with African American students. *The Journal of Negro Education*, 81(2), 148–161.

Howard, G. R. (2007). As diversity grows so must we. *Educational Leadership*, 64(6), 16–22.

Howard, T. C., & Reynolds, R. (2008). Examining parents' involvement in reversing the underachievement of African American students in middle-class schools. *The Journal of Educational Foundations*, 22(1/2), 79–98.

Humes, L. H. (2016). African American storytelling: A vehicle for providing culturally relevant education in urban public schools in the United States [Doctoral dissertation]. Retrieved from https://fisherpub.sjfc.edu/education_etd/264/

Jack and Jill. (2017). *Scope*. Retrieved from http://jackandjillinc.org/

Leary, J. D. (2005). *Crimes against humanity. Post traumatic slave syndrome: America's legacy of enduring injury and healing.* Uptone Press.

Lee, C. C. (2005). Urban school counseling: Context, characteristics and competencies, *Professional School Counseling*, 8(3),184–188.

Lewis, C. W., James, M., Hancock, S., & Hill-Jackson, V. (2008). Framing African American students' success and failure in urban settings: A typology for change. *Urban Education*, 43, 127–153.

Lubienski, S. T. & Crane C. C. (2010). Beyond free lunch: Which family background measures matter? *Education Policy Analysis Archives*, 18(11), 1–43.

Lynn, M., Jennings, M. E., & Hughes, S. (2013). Critical race pedagogy 2.0: Lessons from Derrick Bell. *Race Ethnicity and Education*, 16(4), 603–628.

Mapp, K. (2013). *Partners in education: A dual capacity-building framework for family-school partnership.* SEDL in collaboration with the U.S. Department of Education. Retrieved form http://www.sedl.org/pubs/framework/

Mayfield, V. M., & Garrison-Wade, D. (2015). Culturally responsive practices as whole school reform. *Journal of Instructional Pedagogies*, 16, 1–17.

Moore, J. L. III, & Lewis, C. W. (2012). *African American students in urban schools: Critical issues and solutions for achievement. Educational psychology: Critical pedagogical perspectives.* Volume 4. Peter Lang.

Mubenga, P. (2006). *The struggle of African American students in the public schools [ED491396].* ERIC. Retrieved from http://files.eric.ed.gov/fulltext/ED491396.pdf

Naomi's Program of Excellence. (2017). *About Naomi's program of excellence.* Retrieved from http://npefamily.org/

Rankin, B. H., & Quane, J. M. (2002). Social contexts and urban adolescent outcomes: The interrelated effects of neighborhoods, families, and peers on African American youth. *Social Problems*, 49(1), 79–100.

Schönpflug, U. (Ed.). (2008). *Cultural transmission: Psychological, developmental, social, and methodological aspects.* Cambridge University Press.

Shonkoff, J. P., & Meisels, S. J. (2000). *Handbook of early childhood intervention.* Cambridge University Press.

Swick, K. J., & Williams, R. D. (2006). An analysis of Bronfenbrenner's bio-ecological perspective for early childhood educators: Implications for working with families experiencing stress. *Early Childhood Education Journal, 33*(5), 371–378.

Tamis-LeMonda, C. S., Briggs, R. D., McClowry, S. G., & Snow, D. L. (2008). Challenges to the study of African American parenting: Conceptualization, sampling, research approaches, measurement, and design. *Parenting: Science and Practice, 8*(4), 319–358.

Thompson, G. L. (2003). *How African American parents/guardians assisted their children academically. What African American parents want educators to know.* Praeger.

Tobin, P. K., & Snyman, R. (2008). Once upon a time in Africa: A case study of storytelling for knowledge sharing. *Aslib Proceedings, 60*(2) 130–142.

Trent, S. C., & Artiles, A. J. (1995). Serving culturally deprived students with behavior disorders: Broadening current perspectives. In J. M. Kauffman, J. W. Lloyd, R. A. Astuto, & D. P. Hallahan (Eds.), *Issues in the educational placement of pupils with emotional or behavioral disorders* (pp. 215–249). Erlbaum.

U.S. Department of Education, National Center for Education Statistics. (2003). *NCES Statistical Standards (NCES 2003–601).* Government Printing Office.

Waugh, D. (2012). "The issue is the control of public schools": The politics of desegregation in Prince Edward County. *Virginia. Southern Cultures, 18*(3), 76–94.

Yeung, W. J. J., & Pfeiffer, K. M. (2009). The Black–Caucasian test score gap and early home environment. *Social Science Research, 38*(2), 412–437.

13

SOME LESSONS LEARNED FROM WORKING WITH CHILDREN AND FAMILIES IN DIVERSE COMMUNITIES

Looking Back, Looking Forward

Jim Anderson and Ann Anderson

In this chapter, we trace three decades of working in/with family and community-initiated literacy programs in socioculturally diverse communities in different areas of Canada. We first describe the framework that has informed this work. Next, we briefly review the literature on family literacy, including inherent tensions and differing perspectives. Then we describe the various initiatives and the contexts in which they took place. We identify insights drawn from this work and conclude by proposing a modest agenda for future work with families, in an era of *superdiversity* (Vertovec, 2007).

Framework

We draw on sociohistorical theory (e.g., Vygotsky, 1978; Wertsch, 1991), and its central tenet that learning is initially social, before becoming internalized. That is, supported by more knowledgeable, significant others, individuals learn to use cultural tools such as literacy that are important and valued in their community, *inter-psychologically*. This support or "scaffolding" (Wood et al., 1976) is withdrawn gradually, as individuals become more proficient and able to use the tools *intra-psychologically*, or independently. As Rogoff (2003) cautions, although there is considerable variation in development and learning across cultures "[t]o date, the study of human development has been based largely on research and theory coming from middle class communities in Europe and North America" (p. 4).

Relatedly, we pay attention to the notion of *cultural models* (Holland & Quinn, 1987) of learning and literacy. Cultural models are "theoretical constructs composed of the interconnected ideas, beliefs, goals, and practices shared by members of a cultural group that guide their actions and interpretations of phenomena" (Suizzo et al., 2014, p. 256). For example, while some families believe that children develop literacy naturally by being surrounded by activities and events in their daily lives, by being read to, and by engaging in conversations and discussions, other families emphasize rote memory and practice (e.g., Anderson et al., 2017; Li, 2008).

Bronfenbrenner's bio-ecological model of human development (e.g., Bronfenbrenner & Morris, 2006) also informs our work. He postulated that different systems, each increasingly more distant from the child, influence learning and development. The *microsystem*, most proximal, consists of family members, teachers and so forth; the *macrosystem*, most distal, includes "belief systems, resources, hazards, lifestyles, opportunity structures, life course options and patterns of social change that are embedded in these systems" (Bronfenbrenner, 2005, p. 149). For example, a lack of resources in a community will affect the extent to which families and schools can support children's literacy development, as can prevailing attitudes toward, and beliefs about, literacy.

In our work with immigrant and refugee families for most of whom English was an additional language, we drew on the literature on bilingualism and the benefits of maintaining one's home language. For example, Bialystok and her colleagues documented the cognitive benefits of being bilingual that extend across the life course (Bialystok, 2017). Cummins (1980, 2016) has been a strong proponent of children and families retaining their home language as they learn the dominant language of their community (e.g., English). He proposed the notion of common *underlying proficiency*, postulating that although there are surface-level differences across languages, *interlinguistic resources*—analytic and cognitive skills—transfer from one to the other. In their report to the influential National Reading Panel in the United States, Snow et al. (1998), deduced from research that maintaining the home language facilitated children's learning to read in a second language. Wong-Fillmore (1991, 2000) demonstrated the negative effects on family life and intergenerational communications when children lose their home languages and parents and grandparents are not facile in the new language.

Related Literature

Denny Taylor (1983) brought the concept of *family literacy* into prominence with the publication of her foundational book with that name. Her ethnography involving eight middle-class families documented how young children acquired knowledge and skills through an acculturation process as they were surrounded by, and participated in, literacy activities and events embedded in daily life. Studies with families from socially and culturally diverse communities (e.g., Delgado-Gaitan, 1987; Heath, 1983; Purcell-Gates, 1996; D. Taylor & Dorsey-Gaines, 1988) revealed that children experienced and participated in literacy activities and events prior to formal instruction, although these experiences sometimes did not map on to school literacy as did those of children from "mainstream" homes such as those in Taylor's original study.

Based on studies such as these demonstrating that families can play important roles in children's early literacy development, educators, and others concerned with young children's learning began to develop family literacy programs. Whereas the term *family literacy* originally connoted the naturally occurring, day-to-day literacy practices of families in the contexts of their homes and communities, family literacy programs were designed "to teach literacy knowledge and make use of learner's family relationships and engagement in family literacy practices" (Hannon, 2003, p. 100). These programs proliferated, and although originally there was relatively little assessment or evaluation of their efficacy (Purcell-Gates, 2000; Thomas & Skage, 1998), researchers and program providers responded and began more systematic evaluation of these initiatives.

Several scholars have conducted systematic reviews and meta-studies of research in family literacy programs. In their meta-study, Brooks and colleagues, (2008) examined 19 qualitative and quantitative studies. Although they did not compute effect sizes, as in meta-analyses, they found that in 18 of the 19 studies, children made gains in language and literacy. Interestingly, four of five studies found that gains in children's literacy were maintained post-program.

In their meta-analysis, Senechal and Young (2008) included 16 studies involving more than 1300 children. They divided the studies as follows and reported the effect size of each type of activity: parent/significant other reading to children (.18), children reading to their parents/significant other (.52), and parents/significant other teaching literacy skills such as letter–sound correspondence (1.15). Only the first condition, parents reading to children, did not yield statistically significant results; the overall effect size of the 16 studies was .65, which was statistically significant and considered medium (Cohen, 1988).

Marulis and Neuman (2010) conducted a meta-analysis of studies that examined young children's expressive and/or vocabulary development. Children's vocabulary is a good predictor of their later literacy achievement (Storch & Whitehurst, 2002) and considered crucial in comprehending disciplinary texts that children encounter as they enter elementary school. Marulis and Neuman examined 67 studies involving about 5,900 students, approximately 3,200 in intervention groups and 2,700 in control groups. They found an effect size of .88, which is large (Cohen, 1988).

van Steensel et al. (2011) in their meta-analysis of 30 studies found an effect size of .20, which was statistically significant but is considered small. They noted that small effects may be educationally significant and "non-trivial" (van Steensel et al., 2011, p. 88) but cautioned about the need to have reasonable expectations of the effects of family literacy programs.

As Swain et al. (2014) pointed out, most assessment and evaluation studies of family literacy programs focused on children's language and literacy. In a study that focused on the benefits that might accrue parents/caregivers, they interviewed about 100 parents from 74 programs across England. They found that participants: felt better able to support their children's learning, ascribed greater importance to education, understood schools and education systems more fully, developed social networks, and became more interested in furthering their own literacy development and education. In a subsequent study, Swain and Cara (2019) reported that parents indicated that the programs helped demystify school literacy.

Critiques of Family Literacy Programs

Although family literacy programs benefit children's language and literacy learning and parents indicate that they benefit from them, a number of scholars have critiqued them (e.g., Auerbach, 1989; Crooks, 2017; Reyes & Torres, 2007). Critiques include the following: Vernacular literacies are ignored or invalidated and literacy activities valued in schools are promoted; dominant languages (e.g., English) are favored, and home languages are discouraged; and programs tend to reflect hegemonic Eurocentric, middle-class orientations, and perspectives. Swain and Cara (2019) concluded that these issues persist in some of the family literacy programs that they examined. However, some program developers and providers have attempted to make their programs more socio-contextually responsive; the development of bilingual family literacy programs is an example.

Bilingual Family Literacy Programs

Hirst et al. (2010) reported on a study involving 16 families originally from Pakistan, living in Sheffield, United Kingdom. Families were encouraged to use their first language—Mirupuri, Punjabi, or Urdu. For about a year, a teacher and a cultural worker visited the eight families participating in the family literacy program; the other families served as a control group. Each visit had a particular focus such as emergent writing, oral language, or shared reading. There were no significant differences between the control group and the program group in children's scores on the Sheffield Early Literacy Development Profile (Nutbrown, 1997) at the commencement of the program; at the end of the program, children who had participated in the program scored significantly higher than those in the control group.

In a study involving 42 Chinese Canadian families, Zhang et al. (2010) documented the impact of a bilingual family literacy program on the children's home language and English. During the 2-hour sessions, the teachers had families engage in age appropriate language and literacy activities and provided rhyming books and web-based language and literacy activities for home. Pre- and postcomparisons of the Peabody Picture Vocabulary Test indicated that the children made significant gains in receptive vocabulary; they did not make significant gains on the Expressive Vocabulary Test. Furthermore, children of parents with higher income and more education made greater gains than children whose parents had lower education levels and income.

Boyce et al. (2010) reported on a study with migrant families in the United States that focused on storytelling. Families told stories to children about their day-to-day experiences, which, with the facilitators' support, they made into books for sharing with the children. Compared with a control group, both children and parents expanded their language use including the number of words used and the number of new words used.

Working in Socioculturally Diverse Contexts

Rural, Disadvantaged Community

Early in his career, Jim the first author taught in small, rural, socially disadvantaged communities, often with low educational achievement and expectations. However, his first experience with working in an initiative to address these issues more systematically occurred when he was an assistant superintendent of curriculum and instruction in a rural school district in the Province of Newfoundland and Labrador, Canada, in the late 1980s. A principal of the elementary school in a socioeconomically disadvantaged community, who grew up and still resided there, approached the district, seeking support in developing an "intervention" program to address persistent, systemic issues of low achievement, low expectations, low high school completion rates, and low participation in postsecondary education.

Jim's role was to support the principal and the district's early childhood consultant in developing and implementing the program. To begin, we met with the Parent Advisory Council of the school, social agencies, and parents of young children to identify goals and strategies. The groups decided on a program wherein 4-year-olds and a caregiver would attend monthly half-day sessions in the kindergarten classroom at the school for the year prior to school entry. The early-childhood consultant and the kindergarten teacher collaborated in designing learning centers where the children engaged in age-appropriate activities, supported by parents/caregivers. Ann, the second author, participated as a parent and volunteer.

Norman (1997) interviewed the parents and found that they were overwhelmingly supportive. Anderson et al. (2013) conducted retrospective interviews with 10 of 18 parents who had participated in the initial offering of the program two decades previously, and their findings were similar. Norman also tracked the results of the Canadian Test of Basic Skills Tests administered to Grade 4 students at the school every three years for a decade as follows: 1984, 20th percentile; 1987, 37th percentile; 1990, 30th percentile. In 1993, the year when the original cohort of children from the program was in Grade 4, the class scored at the 50th percentile, the first class at the school to ever achieve that level, which Norman attributed to the effect of the program.

Inner-City Communities

In 1999, the mayor of a small city in the Greater Vancouver area of British Columbia invited Jim and Fiona Morrison, the early childhood coordinator in the local school district to join a community development project in inner-city neighborhoods. Through a series of focus groups, we consulted with families, early-childhood educators, and other school district personnel and developed a family literacy program called Parents[1] As Literacy Supporters (PALS) that we offered in two schools (Anderson & Morrison, 1999). Informed to a large extent by the project in Newfoundland, PALS consisted of monthly 2-hour sessions, each focusing on a particular topic that families had identified they wanted to learn more about (e.g., learning to read, learning mathematics). Sessions began with sharing food, after which an early-childhood educator accompanied the children to a classroom. The facilitators, encouraged parents to share what they had observed about their children's learning since the last session, addressed any concerns or questions that arose and provided an overview of the session. The parents and facilitators then joined the children in the classrooms where they circulated for about an hour among learning centers with developmentally appropriate activities, reflecting the theme of the session (e.g., emergent writing). The children then had a recess break, while the facilitator led a debriefing session with the parents, prompting discussion about which activities went well and which needed improvement, what the children learned, what they (parents) learned, and so on. To culminate the session, each family received a children's book, and other materials to supplement the kit of resources such as markers, paper, crayons, and so forth, that they received at the orientation session.

First Nations Communities

Other schools and districts became interested in implementing PALS, including several First Nations Communities. In particular, one school district in Northern British Columbia embraced the program and, under the leadership of the First Nations Education Coordinator, adapted it to fit the needs of their community. After PALS had run for several years there, we interviewed 20 caregivers (mothers, fathers, grandparents, older siblings) who had participated in the program (Anderson et al., 2007). In general, caregivers felt that they and their children benefited from the program. Fourteen of the participants indicated that they felt better connected and more comfortable in schools, an important finding given the legacy of residential schools in Canada (Hare, 2005). Although the program facilitators incorporated First Nations culture and languages to the extent possible, most of the participants agreed that more needed to be done in that regard.

In another initiative, Gail Stromquist and Janet Stromquist, worked with elders and other Aboriginal educators to redevelop the program into what they called Aboriginal PALS. It is a "culturally responsive family literacy program that gives parents and caregivers new strategies to support their preschool and kindergarten-aged children's learning" (Decoda Literacy Solutions, 2019, para. 1). Various First Nations communities adopted the program, and it continues to be used throughout British Columbia (A. Dhungana, personal communication, May 5, 2020).

Immigrant and Refugee Communities

In 2005, a cultural worker in the school district where PALS originated, approached the program developers with the suggestion that the program be adapted for the Vietnamese families from her community and offered in Vietnamese and English. Working in collaboration with a local elementary school, the school district, and the cultural worker, the program developers, Anderson and Morrison, redesigned the program to align with the needs of the Vietnamese community. The program retained a similar format as the original PALS described earlier, but sessions were offered in English and Vietnamese with the cultural worker co-facilitating. Also, dual-language children's books were provided, and families were encouraged to maintain their home language. Furthermore, an adult English as a Second Language (ESL) component was added to each session at the request of the parents. In response to parents, in the second year of the program, technology was integrated into the adult ESL portion. Perkins (2010) documented the implementation and reported that the program was generally well received and the families valued the learning that occurred. She also reaffirmed the need for creativity and flexibility, the importance of listening to families and communities, the essential role of the cultural worker, and the need for program providers to continue to strive for greater inclusion of families' funds of knowledge (Moll et al., 1992).

Subsequently, other communities began to express interest in the program, and in 2007, the program was offered in five communities in Farsi, Karen, Mandarin, and Punjabi. Results of a mixed-methods study that examined these programs indicated (1) children's early literacy knowledge in English increased significantly, (2) parents appreciated the bilingual format of the program, (3) parents indicated that they learned about Western schooling/pedagogy and felt more comfortable in schools, and 4) families were generally supportive of first language maintenance (Anderson et al., 2011). However, families also (1) wanted more frequent sessions and the program extended to school-aged children, (2) wanted more emphasis placed on school readiness, (3) worried that their children might fall behind in learning English, and (4) asked for more explicit instruction in ways to support their children.

Looking Back

Consulting with Families and Communities

In each of these initiatives, the program developers consulted with families and communities as they developed the programs; indeed, initial requests came from the communities. We see this feature as being important for several reasons. First, we believe programs are more responsive to local needs when the people who will participate in and deliver them are involved from the outset. Second, we think it also promoted greater "buy-in" and ownership and therefore prolonged and sustained attendance at sessions, and subsequently adults' and children's learning (Purcell-Gates et al., 2012). We note that participants in these initiatives chose to attend or not attend sessions of their own volition. Finally, we believe we had an ethical or moral responsibility to consult with families and communities, and programs should not be imposed.

Culture Brokers

Culture brokers are those who have "prior knowledge and trusting relationships with particular communities" (Center for Reducing Health Disparities, 2007, p. 4). In our work with immigrant and refugee families, the cultural workers acted as culture brokers in several ways. First, they had the trust of the communities and were key in making families aware of the program and maintaining communications with them. They acted as co-facilitators of the program, co-planned sessions, identified community practices, translated key materials into participants' home languages and served as translators during the sessions. They helped clarify miscommunications and misunderstandings and indicated when participants' needs were not met. For example, at one site, the cultural worker indicated that the families felt that the facilitators were not providing explicit explanations of key concepts; consequently, the facilitators assumed a more didactic stance, making sure to explain the rationale for various activities. In another instance, the families wanted "homework," or key points from each session to take home in note form, which the cultural worker provided. Of course, the Stromquists, in collaboration with elders and other First Nations educators, were also acting as culture brokers in Aboriginal PALS, as they transformed the original program to fit their communities' needs.

Cultural Models of Learning and Teaching

As noted, communities have different ways of teaching and learning, and this was manifested in different ways in the different contexts. For example, in the PALS in Immigrant Communities project, parents would sometimes insist on modelling for the child how to draw an object, print his or her name, or organize a pattern of objects at the learning centers, before permitting the child to attempt the task independently (Anderson & Morrison, 2011). Of course, such adult involvement is anathematic to the dominant philosophy of early-childhood development and education in North America, where approximation, independence, and risk-taking are assumed, as the way children learn. On the other hand, Friedrich (2016) reported on how the Karen-speaking families with whom she worked did not sit with the children, engaging in activities at the centers, but stood back from them, providing responsive assistance (Rogoff, 2003) as called on by the children.

Home–school Connections

Positive, two-way home–school connections are important in children's learning (Rodriguez-Brown, 2009). Traditionally, schools have utilized information sessions, curriculum nights, and teacher–parent meetings typically scheduled around report cards, and so forth to connect with parents and families. Laureau (1987) found that families in her study in a middle-class neighborhood felt comfortable in school, participated in parent–teacher conferences, and felt a sense of agency in their children's education. However, families in the working-class neighborhood did not feel comfortable or welcomed in school, tended to avoid parent–teacher conferences, and did not feel a sense of agency. One of the positive outcomes of our work is that families generally indicated that they felt more comfortable in school and more confident in supporting their children's learning. For example, a father from a First Nations community commented that his own experiences in school were quite negative, and he was initially reluctant to participate in the family literacy program (Anderson et al., 2007). However, he felt that the focus on families' assets, the inclusion of First Nations culture, and the learning by doing pedagogy, led him to feel welcomed and valued, and encouraged him to continue to be involved in his child's education and the school. Likewise, the families in the rural community indicated that they became more involved in school activities and events, and indeed, some of them said that they took on leadership roles in the parent–teacher association. Also, the immigrant and refugee families reported that they appreciated becoming familiar with Western education systems, pedagogy, and schools, which were sometimes markedly different from those in their homeland.

School Readiness/Transition to School

The notion that families have a responsibility to get children ready for school is quite prominent (e.g., Brown, 2018), although some scholars argue that the opposite should be the case and schools should be ready for children (e.g., Freeman & Powers-Costello, 2011). Although some scholars contest the concept of school readiness, families across the different contexts that we worked in believed that one of the biggest benefits of the program was in helping their children get ready for school. For example, one of the parents interviewed in the rural community stated that

> before this program, a lot of children went to kindergarten, and they [had] absolutely no knowledge—anything regarding colors, numbers, and nothing. But with this way, at least every child got started, like they were a little bit prepared, right?
>
> *(Anderson et al., 2013, p. 40)*

The immigrant and refugee families also emphasized the importance of their children being ready for school, and indeed, some of them suggested an increased focus on school readiness when we asked them about ways that we could improve the program.

Relatedly, families indicated that their children's transition to kindergarten was enhanced because of their participation in the program. They believed that the children developed a relationship with the kindergarten teachers, became familiar with activities and routines similar to those they would encounter in school, and developed friendships with other children, some of which continued outside of the program. Souto-Manning (2018) questioned the appropriateness and efficacy of transition activities such as school tours or orientation sessions, which often position minoritized children, families, and communities as a deficit. However, the minoritized families we worked with believed that their and their children's experiences were valuable in easing transition to formal schooling.

Looking Forward

Although, in general, these initiatives were positively received and families indicated that they benefited, there is still work to do. We next discuss ongoing concerns and issues that we believe need to be addressed.

Funds of Knowledge

Moll et al. (1992) define funds of knowledge as "historically accumulated and culturally developed bodies of knowledge and skills essential for household or individual functioning and well-being" (p. 133). In some instances, we were successful in incorporating families' funds of knowledge, as for example when the facilitators at one site encouraged families to bring in riddles and rhymes in Farsi for a session on oral language development (Friedrich et al., 2014). As well, the Aboriginal PALS program incorporated funds of knowledge from First Nations communities. However, we believe that more consistency is needed, to ensure that facilitators are able to capitalize on the knowledge that families bring. Friedrich (2016) reported there was very little evidence of the Karen refugee families' funds of knowledge, and for example, in the session on oral language, only traditional, Western nursery rhymes were read and songs shared in English, even though singing is a prominent part of the Karen cultural repertoire. We also see funds of knowledge as incorporating teaching and learning strategies, and here, some facilitators struggled with allowing parents to mediate learning in ways that differed from their own philosophy. For example, some were concerned when parents modelled how to draw an object, instead of allowing the child to proceed on his or her own, consistent with dominant

North American perspectives such as those outlined by the National Association of Early Childhood Education.

Diversity in Texts

As noted earlier, we provided dual-language books in English and the first languages of the immigrant and refugee families. These were generally well received and appreciated and parents indicated that they and the children used different approaches in sharing them (e.g., reading the text in their first language [L1] first and then rereading in English the next occasion, the parent reading the text in L1 and the child reading the English text, and so forth). The books were generally high-quality literature; however, few of them allowed the children and families to see themselves or reflected their culture (Bishop, 1990), and in future, this lacuna needs to be addressed. Relatedly, facilitators can work with families to produce their own identity texts as was the case in a project described by L. Taylor et al. (2008) in which English language learners, with the support of family members, developed dual-language texts, which were shared in their kindergarten classroom.

Sustainability

An issue with initiatives such as those we have described is sustainability, as many of them are funded as short-term projects that terminate when funding ends or struggle along through the good graces of the program providers and community supporters (e.g., Purcell-Gates, 2000). The PALS in Immigrant Communities program is still offered in a number of communities and Aboriginal PALS is also still vibrant and relevant. However, despite the relative longevity of these programs and the fact that families see them as valuable (e.g., Anderson et al., 2007, 2011), they are still contingent on short-term funding that entails time-consuming applications each year and bureaucratic accountability that has little to do with efficacy or impact.

Multi-literacies, Multimodality

Although print literacy played a prominent role in the initiatives we described, like most programs for young children, they also reflected a multimodal, multi-literacies perspective (Bezemer & Kress, 2016; Cope & Kalantzis, 2009). For example, picture books were a feature in each, children drew and painted, and rhymes, riddles, songs and so forth were incorporated throughout. As well, First Nations languages were incorporated in Indigenous communities, and home languages were encouraged and promoted with immigrant and refugee families. When we designed the original PALS program, families indicated that they wanted to learn about "computers" and so we designed a session on technology and we provided children's songs in the children's home languages on DVDs when we originally worked with English-language learners. Beyond that, however, technology has not been prominent in the program, as there are continuing tensions around the issue of young children's use of technological devices (e.g., Canadian Pediatric Society, 2017). Given the ubiquity of digital technology and the fact that it is now a part of daily life in many families (Marsh et al., 2017), it is time to revisit this issue and to look at ways of embedding digital tools in family literacy programs.

Conclusion

We believe that the three decades of working with families and in diverse communities we have described demonstrates the potential of contextually responsive programs in supporting children's language and literacy development and learning. Such programs, we propose, can address some of the challenges posed by the superdiversity (Vertovec, 2007) in communities resulting from the unprecedented global movement of people. That is, they can support minoritized children and families as they make the transition to school, which often differs considerably from their country of origin while valuing and utilizing their cultures, experiences, and languages. Our work also demonstrates the need for reflexivity on the part of program developers and providers to ensure that programs continue to evolve and change to meet the needs of families and communities.

Note

1   Grandparents, aunts and uncles, older siblings, and other caretakers often accompanied children. Because families had become familiar with the program name, we retained the wording and use *parents* to signify a range of caregivers.

References

Anderson, J., Anderson, A., Friedrich, N., & Teichert, L. (2017). "You guys should offer the program more often!": Some perspectives from working alongside immigrant and refugee families in a bilingual family literacy program. In C. McLachlan & A. Arrow (Eds.), *Literacy in the early years—Reflections on international research and practice* (pp. 63–78). New York: Springer.

Anderson, A., Anderson, J., & Teichert, L. (2013). Through a rear-view mirror: Families retrospectively evaluate a family literacy program twenty years later. *The School Community Journal*, 23(2), 33–53.

Anderson, J., Friedrich, N., & Kim, J. (2011). *Implementing a bilingual family literacy program with immigrant and refugee families: The case of Parents As Literacy Supporters (PALS)*. Decoda Literacy Solutions. http://www.decoda.ca/wp-content/uploads/PALS-in-Immigrant-Communities-Research-Report-Feb-2011-2.pdf

Anderson, J., & Morrison, F. (2011). Learning from/with immigrant and refugee families in a family literacy program. In A. Lazar & P. Schmidt (Eds.) *Practicing what we* teach: How culturally responsive literacy classrooms make a difference (pp. 30–38). New York: Teachers College Press.

Anderson, J., Morrison, F., Leighton-Stephens, D., & Shapiro, J. (2007, May). *Listening to parents' voices: Working with First Nations communities in a culturally responsive family literacy program* [Paper presentation]. *Annual conference of the Canadian Society for the Study of Education*, Saskatchewan, Canada Saskatoon.

Anderson, J., & Morrison, F. (1999). *The PALS Handbook: Creating and sustaining a culturally responsive family literacy program*. Langley, British Columbia: Langley School District.

Auerbach, E. (1989). Toward a social-contextual approach to family literacy. *Harvard Educational Review*, 59, 165–181.

Bezemer, J., & Kress, G. (2016). *Multimodality, learning and communication: A social semiotic frame*. London: Routledge.

Bialystok, E. (2017). The bilingual adaptation: How minds accommodate experience. *Psychological Bulletin*, 143(30), 232–262.

Bishop, R. S. (1990). Mirrors, windows, and sliding glass doors. *Perspectives*, 6(3), ix–xi.

Boyce, L. K., Innocenti, M. S., Roggman, L. A., Norman, V. K. J., & Ortiz, E. (2010). Telling stories and making books: Evidence for an intervention to help parents in Migrant Head Start families support their children's language and literacy. *Early Education & Development*, 21(3), 343–371.

Bronfenbrenner, U. (2005). *Making human beings human: Bioecological perspectives on human development*. London: Sage Publications.

Bronfenbrenner, U., & Morris, P. A. (2006). The bioecological model of human development. In W. Damon & R. M. Lerner (Eds.), *Handbook of Child Psychology, Vol. 1. Theoretical models of human development* (6th ed., pp. 793–828). New York: John Wiley.

Brooks, G., Pahl, K., Pollard, A., & Rees, F. (2008). *Effective and inclusive practices in family literacy and numeracy: A review of and practices in the UK and internationally*. Reading, UK: CfBT Trust.

Brown, C. (2018). School readiness. In L. Miller, C. Cameron, C. Dalli, & N. Barbour (Eds.), *The SAGE handbook of early childhood policy* (pp. 287–302). London: Sage Publications.

Canadian Pediatric Society. (2017). Screen time and young children: Promoting health and development in a digital world. *Pediatrics & Child Health*, 22(8), 461–468.

Center for Reducing Health Disparities. (2007). *Building partnerships: Key considerations when engaging underserved communities under the MHSA (Monograph No. 2, Center for Reducing Health Disparities)*. Sacramento: University of California, Davis. Retrieved from https://health.ucdavis.edu/crhd/Pdfs/FINAL%20Building%20Partnerships%201.10.pdf

Cohen, J. (1988). *Statistical power analysis for the behavioral sciences* (2nd ed.). Hillsdale, NJ: Lawrence Erlbaum.

Cope, B., & Kalantzis, M. (2009). "Multi-literacies": New Literacies, new learning. *Pedagogies: An International Journal*, 4(3), 164–195.

Crooks, S. (2017). *Family literacy and colonial logics* [Unpublished doctoral dissertation]. Toronto, Canada: University of Toronto.

Cummins, J. (1980). The cross-lingual dimensions of language proficiency: Implications for bilingual education and the optimal age issue. *TESOL Quarterly*, 14, 175–187.

Cummins, J. (2016). Intercultural education and academic achievement: A framework for school based policies in multilingual schools. *Intercultural Education*, 26(6), 455–468.

Decoda Literacy Solutions (2019). *Aboriginal PALS*. Retrieved from https://www.decoda.ca/practitioners/professional-development-community-literacy/pals/aboriginal-pals/

Delgado-Gaitan, C. (1987). Traditions and transitions in the learning process of Mexican American children: An ethnographic view. In G. & L. Spindler (Eds.), *Interpretive ethnography of education* (pp. 332–362). Hillsdale, NJ: Lawrence Erlbaum.

Freeman, N. K., & Powers-Costello B. (2011) Reconsidering readiness. In D. Laverick & M. Jalongo (Eds.), *Transitions to early care and education. Educating the young child* (pp. 137–148). Dordrecht: Springer.

Friedrich, N. (2016). *Making connections: Literacy practices of Karen refugee families in the home, community and family literacy program* [Unpublished doctoral dissertation]. Vancouver, Canada: University of British Columbia.

Friedrich, N., Anderson, J., & Morrison, F. (2014). Culturally appropriate pedagogy in a bilingual family literacy program. *Literacy*, 48(2), 72–79.

Hannon, P. (2003). Family literacy programmes. In N. Hall, J. Larson, & J. Marsh (Eds.), *Handbook of early childhood literacy* (pp. 99–111). London: Sage Publications.

Hare, J. (2005). To 'Know Papers': Aboriginal perspectives on literacy. In J. Anderson, M. Kendrick, T. Rogers, & S. Smythe (Eds.), *Portraits of literacy across families, communities and schools: Intersections and tensions* (pp. 243–264). Mahwah, NJ: Lawrence Erlbaum Associates.

Heath, S. (1983). *Ways with words: Language, life and work in communities and classrooms.* New York: Cambridge University Press.

Hirst, K., Hannon, P., & Nutbrown, C. (2010). Effects of a preschool bilingual family literacy programme. *Journal of Early Childhood Literacy*, 10, 183–208.

Holland, D., & Quinn, N. (1987). *Cultural models in language and thought.* New York, NY: Cambridge University Press.

Laureau, A. (1987). Social class differences in family-school relationships: The importance of cultural capital. *Sociology of Education*, 60(2), 73–85.

Li, G. (2008). *Culturally contested literacies: America's "rainbow underclass" and urban schools.* New York: Routledge.

Marsh, J., Hannon, P., Lewis, M., & Ritchie, L. (2017). Young children's initiation into family literacy practices in the digital age. *Journal of Early Childhood Research*, 15(1), 47–60.

Marulis, L., & Neuman, S. (2010). The effects of vocabulary intervention on young children's word learning: A meta-analysis. *Review of Educational Research*, 80(3), 300–335.

Moll, L., Amanti, C., Neff, D., & González, N. (1992). Funds of knowledge for teaching: Using a qualitative approach to connect homes and classrooms. *Theory Into Practice*, 31(2), 132–141.

Norman, (1997). *The hand that rocks the cradle: An evaluation of the preschool early intervention at St. Mark's School* [Unpublished master's thesis]. St. John's, NL: Memorial University of Newfoundland.

Nutbrown, C. (1997). *Recognizing early literacy development: Assessing children's achievement.* London: Paul Chapman.

Perkins, S. (2010). PALS in Vietnamese: Implementing a bilingual family literacy program. In S. Szabo, M. Sampson, M. Foote, & F. Falk (Eds.), *Mentoring literacy professionals: Continuing the spirit of CRA/ALER after 50 years* (pp. 81–93). Commerce, TX: Association of Literacy Educators and Researchers.

Purcell-Gates, V. (2000). Family literacy. In M. L. Kamil, P. B. Mosenthal, P. D. Pearson & R. Barr (Eds.), *Handbook of reading research, volume III* (pp. 853–870). Mahwah, NJ: Lawrence Erlbaum Associates.

Purcell-Gates, V. (1996). Stories, coupons and the *TV Guide*: Relationships between home literacy experiences and emergent literacy knowledge. *Reading Research Quarterly*, 31(4), 406–428.

Purcell-Gates, V., Anderson, J., Jang, K., Gagne, M., Lenters, K., & McTavish, M. (2012). Measuring situated literacy activity: Challenges and promises. *Journal of Literacy Research*, 44(4), 132–141.

Reyes, L., & Torres, M. (2007). Decolonizing family literacy in a culture circle: Reinventing the family literacy educator's role. *Journal of Early Childhood Literacy*, 79(1), 73–94.

Rodriguez-Brown, F. (2009). *The home-school connection: Lessons learned in culturally and linguistically diverse communities*. New York: Routledge.

Rogoff, B. (2003). *The cultural nature of human development*. Oxford, UK: Oxford University Press.

Senechal, M., & Young, L. (2008). The effects of family interventions on children's acquisition of reading from Kindergarten to Grade 3. *Review of Educational Research*, 78(4), 880–907.

Snow, C., Burns, M., & Griffins, P. (Eds.). (1998). *Preventing reading difficulties in young children*. Washington, DC: National Academy Press.

Souto-Manning, M. (2018). Disrupting Eurocentric epistemologies: Re-mediating transitions to centre intersectionally-minoritised immigrant children, families and communities. *European Journal of Education*, 53(4), 456–468.

Storch, S., & Whitehurst, G. (2002). Oral language and code-related precursors to reading: Evidence from a longitudinal structural model. *Developmental Psychology*, 38(6), 934–947.

Suizzo, M-A., Pahlke, E., Yarnell, L., Chen, K-Y., & Romero, S. (2014). Home based parental support for young children's learning across US ethnic groups: Cultural models of academic socialization. *Journal of Family Issues*, 35(2), 254–287.

Swain, J., Brooks, G., & Bosley, S. (2014). The benefits of family literacy provision for parents in England. *Journal of Early Childhood Research*, 12(1), 77–91.

Swain, J. & Cara, O. (2019). The role of family literacy classes in demystifying school literacies and developing closer parent–school relations. *Cambridge Journal of Education*, 49(1), 111–131.

Taylor, D. (1983). *Family literacy: Young children learning to read and write*. Exeter, NH: Heinemann.

Taylor, D., & Dorsey-Gaines, C. (1988). *Growing up literate: Learning from inner-city families*. Exeter, NH: Heinemann.

Taylor, L. K., Bernhard, J., Garg, S. & Cummins, J. (2008). Affirming plural belonging: Building on students' family-based cultural and linguistic capital through a multiliteracies curriculum. *Journal of Early Childhood Literacy*, 8(3), 269–295.

Thomas, A., & Skage, S. (1998). Overview of perspectives of effective practice. In A. Thomas (Ed.), *Family literacy in Canada: Profiles of effective practices* (pp. 5–24). Welland: Soleil Publishing.

van Steensel, R., McElvaney, N., Kurvers, J., & Herppich, S. (2011). How effective are family literacy programs? Results of a meta-analysis. *Review of Educational Research*, 81(11), 69–96.

Vertovec, S. (2007). Superdiversity and its implications. *Ethnic and Racial Studies*, 30(6), 1024–1054.

Vygotsky, L. (1978). *Mind in society: The development of higher psychological processes*. Cambridge, MA: Harvard University Press.

Wertsch, J. (1991). *Voices of the mind: A sociocultural approach to mediate action*. Cambridge, MA: Harvard University Press.

Wong-Fillmore, L. (1991). When learning a second language means losing the first. *Early Childhood Research Quarterly*, 6, 323–346

Wong-Fillmore, L. (2000). Loss of family languages: Should educators be concerned? *Theory Into Practice*, 39, 203–210.

Wood, D. J., Bruner, J. S., & Ross, G. (1976). The role of tutoring in problem solving. *Journal of Child Psychiatry and Psychology*, 17(2), 89–100.

Zhang, J., Pelletier, J., & Doyle, A. (2010). Promising effects of an intervention: Young children's literacy gains and changes in their home literacy activities from a bilingual family literacy program in Canada. *Frontiers of Education in China*, 5, 409–429.

14

ASSESSMENT PRACTICES IN THE DIVERSE CLASS SETTING

A Fine Balance

Hetty Roessingh

Drucker (1992), prescient in foreseeing a shift to the knowledge economy, underscored the importance of intellectual capital and human resources over natural resources. Such a shift is predicated on high levels of English academic proficiency (EAP) that must be developed in the context of diverse learner needs in the inclusive classroom setting beginning early in children's involvement in K–12 education and sustained over time. Inarguably diversity is increasingly characterized by the participation of English language learners (ELLs), that is the Canadian-born children of immigrants who arrive at school with little developed English language proficiency (ELP). Their English language learning must accelerate over time as curricular demands also accelerate, and more, ELLs are unlikely to be able to transfer linguistic and cognitive information from the first language (L1), which is largely reserved for communicative purposes with close family and community (Roessingh, 2018). The importance of the teaching-learning-assessment cycle for both content understanding and the development of EAP over time becomes clear.

Hattie (2012, 2015) reminds us of the importance of *visible learning*, that is, identifying high-impact teaching approaches through observation, documentation, evaluation and monitoring of student work. These data then feed the cycle of instructional planning aimed at improving student learning outcomes. 'Measuring up' is a complex undertaking in education today. It is also increasingly controversial, contested and politically charged as competing parties seek increasing control over the assessment agenda (Alberta Teachers' Association, 2009; Hunter, 2016). In Alberta and British Columbia, for example, provincially mandated Grade 12 diploma examinations are weighted 70–30 and 60–40, respectively, but there remains a visible gap between the school-based mark and those that students achieve on the exams (British Columbia Ministry of Education, 2016; Calgary Board of Education, 2018). There is a distinct disconnect between achievement outcomes on external, summative assessments *of* learning and the more dynamic, process-oriented and formatives assessment *for* learning in the classroom. This places pressure for accountability at the classroom level from parents, politicians and our educational partners in postsecondary settings.

This chapter begins by providing more information on the needs of ELLs; elaborates on a triad of classroom assessment approaches identified as assessment *of*, *as* and *for* learning; and makes suggestions for strengthening classroom assessment practices for better alignment between classroom and external assessment programs. Classroom-based/teacher-designed learning tasks can be seen through the lens of assessment data that can be utilized in the ongoing/iterative cycle of noticing, planning, teaching, documenting and reflecting with the goal of producing a distinct impact on student learning outcomes (Rintakorpi, 2016). Increasingly, simple online tools can help provide more quantitative information useful for monitoring student growth and achievement over time. While the assessment shortfall in this article is largely concerned with and targets the learning needs of ELLs, other learner profiles in the inclusive class setting such as children raised in poverty are certain to benefit as well.

Diversity in the Classroom: The Increasing Numbers of ELLs

The demographic landscape of the school going population across Canada is shifting rapidly as a consequence of Canada's immigration strategy. Canada primarily seeks to replenish and renew its human resource needs for a complex, competitive global economy by way of attracting a 'brain gain', that is, young, well-educated arrivals who are likely to begin family life with young children on arrival or who are their Canadian-born offspring.

In 2018–2019, Canada welcomed 313,580 immigrants as well as 30,000 refugee arrivals triggered by the Syrian crisis (Statistics Canada, 2019). This is the highest level of immigration in Canada's history and is also the highest level of population growth among the G7 countries. Currently, some 22% of Canadians identify themselves as immigrants. In urban school districts such as Vancouver, Calgary, and Toronto ELLs may compose up to 80% of the demographic makeup of individual schools, and they represent as many as 40 languages and cultural backgrounds (Calgary, n.d.).

In alignment with Canada's immigration policy, the number of immigrants with advanced degrees has steadily increased over the past decade (Keung, 2018), making Canada one of the best educated countries in the world. Immigrant parents have high educational expectations for their children in Canada, as well. The vast majority of new arrivals speak a language other than English and maintain this language with their children at home. Many of these young learners have developed some basic communicative skills in English prior to arrival in kindergarten and will receive some type of ELL support. However, many may not be recognized for language learning support upon arrival at school, sometimes even on the insistence of their parents who believe that immersion and early interaction with native English-speaking (NES) youngsters will better facilitate their children's acquisition of English.

Often referred to as Generation 1.5 in the scholarly literature, perhaps their single most pressing challenge will be to develop EAP at an accelerated pace to compete academically with their NES counterparts at some point in the K–12 trajectory ... it is a fraught journey (Ontario Ministry of Education, 2013). Because their first language (L1) is largely used for communicative purposes within the extended family and ethno-cultural community, it may not provide a strong platform for transfer to academic modes of literacy learning in English. ELLs can acquire basic interpersonal communication skills (BICS: Cummins, 2011) and close the early literacy gap fairly readily and quickly by the end of Grade 2. ELLs even outscore their NES counterparts on measures associated with decoding skills predictive of early reading success (Lesaux & Siegel, 2003) and the lower level developmental skills of printing and spelling associated with early written literacy. These early strengths in language and literacy development may easily be mistaken for the ability to independently develop academic literacy (Roessingh, 2018).

Early dedicated language learning support is likely of only short duration and will miss the important transition from early language and literacy learning to academic literacy development around the Grade 4 year—recognized as the Grade 4 slump (Chall & Jacobs, 2003; Sanacore & Palumbo, 2008) and associated with gaps in academic vocabulary knowledge.

It is important to understand that within the context of the contemporary inclusive classroom there is enormous diversity both among NES and ELLs. Under the mandate of least restrictive learning environment for all children (Alberta Education, 2019), a variety of exceptional needs are represented by approximately 9% of students. Teachers must have a repertoire well beyond 'just good teaching' and know how to differentiate for many different learning needs. This can be an overwhelming demand, especially for entry-level teachers and is elaborated in the section on assessment literacy. However, addressing the learning needs of ELLs inarguably presents the single most pressing challenge for mainstream teachers in supporting the development of EAP. In broad strokes, it is safe to indicate that most ELLs have at least average (or better) academic potential and expectations, many of which will be unfulfilled. Despite an apparent good, early start noted earlier, mounting research evidence in the Canadian context records their academic underachievement beginning by around Grade 4—the aforementioned grade for 'slump'. Ultimately, this undermines their ability to make their rightful contribution in the Canadian societal multicultural tapestry and Canada's ability to compete in the global knowledge-based economy (Miles, 2014; Roessingh & Douglas, 2012a, 2012b; Roessingh & Elgie, 2009).

As noted previously, ELLs are at heightened risk across the educational trajectory (Ontario Ministry of Education, 2013). Their continued representation in the data of under-achieving students as they transition to postsecondary settings underscores the need to attend to their learning needs, most crucially the need to develop EAP beginning early in their educational experiences and sustained over time (DiCerbo et al., 2014).

The Importance of Vocabulary Knowledge

Vocabulary knowledge is at the center of reading comprehension over time (Biemiller, 2001, 2003). August et al. (2005) note that teachers do not allocate sufficient instructional time to focus on academic vocabulary instruction, in particular, the high utility, general academic words that transfer across curricular boundaries. Elementary school practitioners need to address and track students' ongoing EAP throughout the K–12 trajectory and be more mindful of classroom talk that can promote the development of academic language (Ernst-Slavit, & Mason, 2011; Roessingh, 2019).

Developing EAP is a gradual, protracted process that begins early in life. Many academic words are not conceptually difficult and begin to appear in children's writing on expository prompts as early as Grade 2, accelerating sharply to Grade 4. This is an important threshold to attain: moving ahead, those who have attained a critical mass of vocabulary gain traction—recognized as the Matthew Effect (Stanovich, 1986). In short, the rich get richer, the poor fall farther and farther behind.

The samples of student work included in this chapter illustrate the importance of teacher interaction focused on vocabulary learning and strategies for monitoring and tracking the growth in vocabulary knowledge.

Few preservice teacher preparation programs (i.e., BEd degree of teacher licensing programs at universities across Canada) require any course work in working with ELLs in elementary mainstream settings, thus adding a second layer of complexity to the assessment literacy shortfall addressed in the next section.

Teachers' Assessment Literacy

A large body of research identifies teachers' lack of assessment understanding and knowledge—'assessment literacy' (Deluca & Klinger, 2010) as the weak point of their professional capability and responsibility, beginning with their preservice preparation enduring throughout their in-service professional lives (Alberta Teachers' Association, 2014; Crocker & Dibbon, 2008; Hattie, 2015; Kirschkom & Mueller, 2016).

In the initial teacher preparation programs—typically, undergraduate BEd degree programs and continuing through in-service professional development, assessment is consistently identified as an area of need for professional improvement (DeLuca & Klinger, 2010; Popham, 2011). Teachers themselves identify the need to enhance classroom-based approaches to assessment as among the top concerns they have (Alberta Teachers' Association, 2014) in their professional growth needs. In-service teachers especially note they cannot bootstrap their own way toward assessment literacy (Mertler, 2009). Time, an array of professional development opportunities and support for doing action or classroom-based research are all part and parcel of improving assessment literacy and in turn, student learning outcomes. In short, teachers cannot find their own way out of the vicious cycle of ineffective teaching–learning–assessment practices that are not producing a tangible impact on learning outcomes on external assessment programs (assessment *of* learning).

It becomes clear from the above that assessment becomes a juggling act that requires teachers' sensitivity and responsiveness to individual and diverse learning needs in the inclusive mainstream classroom. The needs of ELLs are easily overlooked: early successes mask their ongoing learning needs. DeLuca et al. (2019) provide a very accessible discussion on the complexities of grading practices and policies across Canada. They note that teachers are prepared to reward effort and good behavior, especially for students at risk of failure. This might account for the gap in teachers' assigned school-based marks and externally mandated diploma exams in Grade 12 in English language arts (British Columbia Ministry of Education, 2016; Calgary Board of Education, 2018). ELLs may be especially vulnerable for academic failure if classroom assessment data are not meaningfully communicated and do not offer sufficiently specific feedback for all stakeholders to adjust the learning experiences of students (Miles, 2014). Teachers may therefore inadvertently be doing ELLs a disservice by setting them up for failure in the long run in postsecondary settings where the expectations for academic literacy are suddenly much higher, and the cost of failure dire (Roessingh & Douglas, 2012a, 2012b).

Teachers wrestle with the idea of 'fairness' in assessment practices, reflecting the complex and often conflicting circumstances and pressures associated with assessment (DeLuca et al., 2019). Tomlinson (2000), well recognized for her work on differentiation, suggests four dimensions for differentiated instruction: content, process, product and learning environment. Additional time to complete work (i.e., process), providing scribes, offering various types of scaffolded support, the use of bilingual dictionaries and a process approach that permits multiple drafts of work to be submitted and reworked, and alternate ways of demonstrating understanding (i.e. product) might all be examples of fairness that teachers and scholars advocate for.

Assessment *for, as* and of Learning: Multiple Goals and Perspectives on Assessment

Various forms of assessment, described as assessment *for, as* and *of* learning in the contemporary assessment scholarship (Black & Wiliam 2010; Earl et al., 2015;

Guskey, 2003) focus on the classroom and teachers' and students' growing need to glean ongoing insights into learning outcomes. Over the past 20 years, there has been a distinct shift and emphasis on this multipronged approach to classroom assessment approaches. Researchers emphasize how these work in concert to complement each other in a triad of assessment endeavors, each with its central purpose and need. Ultimately, these should also complement external assessment measures *of* achievement—usually mandated by provincial governments mentioned earlier that focus on maintaining consistency and province-wide standards and to certify individual student achievement.

Assessment *for* learning is any assessment for which the first priority in its design and practice is to serve the purpose of promoting students' ongoing learning. It is formative (Black & Wiliam, 2003) and thus differs from assessment designed primarily to serve the purposes of accountability, or of ranking, or of certifying competence. In their seminal review on formative assessment practices, Black and Wiliam (1998) emphasize that assessment *for* learning can help learning if teachers provide specific feedback and thus enable and empower their students to develop self-assessment skills. This includes articulating clear learning goals, providing information to students on their present position and finally information on how to close the gap. They describe formative assessment as, 'all those activities undertaken by teachers, and/or by their students, which provide information to be used as feedback to modify the teaching and learning activities in which they are engaged' (Black & Wiliam, 1998, pp. 7–8). Importantly, it is not the assessment instrument itself that determines whether it be formative or summative (i.e. assessment *of* learning, elaborated below) but rather what is done with the information in modifying and redirecting instructional decision making and offering feedback to students that will enhance the ensuing teaching ↔ learning ↔ cycle. Stiggins (2006) notes the role of assessment *for* learning in motivating students to work toward learning goals. These same principles can also be applied to peer assessment activities. This further encourages student ownership, agency and autonomy over their own learning goals and can begin at early stages in children's formal schooling involvement.

Assessment *as* learning focuses on the reciprocal, iterative relationship between teaching ↔ learning that views student engagement as a prime opportunity to gather data from learning artifacts that will inform subsequent cycles of teaching. Hattie (2015) refers to this idea as *visible* learning, underscoring the notion that teachers must make use of assessment information to direct instructional decision-making. This type of assessment may be used as teachers' professional development in targeting next steps for instructional planning. When teachers collaborate on documenting and evaluating student work and implementing an instructional intervention and participate in the give-and-take of informed discussion their classroom practices are enhanced and, based on classroom-level data, transformed. In the iterative cycle of planning, teaching, reflecting they theorize for themselves the journey of early literacy learning. As the title of her article suggests, Rintakorpi (2016) emphasizes how pedagogical documentation works as a potent tool for developing early childhood pedagogy and practices.

Assessment *for* and *as* learning becomes 'formative assessment' when the evidence is used to adapt the ongoing work of planning and teaching to meet learning needs (Greenstein, 2010). A process approach with a goal of mastery lends itself to this type of orientation and may include portfolios and projects that capture learning over time and opportunities for feedback and reflection by both teacher and student.

Assessment *of* learning focuses on summative achievement and whether externally imposed or orchestrated within the class setting, the purpose is simply to obtain achievement information for a single assessment moment: a one-time snapshot of what students can do as a consequence of their learning experiences in the classroom. Student artifacts *of* learning as assessment data within the classroom can include any number of measures, including from time to time, standardized instruments such as a vocabulary or reading test. Personal experience indicates that high school–aged ELLs value the feedback that outcomes of such tests can provide. For them, this is tangible evidence that instruction that may not be familiar to them, such as thematically organized units broadly following principles of language through content (LTC) and communicative language teaching (CLT), is, indeed, demonstrating impact on learning outcomes.

A point worth reiterating relates to the use of the same learning task for different assessment purposes. I turn to this next, providing illustrative exemplars of student work and the information that can be gleaned from them by altering the process for the task completion, clarity in task expectation and understanding the student's strengths and learning needs reflected in the work.

Assessment for, as and of Learning: Illustrative Samples for in the Classroom

The classroom holds endless possibilities for task design and student engagement in work for teacher reflection, instructional decision-making and feedback for students that can deepen their own approach to learning. Teacher-prepared crossword puzzles, co-constructed texts along the lines of Language Experience Approach (LEA), word webs, cloze exercises, timed readings paired with Question Answer Relationships (identified as QARs in the literature; Raphael, 1982), writing samples are just a few examples of student work that can be understood through an assessment lens. This offers rich 'data' for teacher professional development, individual reflection and ongoing planning.

Various tools available in the public domain, including puzzlemaker, lexical profiling tools, graded word lists and Flesch-Kincaid reading formula, all help teachers determine the complexity and cognitive demand of learning tasks. Teachers can further decide on types of scaffolding that will enable the student to complete a task. Allowing a student to display their wordplay or flash cards to support completing a crossword puzzle, allowing for coloring and drawing as a type of priming exercise, offering other sorts of visual representations such as picture strips, prewriting strategy activate vocabulary or scribing for a young student to alleviate the cognitive load of generating text all help students produce their best work for us. It is important that we see assessment through the lens of 'can do' performances that engages our learners in authentic-like, purposeful, work they find interesting, challenging, personally and culturally relevant and even fun. Deep processing that links some of the activities noted, especially those that link visual input to language and writing tasks, will further ensure deep learning (Craik & Lockhart, 1972).

For nearly a decade, I have worked as a volunteer tutor for a small group of ELLs, for two hours on Monday evenings. In the following, I provide illustrative samples of linked tasks and a variety of tools mentioned earlier that afford insights into one of the young student's (Partik) learning.

One Monday evening, Partik was sporting a new and very trendy buzz cut. By Sikh tradition, Partik and his cousin, also part of the group, had never cut their hair—at this point it fell well below waist level. My initial thought that Partik might have been bullied or teased at school were not borne out—this was a decision of Partik's own doing for reasons soon to be shared through a good story he had to tell and an adapted LEA approach involving the co-construction of the text that would be usable for further task development and language learning. Furthermore, the experience had been recorded via a series of pictures taken in the hairdressing shop the day before, shown in Figure 14.1. An ideal, *teachable moment* (Baxter, 2007) had landed serendipitously in my hands, as they often do in classrooms. Classroom practitioners, too, sometimes need to recognize these learning opportunities and capitalize on them, leaving planned lessons temporarily aside. At the tender age of just 8, cutting his hair would have been a major decision for Partik: one that his young mother generously allowed him to make on his own. Storytelling is not an easy task. The teller must marshal and mobilize an array of psycholinguistic and metacognitive resources involving knowledge of story grammar, vocabulary and recognition of the listener's relevant knowledge. For young children, transcribing the story for them alleviates the burden of printing and spelling, themselves resource costly and a drain on working memory at this age. An engaged adult listener can also introduce the level of challenge that Vygotsky (1978) noted as crucial to ongoing development (Zone of Proximal Development, ZPD).

An initial conversation following the pictures taken of the haircutting process allowed for adjusting the linguistic input, but also for noting the words in the first language (L1) that do not translate in English (L2). The degree to which young students *translanguage* or access the full range of the sum of both languages is an important insight into their thinking processes. The conversation yielded words such as *rishi* (the knot that secures long, coiled and braided hair at the top of the head), *juda* (the long length of hair to be cut off and donated). It allowed for the introduction of words such as *entire, vacant, donate, product, anxious* and *reaction*.

Figure 14.2 illustrates the transcribed story of 'Partik Cuts His Hair'. The process involved introducing words not in his lexical repertoire that would

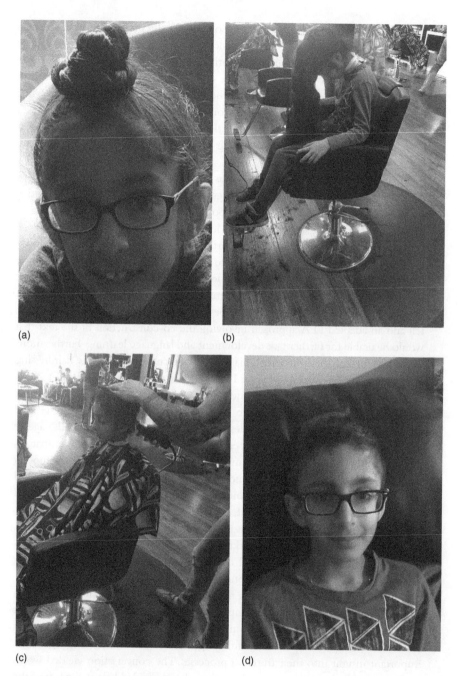

FIGURE 14.1 Partik Cuts His Hair

Partik cuts his hair
~ as told by Partik , February 22, 2016

Yesterday I got my hair cut off. I had never cut my hair before in my entire life. It was longer than waist length. Deciding to cut my hair was a big decision. I thought about it for a long time. I talked to my mum about it.
Yesterday was the big day at last. We went to a walk-in barber shop close to my house. I was so excited to take the vacant chair. The barber had to tell me to take my turn and wait!
The kids' specialist soon got to work on my hair. My mum held my hair finished so the barber could take the juda first. I wanted to donate the juda to kids who have cancer. My juda can be used to make a wig for someone who has lost all their hair. There is a boy in Grade 4 in my school who has cancer, and I was thinking of him when I decided to donate my hair.

Next the barber began to style my hair with his tools : scissors, shaver and hair dryer. He finished by putting on some styling spray and shaping my hair with his fingers. He even gave me some product to use at home.
Today I woke up joyful to go to school. I had not told anyone about my secret plan. I was anxious to get on the bus and see everyone's reaction to my new, cool look. My friends said, 'You look like a random person.' The bus driver did not recognize me! My teacher said, 'You are so handsome!'
I am so happy I made this decision. I am very cool and famous.

Readability Statistics	
Counts	
Words	279
Characters	1066
Paragraphs	5
Sentences	26
Averages	
Sentences per Paragraph	5.2
Words per Sentence	10.7
Characters per Word	3.6
Readability	
Passive Sentences	3%
Flesch Reading Ease	90.1
Flesch-Kincaid Grade Level	3.3

Notes: Fluent rereading of this co-constructed story. Miscues on just two words: *scissors* and *anxious*. Elaborated words given to Partik included *donate, vacant, products, anxious.*

FIGURE 14.2 'Partik Cuts His Hair', transcribed story

lend precision and nuance and at the same time, work the ZPD. A check with the Flesch Kincaid formula tool available online reflects a grade equivalent of 3.3—suitable for the purposes here. The length, at 279 words, is sufficient as well for rereading. (See https://readabilityformulas.com/freetests/six-readability-formulas.php.)

Submitting this text to vocabulary profiling tools would provide further information on lexical difficulty and density.

A story rereading task indicated two miscues (noted), surprisingly the word *scissors* which should be a sight word for Partik, and the word *anxious* a newly introduced word that would be recycled through flash-card play, a crossword puzzle I prepared as well as a cloze activity. It is important to emphasize that reading at grade (3) reflects excellent progress in his learning since joining the Monday tutoring group in his Grade 1 year; however, in the long run, he must achieve at yet a much higher 'bar' (i.e. the upper quartile) if he is to pursue the postsecondary studies and the career goals of his young dreams. He is capable of this with monitored and sustained support crucially traversing the Grade 4 (Sanacore & Palumbo, 2008) and Grade 9 thresholds.

A crossword puzzle, completed with access to the flash cards was completed next. Partik readily completed this task. Teachers can avail themselves of online tools such as Puzzlemaker (http://puzzlemaker.discoveryeducation.com/CrissCrossSetupForm.asp) to generate different types of puzzles.

Finally, a cloze activity (Figure 14.3) recycles and reconstructs the story once again, this time with no access to either the printed version or the flash cards.

Partik cuts his hair

Yesterday I got my hair cut off. I had never cut _m 2_ hair before in my _entire_ life. It was longer _then_ waist length. Deciding to _cut_ my hair was a _big_ decision. I thought about _it_ for a long time. _I_ talked to my mum _about_ it.

Yesterday was the _big_ day at last. We _went_ to a walk-in barber _shop_ close to my house. _I_ was so excited to _sit_ the vacant chair. The _barber_ had to tell me to _wait_ my turn and wait! The _kid_ specialist soon got to _work_ on my hair. My _mum_ held my hair forward _so_ the barber could take the _hair_ first. I wanted to _donate_ the juda to kids _how_ have cancer. My juda _could_ be used to make a _wig_ for someone who has _lost_ all their hair. There _is_ a boy in Grade 4 _in_ my school who has _cancer_, and I was thinking _about_ him when I decided _to_ donate my hair.

Next the _barber_ began to style my _hair_ with his tools: scissors, _cream_ and hair dryer. He _started_ by putting on some _water_ spray and cream, and _cut_ my hair with his _sicces_. He even gave me _hair_ product to use at _home_.

Today I woke up _exicited_ to go to school. _I_ had not told my _secret_ plan to anyone. I _was_ anxious to get on the _bus_ and see everyone's reaction _to_ my new, cool look. _My_ friends said, 'You look _like_ a random person.' The _bus_ driver did not recognize _me_! My teacher said, 'You _are_ so handsome!'

I am so happy I made this decision. I am very cool and famous.

Blank spaces: 50

Independent reading threshold (60%+) = 30+ correct

Instructional threshold (45 – 60%) = 23 – 29 correct

Frustration threshold (less than 45%) = 22 or less correct

FIGURE 14.3 Cloze Activity

In a classroom setting, a cloze activity can be used flexibly for various instructional goals. If used as a learning task (i.e. in the ZPD), the reading passage should be slightly ahead of the students' estimated independent reading level (i.e. instructional level). Partnering students with a more competent peer and promoting talk and discussion around choices for each blank space supports learning. Whole-class discussion on completion of the task is equally important and gives teachers immediate feedback on students' ability to reconstruct text using semantic and syntactic cueing systems and gives students an opportunity to glean insights into their work—an example of assessment *for* learning.

If this task is used as an assessment *of* learning strategy, of course, the reading should be set at the students' estimated *independent* reading level and should be completed unaided.

Taken together, linked tasks that sustain student engagement on a central theme or topic offers rich and varied information to teachers on students' vocabulary knowledge and reading comprehension, the keys to academic success. It gives opportunities for pitching the ball slightly ahead of where the students are currently working, thus resetting the current 'bar'. Teachers need to be vigilant, intentional and keenly aware of how their instructional choices produce an impact on student learning, communicate this information with their students and set realistic, achievable learning goals.

Conclusion

The contemporary elementary classroom is a complex and rapidly evolving one in the face of linguistic and cultural diversity, inclusion of learners with exceptional needs, technology, competing demands in curriculum and new ideas related to pedagogical approaches, and ever-increasing demands for accountability. There is a palpable tension between externally mandated assessment from provincial ministries of education holding the profession to public scrutiny and accountability and teachers' desire to have increased discretion over assessment approaches and choices.

Aligning the pillars of the assessment triad in the classroom can lessen this tension and regain public trust in the work of the teaching profession. For ELLs, in particular the Canadian-born children of immigrants who represent the next generation of Canada's best hopes for a vibrant economy and quality of life for everyone, teaching and learning throughout the educational trajectory are paramount to this endeavor. Good assessment informs good teaching. Given the tools to undertake this work, it is within the purview of all teachers to address the learning gaps that have not diminished over the years and advocate on behalf of their students where additional learning supports are needed over time. Armed with good data, our profession is better prepared to do this work, too. Ultimately it is our community of families and their children we serve and in whose best interest we must conduct our work in classrooms across Canada.

References

Alberta Education. (2019). *Inclusive education*. https://www.alberta.ca/inclusive-education.aspx

Alberta Teachers' Association. (2009). *Real learning first: The teaching profession's view of student assessment, evaluation and accountability for the 21st century* (Issues in Education, #7). https://www.teachers.ab.ca/SiteCollectionDocuments/ATA/Publications/Student-Assessment/PD-75-5%202009.pdf

Alberta Teachers' Association. (2014). *PD survey 2014*. https://www.teachers.ab.ca/SiteCollectionDocuments/ATA/Publications/Professional-Development/PD-183%20PD%20Survey%202014_2015-07_Web.pdf

American Academy of Pediatrics. (2017). *Handheld sscreen time linked with speech delays in young children*. www.sciencedaily.com/releases/2017/05/170504083141.htm

August, D., Carlo, M., Dressler, C., & Snow, C. (2005). The critical role of vocabulary development for English language learners. *Learning Disabilities Research and Practice*, 20(1), 50–57. doi:10.1111/j.1540-5826.2005.00120.x

Baxter, S. (2007). *Teachable moments*. A Place of Our Own. http://aplaceofourown.org/question_detail.php?id=101

Biemiller, A. (2001, Spring). *Teaching vocabulary: Early, direct, sequential*. American Educator. https://www.aft.org/periodical/american-educator/spring-2001/teaching-vocabulary

Biemiller, A. (2003, Spring). *Oral comprehension sets the ceiling for reading comprehension*. *American Educator*. http://www.aft.org/periodical/american-educator/spring-2003/oral-comprehension-sets-ceiling-reading

Black, P., & Wiliam, D. (1998). Assessment and classroom learning. *Assessment in Education: Principles, Policy and Oractice*, 5(1), 7–74. doi:10.1080/0969595980050102

Black, P., & Wiliam, D. (2003). In praise of educational research: Formative assessment. *British Educational Research Journal*, 29(5), 623–637. doi:10.1080/0141192032000133721

Black, P., & Wiliam, D. (2010). Inside the black box: Raising standards through classroom assessment. *Kappan Magazine*, 92(1), 81–91. http://journals.sagepub.com/doi/pdf/10.1177/003172171009200119

British Columbia Ministry of Education. (2016). *English 12. Report to schools*. https://www.bced.gov.bc.ca/exams/pdfs/1606en_rt.pdf

Calgary. (n.d.). *Diversity in Calgary: Looking forward to 2020*. https://www.calgary.ca/CSPS/CNS/Documents/Social-research-policy-and-resources/diversity-in-Calgary.pdf?noredirect=1

Calgary Board of Education. (2018). *English language arts 30-1 Diploma Examination Results*. https://www.cbe.ab.ca/about-us/provincial-tests-and-reports/Documents/2017-18-Grade-12-English-Language-Arts-30-1.pdf

Chall, J., & Jacobs, V. (2003, Spring). *Poor children's fourth grade slump*. American Educator. http://www.aft.org/periodical/american-educator/spring-2003/classic-study-poor-childrens-fourth-grade-slump

Craik, F., & Lockhart, R. (1972). Levels of processing: A framework for memory research. *Journal of Verbal Learning and Verbal Behavior*, 11(6), 671–684. http://www.sciencedirect.com/science/article/pii/S002253717280001X

Crocker, R., & Dibbon, D. (2008). *Teacher education in Canada: A baseline report*. Society for the Advancement of Excellence in Education. http://s3.amazonaws.com/zanran_storage/www.saee.ca/ContentPages/42969797.pdf

Cummins, J. (2011). Literacy engagement: Fueling academic growth for English learners. *The Reading Teacher*, 65(2), 142–146. http://onlinelibrary.wiley.com/doi/10.1002/TRTR.01022/epdf

DeLuca, C., & Klinger, D. A. (2010). Assessment literacy development: Identifying gaps in teacher candidates' learning. *Assessment in Education: Principles, Policy & Practice*, 17(4), 419–438. doi:10.1080/0969594X.2010.516643

DeLuca, C., Cheng, L., & Volante, L. (2019). Grading across Canada: Policies, practices and perils. *Education Canada*, 59(1), 22–25. https://www.edcan.ca/articles/grading-across-canada/

DiCerbo, P., Anstrom, K., Baker, L., & Rivera, C. (2014). A review of the literature on teaching academic language to English language learners. *Journal of Educational Research*, 84(3), 446–483. doi:10.3102/0034654314532695

Drucker, P. (1992, September–October). The new society of organizations. *Harvard Business Review*. https://hbr.org/1992/09/the-new-society-of-organizations

Earl, L., Volante, L., & DeLuca, C. (2015). Assessment for learning across Canada: Where we've been and where we're going. *Education Canada*, 55(2). http://www.cea-ace.ca/education-canada/article/assessment-learning-across-canada

Earl, L. (n.d.). Assessment for learning; Assessment as learning: Changing practices means changing beliefs. *Assessment and Learning*, (2). http://wlts.edb.hkedcity.net/fileman-ager/file/AandL2chapter/A&L2_(1)%20Lorna.pdf

Ernst-Slavit, G., & Mason, M. R. (2011). "Words that hold us up": Teacher talk and academic language in five upper elementary classrooms. *Linguistics and Education*, 22, 430–440. doi:10.1016/j.linged.2011.04.004

Greenstein, L. (2010). Chapter one: The fundamentals of formative assessment. In L. Greenstein, *What teachers really need to know about formative assessment*. Alexandria, VA: ASCD. Retrieved from http://www.ascd.org/publications/books/110017/chapters/The-Fundamentals-of-Formative-Assessment.aspx

Guskey, T. (2003). How classroom assessments improve learning. *Educational Leadership*, 60(5), 6–11. Retrieved from http://www.ascd.org/publications/educational-leader-ship/feb03/vol60/num05/How-Classroom-Assessments-Improve-Learning.aspx

Hattie, J. (2012). *Visible learning for teachers: Maximizing impact on learning*. Routledge. http://thequohaslostitsstatus.weebly.com/uploads/5/4/2/3/54231535/_visible_learning_for_teachers.pdf

Hattie, J. (2015, October 28). *We aren't using assessments correctly*. EdWeek. Retrieved from http://www.edweek.org/ew/articles/2015/10/28/we-arent-using-assessments-cor-rectly.html

Helm, J., Beneke, S. & Steinheimer, K. (1997, Summer). Documenting children's learning. *Childhood Education*, 73(4), 200–205. doi:10.1080/00094056.1997.10521093

Hunter, J. (2016, May 26). *Provincial exams scaled back, more emphasis on class results in BC*. Globe and Mail. http://www.theglobeandmail.com/news/british-columbia/fewer-provincial-exams-more-in-class-assessment-in-bc-to-come-next-year/article30178911/?cmpid=rss1

Keung, N. (2018, February 1). Immigrants are largely behind Canada's status as one of the best education countries. *The Star*. https://www.thestar.com/news/immigration/2018/02/01/immigrants-are-largely-behind-canadas-status-as-one-of-the-best-educated-countries.html

Kirschkom, M., & Mueller, J. (2016). What should Canada's teachers know? Teacher capacities: Knowledge, beliefs, and skills. *Canadian Association for Teacher Education*. Retrieved from https://www.researchgate.net/profile/Lynnette_Driedger-Enns/pub-lication/318960947_Negotiating_Personal_Knowledge_on_Professional_Knowledge_Landscapes_The_Becoming_of_Teachers/links/59884a80aca27266ada47828/Negotiating-Personal-Knowledge-on-Professional-Knowledge-Landscapes-The-Becoming-of-Teachers.pdf

Klinger, D., Volante, L., & DeLuca, C. (2012). Building teacher capacity within the evolving assessment culture in Canadian education. *Policy Futures in Education*, 10(4), 447–460. http://journals.sagepub.com/doi/abs/10.2304/pfie.2012.10.4.447

Klinger D. A., Deluca C., & Miller S. (2008). The evolving culture of large-scale assessments in Canadian education. *Canadian Journal of Educational Administration and Policy*, 76, 1–34. Retrieved from https://eric.ed.gov/?id=EJ807064

Lesaux, N., & Siegel, L. (2003). The development of reading in children who speak English as a second language. *Developmental Psychology*, 39(6), 1005–1019. https://pdfs.semanticscholar.org/b0c7/38401bc23cba8f6958dd9a16ad1fc2a76ead

Leung, D. (2009). Developing formative teacher assessment: Knowledge practice and change. *Language Assessment Quarterly*, 1(1), 19–41. doi:10.1207/s15434311laq0101_3

Mertler, C. A. (2009). Teachers' assessment knowledge and their perceptions of the impact of classroom assessment professional development. *Improving Schools*, 12(2), 101–113. doi:10.1177/1365480209105575

Miles, J. (2014). *Lost in transition? The impact of early inclusion on the transitional high school experiences and distal academic outcomes of ELLs* [Master's thesis]. Werklund School of Education, University of Calgary. doi:10.11575/PRISM/26789

Ontario Ministry of Education. (2010). *Growing success: Assessment, evaluation, and reporting in Ontario schools*. Queen's Printer for Ontario. http://www.edu.gov.on.ca/eng/policyfunding/growSuccess.pdf

Ontario Ministry of Education. (2013). *Canadian-born English language learners* (Capacity Building Series, 31). http://www.edugains.ca/resourcesLNS/Monographs/CapacityBuildingSeries/CBS_CdnBornELL.pdf

Popham, W. (2011a). Assessment literacy overlooked: A teacher educator's confession. *The Teacher Educator*, 46(4), 265–273. doi:10.1080/08878730.2011.605048

Popham, W. (2011b, February 23). Formative assessment—A process, not a test. *Education Week*. http://www.edweek.org/ew/articles/2011/02/23/21popham.h30.html?t

Raphael, T. (1982). Question-answering strategies for children. *The Reading Teacher* 36(2), 186–190. https://www.jstor.org/stable/i20198169

Rintakorpi, K. (2016). Documenting with early childhood education teachers: Pedagogical documentation as a tool for developing early childhood pedagogy and practices. *Early Years*, 36(4), 399–412. doi:10.1080/09575146.2016.1145628

Roessingh, H. (2018). Unmasking the early language and literacy needs of ELLs. *BC TEAL Journal*, 3(1), 22–36. http://ejournals.ok.ubc.ca/index.php/BCTJ/article/view/276

Roessingh, H. (2019). Read-alouds in the upper elementary classroom: Developing academic vocabulary. *TESOL Journal*, 11(1), e445. doi:10.1002/tesj.445

Roessingh, H., & Douglas, S. (2012a). English language learners' transitional needs from high school to university: An exploratory study. *Journal of International Migration and Integration*, 13(3), 285–301. doi:10.1007/s12134-011-0202-8

Roessingh, H., & Douglas, S. (2012b). Educational outcomes of English language learners at university. *Canadian Journal of Higher Education*, 42(1), 82–97. doi:10.1007/s12134-011-0202-8

Roessingh, H., & Elgie, S. (2009). Early language and literacy development among young ELL: Preliminary insights from a longitudinal study. *TESL Canada Journal*, 26(2), 24–45. http://www.teslcanadajournal.ca/index.php/tesl/article/view/413

Sanacore, J., & Palumbo, A. (2008.) Understanding the fourth-grade slump: Our point of view. *The Educational Forum*, 73(1), 67–74. http://www.tandfonline.com/doi/pdf/10.1080/00131720802539648?needAccess=true

Stanovich, K. (1986). Matthew effects in reading: Some consequences of individual differences in the acquisition of literacy. *Reading Research Quarterly*, 21(4), 360–407. https://my.psychologytoday.com/files/u81/Stanovich__1986_.pdf

Statistics Canada. (2019, July). *Canada's population estimates: Age and sex*. https://www150.statcan.gc.ca/n1/daily-quotidien/190930/dq190930a-eng.htm

Stiggins, R. J. (2002). Assessment crisis: The absence of assessment for learning. *Phi Delta Kappan*, 83(10), 758–765. doi:10.1177/003172170208301010

Stiggins, R. J. (2006). Assessment for learning: A key to student motivation and learning. *Phi Delta Kappa*, 2(2), 1–19. http://downloads.pearsonassessments.com/ati/downloads/edgev2n2_0.pdf

Tomlinson, C.A. (2000). *Differentiation of instruction in the elementary grades [ED443572]*. ERIC. http://www.ericdigests.org/2001-2/elementary.html

Vygotsky, L. S. (1978). *Mind in society: The development of higher psychological processes*. Cambridge, MA: Harvard University Press.

Volante L., & Jaafar, B. S. (2008). Profiles of education assessment systems worldwide: Educational assessment in Canada. *Assessment in Education*, 15(2), 201–210. doi:10.1080/09695940802164226

Western and Northern Canadian Protocol for Collaboration in Basic Education. (2006). Three purposes of assessment. In L. Earl & S. Katz (Eds.), *Rethinking classroom assessment with purpose in mind: Assessment for learning, assessment as learning, assessment of learning* (pp. 27–66). Winnipeg, MB: Manitoba Education, Citizenship and Youth.

15

DIVERSITY AS THE NORM

Teaching to and Through Superdiversity in Postsecondary Indigenous Education Courses

Nikki L. Yee and Sara Florence Davidson

The premise of this chapter is that diversity is normal, or commonplace (Wessendorf, 2013), whether it is neuro-diversity, cultural diversity, or differences in socioeconomic status, gender, or experiences of the world. Scholars have recognized that diversities have become heightened and complex (i.e., superdiversity) as they intersect with one another in a world with increased movement between nations (Foner et al., 2019). We extend this definition of superdiversity to also include varied and complex familial histories, communities, and Indigenous Nations. Teaching to and through superdiversity is an ongoing challenge, given educational contexts shaped by colonialism in North American settings. As two diverse educators facilitating learning opportunities with Indigenous and decolonizing perspectives (e.g., Archibald, 2008; Brayboy & Maughan, 2009) in mandatory Indigenous education courses for teacher candidates (TCs), we have embraced the normalcy and value of superdiversity in ourselves, our teaching, and our students. In this chapter, we consider some of the reflective, contextual, and practical considerations we have observed to be foundational to presenting Indigenous and decolonizing perspectives while embracing superdiversity among Indigenous (and all) Peoples in these courses.

In the context of superdiversity, we wish to acknowledge the complexity and intersectionality of Indigenous communities and Nations. We use the term *Indigenous* inclusively to refer to diverse First Nations, Inuit, and Métis Peoples (Younging, 2018). We use this term not to erase differences but to respectfully acknowledge the Original Peoples in the land known as Canada who have survived targeted colonial programs through diverse personal and cultural strength and resiliency. We acknowledge diversity between Indigenous Nations by noting specific cultural or community affiliations where possible. At times, we refer to *Indigenous (and all) Peoples* to recognize that although colonial impacts vary drastically between Indigenous and non-Indigenous communities, we are on a shared journey of (re)imagining our relationship to one another, for the benefit of all peoples (Donald, 2009; Smith, 2012). We name Indigenous Peoples first to prioritize their perspectives, even as we recognize this connection. In this way, we hope to appropriately recognize superdiversity within Indigenous cultures and communities, and within both Indigenous and non-Indigenous positionalities in relation to colonialism, while bringing people together in relationship with one another going forward.

We see our identities as an embodiment of the superdiversity that we address in this chapter. Sara's identity as a Haida/settler educator and scholar informs not only the pedagogy she brings to the classroom but also how her instruction is received and interpreted. Likewise, Nikki's background as a special educator and scholar of Chinese and Mennonite lineage creates affordances and limitations in terms of the learning opportunities she can facilitate. We differ in our experience in teaching Indigenous education course work to teacher candidates; Sara's experience is quite extensive, while Nikki is more of a novice. We are acutely aware that even a deep-rooted understanding about particular perspectives or narratives does not equate with authority (Archibald, 2008). Thus, we have found that an authentic engagement with one another and a commitment to long-term collaboration expands the possibilities for our thinking and for our teaching. In this chapter, we provide examples from our collaborative conversations to highlight how we have addressed superdiversity from our own diverse positionalities.

Mandatory postsecondary Indigenous education courses have developed within specific national and provincial contexts in British Columbia (BC), Canada. On the national level, Canada's Truth and Reconciliation Commission (TRC) has highlighted the need for Indigenous content in teacher education programs to promote reconciliation (TRC of Canada, 2015). Building on this, a key component of the revised BC curriculum includes Indigenous content and perspectives across all curricular areas (BC Ministry of Education, 2019). Therefore, teacher education programs in BC include mandatory Indigenous education content that is taught by Indigenous and non-Indigenous instructors to diverse, but largely non-Indigenous teacher candidates (Hare, 2015). In these courses, we interpret our responsibility as prompting critical engagement with colonial narratives so that TCs are knowledgeable about the scope and impacts of colonial policies. Then TCs may be better prepared to build the kind of relationships envisioned by the TRC and that have been shown to support the achievement and well-being of Indigenous students and communities (Castagno & Brayboy, 2008).

Thus, a key objective of our work as teacher educators is to have TCs critically examine colonial narratives. Colonialism may be understood as an ongoing, culturally embedded paradigm that perpetrates physical and psychological violence on Indigenous Peoples to facilitate the dispossession of Indigenous lands (Cote-Meek, 2014; Pidgeon, 2009). It is maintained, in part, through social rationalizations that include the division and essentialization of Indigenous (and all) Peoples (Deloria, 1970), so that the nuances of superdiversity are reduced to a series of simplistic exchanges between caricatures. Despite the major impacts of colonialism on Indigenous Peoples, and to a lesser degree on all Peoples (Donald, 2009; Smith, 2012), the pervasive and culturally embedded nature of colonialism makes it difficult to detect by people within a colonial culture (Wolfe, 2006). Its invisibility is partly due to the normalization that occurs through the retelling and enactment of colonial narratives, the deeply embedded social stories that implicitly and explicitly reinforce and perpetuate colonial logics (Donald, 2009).

Learning about colonial history may surface intense emotions such as anger, guilt, shame, defensiveness, or helplessness (Donald, 2009). Indigenous and decolonizing perspectives may challenge learners' conceptions of themselves as embedded in romanticized familial and cultural histories (Restoule & Nardozi, 2019). Other students may experience trauma or retraumatization from stories of historical and contemporary colonial violence (Cote-Meek, 2014; Pidgeon, 2019). Furthermore, postsecondary institutions themselves have been heavily critiqued for their perpetuation of colonial structures and values (Pidgeon, 2019). Emotionally charged confrontation constantly threatens to sabotage learning and personal well-being for Indigenous (and all) students within these spaces (Cote-Meek, 2014).

In this context, Indigenous education courses are meant to help TCs find a solid basis for being able to understand themselves as teachers, in relation to colonial narratives, Indigenous perspectives, and decolonizing potentials. Possibilities for both critique and (re)imagination are largely dependent on personal positioning in relation to colonialism and Indigenous cultural paradigms, and contextual limitations. We have found several pedagogical approaches useful to support this kind of learning. In this chapter, we describe how we have navigated this contested space by enacting reflection, creating inviting contexts, and strategically using key practices to support TCs' learning in relation to Indigenous education.

We wish to emphasize that because of our own diversity, *the way we engage with Indigenous perspectives and decolonizing possibilities is fundamentally different.* There is no one pedagogical recipe that is going to support every educator (Castagno & Brayboy, 2008) because educators themselves are superdiverse. As such, we describe important considerations and inspirational examples emerging from a collaborative conversation between us, to show how we have taken up these ideas from our own positionalities. We have used this strategy as way to discuss the similarities and differences that flow from how we understand what it means to be educators who engage with Indigenous education:

SARA: … I don't think [Indigenous education] looks a particular way. And I don't think it can ever really be achieved. We're constantly in relationship with it… . I think we can do all of "the things" we're supposed to do and not be doing it… . if you are not fully committed and engaged with the ideas and continuing to interrogate your practice, you're not doing it. And it looks different for everybody… . I think that going to the lists is a great place to start, but we still need to read the books and decide if they work best for the students in our classroom, the community that we're working in. We need to be active in engaging with it.

NIKKI: … to me, Indigenous education is about thinking critically about what you're doing, with respect to Indigenous and decolonizing perspectives, in a nutshell …

By embracing our own superdiversity, we hope to challenge readers to examine their own ideas of what it means to teach Indigenous education. We offer this chapter as a collaborative example of how we have taken up this kind of engagement with Indigenous education in a postsecondary teacher education program using reflection, context, and practice.

Reflection

We see teaching as a fundamentally humanizing endeavor where we build from diverse ideas to co-construct knowledge and understanding about the world. In alignment with particular learning theories, we see the identities, values, and beliefs students and teachers bring to the learning context as integral facets of their humanity, germane to learning (Archibald, 2008; Butler et al., 2017). Thus, education becomes a partnership where the interaction between educators' and learners' humanity shapes the kind of learning that can be facilitated in a classroom at any given time. Reflecting on our holistic human experience and that of our students opens opportunities for learning and teaching through authentic engagement with diverse peoples, perspectives, cultures, and social histories.

As such, we have found it useful to first reflect on our ourselves as educators. We think about our own identities and cultural grounding, and critically consider our own pedagogical stance and positionality in relation to colonialism and Indigenous cultures. For some people, this kind of reflection may happen as a culturally ingrained component of learning (Archibald, 2008). Others may need to be more intentional about this process (e.g., Nicol & Korteweg, 2010; Zinga, 2019). Understanding our own identities and cultural touchstones allows us to ground ourselves in relation to the contentious narratives that emerge in Indigenous education courses (Cote-Meek, 2014). This clear vision of self and purpose can provide a core orientation from which to sensitively respond to students' questions, concerns, or intense emotions, as they emerge (Fairbanks et al., 2010). Our teaching becomes adaptable to the needs of TCs who will soon be journeying with students through a colonial system. At the same time, this grounding provides a sense of security that allows us to open and expand our thinking. In one of our conversations, we reflected on how we saw our identities as impacting our teaching:

NIKKI: I think about my identity as being a mixed person, and that informs my teaching in two ways. First is this idea I call "invisible minority" and what that means to me is that people don't immediately identify me … as a minority or a racialized person, so I'm invisible in that sense. At the same time, I have that sensitivity to racialization and marginalization. So I have this insider/outsider view that gives me the opportunity to understand and address the challenges people are facing in terms of the narratives informing their thinking. And then the other piece is that in many ways I was born into a space where people already were working across diversity … that's just normal to me… . So I want to have a space where people can come together across diversity, … and they can feel comfortable to really open up and really, truthfully say, this is the colonial narrative that I'm struggling with, and that is something that we can work on in the space. So that's how I teach who I am.

SARA: For me it is so different. At the beginning of the course, I remind students, "when you're talking about Indigenous People, you're talking about my father, you're talking about my nieces and nephews, you're talking about my cousins," to connect to the fact that we are human beings and to create an expectation of being respectful… . And then there's another point, part way through the course, when they become frustrated with my high expectations. So at that point I share with them how much is at stake for me teaching this course. As a person of mixed-Haida ancestry, I am representing my family, my community, my Nation … I'm representing all of these different people, and I'm accountable to them. So I need to know I've done everything in my power to support their learning. And I would say that my identity adds a level of pressure because I recognize these obligations, that many students are not aware of or don't even truly understand, run beyond the classroom. But I feel that talking about it might provide an example of how things are different for different people.

As demonstrated through our conversation, reflection on our own identities, and personal histories and relationships relative to Indigenous and decolonizing perspectives has been key to our orientation as educators in the postsecondary Indigenous education courses we have taught. Our superdiverse positionalities limit and open different possibilities for teaching. Perhaps this point speaks to the critical importance of collaboration, and challenges administrators to consider how to structure Indigenous education courses so that greater affordances can be offered across course sections. In our collaboration, we used this initial reflection as a springboard to consider the kind of contexts that could inspire learning.

Context

Creating inviting contexts is the second crucial consideration of our instruction. Inviting contexts are key to creating a classroom environment where TCs are able to engage with Indigenous and decolonizing perspectives that transcend entrenched colonial narratives (e.g., Brant-Birioukov et al., 2020; Zinga, 2019). Furthermore, we expect the kinds of relationships, attitudes, and mindsets that we nurture within the course can serve as foundations for TCs as they enact relationships across cultural communities in their subsequent roles as teachers (Restoule & Nardozi, 2019). As such, in this section, we elaborate on the importance of creating ethical spaces of engagement to cultivate a respectful web of relationships across diverse cultural paradigms and experiences of colonialism.

Ethical Space of Engagement

An ethical space of engagement is essential for people in colonial societies to communicate across diverse social, historical, and political experiences (Donald, 2009; Ermine, 2007). Power differentials are inherent in systems of colonialism, and as such, educators must deliberately create contexts where all learners will have an opportunity to ethically engage in the development and exchange of ideas to co-construct knowledge (Battiste, 2013; Donald, 2009). Importantly, our preoccupation here is not with safe space, but with ethical space. We do not wish to create a safe space for learners to give voice to colonial narratives (Restoule & Nardozi, 2019), or where, as Sara has encountered, students seem to conflate the feeling of "safety" with being "comfortable" (as suggested by Arao & Clemens, 2013). Instead, we wish to create an ethical space of engagement that Cree scholar Willie Ermine (2007) describes as "a venue to step out of our allegiances, to detach from the cages of our mental worlds and assume a position where human-to-human dialogue can occur" (p. 202). We hope an ethical space allows students to move beyond colonial assumptions to engage with Indigenous perspectives in a transformative way.

An ethical space of engagement in a postsecondary Indigenous education classroom may allow TCs to build from Indigenous and decolonizing perspectives to examine their own identity and beliefs in relation to curricular content. For non-Indigenous TCs, this approach supports engagement with Indigenous perspectives and decolonizing possibilities (e.g., Brant-Birioukov et al., 2020; Iseke-Barnes, 2008), while Indigenous TCs require an ethical space to explore how their own diverse identities and paradigms fit within Western educational contexts (e.g., Brayboy & Maughan, 2009). These transformative experiences are only possible where space is opened for an ethical cross-cultural exploration of ideas and practices.

In our own practices, we have opened ethical spaces of engagement primarily by focusing on relationships, which we describe in the following section. Our objective is always to orient learners toward a compassionate opening of hearts and minds in relationship with diverse perspectives. Of course, there may be students who do not take up these opportunities, despite our efforts to provide multiple points of engagement. In these cases, we increase prompts, feedback, or opportunities to learn from perspectives that will encourage ethical engagement across superdiversity.

Relationships

Ethical spaces of engagement are only valuable when they are energized by a network of respectful relationships. Relationships are foundational to much of our work in Indigenous education, whether it is examining or (re)imagining the societal relationships between Indigenous and non-Indigenous Peoples (e.g., Battiste, 2013; Donald, 2016; Pidgeon, 2019), developing personal relationships across diversity (e.g., Christian & Freeman, 2010), or determining our own relationship to course content (e.g., Brayboy & Maughan, 2009; Hanson, 2019). Positive relationships between educators and students have been shown to support learning across educational experiences (Castagno & Brayboy, 2008; Cote-Meek, 2014). In Indigenous education courses, we see respectful relationships as crucial for students to authentically engage with content that may threaten their identities and existing relationships to familial histories and understandings of where they fit in the world (Aveling, 2006; Cote-Meek, 2014; Restoule & Nardozi, 2019). Other students may perceive a risk of violent opposition to views expressed in class. Thus, cultivating respectful relationships across cultural paradigms and experiences of colonialism requires a clear and intentional understanding of both the nature of relationships and what it means to demonstrate respect across diversity. This understanding of relationships informs how we interact with our colleagues, students, and local Indigenous communities and shapes the capacities we wish to develop in our students.

Relationships may be enacted in a way that is respectful, or mutually uplifting and affirming for individuals across diversity. In particular, demonstrating respect may require taking responsibility for our own past, present, and future words and actions in relation to other people (Kirkness & Barnhardt, 1991; Pidgeon, 2019). In our classes, we enact responsibility by creating a safe environment for diverse, and especially vulnerable students. Sara sees her relationship to students flowing from her diverse identity and responsibility to her family, clan, and the Haida Nation. She described how she talks about her expectations:

> [A]t the beginning of course, I talk about the kinds of topics we will cover and how we will structure our conversations, ask questions, talk about people's discomfort … I'm thinking about the most vulnerable people in my class at that point… . I feel that I have an obligation to … create a safe space for those people who have the most to lose as a result of some of the

conversations and issues that might emerge from the course. My primary responsibility is that people are not re-traumatized, so I really do focus, in the case of Indigenous education, on the safety of Indigenous students ...

In this case, Sara prioritizes what she understands to be her responsibility towards Indigenous (and all) students through her creation of an ethical space of engagement. This responsibility is directly informed by Sara's identity as a Haida educator and by the kinds of ethical spaces her parents created within their family. Furthermore, Sara creates these spaces in response to her own experiences with being Indigenous in contested classroom spaces (e.g., Pidgeon, 2019).

Respectful relationships may also be demonstrated through reciprocity, where each party in the relationship stands to benefit from engagement with one another (Kirkness & Barnhardt, 1991). This approach can diminish the exploitive nature of colonial encounters and recognizes the value of diverse contributions. Nikki described how she discusses respect and enacts reciprocity in her classroom:

> I like to co-construct ideas about respect. I have learned that people across diverse cultures don't always have the same ideas about what it means to be respectful... . I have found that to be powerful. For one thing, it's showing value for diverse ideas. And it gives us that opportunity to talk about, "this is how I want to be treated when I come to class." ... And then of course the other thing is that I bring food... . The reason why I do that, and I tell them explicitly, is ... in terms of reciprocity... . I wanna demonstrate to them that I value their ideas, and I expect them to give me ideas that are going to help me grow as a person as well, and in my own decolonizing journey.

Nikki has focused on reciprocity as a key foundation for the kinds of relationships she wishes to enact through the ethical space of engagement in her course. As a non-Indigenous educator, she feels that reciprocity gives her a tangible way of demonstrating respect, appreciation, and gratitude to Indigenous (and all) Peoples across diverse cultures, classes, genders, and power structures. Her identity as a non-Indigenous teacher educator informs how respectful relationships are conceptualized and enacted.

As instructors of Indigenous education courses in the teacher education program, we have deeply considered the importance of creating inviting contexts through an ethical space of engagement that supports respectful relationships. Although we both value the importance of inviting contexts, we have built on notions of respect, responsibility, and reciprocity in different ways as a result of our own diverse identities. In these contexts, learners are able to take risks in their exploration of Indigenous perspectives and decolonizing possibilities.

Practice

Once we establish our own positionality in relation to Indigenous and decolonizing perspectives and have considered how we might create inviting contexts, we attend to the specific pedagogical approaches we might use to support TCs in their understanding of Indigenous education. In examining our activities across several iterations of Indigenous education courses, we distilled four distinctive approaches that we have found to encourage deep engagement with Indigenous and decolonizing perspectives. Specifically, our courses emphasize diverse perspectives and resources, arts and literature, co-constructing knowledge, and place-based learning.

Diverse Perspectives and Resources

We very carefully consider the resources we incorporate into the Indigenous education course. As is typical practice for many Indigenous pedagogical approaches, we work to prioritize Indigenous perspectives emerging from the territories where we teach (Brayboy & Maughan, 2009; McInnes, 2017). We do this both to show and model respect to the Nations hosting us on their traditional territories and in an effort to build on local perspectives to shape our, and our students', engagement with the land where we live and work. Furthermore, we hope local Indigenous students might find a point of connection in the resources that we center.

We balance these local teachings with diverse Indigenous perspectives on broader educational issues to help students connect with Indigenous Peoples and paradigms and push against essentializing notions of Indigenous experiences and scholarship. We want to demonstrate that superdiversity extends into Indigenous communities by highlighting the rich diversity of Indigenous scholarship and pedagogical approaches (e.g., Archibald, 2008; Donald, 2016), and how these may be interwoven with Western educational systems (e.g., Barnhardt & Kawagley, 2005; Battiste, 2013). Our practice reflects these ideas through simple things we do like playing videos of diverse Indigenous music while students file into class. Incorporating a range of resources can help students connect to the course content and learn from superdiversity among Indigenous cultural paradigms and individual perspectives.

In addition, we purposefully and strategically incorporate non-Indigenous perspectives into our courses. We want to demonstrate how non-Indigenous Peoples might engage with Indigenous and decolonizing perspectives (e.g., Chung, 2012; Regan, 2010) to provide inspirational examples for non-Indigenous students and hopeful possibilities for Indigenous students. Furthermore, students tend to take up some of the challenging ideas inherent in Indigenous education differently based on who is presenting them (Hare, 2015). In Sara's experience, students may be more open to self-examination of problematic colonial narratives if prompted to do so from speakers they perceive as being similar to themselves. By emphasizing a high level of diverse perspectives, we hope to maximize student engagement with the content and facilitate transformational learning for superdiverse TCs in the teacher preparation program.

Arts and Literature

We have found incorporating arts and literature useful to build on the diversity of students and heighten holistic engagement with Indigenous and decolonizing perspectives, within an ethical space of engagement. In our Indigenous education courses, we have used various activities that build from art and literature because they offer students multiple points of entry. We might provide stories by Indigenous authors to teach a particularly sensitive topic, such as residential schools, or use a choice of songs, visual arts, or multimedia presentations to support concept attainment about complex topics like colonialism. The interpretive nature of arts and literature allows students to bring their previous expertise and experiences into their exploration of Indigenous and decolonizing perspectives (Archibald, 2008).

Arts and literature may also more easily provoke an emotional connection or response to course content, so that students deeply engage with Indigenous and decolonizing perspectives not only from an academic point of view but from an affective stance as well (as per Newhouse, 2008). Sara observed this when she integrated memoirs and historical fiction by Indigenous authors into her course readings. Art and literature seem to be perceived as nonthreatening and thus create conditions whereby students are more open to examining their own knowledge, beliefs, and attitudes to support their future teaching of Indigenous content in a compassionate and knowledgeable way (Strong-Wilson, 2007).

Importantly, students' engagement with arts or literature may cultivate reflexive sensitivity to diverse perspectives and experiences of colonialism and answer many of their basic questions even before they come to class. Their discussions in class can then build on the rich and diverse perspectives their classmates and instructors may share. By nurturing this mindset through literature and the arts rather than direct personal engagement, instructors and other students are saved the emotional energy required to address colonial narratives that diminish the value of diverse peoples. Thus, arts and literature provide an opportunity for students to create meaningful connections between their previous experiences and course content so that they can delve deeper into questions around Indigenous and decolonizing perspectives while maintaining positive relationships in class.

Co-constructing Knowledge

Perhaps just as important, we have found that co-constructing knowledge is a powerful strategy to facilitate learning. Our understanding of co-constructing knowledge runs parallel to what Onondaga scholar David Newhouse (2018) describes as an Anishinaabe concept of debwewin whereby complex understandings might emerge when we see things from multiple perspectives and understand the relationships among perspectives. Co-constructing knowledge in the postsecondary Indigenous education courses encourages students to actively engage with course content and take responsibility for this kind of content in their learning and teaching.

Co-constructing understandings of complex phenomena together with TCs facilitates their active engagement with course content in several ways. Not only are students' experiences of the world used to inform our understanding of education, but students can also surface their own struggles and see how diverse people think about critical issues. They might begin to understand how their positionality extends beyond their own personal identities but also shapes the social context for Indigenous (and all) Peoples. Furthermore, it helps TCs see themselves as capable of grappling with important educational and social questions.

Opportunities to co-construct knowledge may be embedded in activities that support TCs' sense of autonomy. Specifically, students can explore topics relevant to their personal growth when learning activities incorporate meaningful choices (Butler et al., 2017). These activities may help TCs take responsibility for their engagement with Indigenous and decolonizing perspectives within the course. However, in the longer term TCs may carry this sense of personal responsibility into their classrooms and the world, creating their own ethical spaces of engagement and uplifting classroom contexts for Indigenous (and all) students. In this way, co-constructing knowledge about Indigenous and decolonizing perspectives supports and builds on the superdiversity in our classrooms, but also has the potential to cultivate a sense of agency so that TCs are able to see themselves enacting decolonizing possibilities.

Place-based Learning

Place-based learning is a key approach emphasized in Indigenous (Cajete, 1994) and decolonizing (Calderon, 2014) pedagogies. We understand place-based learning as a pedagogical approach that "puts animals, plants, and landscapes in the active role of teacher and therefore results in a more holistic and integrated understanding of phenomena" (Marker, 2003, as cited in Brayboy & Maughan, 2009). Extending beyond environmental education, Mexican and Tigua scholar Delores Calderon (2014) discusses how place-based education can disrupt settler identities by centering Indigenous perspectives and incorporating critical perspectives that examine relationships to the land within a colonial context. As such, we feel it is important to model this pedagogy for TCs, and to provide meaningful opportunities for them to co-construct knowledge in relation to, and in relationship with place. In our courses, we facilitate multiple place-based learning opportunities to support TCs' personal and diverse explorations of Indigenous and decolonizing perspectives.

Similar to the arts and literature, place-based approaches seem to open TCs to learning about Indigenous and decolonizing perspectives in ways that are less confrontational, but equally as challenging. For example, in Sara's class, students are invited to adopt the perspective of an ancient object in the environment witnessing how peoples' relationship to the land has shifted from the past to present, and into the imagined future. Nikki took her class to a nearby forested area to contemplate the impacts of colonial history. These kinds of activities help students to deeply reflect on the impacts of colonialism on Indigenous individuals, families, and communities. Sometimes we worry that TCs will not seriously engage with these activities. But more often than not, TCs are able to recognize the human impacts of broad social histories, government policies, and social narratives, bringing tangible meaning to abstract ideas. Once brought to this personal level, we find that students may be more likely to critically examine their own ideas, and commit to (re)imagining new ways of relating to one another.

We have already provided several specific examples of how we incorporate diverse perspectives, use arts and literature, co-construct knowledge, and structure activities using place-based approaches in our teaching of Indigenous education. We provide a final example that builds from all four approaches described, while also reinforcing a space of ethical engagement, as students deeply reflect on course content in relationship with one another:

SARA: … the activity that I have found has had the biggest [impact] … has been switching to a small group inquiry using a First Peoples' Principle of Learning. Because I think one of the biggest challenges in Indigenous education is that people want the pre-made lesson plan. They want the checklist, or "Top 10 things to achieve reconciliation in your classroom," and it can't be done in that way… . [So] I give them the question, "What does it mean to plan, teach, and learn while being guided by this First Peoples Principle?," and [ask them to think about this] … throughout the course… . "How does my principle play a role in my understanding of Missing and Murdered Indigenous Women?" and "how does it connect to this article on place-based learning?" And really thinking about that and having that conversation with their inquiry groups. Part of the inquiry is a visual representation of their learning about the principle. I [also] have a little framework they fill out, [which asks] "which articles helped you to understand this principle more?", "which experiences helped you understand this principle?", "what does it mean to plan a lesson through the lens of this principle?" And when they come together at the end they do these 20-minute presentations about what they learned about their principle throughout the course. I have learned something from every one of those presentations.

This example highlights how Sara was able to create one activity to support student learning and engagement in multi-faceted ways. The activity provided multiple points of entry for diverse students to engage with course content, and built on the diverse resources in the course, including the arts. It also provided opportunities for students to co-construct knowledge through their exploration of course content using Indigenous pedagogical perspectives. Place-based learning occurred through the educational values that Indigenous Peoples in BC have identified as important. In this way, Sara was able to use one multi-faceted activity to address superdiversity within her Indigenous education course.

Conclusion and Future Directions

In this chapter we have provided our own examples of how instructors of Indigenous education courses can build on the rich interactions between superdiverse identities and perspectives. Indeed, we feel that this is an integral part of modelling a decolonizing approach to education that works to transcend essentializing notions of who people are and how we should act in the world. Reflecting on the ways our own identities shape our teaching helps us to be intentional about shaping the contexts we create for learning through ethical spaces of engagement and the relationships that may emerge. These ideals are further enacted through pedagogical approaches that flow from that context.

There is still much for us to learn and contemplate in this vein of research. Although scholars are building a body of research that examines pedagogy in postsecondary Indigenous education courses (e.g., Brant-Birioukov et al., 2020; Hare, 2015; Nicol & Korteweg, 2010), more research may be needed to tease apart key aspects of practice. More research on superdiversity among instructors in teacher education programs might shed light on how pedagogy interacts with diverse identities and positionalities in relation to colonialism. This vein of research might be strengthened by further inquiry into the impact of these approaches on TCs in the short term and as they become teachers in the future. It is our hope that further research might strengthen practices within mandatory Indigenous education courses for TCs, and ultimately improve educational contexts for Indigenous (and all) students.

References

Arao, B., & Clemens, K. (2013). From safe spaces to brave spaces: A new way to frame dialogue around diversity and social justice. In L. Landreman (Ed.), *The art of facilitation: Reflections from social justice educators*. Sterling, VA: Stylus Publishing.

Archibald, J. (2008). *Indigenous storywork: Educating the heart, mind, body, and spirit*. Vancouver, BC: University of British Columbia Press.

Aveling, N. (2006). 'Hacking at our very roots': Rearticulating white racial identity within the context of teacher education. *Race Ethnicity and Education*, 9(3), 261–274. doi:10.1080/13613320600807576

Barnhardt, R., & Kawagley, A. O. (2005). Indigenous knowledge systems and Alaska Native ways of knowing. *Anthropology & Education Quarterly*, 36(1), 124–148.

Battiste, M. (2013). *Decolonizing education: Nourishing the learning spirit*. Saskatoon, SK: Purich Publishing Ltd.

BC Ministry of Education. (2019). *BC's new curriculum: Curriculum overview*. Retrieved from https://curriculum.gov.bc.ca/curriculum/overview

Brant-Birioukov, K., Ng-A-Fook, N., & Llewellyn, K. R. (2020). Re-storying Settler teacher education: Truth, reconciliation, and oral history. In K. R. Llewellyn & N. Ng-A-Fook (Eds.), *Oral history, education, and justice: Possibilities and limitations for redress and reconciliation* (pp. 107–131). New York: Routledge. doi:10.4324/9781315179278-7

Brayboy, B. M. J., & Maughan, E. (2009). Indigenous epistemologies and teacher education: The story of bean. *Harvard Educational Review*, 79(1), 1–21.

Butler, D. L., Schnellert, L., & Perry, N. E. (2017). *Developing self-regulating learners*. Toronto, ON: Pearson Canada.

Cajete, G. (1994). *Look to the mountain: An ecology of Indigenous education. first edition*. Durango, CO: Kivaki Press.

Calderon, D. (2014). Speaking back to manifest destinies: A land education-based approach to critical curriculum inquiry. *Environmental Education Research*, 20(1), 24–36. doi:10.1080/13504622.2013.865114

Castagno, A. E., & Brayboy, B. M. J. (2008). Culturally responsive schooling for Indigenous youth: A review of the literature. *Review of Educational Research*, 78(4), 941–993. doi:10.3102/0034654308323036

Christian, D., & Freeman, V. (2010). The history of a friendship, or some thoughts on becoming Allies. In L. Davis (Ed.), *Alliances: Re/envisioning Indigenous—non-Indigenous relationships* (pp. 376–390). Toronto: University of Toronto Press.

Chung, M. (2012). *The relationship between racialized immigrants and Indigenous peoples in Canada: A literature review* [Unpublished master's thesis]. Ryerson University, Toronto, ON.

Cote-Meek, S. (2014). *Colonized classrooms: Racism, trauma and resistance in post-secondary education*. Black Point, NS: Fernwood Publishing.

Deloria, V. (1970). Power, sovereignty, and freedom. In V. Deloria (Ed.), *We talk, you listen* (pp. 114–137). New York, NY: Macmillan.

Donald, D. (2009). *The pedagogy of the fort: Curriculum, Aboriginal-Canadian relations, and Indigenous métissage* [Doctoral dissertation]. University of Alberta.

Donald, D. (2016). From what does ethical relationality flow? an Indian act in three artifacts. In J. Seidel, & D. W. Jardine (Eds.), *The ecological heart of teaching: Radical tales of refuge and renewal for classrooms and communities* (pp. 10–16). Bern, Switzerland: Peter Lang.

Ermine, W. (2007). The ethical space of engagement. *Indigenous Law Journal*, 6(1), 193–203.

Fairbanks, C. M., Duffy, G. G., Faircloth, B. S., He, Y., Levin, B., Rohr, J., & Stein, C. (2010). Beyond knowledge: Exploring why some teachers are more thoughtfully adaptive than others. *Journal of Teacher Education*, 61(1–2), 161–171. doi:10.1177/0022487109347874

Foner, N., Duyvendak, J. W., & Kasinitz, P. (2019). Introduction: Super-diversity in everyday life. *Ethnic and Racial Studies*, 42(1), 1–16. doi:10.1080/01419870.2017.1406969

Hanson, K. (2019). The First Peoples principles of learning: An opportunity for settler teacher self-inquiry. *LEARNing Landscapes*, 12, 125–137.

Hare, J. (2015). "All of our responsibility": Instructor experiences with required Indigenous education courses. *Canadian Journal of Native Education*, 38(1), 101–120.

Iseke-Barnes, J. (2008). Pedagogies for decolonizing. *Canadian Journal of Native Education*, 31(1), 123–148.

Kirkness, V. J., & Barnhardt, R. (1991). First Nations and higher education: The four R's—respect, relevance, reciprocity, responsibility. *Journal of American Indian Education, 30*(3), 1–15.

McInnes, B. D. (2017). Preparing teachers as Allies in Indigenous education: Benefits of an American Indian content and pedagogy course. *Teaching Education, 28*(2), 145–161. doi:10.1080/10476210.2016.1224831

Newhouse, D. (2008). Ganigonhi:Oh: The good mind meets the academy. *Canadian Journal of Native Education, 31*(1), 184–197.

Newhouse, D. (2018, Fall). Debwewin: To speak the truth—nishnabek de'bwewin: Telling our truths. *Academic Matters*(Fall), 13–17.

Nicol, C., & Korteweg, L. (2010). Braiding teacher lives into relation: The steps and dilemmas of culturally responsive teacher education in Canada. In L. B. Erickson, J. R. Young, & S. Pinnegar (Eds.), *The eighth international conference on self-study of teacher education practices, navigating the public and private: Negotiating the diverse landscape of teacher education* (pp. 183–187). Provo, UT: Brigham Young University.

Pidgeon, M. (2009). Pushing against the margins: Indigenous theorizing of "success" and retention in higher education. *Journal of College Student Retention, 10*(3), 339–360.

Pidgeon, M. (2019). Contested spaces of Indigenization in Canadian higher education. In H. Tomlins-Jahnke, S. D. Styres, S. Lilley, & D. Zinga (Eds.), *Indigenous education: New directions in theory and practice* (pp. 205–229). Edmonton, AB: University of Alberta Press.

Regan, P. (2010). *Unsettling the settler within: Indian residential schools, truth telling, and reconciliation in Canada.* Vancouver, BC: University of British Columbia Press.

Restoule, J., & Nardozi, A. (2019). Exploring teacher candidate resistance to Indigenous content in a teacher education program. In H. Tomlins-Jahnke, S. D. Styres, S. Lilley & D. Zinga (Eds.), *Indigenous education: New directions in theory and practice* (pp. 311–337). Edmonton, AB: University of Alberta Press.

Smith, L. T. (2012). *Decolonizing methodologies: Research and indigenous people.* New York, NY: Zed Books.

Strong-Wilson, T. (2007). Moving horizons: Exploring the role of stories in decolonizing the literacy education of white teachers. *International Education, 37*(1), 114–131.

Truth and Reconciliation Commission of Canada. (2015). *Honouring the truth, reconciling for the future: Summary of the final report of the Truth and Reconciliation Commission of Canada.* Winnipeg, MB: Truth and Reconciliation Commission of Canada.

Wessendorf, S. (2013). Commonplace diversity and the 'ethos of mixing': Perceptions of difference in a London neighbourhood. *Identities: Ethnography, Diversity and Urban Space, 20*(4), 407–422. doi:10.1080/1070289X.2013.822374

Wolfe, P. (2006). Settler colonialism and the elimination of the Native. *Journal of Genocide Research, 8*(4), 387–409. doi:10.1080/14623520601056240

Younging, G. (2018). *Elements of Indigenous style: A guide for writing by and about Indigenous peoples.* Edmonton, AB: Brush Education.

Zinga, D. (2019). Teaching as the creation of ethical space: Indigenous student learning in the academy/university. In H. Tomlins-Jahnke, S. D. Styres, S. Lilley & D. Zinga (Eds.), *Indigenous education: New directions in theory and practice* (pp. 277–309). Edmonton, AB: University of Alberta Press.

Conclusion

TEACHING AND TEACHER EDUCATION IN AN ERA OF SUPERDIVERSITY

Challenges and Opportunities

Lilach Marom, Caroline Locher-Lo, April Martin-Ko, Monica Shank Lauwo, Zhuo Sun, and Kwesi Yaro

The chapters in this book engage in multiple ways with the concept of superdiversity (Vertovec, 2007, 2019) in the North American context of K–12 schooling and teacher education. As illustrated in the introduction chapter, the concept of superdiversity (Meissner & Vertovec, 2015; Vertovec, 2007) highlights the need for new theoretical and methodological tools to unpack the rapid changes in modern societies that lead to ever-changing social formations. It articulates the need to move away from simplistic understandings of diversity grounded in wide ethnic categories, to a more nuanced analysis of the "diversification of diversity" (Vertovec, 2007) and how it is manifested in multiple locations. The concept of superdiversity further explores public conceptions about diversity and migration that emerge in relation to rapid societal changes (Vertovec, 2019). As such, superdiversity is highly applicable to educational researchers and practitioners alike, as it calls us to examine the changing composition of educational institutions and to ask how human relations could be nourished in superdiverse educational spaces.

The final stages of the production of this book were disrupted by the COVID-19 pandemic; as we write this concluding chapter (Spring 2020), it is not at all clear what the day will bring and how the world, in general, and higher education and K–12 schooling, in particular, are going to look on the other end. What is clear already is a rise in public perceptions that look for "someone to blame" and a shift away from global collaboration toward national and communal segregation. While national and international tensions are on the rise, it is important to note that there is also an increase in solidarity in and between communities.

Public servants, in particular, have risen to the task, including teachers and faculty members, who have been engaged in creative ways to ensure the continuity of education for all students.

The crisis also exposes our interdependence, and the necessity of global cooperation in order to overcome global challenges. This situation, once again, demonstrates that our social structures are fragile and that public perceptions are highly susceptible to manipulations. In such a complex context of superdiversity, more than ever, we need to reimagine the role of education in order to navigate current and future challenges. This is not an easy task, as the authors in this book remind us, and there is much to fix in our educational institutions. But it also gives us hope that in the global pendulum swinging between separation and collaboration, education for superdiversity could add to the forces that aim to foster collaborative relations across differences.

The global pandemic is also a reminder that any analysis of diversity should not only focus on identity recognition (even when identity is seen in a complex, nuanced, and interactional way) but rather should be tied to an analysis of a global neoliberal education market. Varghese et al. point to "the dearth of attention in the superdiversity scholarship to the larger justice projects and the racial and neoliberal hierarchies" (p. 87). It is alarming to see how discussions on education in a pandemic context are entangled with economic considerations. Not only universities but also public school systems are mourning the decline in the number of international students as a loss in revenues while universities weigh economic gains against the safety of students. We must ask, how can we educate for superdiversity in an environment in which education is seen as a competitive commodity?

The concept of superdiversity is constantly evolving and has been taken on in multiple ways and fields (Vertovec, 2014). As Vertovec (2014) himself acknowledges: "It is likely a—hopefully useful—placeholder until we develop more enhanced terms, theories and perspectives with which to depict and interpret the multiple modes and impacts of current forms of societal complexification" (p. 4). The authors in this book have engaged in this process by using the frame of superdiversity in multiple geographical locations, in the context of K–12 schooling and teacher education, through different methodologies and with relations to diverse aspects of education (such as language education and Indigenous education).

Each chapter presents unique considerations and implications since there is never one-size-fits-all in education, especially when considering the superdiversity in our communities and education systems. However, there are some threads that are weaved throughout the book, highlighting main challenges in education for superdiversity. Multiple authors discuss issues of marginalization and unchecked Whiteness in education; criticize simplistic notions of diversity, multiculturalism, and multilingualism; address tensions between Indigenous education and multicultural discourses; and challenge the colonial structures and narratives underlying Western education institutions.

These themes correspond with the five main principles for moving "from a diversity stance to a superdiversity lens" articulated in the introduction chapter (Li et al., p. 12). These principles include urging teachers and teacher educators to engage deeply in decolonizing processes, moving beyond simplistic notions of multiculturalism to engagement with superdiversity and social justice, supporting diverse learners while acknowledging the multiplicity of backgrounds, and belonging that underlie educational spaces, and drawing on the multilingual, multicultural and transnational repertoires that students and preservice teachers carry. In the conclusion section, we return to these five principles and map corresponding strategies that could support justice-oriented and inclusive education for all students, families, and communities across global and local boundaries.

Section I: Contexts of Teacher Education in a Superdiverse World

One main notion that is highlighted in Section I, particularly in the chapters of Bennett and Varghese et al., is the dominance of Whiteness that is embedded in the design and policies of teacher education programs. This dominance, according to Bennett's empirical study, is prevalent in the minds of White preservice teachers, who are the majority in most mainstream teacher education programs. Similarly, Taylor and Varghese et al. demonstrate how White dominance is reflected in an embodied sense of entitlement that many preservice teachers hold. Both Bennett and Varghese et al. indicate discord between the sense of entitled unchecked Whiteness and the urgency of creating a multilingual and multicultural core in teacher education. These authors argue that even when teacher education programs have diversity plans, these are often approached as "add-ons" and this message is received by preservice teachers and reproduced by them when they enter the field. For instance, Li refers to research (Pezzetti, 2017) in which teachers who claim a commitment to diversity in fact lack the understanding or fluidity necessary to effectively teach in superdiverse classrooms.

While Whiteness has problematically been granted the notion of neutrality and universality in K–12 schooling and teacher education (see Varghese et al.), the concept of superdiversity urges us to move beyond a simplistic binary in the conceptualization of Whiteness (Whites vs. people of colour). Superdiversity asks us to unpack the nuanced, distinct, and intersecting ways in which diverse groups are positioned in relation to Whiteness (Crenshaw, 1990). For example, Li demonstrates that refugee students often experience interrupted schooling, financial pressures, or a traumatic past, as well as confusion within a novel education system; whereas children of transient migrants rarely encounter teachers who are equipped with the pedagogical competence or adequate curricular resources to provide students with meaningful support to utilize their transnational experience. While students of both groups are likely not to be White, since many waves of recent immigration hail from the East and might share similar ethnicity or country of origin, their experiences are distinct and thus require different pedagogies and strategies.

A related theme in Section I is that in both the United States and Canada, teacher education programs do not necessarily acknowledge and reflect differences in culture, language, and social class. Often, cultural and linguistic diversity is not emphasized or pedagogically addressed. Curriculum and pedagogy are still mostly shaped by Eurocentric theories and practices; therefore, even when programs use terminologies of diversity, they frequently uphold notions of assimilation and integration.

A second main theme in Section I focuses on language policies and their implications. Varghese et al. argue that language policies can be tools to enhance racial and social justice but can also implicitly and explicitly serve the neoliberal agenda of cultural assimilation. For example, they demonstrate that language education policies in the United States, such as the lack of a federal mandate for bilingual education, often serve as a means of neutralizing or suppressing minority languages and the associated cultures. Such policies negatively affect the school experiences and retention of linguistic minority students and their families. Varghese et al. further argue that even with an increasing number of bilingual preservice teachers, there is not enough awareness and support in teacher education to draw upon and enhance these multilingual repertoires. It seems that instead of educating for superdiversity, many teacher education programs still follow models of linguistic assimilation.

The tendency to promote linguistic assimilation is also reflected in the K-12 system in which, often, educational institutions do not see the unique needs of transnational learners as a priority, leaving students with a lack of sense of belonging and engagement. As Li explains, this may lead to feelings of Othering that are experienced among linguistic minority groups, ranging from "involuntary immigrant [refugee]" to "transilient global [elite]" students (Li, p. 7). Whether multilingual students come from affluent or marginalized backgrounds, they are all confronted with sociolinguistic challenges due to linguistic and cultural barriers. Multilingual students may experience a lack of validation of their repertoire of existing linguistic and cultural knowledge in a dominant pedagogical space in which they are perceived as language learners. The authors in Section I collectively demonstrate that in order to foster inclusive education in a superdiverse context, a systemic, institutional, and pedagogical shift has to happen in both teacher education and K–12 system.

Finally, a core theme in Section I relates to Indigenous education. The chapters by Taylor and Hare urge educators and policy makers to acknowledge the unique place of Indigenous education within the context of superdiversity. In spite of Indigenous Peoples' roles as the original inhabitants of Turtle Island and stewards of the land, post-contact colonial Western institutions have marginalized Indigenous communities and aimed to erase their histories, cultures, and languages. Indigenous students have been facing ongoing forms of discrimination in North American educational institutions as well as elsewhere such as Australia and New Zealand, from the notorious residential schools to the continuous marginalization of their cultures, knowledge systems, and languages in the public school system (Regan, 2010).

The unique position of Indigenous Peoples, that was publicly recognized in Canada in the Truth and Reconciliation Commission's Final Report and its 94 "Calls to Action" (Truth and Reconciliation Commission of Canada, 2015), entails that Indigenous education should have a distinct and central place in the school system and should not be conflated with other issues of diversity (as important as they may be). Indeed, Taylor and Hare warn us against reducing the fundamental focus of decolonization and Indigeneity to overarching realms of antiracism, plurality, inclusion, equity, or social justice. While students of marginalized groups face multiple challenges in a Western school system that is underlined by White, middle-class structures and values, Indigenous students face distinct challenges that should be addressed as such.

Furthermore, Indigenous education is not only about addressing ongoing settler colonialism but also about incorporating Indigenous epistemologies, forms of knowledge, and traditions into Western education systems. Hare explains that there are fundamental differences between Indigenous ontology and epistemology and those of Western cultures in how one understands and lives in the world. She demonstrates how even teacher education programs that intend to bridge mainstream education with Indigenous education often overlook the fundamental ontological and epistemic differences between these diverse systems.

Teacher education programs often rely on Indigenous preservice teachers to navigate and bridge this divide, which may result in a colonized space in which Indigenous preservice teachers are expected to act "as teachers" for both faculty and fellow students. The authors argue that *all* preservice teachers need to acquire dispositions, knowledge, and strategies to incorporate Indigenous worldviews during teacher education programs. Preservice teachers also have to be prepared to address resistance that might occur in their classrooms when attempting to include Indigenous knowledge and perspectives for a mainly non-Indigenous student body.

The authors call to integrate Indigenous epistemologies and ways of knowing as a central tenet that underlies education in a superdiverse context. In this sense, education for superdiversity could be understood as an invitation to unlearn colonialism and unpack the ways colonialism has shaped the fundamental structures and relations in North America (Donald, 2009). This starting point is needed in order for education to be truly inclusive and transformative.

Section I Implications for Practice

In Section I, a wide spectrum of strategies and implications for K–12 schooling and teacher education are presented. When it comes to teacher education programs, the authors argue that culturally responsive pedagogies (Ladson-Billings,

1995) should be reframed as a fundamental backbone of teacher education rather than be delivered as a mere "add-on." Teacher education programs should be spaces for fostering relationships, mediation, mutual understanding, and heartfelt reconciliation through culturally and linguistically responsive pedagogies. For example, Varghese et al. suggest placing dual language teacher education within the realm of regular teacher education programs and introducing reflexivity as a transformative way of learning and teaching.

The authors suggest that an important starting point for developing culturally and linguistically responsive teaching is to develop a critical stance that recognizes power relations and hierarchies in society and how they are reflected in educational institutions. Such a standpoint is needed to disrupt covert and overt forms of societal injustice. This is a reflective-analytical process that must be connected to one's racial, linguistic, and class locations, as well as to the intersection of privileges and marginalization that one's position entails. Bennett demonstrates that, to carry out this process, preservice teachers must reflect on and challenge the entitlement of Whiteness.

Taylor and Hare particularly highlight implications for the practice of Indigenous education. For example, Hare suggests educational sovereignty for Indigenous teacher education, which means the right to "shap[e] curriculum and policy" (p. 48) for both Indigenous and non-Indigenous students, as a priority. Similarly, Taylor stresses that all preservice teachers must acknowledge that the ongoing marginalization of Indigenous students is deeply rooted in Canadian policies and institutions and commit to Indigenous education beyond symbolic additions.

Both Hare and Tylor pose a radical call for transforming teacher education into a space of renewal that breaks institutional barriers in order to achieve "self-determination, nationhood, and transformation of [the] educational system" (Hare, p. 41). This process could be realized through multiple changes on all levels of teacher education programs, such as: validating Indigenous preservice teachers' experiences and knowledge (without forcing them to "educate" their peers and faculty) and by decolonizing the curriculum. The authors also highlight the importance of Indigenous educators serving as role models to Indigenous students, since they can intrinsically resonate with Indigenous students' languages, cultures, and perceptions. Indigenous educators are also important as role models to all students as they can enrich and challenge the normative perceptions and knowledge that mainstream teachers tend to have.

Last but not least, when considering K–12 education in superdiverse contexts, Li argues that schools should challenge the notion of educating the future citizens of a single country and instead, recognize that students' sense of being and belonging may cross state boundaries (Levitt & Schiller, 2008) or reside in complex spaces within them (such as Indigenous students who are members of their Nations as well as Canadian citizens). Li suggests that teachers embrace students' transferable knowledge, identity fluidity, and needs for global adaptability rather than force local acculturation. In a superdiverse classrooms, curricula should convey a fuller appreciation of the socioeconomic, sociopolitical, and ecological contexts of all learners.

Drawing on the chapters in Section I, we may begin to imagine how teacher education programs that are grounded in superdiversity might look. We imagine spaces in which Indigenous and non-Indigenous preservice teachers could bring their own conceptions of what knowledge is and question how knowledge is produced while exploring underlying structures of colonialism and other forms of marginalization. Preservice teachers should be encouraged to connect to their own family histories and explore their relationships with Indigenous communities and their land. Such educational spaces should draw on the knowledge of Elders and knowledge keepers, and on traditions such as land education and storytelling (Archibald, 2008). Furthermore, teacher education programs should invite all preservice teachers to draw on their cultural and linguistic knowledge and exchange it in a reciprocal way, while unpacking tensions and intersections that underlie superdiverse spaces.

Section II: Research on Teacher Education in a Time of Superdiversity

The contributors of Section II, who focus particularly strongly on linguistic diversity, emphasize the importance of cultivating an asset-based approach amongst all educators. Asset-based approaches position superdiversity (including multilingualism/plurilingualism) as a resource and opportunity, rather than a deficit. Each author brings their particular orientation to understanding what an asset-based approach looks like, resulting in complementary perspectives that collectively address educators' pedagogies and practices, beliefs, attitudes, and dispositions.

Moore's asset-based orientation, for example, is about cultivating plurilingual and pluricultural practices and dispositions. This involves drawing on full linguistic repertoires, multiple worldviews and knowledge systems, and building bridges between schools, families, and communities by embracing learners' cultures, knowledges, and practices in school-based learning. Smith and Hajek employ culturally and linguistically responsive pedagogies as their framing of asset-based approaches, including the importance of educators having critical multilingual and multicultural awareness. Taking a more explicitly equity- and social justice–oriented approach, Gagné draws on frameworks of teaching for equity (Grudnoff et al., 2017) and intercultural teaching competence (Dimitrov & Haque, 2016).

A related core interest represented in Section II is bringing pluralistic approaches to linguistic diversity—and superdiversity more generally—into mainstream teacher education. These chapters loudly articulate the need to prepare *all* teachers with the assumption that their students will be linguistically and culturally diverse and that this diversity is a resource. A refrain echoing throughout these chapters is that many mainstream teachers feel ill equipped to support multilingual learners and that they lack foundational knowledge of working with English language learners (ELLs). These chapters also point to a general disconnection in North American schooling between teachers' identities (predominantly White and English-dominant) and students' identities (predominantly people of colour and multilingual).

The commitment to centering pluralistic approaches in mainstream teacher education is about unsettling White, monolingual English-speaker normativity and acknowledging diversity as mainstream in superdiverse contexts. As de Jong points out, non-language-specialist teacher educators must play an important role in bringing pluralistic approaches to linguistic diversity into mainstream teacher education, particularly if ELL-responsiveness is to be integrated or infused across the entire program. Sterzuk finds that critical language education courses, practicum placements with mentor teachers who espouse critical orientations towards language, and fieldwork in particularly diverse classrooms (especially when supported by a critical mentor) are potential means of supporting pluralistic orientations towards language. Throughout the Section II chapters, authors stress the importance of professional development relating to supporting ELLs (see de Jong) and to issues of equity and diversity (see Gagné) for *all* teacher educators regardless of their area of specialization.

All five chapters in Section II move away from monolingual orientations and position multilingual linguistic repertoires as the normative starting point. The authors argue for a multilingual orientation to inform language policies in schools and classrooms, not only in the teaching of language but also across other curriculum disciplines. Representing markedly different institutional, political, and demographic contexts (preservice teacher education programs in Ontario, Saskatchewan, and Florida; in-service teachers in British Columbia and the southwestern United States), contributors in Section II make it clear that different contexts call for different strategies, cautioning against one-size-fits-all approaches. They emphasize that the task of mainstreaming pluralistic approaches to language is necessarily interdisciplinary work, requiring bringing ELL-responsiveness and plurilingual pedagogies into non-language subjects in both preservice teacher education programs and K–12 educators schooling contexts.

Section II Implications for Practice

Since shifting pedagogy can never be a purely technical endeavor, asset-based approaches necessarily involve shifts in educators' beliefs and dispositions in order to sustain linguistically and culturally responsive pedagogy in moment-to-moment teaching and interactions. Admittedly, shifting beliefs and dispositions are exceedingly difficult to do and must be a central objective of both preservice and in-service teacher education. The chapters in Section II call our attention to the urgency for teacher education programs to cultivate critical perspectives among teachers, including critical multilingual and multicultural awareness. Such critical understandings (which can lead to critical dispositions) include problematizing standardized notions of what constitutes "legitimate" academic English, and engaging with questions of power, colonialism, racism, and intersectional injustices pertaining to language use.

The five chapters in Section II call on educators to move away from deficit perspectives to asset-based approaches to diversity, through paradigm shifts in their pedagogical practices, beliefs, attitudes, and dispositions. This call has important implications for teachers, teacher educators, and educational institutions. At the heart of an asset-based approach is a commitment to bringing learners' full linguistic, semiotic, and cultural repertoires into their learning experiences, and to positioning linguistic and cultural diversity as a foundational resource in the development of literacy, disciplinary knowledge, and various skills and competencies. As Moore's chapter demonstrates, this ideally involves collaborations between teachers, learners, families, and communities, with teachers and schools recognizing the important informal education that occurs outside of formal schooling.

In addition to incorporating multilingualism into teaching and learning, an asset-based approach also entails embracing students' diverse knowledge systems, and their connections to the land and their communities, into the processes of learning and co-construction of knowledge. This is a pedagogical manifestation of superdiversity that could affirm Indigenous students' connection to their nations, cultural knowledge, and languages, as well as supporting settler and immigrant students in navigating their family roots, languages, and transnational relations. These chapters encourage us to make such pluralistic approaches the pedagogical norm in all schooling environments, and across the curriculum. This is exemplified the plurilingual and pluricultural approach to STEAM (science, technology, engineering, arts, mathematics) that Moore proposes, as well as in Smith and Hajek's call to prepare teachers to enact culturally and linguistically responsive pedagogical practices.

Section II makes clear that the pedagogies, beliefs, and dispositions associated with asset-based approaches require teachers to have growth mindsets and be lifelong learners. Part of nurturing this could include supporting teachers to become researchers of their own practices, classrooms, and experiences, as well as supporting teachers to participate in professional learning communities that foster collaboration and sharing of ideas, challenges, and promising practices (Moore demonstrates what such practices might look like).

The chapters of Section II also have important implications for preservice teacher education programs, and ways of ensuring that all preservice teachers are adequately prepared to teach for superdiversity. By examining multilayered contextual factors, both Gagné and de Jong point to the interplay of policy, institutional, program-based, and instructor-dependent factors that impact possibilities for centering issues of diversity and equity in mainstream teacher education.

This serves as an important reminder that, in addition to focusing efforts at the pedagogical level, broader program-based, institutional, and policy transformation is essential. Ontario's 2013 Enhanced Teacher Education policy, mandating that all teachers be prepared to work with linguistically, culturally, and racially diverse students (Gagné, p. 111), and Florida's requirement since 2003 that all elementary preservice teachers graduate with an English for Speakers of Other Languages endorsement (de Jong, p. 205), are examples of policies that have supported greater attention to superdiversity in mainstream teacher education programs. Other provinces and states can learn from such diversity-oriented teacher education policies.

With regards to language-related aspects of teacher education, de Jong and Gagné's examinations of different models for infusing ELL considerations into mainstream teacher education speak to possibilities and challenges for bringing pluralistic approaches to linguistic diversity into the mainstream. Their respective chapters demonstrate that ELL-related professional development for all teacher educators is essential, regardless of subject area, in order to infuse ELL expertise across teacher education programs. However, as Gagné points out, the prevalence of precariously employed sessional instructors is one barrier to such professional development, due to high turnover and lack of remuneration for work they do beyond teaching.

In addition to the infusion of ELL-related considerations across the teacher education curriculum, both Gagné and de Jong insist on the importance of having specialized, stand-alone courses on supporting ELLs that are mandatory for all teacher candidates. This requirement, if applied to all teacher education programs in North America, would be an enormous asset in working towards more linguistically and culturally inclusive mainstream classrooms. While infusing ELL expertise into all mainstream teacher preparation courses is imperative, de Jong cautions against ELL-infused mainstream programs replacing specialized programs preparing ELL specialist teachers, which remain essential in maintaining high standards for discipline-based professional expertise supporting ELLs in schools.

Sterzuk, Gagné, and de Jong all point to the critical importance of field/practicum experiences with ELLs as part of the effort to prepare all teachers for superdiversity. Indeed, field experiences involving working with ELLs are formative opportunities to shape teacher candidates' expectations, beliefs, practices, and dispositions while supporting the normalization of diversity. Sterzuk also emphasizes that having mentor teachers who understand and are experienced in working with cultural and linguistic diversity is key to supporting teacher candidates in developing this mindset during the practicum. Efforts should be made to ensure that all teacher candidates have opportunities to teach in richly multilingual, superdiverse contexts, with pluralistically oriented mentor teachers, as part of their field experiences in mainstream teacher education programs.

Moving forward, there is an ongoing need to focus on how to embody diversity and equity within teacher education programs themselves, in addition to preparing teacher candidates to be diversity- and equity-oriented educators in their future classrooms. Perhaps, in part, because of the ongoing predominance of White, English-dominant teacher candidates in many North American teacher education programs, the development of teacher education programs that are themselves linguistically and culturally responsive has been less an emphasis than preparing teachers to be linguistically and culturally responsive in their future K–12 classroom contexts. This speaks to the need for teacher education programs to critically model what asset-based and pluralistic approaches to education look like within teacher education.

There is also an urgent need to expand efforts to diversify the teaching force, including recruiting a more diverse pool of applicants for teacher education programs. Gagné details some efforts to recruit a more diverse and representative student body at Ontario Institute for Studies in Education (OISE), University of Toronto, including outreach to secondary schools to support underrepresented groups (such as Black and Indigenous students) to imagine themselves as future teachers, and embedding in the application process opportunities for applicants to write about connections between their multiple identities and the kinds of teachers they want to be.

Finally, there is an ongoing need to frame struggles towards more pluralistic approaches to linguistic and cultural diversity with both antiracist and Indigenous lenses. In Section II, Moore models how Indigenous perspectives and First People's Principles of Learning can be integral to plurilingual and pluricultural pedagogies. Gagné calls for an intersectional approach to diversity and equity, describing how early attempts at ESL infusion at OISE led to the recognition that a focus on linguistic and cultural diversity needed to expand to more complex and intersectional understandings of diversity. An intersectional approach to diversity and equity must centrally entail attention to issues of Indigeneity and colonialism and not just dimensions of diversity resulting from waves of migration and transnationalism. Indeed, issues relating to linguistic, cultural, and racial diversity, as well as Indigeneity and settler colonialism, are overlapping and interdependent (and sometimes in tension), and approaches to addressing pluralism in teacher education must take into account the intersectional nature of superdiversity.

Section III: Engaging Practices for Educators for Superdiversity

Chapters in Section III identify local responses from various types of educational programs to the macro context of globalization and transnational migration. A shared sentiment among the classroom practitioners portrayed in these chapters is a strong sense of perplexity and inadequacy when they attempt to establish an authentic relationship with students and their families amidst radical disparities of social and cultural upbringings. This is hardly surprising considering that teacher education programs traditionally have reflected Eurocentric, White, middle-class perspectives, and attracted mostly White middle-class preservice teachers. For instance, Anderson and Anderson capture family literacy program facilitators' struggle with understanding immigrant parents' culturally oriented interactions with their children that appeared discrepant from dominant North American perspectives. Similarly, the mainstream teachers from Que and Li's Newfoundland and Labrador–based study expressed their feeling of unpreparedness in supporting refugee students academically with little knowledge about their educational experience prior to immigration.

The frame of superdiversity suggests that this troubling sentiment, which many teachers share, accelerates in response to rapid demographic changes, in which the relatively homogeneous dynamic of established settler communities become complicated by drastic changes of demographics under increased and more diverse recent global mobility (Vertovec, 2019). However, the core of this sense of perplexity is rooted in teachers' essentialized interpretation of difference. Some teachers see themselves as "outsiders" to their students' cultural norms and linguistic repertoires and assume fixed simplistic dichotomies in their classrooms such as Indigenous/settler, ELL/native English speaker, refugee/citizen. This is in addition to consistent underlying disparities between the mainly White teaching force and their students who are in many cases predominantly people of colour (see Edwards & White). However, such dichotomies cannot capture the nuances of classrooms and are unhelpful to understanding education in a global, transnational context of superdiversity, in which students and teachers can belong to multiple linguistic, ethnic, cultural, and national communities.

Acknowledging the pluralism that underlies current classrooms, Section III authors imply that educators should shift their mission statement from integrating learners into the mainstream community to constructing a community of learners with shared understanding and respect for difference and diversity. The underpinning guideline to this change is an understanding of identity and belonging from a dynamic, multidimensional perspective. When teachers have an enhanced awareness of the multidimensionality of identity and allegiance, they can foster authentic connections with students on the basis of shared priorities. These include addressing the needs of the local community, negotiating shared goals, ameliorating tensions between communities, and working toward reconciliation and empowerment.

Similar to the authors in Section II, the authors in Section III also highlight how socioculturally framed, asset-based pedagogies can be woven into classroom practices in order for teachers to further facilitate learners' investment and engagement in classrooms. Roessingh, for instance, demonstrates how a young ELL learner gained confidence and control over his English learning process along with a rapid development of his vocabulary repertoire after Roessingh intentionally developed the learning and assessment materials closely around the student's culturally/religiously pertinent experience (i.e., hair-cutting) and allowed space for first language use in his oral/written practice. Roessingh's practices of holistic ELL teaching echo Li's (2020) call for educators to transcend the conception of learner agency as an individual effort. Instead, she proposes a sociocultural approach to learner agency that depicts the mechanism of agency construction as dynamically interweaved with the "availability of economic, cultural, and social resources within the learners' particular physical environment and networked space" (Li, 2020, p. 35).

Other authors in Section III (e.g., Anderson & Anderson; Edwards & White) enumerate some practical approaches to incorporating students' cultural model of learning and family funds of knowledge into existing educational programs and classrooms. They call on educators to embrace epistemological openness towards diverse home/community-based resources. Reflecting on their work with immigrant and refugee communities, Anderson and Anderson encourage family literacy program facilitators to allow parents to mediate learning in ways that may not be aligned well with the dominant philosophy/pedagogy of early childhood development in North America (e.g., parents insisting on modeling how to complete a task for a child rather than allowing the child to proceed independently). Similarly, Edwards and White highlight the existence of multiple parenting styles and needs among African American parents. They suggest, for example, inviting parents to tell their family stories to establish a starting point for mainstream educators to create relationships with families.

Finally, authors in this section (e.g., Edwards & White; Que & Li; Yee & Davidson) demonstrate shortfalls of some teachers' symbolic enactment of multicultural, antiracism, and decolonizing policies when they refrain from incorporating students' lived experience of poverty, racism, and violence as sources of curriculum and instructional materials. Educational policies and practices that embrace superficial multiculturalism (or, "symbolic antiracism" in Que & Li) without social justice–oriented actions, may result in students' further exclusion from classroom-based learning. When "the contemporary challenge that many immigrant and otherwise marginalized and displaced students and families experience" (Rodriguez, 2013, p. 100) remains unspoken to, students will not be able to meaningfully engage in pedagogical interactions, nor will they deem the classroom as a safe, inclusive space to belong to.

As an alternative, Edwards and White argue that it is important for mainstream educators and teachers to maintain lively discussions on various dimensions of diversity and construct cogent counter-narratives against historical and existing inequalities before they can develop transforming instructional practices to engage with African American students. Similarly, Yee and Davidson propose to utilize the rich interpretive power of art and literature for dealing with contentious issues. For example, they suggest classroom teachers offer stories by First Nations authors as an entry point to teach topics such as residential schools or colonialism. The earlier-outlined approaches exemplify critical, asset-based practices that serve transformative power for learners of immigrant, refugee, Indigenous, as well as other historically minoritized backgrounds. These approaches connect to Zipin's (2009) argument for an expansion of the existing Funds of Knowledge framework to include the knowledge and epistemologies that derive from the adversity students and their families experience, or in his term, the "dark funds of knowledge". While teachers might be worried to incorporate sensitive discussions that might arise negative emotions in their classrooms, Zipin demonstrates that it is both ethical and pragmatic to "engage learners through familiar social-cultural resonances" (p. 319).

Section III Implications for Practice

An immediate implication that emerges from chapters in Section III relates to the structures and practices of contemporary teacher education programs. Teacher education programs need to prepare preservice teachers for superdiverse classrooms, in which they might experience discomfort when confronted with sensitive and controversial issues. To do it, preservice teachers need to be equipped with both conceptual and practical tools to frame students' "dark funds of knowledge" in constructive, empowering manners without potential re-traumatization.

Much as asset-based pedagogical practices offer opportunities for supporting educational equity across the various educational programs that are represented in this section, caution still needs to be exercised by teacher educators and classroom practitioners to critically review the nature of community/family-based resources and thoughtfully frame them in instructional practices in order to avoid reproducing social exclusion in classrooms. Practices that perpetuate "tokenism" of diverse students require problematization. For example, continuously asking an Indigenous student within a classroom of settlers to speak about their own or family members' lived experiences relating to residential schools or the ramifications of colonization, imposes emotional labour onto students (Pleasant, 2016).

Furthermore, practices that encourage educators to investigate broad approaches to trauma-informed practices must reach beyond simply focusing on technical and behavioral interventions to alternatives which allow introspection and ethical responses to students' lifeworlds that exist in multiple layers of identity (Rocha & Ruitenberg, 2019). For the teachers in Que and Li's study such introspection and ethical response entail holding their judgement that refugee students are deprived of voices due to the language barrier.

Another implication for classroom practitioners is to further reconfigure the instructional and assessment context to better facilitate students' integration of existing knowledge systems and skill sets. For example, as an alternative to language-based assessment, teachers can incorporate different modes of communication (e.g., drawing, online posting, vlog) into the classroom routine, which may help refugee students feel better supported and therefore more capable and willing to express their needs and aspirations. Moreover, as Roessingh illustrates there is room for assessment to exist *"for* and *as* learning [rendering] a reciprocal iterative relationship" (pp. 273) between teaching and learning.

Moving away from assessment "of learning" to more diverse assessment models also opens up the potential for reciprocal relations among teachers and students. Roessingh briefly alludes to "pedagogical documentation" (p. 274) as one of these possibilities. This practice, inspired by the educational model from Reggio-Emilia Italy, is now utilized by early childhood educators globally. Pedagogical Narration is seen as an ongoing process where learning emerges as "living" engagement between student, educator, and pedagogical processes. Assessment tools such as this stretch beyond the "reflective" to "reflexive" (Berger, 2015) and provide an avenue for teachers to engage with the unfolding complexities that exist in learning environments where numerous intersectionalites present continuous "becomings" for both teachers and students.

Overall, the practices identified in Section Three reflect an emerging, yet incomplete, shift from diversity to superdiversity in the conceptualization of education in mainstream North American educational institutions. While pluralistic understanding of knowledge is becoming more prevalent and is supported by changes in curriculum, pedagogy, and assessment, the work is not complete. There is still a persistent need for teacher educators, program developers, and teachers to commit to critical awareness and reflexive practices to avoid perpetuating power imbalances and social inequities that still underlie educational spaces.

Concluding Thoughts

King and Bigelow (2018) argue that the least explored avenue of superdiversity is the "practical and policy implications of the construct" (p. 460). In this chapter, we have tried to answer their call by suggesting practical implications as to how to translate the concept of superdiversity into the context of K–12 and teacher education in North America.

While we suggest multiple strategies and practices that teachers and teacher educators can adopt when working in superdiverse educational contexts, we are aware that some changes can only occur when supported by a shift in institutions, policies, and funding. For example, increasing the funding for public schools is crucial to better support students in superdiverse classrooms. Similarly, changes are needed in admission policies and structures of teacher education programs to increase the accessibility and success of preservice teachers from marginalized communities. There is also a need for institutions to move away from business models, for teachers and teacher educators to be prepared to address the challenges that superdiversity poses. The current economic crisis in many Western educational institutions exposes the depth in which educational processes are subjected to market considerations.

As demonstrated in many of the chapters, individual teachers, schools, and teacher education programs can create initiatives that could eventually lead to wider changes. Hence, there are always ways for educators to create more accessible and inclusive spaces for their students. As many authors argue, a necessary starting point for educational change is for educators to be willing to reflect on their biases, develop their critical dispositions, create relationships with students and communities, and rethink their pedagogy, curriculum, and assessment.

Recent research on public perceptions in the context of superdiversity demonstrates that when people interact with each other on a daily basis and on a levelled field, they develop positive dispositions toward each other (Dovidio et al., 2008; Vertovec et al., 2017a). Schools are prime sites in which such interactions could be nourished, particularly when in other public and online spaces, animosity between communities and individuals is on the rise. Furthermore, as negative stereotypes are easily spread via social media outlets (Vertovec, 2018) schools and teacher education programs have an important role in addressing tensions and controversial topics in critical, supportive, and reflective ways.

While the frame of superdiversity cannot provide ultimate educational solutions or prescriptions that can apply to all contexts, we believe that there is a lot to take from the chapters in this book that could guide teacher educators, teachers, and other practitioners who are interested in reflecting on their practice and in creating more supportive and engaging educational spaces with their students. We hope that this book will open spaces for further conversations, collaborations, and creations. In this hope we draw on the great Paulo Freire (2018), who wrote in the final chapter of the *Pedagogy of the Oppressed* (in the Portuguese original): "If nothing remains of these pages, something, at the very least, we hope will endure: our trust in the people. Our faith in people to create a world where it is less difficult to love." (cited in Kohan, 2021)

References

Archibald, J. A. (2008). *Indigenous storywork: Educating the heart, mind, body, and spirit.* Vancouver, BC: University of British Columbia Press.

Berger, I. (2015). Pedagogical narrations and leadership in early childhood education as thinking in moments of not knowing. *Journal of Childhood Studies, 40*(1), 130–147.

Crenshaw, K. (1990). Mapping the margins: Intersectionality, identity politics, and violence against women of color. *Standford Law Review,* 43, 1241–1299.

Dimitrov, N., & Haque, A. (2016). Intercultural teaching competence: A multi-disciplinary model for instructor reflection, *Intercultural Education,* 27(5), 1–20. doi:10.1080/14675986.2016.1240502

Donald, D. (2009). Forts, curriculum, and Indigenous Métissage: Imagining decolonization of Aboriginal-Canadian relations in educational contexts. *First Nations Perspectives,* 2(1), 1–24.

Dovidio, J. F., Glick, P., & Rudman, L. A. (Eds.). (2008). *On the nature of prejudice: Fifty years after Allport.* Hoboken, NJ: John Wiley & Sons.

Freire, P. (2018). *Pedagogy of the oppressed*. London, UK: Bloomsbury Publishing.

Grudnoff, L., Haigh, M., Hill, M., Cochran-Smith, M., Ell, F., & Ludlow, L. (2017). Teaching for equity: Insights from international evidence with implications for a teacher education curriculum. *The Curriculum Journal*, 28(3), 305–326. Retrieved from http://dx.doi.org/10.1080/09585176.2017.1292934

King, K. A., & Bigelow, M. (2018). Multilingual education policy, superdiversity, and educational equity. In A. Creese & Adrian Blackledge (Eds.), *Routledge handbook of language and superdiversity* (pp. 359–472). London, UK: Routledge

Kohan, W. (2021). *Paulo Freire: A Philosophical Biography*, trans. Samuel D. Rocha, Bloomsbury.

Ladson-Billings, G. (1995). But that's just good teaching! The case for culturally relevant pedagogy. *Theory Into Practice*, 34(30), 159–165.

Levitt, P., & Schiller, N. (2008). Conceptualizing simultaneity. In A. Portes & J. DeWind (Eds.), *Rethinking migration: New theoretical and empirical perspectives* (pp. 181–218). New York, NY: Bergbabn Books.

Li, G. (2020). Principles for developing learner agency in language learning in a new eduscape with COVID-19. 英语学习 [English Learning], 8, 33–43.

Meissner, F., & Vertovec, S. (2015). Comparing superdiversity. *Ethnic and Racial Studies*, 38(4), 541–555.

Pezzetti, K. (2017). 'I'm not racist; my high school was diverse!' White preservice teachers deploy diversity in the classroom. *Whiteness and Education*, 2(2), 131–147.

Pleasant, A. Mt. (2016). Emotional labor and precarity in Native American and Indigenous studies. *English Language Notes*, 54(2), 175–181.

Regan, P. (2010). *Unsettling the settler within: Indian residential schools, truth telling, and reconciliation in Canada*. Vancouver, BC: University of British Columbia Press.

Rocha, A. M. V., & Ruitenberg, C.W. (2019). Trauma-informed practices in early childhood education: Contributions, limitations and ethical considerations. *Global Studies of Childhood*, 9(2), 132–144.

Rodriguez, G. M. (2013). Power and agency in education: Exploring the pedagogical dimensions of funds of knowledge. *Review of Research in Education*, 37(1), 87–120.

Truth and Reconciliation Commission of Canada. (2015). *The Truth and Reconciliation Commission of Canada: Calls to Action*. http://trc.ca/assets/pdf/Calls_to_Action_English2.pdf

Vertovec, S. (2007). Superdiversity and its implications, *Ethnic and Racial Studies*, 30(6), 1024–1054.

Vertovec, S. (2014). Reading 'Superdiversity'. In B. Anderson, & M. Keith (Eds.), *Migration: A COMPAS anthology*. COMPAS: Oxford. http://compasanthology.co.uk/wp-content/uploads/2014/02/Vertovec_COMPASMigrationAnthology.pdf

Vertovec, S. (2018, November 6). *Dynamics in the public understanding of diversity [Keynote Lecture]*. Livable Diversity Summit, Melbourne, Victoria, Australia. https://www.mmg.mpg.de/steven-vertovec

Vertovec, S. (2019). Talking around superdiversity. *Ethnic and Racial Studies*, 42(1), 125–139.

Vertovec, S., Schmid, K., Wölfer, R., Swart, H., Christ, O., Al Ramiah, A., & Hewstone, M. (2017a). The "wallpaper effect" revisited: Divergent findings on the effects of intergroup contact on attitudes in diverse versus nondiverse contexts. *Personality and Social Psychology Bulletin*, 43 (9), 1268–1283.

Vertovec, S., Schmid, K., Wölfer, R., Swart, H., Christ, O., Al Ramiah, A., & Hewstone, M. (2017b). The "wallpaper effect" revisited: Divergent findings on the effects of intergroup contact on attitudes in diverse versus nondiverse contexts. *Personality and Social Psychology Bulletin*, 43(9), 1268–1283.

Zipin, L. (2009). Dark funds of knowledge, deep funds of pedagogy: Exploring boundaries between lifeworlds and schools. *Discourse: Studies in the Cultural Politics of Education*, 30(3), 317–331.

INDEX